Politicisation of Hindu Religion in Postmodern India

Politicisation of Hindu Religion in Postmodern India

An Anatomy of the Worldviews, Identities and Strategies of Hindu Nationalists in Bharatiya Janata Party

J. KURUVACHIRA

RAWAT PUBLICATIONS
Jaipur • New Delhi • Bangalore • Mumbai • Hyderabad • Guwahati

ISBN 81-316-0134-X

Published by
Prem Rawat for **Rawat Publications**
Satyam Apts, Sector 3, Jawahar Nagar, Jaipur 302 004 (India)
Phone: 0141 265 1748 / 7006 Fax: 0141 265 1748
E-mail: info@rawatbooks.com
Website: www.rawatbooks.com

New Delhi Office
4858/24, Ansari Road, Daryaganj, New Delhi 110 002
Phone: 011 2326 3290

Also at Bangalore, Mumbai, Hyderabad and Guwahati

Typeset by Rawat Computers, Jaipur
Printed at Chaman Enterprises, New Delhi

Contents

Preface

The politics of religious identity has gained unprecedented influence over the Indian masses in the recent decades, and the rise of the Bharatiya Janata Party (BJP, 'Party of the Indian People') in Indian political scenario is a pure manifestation – a crystal clear manifestation of it. In fact, in postmodern India there is no political party that has challenged the bedrock of Indian secularism, democracy and cultural pluralism as the BJP. In 1980 the ex-Jana Sanghis created the BJP in order to push forward the ideals of Hindu cultural nationalism using political power and influence. Since then the country has been witnessing a gradual unpacking of a 'hidden agenda', namely, that of creating a Hindu *rashtra* (nation) in India, under the direction of the BJP leaders at the dictates of their ideological mentor, namely, the Rashtriya Swayamsevak Sangh (RSS, National Volunteer Association), and by cashing in on the religious sentiments of the majority religious community. Sixteen years after the inception of the party, the BJP became big enough to form a coalition government in New Delhi with a large number of regional partners, called National Democratic Alliance (NDA), first in 1996 for 13 days, then in 1998 and again from 1999 to 2004.

This study is an 'anatomy' of the worldviews, as well as of the identities and strategies of five leading Hindu right-wing political leaders in the BJP who have left a 'mark' on India's history through their political philosophy, communalist and militant activities, strict adherence to Hindu cultural nationalism and politicisation of Hindu religion. The BJP leaders analysed in this study are: Atal Bihari Vajpayee, the former Prime Minister of India, Lal Krishna Advani, the former Deputy Prime Minister of India and Union Home Minister, Murli Manohar Joshi, the former Union Human Resource Development (HRD) Minister, Arun Shourie, writer, scholar, journalist, political thinker and Union Cabinet Minister who held a number of portfolios in a row, and Narendra Modi, who is currently the Chief Minister of Gujarat. All these personalities have been also leaders of prominence in the BJP and have played a major role in its growth during the past 26 years of its history. In addition, they have also held such important posts in the party as, national presidents, general secretaries, executive committee members, 'think-tanks', etc. This fact makes the study of these personalities important, in as much as they embody to a great extent *what the BJP stands for*. Hence our study will deal with their ideological background, attitude towards Hindu cultural nationalism, religious minorities of India, secularism, democracy, cultural pluralism, political ethics, human rights, etc.

A word about the methodology followed in this study: as already stated, the present study is an exposé of the worldviews of five leading contemporary political leaders in the BJP, namely, Atal Bihari Vajpayee, Lal Krishna Advani, Murli Manohar Joshi, Arun Shourie and Narendra Modi. I have based my study mainly on their writings, speeches and statements, reports of fact-finding teams and commissions, and archival materials. Wherever found it opportune, I have engaged in some comparisons with European fascism, especially Hitler's Nazism.

Since all the personalities analysed in this study are still living and are active in politics, one cannot conclude anything definitely about their worldviews. As free human beings they can still alter their ideas, correct or enhance previous statements, beliefs and convictions or even totally reverse their positions – it is especially possible in politics which is such a volatile sphere as far as ideologies are concerned. Hence, in this study I have followed a self-imposed time limit up to 30 June 2006.

The present study belongs essentially to the field of political philosophy, but the subject-matter may overlap History, Sociology and Religious Studies. The methodology used will range from expository, descriptive, analytical to evaluative. For the sake of space, following a contemporary trend in scientific methodology, I have abbreviated the titles of all the books and articles which are long, even when references are made to them for the first time. However, the bibliography contains the full titles with the essential details of publication. For this study a range of materials have been made use of from scientifically written research works to journalistic writings. Since the study deals with current history, I had to depend a great deal on a variety of serious-minded magazines and newspapers for the source material. But I have made sure to consult a variety of them in order to get as objective a picture of the subject-matter as possible. For some of Indian concepts and Indian proper names the reader will notice variant spelling. The German texts cited in this study are given a free English translation by the author. There is a glossary which explains all the important technical terms, expressions and concepts. The abbreviation contains explanations for frequently used acronyms.

Finally, I am indebted to several persons who have helped me in carrying out this study. In the first place, I place on record the encouragement and support given by T. Mulayinkal and J. Poonthuruthil in my research. I thank the staff and the students of Salesian College of Higher Education, Dimapur, especially V. Palathingal, the Director, and R.K. Guangdiat Nicholas, the Principal, for providing me the time necessary for pursuing this project by freeing me for some months of the year from my academic responsibilities. I thank Jnanadeepa Vidyapeeth, Pune; Salesian College, Dimapur; Kristu Jyoti College, Bangalore; Connemara Library, Chennai; Otto Hopfenmüller Library, Shillong; Jawaharlal Nehru University, New Delhi; Madras University, Chennai; Salesian Pontifical University, Rome; Pontifical Gregorian University, Rome; Heinrich Heine Antiquariat, Düsseldorf, Germany, Catholic Bishops Conference of India (CBCI) archives, New Delhi; National Archives of India (NAI), New Delhi; Nehru Memorial Museum and Library (NMML), and India Office Collections, British Library, London, for making available to me their library and archival materials and facilities. I thank in a special way Mons. H. Ewald, Herr Fleischauer, J. Rudolf, T. Martinek and C. Shaeffer, Germany, who helped me in many ways in finding several important original writings on Adolf Hitler and Nazism. My gratitude is also due to J. Kallarackal and C. Kottarathil who gathered immense patience while reading through the entire manuscript and thereby gave their valuable suggestions as for as improvement in language and style is concerned. Finally, I thank Rawat Publications, Jaipur for graciously undertaking the publication of this study.

30 June 2007 **J. Kuruvachira**

Abbreviations

ABVP	Akhil Bhraratiya Vidyarthi Parishad
AIDWA	All India Democratic Women's Association
BJP	Bharatiya Janata Party
BJS	Bharatiya Jana Sangh
BORI	Bhandarkar Oriental Research Institute
CBI	Central Bureau of Investigation
CBSE	Central Board of Secondary Education
CSDS	Centre for the Study of Developing Societies
DAV College	Dayananda Anglo-Vedic College
EBC	Economically Backward Class
EVFUSA	Ekal Vidyalaya Foundation of USA
FISI	Friends of India Society International
FSL	Forensic Science Laboratory
FTS	Friends of Tribal Society
Gitarahasya	Srimad Bhagavadgita-Rahasya or Karma-Yoga-Sastra
HDI	Human Development Index
HMS	Hindu Maha Sabha
HRD	Human Resource Development
HSC	Hindu Student's Council
HSS	Hindu Swayamsevak Sangh
HSS-UK	Hindu Swayamsevak Sangh-UK
IAS	Indian Administrative Service
ICHR	Indian Council of Historical Research
ICSSR	Indian Council of Social Science Research
IGNCA	Indira Gandhi National Centre for Arts
IIT	Indian Institute of Information Technology
IRDF	India Development Relief Fund

ISI	Inter Service Intelligence of Pakistan
I.S.K.CON	International Society for Krishna Consciousness
L/P&J	Legal, Public and Juridical [documents]
MISA	Maintenance of Internal Security Act
MLA	Member of Legislative Assembly
MP	Member of Parliament
NAAC	National Accreditation Assessment Council
NAFRE	National Alliance for Fundamental Right to Education
NAI	National Archives of India
NCERT	National Council for Educational Research and Training
NCF	National Curriculum Framework
NDA	National Democratic Alliance
NGO	Non Governmental Organisation
NHRC	National Human Rights Commission
NMML	Nehru Memorial Museum and Library
NRI	Non Resident Indian
NSDAP	*Nationalsozialistische Deutsche Arbeiterpartei* (The National Socialist German Worker's Party)
OBC	Other Backward Classes
OFBJP	Overseas Friends of the BJP
OTC	Officers' Training Course [for RSS functionaries]
PIO	People of Indian Origin
POTA	Prevention of Terrorism Act
RSS	Rashtriya Swayamsevak Sangh
SA	*Sturmabteilungen* (Stormstroopers, the 'storming department' of Hitler's Nazi regime')
SAARC	South Asian Association of Regional Co-operation
SAHMAT	Safdar Hashmi Memorial Trust
SC	Scheduled Caste
SIUK	Sewa International-UK
SPD	Sozialdemokratische Partei Deutschlands (The Socialist Party of Germany)
SS	*Schutzstaffel* (Security guard; the security service wing of Hitler's Nazi regime)
SSA	Sarva Shiksha Abhiyan
ST	Scheduled Tribe
UGC	University Grants Commission
UNDP	United Nations Development Project
UPA	United Progressive Alliance
VHP	Vishva Hindu Parishad
VHPA	Vishva Hindu Parishad of America

Introduction

Hindu cultural nationalism in India has grown prodigiously from a dormant and apparently minor communal presence to a vast movement in the country within a short span of time. However, the genesis of Hindu nationalism as an ideology is to be traced to the socio-religious movements initiated by the elite groups of Hindu society between the 1870s and 1920s as reaction against British colonialism, Christianity and Islam, and as an effort to build up self-esteem among Hindus. In such a state, the role of important Hindu organisations like, the Arya Samaj ('Noble Society' or 'Society of Aryas', 1875), the Hindu Mahasabha (HMS, 'Hindu Great Assembly', 1915), the Rashtriya Swayamsevak Sangh (RSS, 1925), Akhil Bharatiya Vidyarthi Parishad (ABVP, 'All India Student Council', 1948), etc., is significant. The latter part of the 20th century saw the mushrooming of more Hindu nationalist, communal and militant organisations, such as, the Bharatiya Jana Sangh (BJS, 'Indian People's Association', 1951), Vanavasi Kalyan Ashram (VKA, 'Forest Dweller Prosperity Centre', 1952), Bharatiya Mazdur Sangh (BMS, 'Indian Worker's Association', 1955), Vishva Hindu Parishad (VHP, 'World Hindu Council', 1964), Shiv Sena ('Army of Shiva',1966), Deendalyal Research Institute (1972), Seva Bharati ('Service Organisation', 1979), Bharatiya Janata Party (BJP, 1980), Bajrang Dal ('Team of Hanuman', 1984), Dharam Sansad ('Religious Parliament' 1984), Durga Vahini ('Brigade of the Goddess Durga, early 1990s), Swadeshi Jagran Manch, 1991 etc. Practically all these organisations, associations and movements and several others like them, together form the Sangh Parivar ('Family of the RSS') with the

RSS as their 'parent' body. But of all these organisations it is the BJP that has had the greatest success as a political party. Currently, it represents the political face of Hindu cultural nationalism with a mass base. It has succeeded to form governments in several States of India and even headed a coalition government – the National Democratic Alliance (NDA) – in New Delhi from 1998 to 2004. This makes the study of its prominent leaders and their worldviews a noteworthy project.

The Sangh Parivar openly espouses Hindu *rashtra* (nation) as central to its ideology. Hindutva or Hindu cultural nationalism by definition assumes that, in India, Hindus are not just a religious community among many, like the Muslims and the Christians, but a nation by themselves with Hinduism as the unifier. They envisage India as one nation with one culture, one religion and one language, and for them the terms 'Hindu' and 'India' are inter-changeable.[1]

Basically, Hindu nationalists maintain two views with regard to the concept of Hindu *rashtra*. There is one group which argues that India is a Hindu nation from time immemorial, while the other holds that India is not yet fully a Hindu nation in the real sense of the term, but there is a need to make it one. Those who hold the former view argue that all Indians as Hindus, even those who profess other faiths. For instance, in 2003, K.S. Sudarshan, the RSS chief, stated in Amristar that all Muslims living in India are Hindus and all Sikhs are Hindus.[2] In 2005 in the meeting of the BJP's National Executive in Chennai, L.K. Advani stated in his presidential address: "We must remember that the BJP is not merely a political party. Our mission is larger. We are committed to preserve and protect the soul of India, its culture, its civilisational values and ethos"[3] – which according to him is Hinduism. On 31 December 2005 the newly elected BJP president Rajnath Singh in an interview reiterated that he would brook no dilution of the Hindutva ideology.[4] In January 2006 in the meeting of the Chief Ministers of the BJP-ruled States the issue of Hindutva was a major theme and the participants affirmed their faith in Hindutva and took note of the fact that the BJP as a political party is moving towards Hindutva.[5]

The premise on which the official BJP functions is that India is not yet a Hindu *rashtra* but the Hindus need to work towards realising that goal, especially through the mobilisation of the masses and judicious use of political power. For this purpose they politicise Hinduism in order to win elections. Political observers opine that for all practical purposes Gujarat is already a 'Hindu *rashtra* in one State'. Similar experiments are being carried out in other Sates also where the BJP is in power and new Hindutva labs are emerging in India of which Goa is the typical example. The State is steadily seeing a Hindu-Muslim, Hindu-Christian divide.[6] Way back in 1963, Donald Eugene Smith, American political scientist, wrote that it is far too early to dismiss the possibility of a future Hindu State in India, although the possibility does not appear a strong one. The secular State has far more than an even chance of survival in India.[7]

Vidya Bharati, the RSS controlled educational network and its affiliated institutions continue to indoctrinate young minds with ideas of Hindu cultural nationalism. The RSS mouthpieces like *Organiser, Panchajanya*, publishing houses like Voice of India, thrive; and T.V channels like 'Sadhna' continue to drum up the Hindu nationalist propaganda.

Today BJP has emerged as a national party with strong right-wing tendencies which seriously threaten the existence of the minority communities of India. Confronting the minorities is central to BJP politics because they are seen as major obstacles to the realisation of the Hindu *rashtra*. By minorities they mean, especially the Muslims, Christians, Communists, Dalits and Tribals. In 2002 the former Prime Minister of India, V.P. Singh said: "I expect the propaganda of the Hindutva organisations to be relentless. They inflame passions while fighting elections [....] RSS *shakhas* [branches] all over the country are working continuously. Ultimately what they are aiming at is authoritarian rule. Then not only will the minority be targeted, but also those who do not agree with them. You will be declared as anti-national and treated thus. They are already doing it in the case of minorities."[8]

Hindutva ideologues are relentlessly spreading false and misleading notions about the minorities. For instance, the noted journalist and RSS ideologue M.V. Kamath, argues that Christians are not a helpless minority in India. Behind the small minority of Christians there is the unspoken might of the Catholic Church and the power of the Vatican empire, not to speak of the strength of the Baptist, Methodist, Anglican and other Christian/s groups in Europe and the United States.[9] Giriraj Kishore, a senior VHP leader, alleges that the Christians are worse than Muslims in matters of converting. They go around desecrating Hindu gods and asking tribals to accept Jesus Christ. He calls them sugar-coated people who pretend to be harmless when they are against Hinduism.[10] In July 2003 the RSS resolution adopted at the Kanyakumari conclave, alleged that there is a clever nexus between Christian missionaries and militants in Northeast India.[11]

According to John Dayal, the national convenor of the United Christians Forum for Human Rights, Christians trace the violence against them to the BJP's ascent to power.[12] In 2000 the then Archbishop of Delhi and the head of the Catholic Bishop's Conference of India (CBCI), Alan de Lastic, said: "This is the gravest challenge our community has faced in 53 years since independence. India has a glorious heritage but I worry about its future".[13]

It is argued that complacency, indifference and apathy seem to be the three negative virtues which many Indians cultivate assiduously. There is too much of *tamasic* (darkness, sluggishness, inactivity) spirit in them. This is especially manifested after the general elections of 2004. Since the BJP-led NDA government was voted out of power, many relax with the false conviction that the country has been saved forever from the clutches of Hindu communalism, militancy, fundamentalism and nationalism. This has affected even the most gifted and the indomitable activists against Hindutva. Unfortunately, little do they realise that BJP is bidding time to return to power. The BJP's electoral defeat in 2004 was not total and it is still acting as one of the major forces in Indian politics.

Hindutva is already a vast movement in India and among the Hindu diaspora, and it cannot be routed just by an electoral defeat, and that too, won with a small margin. There are still many people in the country who take Hindutva casually and boast of the achievements of the Hindutva governments without being truly aware of their ulterior motives. Others dismiss the BJP as just another harmless political party in the political horizon of India. There are still others who refuse to admit, often due to ignorance, that even in the Congress and other political parties there are hardcore votaries of the Hindutva ideology. In fact, it is no exaggeration to say that even the present UPA government is not free from such elements, and many in this government have won the elections playing the Hindu card.

On 5 April 2005 BJP celebrated the silver jubilee of its foundation. Way back in 1980, Vajpayee, as the first national president of the BJP had said: "I can say with confidence about the future: Darkness will be dispelled, the sun will rise and the Lotus shall bloom".[14] The salient point of his speech was carried by *BJP Today* in April 2005. Vajpayee had also added that the BJP would cross many 'proud milestones' in the future.[15] In April 2006 Advani was seen touring the country on a *rath* ('chariot') with the intention of making the lotus bloom again. The powerful and articulate Venkaiah Naidu, a former president of the BJP, also stated that lotus will bloom again and that they will comeback to power. He even publicly declared that the BJP will not sit in the opposition for five years.

The youth occupy a prominent part of the main targets of the BJP in order to revive its fortunes in the political field. It was emphasised on the occasion of the silver jubilee celebrations of the founding of the BJP in April 2005. "We must take multiple steps to strengthen the BJP's appeal to the youth and make our Party the voice and choice of Young India. The urgency of this task is self-evident when one considers that 65 per cent of India's population today is less than 35 years of age".[16] Thus, the ideology of the Sangh Parivar is very much alive and the fantasy that India belongs to the Hindus alone still lingers on in their minds.

Political observers say that there is a 'division of labour' among the various members of the Sangh Parivar to achieve their goal of the Hindu *rashtra* – RSS is 'cultural', VHP is 'religious'; BJP is 'Political'; Bajrang Dal is 'mass-base'; ABVP is youth sector; Rashtra Sevika Samiti, Mahila Vihbag (of the VHP) and Durga Vahini are women's wings.

Atal Bihari Vajpayee, the former Prime Minister of India, may have declared that he may not be available for active politics in the future. But given a chance he might be willing to enter the parliament for another term. Advani's *rath* still rolls on and his destination is obviously New Delhi. In fact, on 31 December 2005 while stepping down as the president of the BJP he said that he is still in the race and that he has no intention to bow out of electoral politics.[17] The former Human Resource Development (HRD) Minister Murli Manohar Joshi has some unfinished tasks in his saffronisation of Indian education and cultural institutions, and he would seize any opportunity to complete it. Arun Shourie still nurtures his dislike towards all minorities, and now that he is free from administrative responsibilities, he can once again concentrate on targeting the minorities and the secularists of India through his writings.

Narendra Modi reigns supreme in Gujarat as the icon of Hindu communalism and is dreaming of occupying the Prime Minister's or Home Minister's chair in New Delhi, if the BJP returns to power at the Centre in the near future.

The Sangh Parivar backed the making of the film "Dara Singh the Hero" to counter the film "Murder of a Missionary" – based on the life of the Australian Missionary Graham Stains who was burnt alive with his two sons in Orissa on 23 January 1999. It was nothing but an attempt by the Sangh Parivar to make a hero out of somebody who has been held guilty of heinous crimes.[18] He was even proposed as a candidate for the Uttar Pradesh Assembly elections of 2003 by the Dara Shri Dharmaraksha Sena from two constituencies.[19] Dilip Singh Judeo continues his role as the 'high priest' of many *shuddhi* (re-conversion) ceremonies in Chhattisgarh.

The new BJP president Rajnath Singh has called on all the BJP-ruled States to pass the anti-conversion law. In the 2006 Assam Assembly elections the BJP secured ten seats. The RSS has proved that it can make even the iron man Advani bend, as is evident from the episode of Advani's rhetoric on Jinnah's secularism and its aftermath in which Advani had to surrender to the pressure of the RSS and resign as the president of the BJP. This shows that it is the RSS which is in control of the politics of the Sangh Parivar – and it is not a good news for the secularists of India.

In Madhya Pradesh the Christians are constantly under harassment and attack by Hindu right-wing groups.[20] In 2004 it was decided that the VHP will triple its service projects in *vanavasi* (literally 'forest dweller', tribal) areas of the country by 2006 which is the birth centenary of M.S. Golwalkar, the second RSS *sarsangchalak* (supreme leader).[21] In December 2005 Cardinal Telesphore Toppo's effigy was burned in various parts of Jharkhand because he expressed his displeasure about the proposed anti-conversion bill in the State.[22] On 29 January 2006 Catholic bishop of Vasai Rev. Thomas Dabre and some of his priests were attacked by Bajrang Dal and Vanavasi Kalyan Parishad.[23] In Rajasthan, the attacks on the Christians and Dalits are on the increase since 2005 and on 3 March 2006 Hindu extremists offered Rs 11 lakhs each on the heads of the Archbishop Thomas, founder of Emmanuel Mission International, and his son the Rev. Dr Samuel Thomas, president of the organisation.[24] But the local people of Rajasthan gave a vivid picture of the anti-minority attitude in the State. When interviewed some of the people said: "what is happening here reveals the real face of the BJP government in the State".[25] In April 2006 Rajasthan Assembly passed the anti-conversion bill.[26] During the Shabari Kumbh Mela in the Dangs (Gujarat) from 11-13 February 2006 hate and venom were spewed on the Christians and the resolution was taken to ensure that a national law to ban conversions is passed. Many right thinking people called it a 're-conversion fair';[27] the inflammatory slogan frequently heard at Dangs was '*Hindu jago, Christi bhago*' ('arise Hindus, throw out the Christians').[28] In March 2006 the Divine Retreat Centre in Kerala came under CBI enquiry. Among other things, the centre was accused of financial irregularities and scandals of various sorts. On 1 April 2006 the Modi government gave marching orders to Catholic nuns who selflessly served the leprosy patients for 57 years at the Leprosy Hospital in Ahmedabad.[29]

In 2006, when Pope Benedict XVI told India's new ambassador to the Vatican that efforts in some States in India to outlaw conversions were unconstitutional and should be rejected, there was strong reaction from the Sangh Parivar and it accused the Pope of interfering in India's internal affairs.[30] The BJP president Rajnath Singh even wrote a letter to the Pope in protest.[31]

The annual Country Report on Human Rights Practices for 2003 released by the then US Secretary of State Colin Powel described the BJP thus: "a Hindu nationalist political party with links to Hindu extremist groups that were implicated in violent acts against Christians and Muslims".[32] Hindu Diaspora funds flow into the coffers of the Sangh Parivar to support its programmes and pogroms. Anti-conversion law still prevails in Madhya Pradesh, Orissa, Chattisgarh, Gujarat and Arunachal Pradesh. Praful Bidwai reminds us that Hindutva is concentrated in the very persons of leaders like Advani, Narendra Modi and Uma Bharati. It speaks loudly even when they are silent,[33] and all of them, and several others like them, are very active in politics. From all these it is clear that there is a belligerent attitude against the minorities and the atrocities against them go on unabated, even though government in New Delhi is led by the Congress. Hence one may ask where is the reason for complacency about the implementation of Hindutva agenda?

Hindutva ideologues are trying to give to Hinduism a new identity which most Hindus do not accept. But, as Bhaskar Ghose says, that may not be an identity which all Hindus believe; many devout Hindus do not and may even find it obnoxious, but that identity is loudly attributed to all Hindus, through public speeches and skilful use of the media. Adolf Hitler did that in Germany in the 1930s. Hitler was able to get most Germans see Germany as *he* saw it, and Germans as *he* saw them. That was also what the media of the day presented, for Hitler made sure that they did. But the identity so created was false.[34] S.M. Pandya, the head of the department of Sanskrit in St. Xavier's College, Ahmedabad, expressed a similar view in 1998 when he said: "I am very well aware that now a days true Hindutva is attacked by pseudo-Hinduism imported by the cow-belt Hindutva. [....] As a knower and follower of real Hinduism, I should make it quite clear that Hindu religion was never hostile to anyone either in history or in practice".[35]

Indian history reminds us that Hindu nationalism has come back periodically to disturb the peace and tranquillity of the country and to hinder its progress. by fact, the number of Hindu nationalist organisations is increasing in leaps and bounds. Hence as long as organisations like, the RSS, VHP, Shiv Sena, BJP, Bajrang Dal, Hindu Jagran Manch, and the Sangh Parivar as a whole do not stop their anti-national, communalist and fundamentalist orientations and engage in useful and productive activities, there are good reasons not to be complacent about the state of affairs, and to go on without respite, with the fight against Hindu communalism, fundamentalism and nationalism.

What is BJP? What is its ultimate aim? Who really controls this party? Have Indians given a serious thought to these questions? As K.N. Panikkar has rightly observed, the overthrow of the BJP government in the general elections of 2004 does not automatically mean the end of the communal influence. It would persist in the administration and continue to be felt in institutional practices.[36] He goes on to add that fascism and communalism would come to stay if the social, educational and cultural structures are affected by them. Therefore, it is imperative that they be dismantled by using the right means, including legal interventions. A communal political party may have been defeated at the hustings but by that the country has not been cleansed of the communal ideology. It is still alive and active. Panikkar maintains that the secular forces have been, so to say, gifted with a golden and perhaps the last opportunity to countermand communalism, to dismantle its ideological structures to undermine its social ascendancy and to marginalise its political influence. Another such opportunity may not materialise at all.[37]

Many political analysts argue that politically we are getting back to the same context that existed in the country in the late 1980s and early 1990s. Speaking in the context of the twin *rath yatras* announced by the BJP in early 2006, Venkitesh Ramakrishnan said that by any yardstick the new campaign of the BJP can turn out to be the biggest threat posed by the principal opposition to the UPA government. The Sangh Parivar perceives parallels between the policies of the former Rajiv Gandhi-led Congress government and those of the present UPA.[38]

If what is happening in the BJP is true, the organisation is in an advanced stage of decay with in-fights, internal power struggles and ideological uncertainty. Neena Vyas holds that all the factors that make for a Bollywood pot-boiler have come into full play in the BJP – sex, money, murder, drugs, perhaps even poison, corruption, indiscipline and defiance.[39] Still do not write it off as a political party that has run its course. Communal forces and insidious communalism can always rise like the Phoenix. In 1932 Hitler was written off by all political analysts as a non-entity. But he soon came back with vengeance and rose like a star in the political horizon of Germany. Today, BJP is seeking a new strategy to return to power. It may even emerge as a new political party with a new name, just as Jan Sangh appeared as BJP in 1980 when the former was no longer relevant. The RSS, the 'parent' of many communal organisations might abandon BJP and give 'birth' to a new Hindu fundamentalist party to carry forward its subversive agenda of creating a Hindu *rashtra* in India. Since the last century, on an average, in every 25-30 years, India has produced a new Hindu communal political party: first it was the Hindu Mahasabha, followed by the Bharatiya Jana Sangh, and then the Bharatiya Janata Party. Perhaps time is ripe for founding another Hindu communalist and fundamentalist party, if we go by the trends in Indian political history.

Amulya Ganguli observes that a pernicious fascist doctrine never dies out. It can retreat into the woodwork, but bids its time till the moment is opportune enough for it to raise its ugly head. In Europe the end of World War II ensured a long respite from the horrors of the holocaust under the Nazis. But today if it has reappeared in Europe as – Neo-Nazism (*Neonazismus*) and right-wing extremism (*Rechtsextremismus*) – it means that fascism has found new enemies. This time it is not the Jews but the black and brown immigrants.[40]

If Hindutva gains the upper hand in Indian society, many values are at stake for the country. We are told that under the Nazis very few Jews suspected the tragedy that was in store for them. Many did not take the *Judenpolitik* (Jewish politics) of the Nazis seriously. But once they came to power the 'Stormstroopers' (*Sturmabteilungen*, SA) had no inhibitions to deal with the Jews.[41] It is the same with the Indian scenario. Many in India are still complacent about the danger which Hindu nationalism pauses to the country's democracy, secular values and cultural pluralism. Mani Shankar Aiyar observes that we are faced with a replay of the challenge that Jawaharlal Nehru faced between 1949 and 1951,[42] and goes onto add that the hard secular line of Nehru is the only way of corking the communal genie for the foreseeable future.[43]

Mani Shankar Aiyar is perhaps one of the few contemporary Indians who can correctly read the pulse of Indian politics. He is also one of the most credible and fearless secularists and brilliant political thinkers we have in the country today. According to him, a hard secular response is imperative to Hindutva, and it is not enough to be secular, but one must also be actively anti-communal.[44] Definitely, Aiyar has struck the nail aright out has hit it on the head!

Unalloyed secularism – secularism in the true sense of the term is the only thing that can save India from Hindu cultural nationalism. To promote it lip service is not enough. We need to analyse facts and events correctly with foresight and get down to work and avoid any form of complacency, for the danger from Hindu communalism may be in respite, but definitely not over. A counter propaganda is required to instruct, warn and prepare the citizens, especially the youth, in order to fight the insidious cultural nationalism of Hindutva. Gurcharan Das says that a major failure of contemporary Indian public life is that we do not have voices of moderates, Hindus or Muslims. We only hear the shrill voices of extremists at both ends.[45]

The crisis in our country is essentially intellectual and ideological. It is more mental than physical. The present study makes an attempt to remind the Indians about this, and the author has made a careful analysis of the worldviews of the five leading BJP political leaders in order to demonstrate the depth of intellectual, ideological and mental crisis we are in as a nation.

Notes

1. For further information on these topics read the author's earlier writings, especially J. Kuruvachira, *Roots of Hindutva. A Critical Study of Hindu Fundamentalism and Nationalism*, New Delhi, 2005; ID., *Hindu Nationalists of Modern India. A Critical Study of the Intellectual Genealogy of Hindutva*, Jaipur, 2006.
2. See *The Telegraph*, 4 February 2003; *The Indian Express*, 30 January 2003.
3. L.K. Advani, "National Security in Jeopardy", 17.
4. See "No Dilution of Hindutva", 26.
5. See "BJP-ruled States urged to address RSS concerns", 5.
6. For details of the events of March 2006 and the problem relating to the Hindu-Muslim. Hindu-Christian, divide see D. de Souza, "Goa New Hindutva Lab", 24-29.
7. D.E. Smith, India's Secular State, as cited in K.N. Panikkar, *Before the Night Fall*, 59, Princeton, 1963, 501 .
8. V.P. Singh, "Hindus are Next", 32.
9. See *Daily*, 12 July 2000.
10. See S.N. Bhaumik, "Hawk Flock", 27.
11. See *News Time*, 9 July 2003.
12. See S.N. Bhaumik, "Hawk Flock", 26.
13. S.N. Bhaumik, "Hawk Flock", 26.
14. "'The Lotus will Bloom'", 6.
15. See "BJP Upbeat about Its Future", 4.
16. "BJP Destined to be Stronger for a Stronger India", 14.
17. See "Still in the Race", 29.
18. See *The Pioneer*, 3 November 2003.
19. See *The Indian Express*, 22 January 2003.
20. See "Bishop Deplores Harassment of Christians", 46; S.K. George, "Christian Women paraded naked in MP", 11.
21. See "VHP to Triple Its Service Projects in Vanavasi Areas", 12.
22. See "CBCI Decries Burning of Cardinal's Effigy", 13.
23. See "Attack on Bishop a New Strategy", 27-28.
24. See M. Scaria, "Christians at the Receiving end in Rajasthan", 8.
25. See M. Scaria, "Christians at the Receiving end in Rajasthan", 9.
26. See "Rajasthan Passes Anti-Conversion Bill", 5.
27. See C. Prakash, "Anti-Conversion Law. Gujarat Govt. in Limbo", 32; J. Crasta, "Hindutva Ado about Nothing", 18-22.

28. See "'Untold Story of Hindujaan'", 18-19.
29. See C. Prakash, "Nuns Get Marching Orders", 24-26.
30. See "Pope Interferes in India's Internal Affairs", 10.
31. For the full text of Singh's letter to the Pope see "Rajnathji Lodges Protest with the Pope", 11.
32. "A Longstanding but Flawed Democracy", *The Statesman*, 27 February 2004.
33. See P. Bidwai, "The BJP's Second Mascot", 120.
34. B. Ghose, "Questions of Identity", 90-91.
35. S.M. Pandya, "A New Way of Living One's Religious Faith", 75.
36. See K.N. Panikkar, "Down, but not Out", 123.
37. See K.N. Panikkar, "Down, but not Out", 124.
38. See V. Ramakrishnan, "Yatra Challenge", 26. The *Rath Yatra* of Advani in 2006 proved to be a failure.
39. See N. Vyas, "BJP in a State of Siege", 11.
40. See A. Ganguli, "The Fuehrer Rides Again", *The Hindustan Times*, 20 May 2002.
41. See W. A. Frank, "Wer Jude ist Bestimme Ich", 316.
42. See M.S. Aiyar, *Confessions of a Secular Fundamentalist*, 37.
43. See M.S. Aiyar, *Confessions of a Secular Fundamentalist*, 36-37.
44. See M.S. Aiyar, *Confessions of a Secular Fundamentalist*, 18.
45. See G. Das, *The Elephant Paradigm*, 80.

I

Atal Bihari Vajpayee
Unmasking His Hindutva Hardliner Identity

Atal Bihari Vajpayee was born in a Brahmin family in Gwalior, Madhya Pradesh, on 25 December 1924 to Krishna Bihari Vajpayee and Krishna Devi. He was educated at Victoria College (now Laxmi Bai College), Gwalior, and later at Dayanand Anglo Vedic (DAV) College, Kanpur, Uttar Pradesh, where he took his Masters degree in Political Science.[1]

Vajpayee started his career as a journalist and a social worker. He was the general secretary of the Arya Kumar Sabha, a youth branch of the Arya Samaj, in Gwalior;[2] then joined the Rashtriya Swayamsevak Sangh in 1944.[3] He edited *Hindu Rashtra Dharma,* a Hindi monthly, the RSS Hindi weekly *Panchjanya,*[4] and also the dailies *Veer Arjun* and *Swadesh.*[5]

Vajpayee worked as private secretary to Shyama Prasad Mukherjee (1901-1953), the founder of the Bharatiya Jan Sangh and was its president from 1967-1977. Vajpayee was elected to the Parliament in 1957 as a Jana Sangh candidate and was also the leader of the same parliamentary party from 1957-1977.[6]

Vajpayee was the co-founder of the Janata Party and the founding president of the Bharatiya Janata Party from 1980-1986, and leader of the BJP parliamentary party from 1980-1984, 1986-1991 and from 1993-1996. He served in such capacities as external affairs minister during the Janata Party government (1977-1979) and leader of the opposition in parliament in 1993. He was conferred the second highest civilian award *Padma Vibhushan* in 1992 and the 'Best

Parliamentarian Award' in 1994.[7] He became the Prime Minister of India for thirteen days from 16 to 28 May 1996, a second short term from 19 March to April 1998 and again from October 1999 to May 2004.[8] Besides being a politician, Vajpayee is an orator, poet and a scholar and there are several literary works to his credit.[9]

Vajpayee's Concept of Hindutva

Vajpayee's concept of Hindutva is ambiguous as it is seldom clearly and publicly articulated. He claims that Hindutva presents a broad, all-encompassing view of human life. According to him, the ideology is liberal, liberating and implies no ill-will or hatred or violence against any community on any ground. Citing a verdict of the Supreme Court of India in 1995, which 'defined' Hindutva as a 'way of life',[10] Vajpayee argues that Hindutva connotes a noble and elevating way of life. Thus he interprets Hindutva as *Bharatiyata* or 'Indianness': "Hindutva and Bharatiyata have the same meaning. But I would prefer to say Bharatiyata";[11] "This Indianness or *Bharatiyata* (which is not different from Hindutva) is what we should all celebrate and further strengthen."[12] However, Vajpayee laments that today secularism is being pitted against Hindutva under the belief that the two are antithetical to each other, which according to him is incorrect and untenable.[13] He further claims that India has been secular since the beginning of known history.[14]

Vajpayee Image as a Moderate

There is an appalling ignorance both in India and abroad concerning the real political identity of Vajpayee, and consequently, he is often projected as a moderate and secularist. BJP frequently utilised his image for several years with great electoral dividends. In the past, people erroneously considered Vajpayee as 'the right man in the wrong party' and he himself took advantage of his so-called 'soft image' for political mileage. For example, on 27 May 1996 during the non confidence motion debate he said in Parliament: "During the course of this debate a remark has been made repeatedly that Vajpayee is a good person, but the party is not good".[15] In the general elections of April-May 2004, the BJP exploited Vajpayee's misleadingly 'soft' image by promoting a personality cult around him. The national executive meeting of the BJP held in Mumbai in June 2004 endorsed this cult and even acclaimed him as one of the best Prime Ministers of India. L.K. Advani in his speech affirmed: "We were blessed with the leadership of Shri Atalji, who was universally hailed as one of the best prime ministers India has seen."[16]

However, a closer look at Vajpayee's profile and political strategies will reveal another facet of this so-called 'soft image'. Vajpayee is, in reality, the right man in the right party, namely the BJP, which is a political party that is nationalist, communal, anti-secular and fundamentalist, and a re-incarnation of the Jan Sangh, the political wing of the RSS and a close ally of several communal and militant right-wing Hindutva organisations like the Vishva Hindu Parishad and Shiv Sena.[17]

The Arya Samaj Background of Vajpayee

Vajpayee is one of the political leaders whose commitment to Hindu nationalism was derived, first of all, from the Arya Samaj. Many scholars consider Arya Samaj, as the one of the spiritual and intellectual progenitors of the RSS and its offshoot the BJP.[18] Vajpayee himself admits that he was closely associated with this organisation right from his early days. On 31 March 1998 he said: "During my childhood, I came into contact with the Arya Samaj first".[19] At one time he was the general secretary of the Arya Kumar Sabha of Gwalior.[20] The Dayanand Anglo-Vedic College where Vajpayee received higher education was then the nerve centre of the Arya Samaj.[21]

Arya Samaj, founded by Swami Dayananda Saraswati in 1875, was one of the foremost aggressive Hindu organisations in the late 19th and early 20th centuries. The Samaj was a crusading reform movement in Hinduism based on the slogan 'back to the Vedas'.[22] It sought to 'strengthen' Hinduism especially by opposing Islam and Christianity and introducing proselytisation and re-conversion (*shuddhi*) into Hinduism. It opposed caste system, idolatry, untouchability and animal sacrifice and promoted female education and inter-caste marriages, and at the same time it also upheld the sacredness of the cow, infallibility of the Vedas, doctrines of *karma* and rebirth.[23]

Arya Samaj propagated Hindi as the *Aryabhasa* (the language of the Aryans) in the Arya Samaj parlance.[24] The organisation considered Muslims and Christians as aggressors and foreigners and fought tooth and nail against them. It was said: "In the Arya Samaj the Christian Missionary has an avowed enemy."[25] The *shuddhi* or re-conversion movement and the relentless 'war' against the Muslims and Christian missionaries spearheaded by it inspired several other Hindu organisations to follow its example. L.K. Advani says: "One of the cardinal planks of the Arya Samaj programme is *shuddhi* (re-conversion)".[26] Speaking about Arya Samaj, C.F. Andrews observed that the Arya Samaj has been from the first 'decidedly militant in spirit and policy'.[27] Koenraad Elst, a pro-Hindutva writer, admits that the first truly public and sustained polemical attack on Christianity and Islam was mounted by Swami Dayananda Saraswati, the founder of the Arya Samaj. He considers Arya Samaj as a fundamentalist movement in the true sense of the term.[28] Elst adds that the *shuddhi* movement it spearheaded undeniably contributed to the present-day Hindu-Muslim polarisation.[29] In 1927 Arya Samaj created the *Arya Vir Dal* ("Arya Heroes' Organisation") which took up training in physical self-defence in an exact parallel with the contemporaneous RSS.[30]

Mahatma Gandhi repeatedly denounced the Arya Samaj as fanatical.[31] Krishna Kumar, a scholar of Hindu nationalism in India, observes that the Arya Samaj looms so large on the intellectual and social scene of the late nineteenth century northern India that it is unnecessary to establish linkages between the major tenets and concerns of the Arya Samaj and discrete currents of thought and expression available to individuals growing up during that period.[32] The Arya Samaj produced many prominent Hindu nationalists like Bal Gangadhar Tilak (1856-1920), Swami Shraddhannda (1856-1926) and Lala Lajpat Rai (1865-1928). It influenced Hindutva ideologues like Vinayak Damodar Savarkar (1883-1966) and Madhav Sadhashiv Golwalkar (1906-1973), and inspired Hindu nationalist organisations like the Hindu Mahasabha, Jan Sangh, RSS and VHP. O.P. Tyagi who proposed the anti-missionary Freedom of Religion Bill as a Jana Sangh politician under the Janata government in 1978 was an Arya Samaji.[33] Thus, Vajpayee is greatly indebted to Arya Samaj for his legacy of anti-secularism, anti-minoritism, conservative views on Hindu life and practices and Hindu nationalist ideology.

The RSS Roots of Vajpayee

According to some scholars, the two key organisations of the Hindu-right in pre-independence India were the Hindu Mahasabha[34] and the RSS. However, the most powerful Hindu organisation to emerge in post-independence India has been the RSS. It was founded by Keshav Baliram Hedgewar (1888-1940) in Nagpur in 1925. The RSS has lent its organisational skills to two political parties, the Jana Sangh and its de facto successor, the BJP.[35]

RSS is an activist Hindu nationalist movement that aims at making India a Hindu *rashtra*. Hinduism, for the RSS is another name for nationalism.[36] It built a powerful nationwide network under the leadership of M.S. Golwalkar, the successor of Hedgewar. RSS strives for the restoration of the so-called lost Hindu culture, sees Muslims and Christians as invaders and foreigners and Communists as enemies of the Hindu *rashtra*. It insists on self-discipline and character-building, has a paramilitary organisation and hierarchical set-up which many critics see as aspects of its fascist tendencies.

Walter K. Andersen and Shridhar D. Damle who have made a careful study of the RSS observe that the RSS training ideally starts in pre-adolescence and becomes more ideologically oriented during adolescence. Youth is a period when the individual is particularly susceptible to ideological appeals. The RSS expects of its members something very close to religious zeal, demanding from them strict self-control, disciplined activity and identification with the group. A system of myths, rites and symbols are created to help fuse the individual's identity to the larger Hindu community, which the RSS claims to represent.[37] Sumit Sarkar notes that since seven decades or so the RSS has been concentrating on catching boys very young and instilling in them an unquestioning, total discipline: through paramilitary drill, carefully devised games, a repertoire of simple stories and heavy doses of pseudo-history.[38]

The Hitler Youth (*Hitlerjugend*)[39] had a similar method of training the young generation. The Nazis indoctrinated young members of the party with Nazi ideas on leadership, race, discipline and military values. It sent young people to summer camps at which physical fitness, rifle practice, and team building games were given much importance. This organisation became a very important means of bringing young people into the Nazi party. After 1933, the

Hitler Youth became a key Nazi youth movement, which every young German was required to join.[40]

Vajpayee joined the RSS in the 1940s. He came in contact with the organisation while he was still a member of the Student Federation of India.[41] According to Vajpayee, the RSS is a good organisation that teaches discipline and inspires people to do something every day for the country.[42] For a time he was also a devoted RSS *pracharak*.[43] The *pracharaks* are full-time workers selected from amongst most devoted workers of high integrity, whose mission is to serve the society through the Sangh and who, of their own free will, dedicate themselves to the cause without receiving any remuneration.[44] Some even considered Vajpayee as third in lineage after M.S. Golwalkar and Deen Dayal Upadhyaya (1916-1968) in the RSS 'hierarchy', which is no ordinary designation. In 1946 he was sent to Uttar Pradesh as a *vistarak* and quickly began working for the newspaper of Deen Dayal Upadhyaya, becoming the editor of *Rashtra Dharma* in 1948-1949 and later of *Panchjanya*, one of the mouthpieces of the RSS. In 1977, when the Janata Party formed the first non-Congress government in New Delhi, the RSS approved the merger of the Jan Sangh in the new party, and among the three *swyamsevaks* from the Jana Sangh who got cabinet berths was Vajpayee.[45] Even as the Prime Minister of India, Vajpayee affirmed his commitment to the RSS ideology and in keeping with the RSS tradition each year he offered his *gurudakshina*.[46] He consistently defended the RSS during his political career as an organisation which, according to him, has nothing to do with communal riots,[47] and one of the obvious examples of this was during the motion of confidence in Parliament on 27 May 1996.[48] In December 2004 Vajpayee chided the opponents of the RSS for criticising the organisation and challenged them to create, if they can, a single organisation which is as strong as the RSS.[49]

For the RSS 'Hindu' and 'Indian' are synonymous.[50] In the history of the RSS there have been cases of many RSS members being arrested for manufacturing bombs and other weapons.[51] The RSS argues that it has the best of instruments to set right the malady of the nation and the instruments are the swayamsevaks.[52] The RSS sees Hindus alone as the legal citizens of India. It argues that the non-Hindus may stay in the country but wholly subordinated to the Hindu nation, claiming nothing, deserving no privileges, far less any preferential treatment, not even citizen's rights.[53] Adhering to this tradition, the RSS said in Bangalore on 18 March 2002: "Let Muslims understand that their real safety lies in the goodwill of the majority."[54] Vajpayee was the Prime Minister of India then and there was no voice of dissent from him. His silence was an indicators of approval of the RSS policy.

Khushwant Singh, the noted journalist and secularist, states that in 1990 the RSS had over one million members who included, among others, Atal Bihari Vajpayee. He considers the RSS as a Hindu militant and communal organisation which propagates the cause of a Hindu rashtra. It is anti-Muslim, anti-Christian, anti-Left and anti-Gandhi, and follows fascist methods to strengthen the organisation and could be dismissed as a lunatic group. Its political offshoots are the Jana Sangh and today's Bharatiya Janata Party.[55]

Thus the ideological indebtedness of Vajpayee to the RSS is devoid of any ambiguity. According to Krishna Kumar, the Arya Samaj and the RSS are the two major ideologies that have led to the Hindu revivalist or 'fundamentalist' ideology in modern India.[56] Vajpayee's roots are deep in *both* these organisations.

Vajpayee and the Bharatiya Jana Sangh

Bharatiya Jana Sangh was founded by Shyama Prasad Mukherjee in 1951 as an initiative of the RSS to have a political party of its own. It stands for Hindu cultural nationalism and its fundamentals are: one country, one nation, one culture and the rule of the Hindu law.[57] Jana Sangh maintained that Hindi should be the national language, Sanskrit is to be the repository of Indian culture, education needs to be given on the basis of Indian culture, and military training has to be a part of the higher educational curriculum.[58] It pressed for the total prohibition of cow slaughter and together with the RSS organised the Anti-Cow Slaughter Day on 26 October 1952 and began the collection of signature and petitions for a total ban on cow slaughter in India.[59]

Though the political ancestor of the Jan Sangh is the Hindu Mahasabha,[60] its ideological and organisational ancestor is the RSS.[61] Golwalkar picked up his staunch and tried workers to join the new political party founded by Shyama Prasad Mukherjee. Christophe Jaffrelot says: "Golwalkar, having made sure that Mukherjee was in full agreement with the ideals of the Hindu Rashtra, 'chose some of [his] colleagues – staunch and tried workers' – to assist him".[62] It also had members from Arya Samaj and Hindu Mahasabha. Thus the existence of the Jana Sangh enabled the RSS to be represented in party politics.

Before joining the Jana Sangh, Vajpayee was for a time attracted by the Communist ideology. But when, as he alleges, the Communist Party accepted the partition of India on the basis of religion and called it a right of self-determination, he could not go along with it.[63] Later he followed Deen Dayal Upadhyaya into the Jana Sangh where Shyama Prasad Mukherjee made him the party's secretary. Among the twenty-nine members of the Working Committee of 1954 were a number of RSS men, and one of them was Vajpayee.[64] By the mid 1950, the RSS members had already asserted their sway over the party and from that point onwards it was reshaped in the mould of the RSS and its role adapted to conform to the division of labour within the Sangh Parivar. This led Jaffrelot to call the Jana Sangh the replica and auxiliary of the RSS.[65] In 1958 the team expanded when four veteran *pracharaks*, deputed by the RSS were entrusted with organising the party. Vajpayee was sent to Delhi headquarters, where he assisted Upadhyaya; Balraj Madhok was given the north (Jammu and Kashmir, Punjab, Himachal Pradesh and Delhi) and J.R. Joshi the Dravidian south; the western area was entrusted to Sunder Singh Bhandari.[66] Jaffrelot maintains that the participation of some swayamsevaks in the work of the Jana Sangh and their subsequent takeover of the party was part of the elaborate division of labour within the membership of the RSS. It was application in party politics of the principle that the social and psychological reform of Hindu society was needed to provide the cultural basis for the Hindu rashtra.[67]

There was an over-representation of the upper castes, especially the Brahmins, and the Banyas in the Jana Sangh, and Hindu *rashtra* was its political agenda. But in ideology and general organisation it was an extension of the RSS and appealed primarily to Hindu ethno-religious feelings. It stood for the promotion of Hindi as the national language, cow protection and fight against Christian missions. In 1954 the Jana Sangh launched an 'anti-Foreign Missionary Week' protest movement in Madhya Pradesh,[68] the home state of Vajpayee. Craig Baxter observes that the Jana Sangh saw dangers from Christian missionary activity not only in the State of Madhya Pradesh and Madhya Bharat (Central India) but also among the tribals of Assam, Bihar and Orissa.[69]

In 1962 in Uttar Pradesh, the Jana Sangh was prevented from *openly* resorting to Hindu slogans during the election campaign. But the party confined its use of militant Hindu arguments to its door to door propaganda, a method which the density of its network of militants made it possible.[70] In most of its policies Jana Sangh was communal. In 1966-1967 the party raised the issue of cow protection to build up the Hindu vote and projected the cow as the symbol of Hindu identity.[71] 'A vote for the Jana Sangh is a vote for the protection of the cow' was its slogan. It also circulated a pamphlet, the cover of which showed Jawaharlal Nehru killing a cow with a sword.[72]

In 1957 Vajpayee got elected to the Parliament as Jana Sangh candidate from Balrampur.[73] In the late 1960s and early 1970s Jana Sangh demanded indianisation of the minorities especially the Muslims and the Christians of India, which Indira Gandhi denounced as the fascism of the Jana Sangh and compared it to Hitler's persecution of the Jews.[74] After the assassination of Upadhyaya, Vajpayee was elected president of the Jana Sangh in 1967 which post he held till 1977. The surveys relating to the elections of the 1960s situate the main supporters of the Jana Sangh in the higher castes and the professional, white-collar, merchant and other middle class groups. A research carried out by the Centre for the Study of Developing Societies (CSDS) in 1967 revealed that Jana Sangh remained firmly anchored in the 'middle-world' mostly among the higher castes and those with 'white collar' jobs.[75] Many historians argue that Nazi propaganda appealed persuasively to the middle class and it targeted middle class voters and that Nazi ideas had a sympathetic hearing in middle class areas of the cities and in rural areas.[76] Jana Sangh followed a similar pattern of creating a support base for the party – which is being continued by the BJP to this day.

In 1977 Jana Sangh decided to *conceal* the more aggressive features of their nationalism, especially its attitude towards the minorities. In 1977 Jana Sangh merged with Janata Party and in the general elections the latter was victorious with a sizeable representation of the Jana Sangh.[77] Vajpayee was given the external affairs ministry in the Morarji Desai government. During the debate in the Lok Sabha the ex-Jana Sanghis defended cow protection under the Morarji Desai government.

Jana Sangh was a militant Hindu party. A sanskritised Hindu, cow protection and fight against Christian missionaries were parts of the strategy of Jana Sangh right from its existence. The highly controversial report of the Niyogi Commission set up to enquire into Christian missionary activity in Madhya Pradesh is still repeatedly and 'reverently' cited by Sangh Parivar spokespersons and publications. The Jana Sangh-led Madhya Pradesh government of 1967-1968 implemented some of the recommendations of the Niyogi Committee (1956) and imposed a strict test for proving voluntary choice on Christian converts.[78] Jana Sangh also accused the Christians of being involved in the insurgency movement in the Naga Hills of Northeast India.[79] Under the post-Emergency Janata government with a strong Jan Sangh component the destruction of some churches in what was then the Union Territory of Arunachal Pradesh became the occasion for a law in 1978 which made the erection of places of worship subject to administrative permission in that region. A private bill to ban conversions in India was also moved in December 1978 and was supported by the then Prime Minister Morarji Desai. But it had to be dropped in the face of opposition from the Christians and others.[80]

Thus Jana Sangh was a political party that had strong links with the RSS. Right from the early days the Jana Sangh and the RSS were accused of being fascist organisations established on the pattern of Hitler's Nazi party.[81] Nehru, the first Prime Minister of India, said: "If there is any organisation in India which is really communal it is the Jan Sangh".[82] V.S. Naipaul describes the Jana Sangh as a party which seeks a nuclear armoury for India, and combines that with a programme for protecting the holy cow (free fodder for cows, homes for old cows) which might at first be dismissed as a joke. But it isn't a joke but an idea that touches many Hindu-hearts especially the middle class.[83] It was while Vajpayee was the Prime Minister of India that the BJP-led government succeeded in installing the portraits of the founder of the Jana Sangh, Shyama Prasad Mukherjee and that of the Hindu Mahasabha leader V.D. Savarkar in the Central Hall of Parliament.

History reminds us that religious fundamentalism often craves for power and political influence. There was an almost exact parallel between the propaganda and the organisational campaigns of the RSS and those undertaken by the Jana Sangh.[84] For the Jana Sangh, neither Christians nor Muslims are citizens of the Hindu nation. As a political party it kept itself away from the secular and the liberal traditions as established by Mahatma Gandhi and Jawaharlal

Nehru, and became preoccupied with the ideology of militant Hindu nationalism of the RSS and the orthodoxy of the Hindu Mahasabha.[85]

According to Baxter, Jana Sangh epitomises three conflicts that exist in India: The Dravidian-Aryan cultures, Hindu-Muslim, and modernism and traditionalism (Westernisation and Sanskritisation), and in all the three the party takes a specific stand, though often internally divided over the issue.[86]

Vajpayee and the Bharatiya Janata Party

The Bharatiya Janata Party is a re-incarnation of the Bharatiya Jana Sangh. On the 25th anniversary of the founding of BJP in 2005, Advani reminded his party members of this fact. He said: "The BJP is today 25 years old. But our political *yatra* actually commenced way back in 1951 when Dr Shyama Prasad Mukherjee founded the Bharatiya Jana Sangh".[87] In 1980 the Jana Sangh decided to go alone and reconstitute itself as a new independent all India party. Senior leader of the erstwhile Jana Sangh, Vajpayee became the founding President of BJP in 1980. As Jaffrelot affirms: 'The ex-Jana Sanghis created a Bharatiya Janata Party (BJP) – Party of the Indian People – through which they aspired to inherit the mantle of the Janata Party".[88]

On 5 April 1980 the Bharatiya Janata Party was inaugurated. While emphasising 'secularism' Vajpayee, its founding president, insisted that its secularism is different from Congress secularism which he alleged was biased in favour of the minorities in order to create vote banks.[89] However, on the 24th anniversary of the launching of the BJP on 5 April 2004 Jagdish Prasad Mathur and Ashwini Kumar spoke of the BJP as a movement launched in 1926/1927, during the second and third years of the existence of the RSS for achieving *Param Vaibhav* ('Pinnacle of Glory') for the motherland.[90] Again, concerning the BJP-RSS link Advani said: "In 1980, when we were in the Janata Party, that party decided that none of its members would have anything to do with the RSS. It is this decision that led to the formation of the BJP."[91] There is not an iota of doubt that the BJP is the political wing of the RSS.

After the electoral debacle of the BJP in 1984 which won just 2 seats, the party decided to rehabilitate the basic characteristics of the Jana Sangh, such as the appointment of a single general secretary at the national level and the state and of an organising secretary with responsibility for each district. Thus in 1985 L.K. Advani became the party's sole general secretary. He also had the confidence and support of the RSS. In May 1986 Advani became the party president and he appointed three veteran RSS men to the posts of general secretary: K.N. Sahani, a member of the RSS since the 1940s and a *pracharak* in Kashmir before the partition and in Punjab, his home State, between 1949 and 1953; Murli Manohar Joshi, a professor in physics at the University of Allahabad and a *pracharak* who had been elected to the Lok Sabha in 1977; and Krishna Lal Sharma a member of the RSS since 1942 and a *pracharak* since 1946. Other important posts were given to people with RSS background.[92] In 1988 the representation of the RSS in the top levels of the BJP was bolstered by the appointment of K.N. Govindacharya to the new post of political secretary of the BJP president.[93] Thus the re-establishment of the relationship between the RSS and the BJP was complete. It was a repetition of early RSS-Jana Sangh relationship. Like the RSS, the VHP also networked with the BJP. The BJP then entered into alliance with Shiv Sena, another Hindu militant organisation especially on the Ayodhya temple issue.[94]

In 1986 Advani as president of the BJP called for a ban on cow slaughter, a uniform civil code, and the abrogation of the Article 370 of the Indian Constitution, thus returning to issues which had been earlier exploited by the Jana Sangh. In January 1987 at the BJP's National Council in Viyayawada he spoke of the 'danger of minoritism' and 'pseudo secularism'.[95] In the election campaigns of the BJP, the RSS always played an important role. In Madhya Pradesh, for instance, the persistence of the network of activists trained by the RSS and at the same time serving as a basis for the BJP was apparent from the lists of candidates in the elections of 1980 and 1985.[96]

In 1990 the RSS and the VHP prevailed upon BJP to withdraw their support to the V.P. Singh government. 'Mandir' (temple) and 'Mandal' (Mandal Commission report) were the two issues before them – the former mobilised the Hindus in the name of building the Ram temple at Ayodhya, and the latter brought further support of the upper castes as the Mandal Commission report recommended reservation of 27 per cent posts in the central administration and public corporations for Other Backward Classes (OBC).[97]

Hindutva is evidently the central political agenda of the BJP. It was reiterated in no uncertain terms on a number of occasions. For example, Venkaiah Naidu in his presidential address during the national executive meeting of the BJP in Mumbai from 22-24 June 2004, said: "There is once again speculation in a section of the media that the BJP is gong back to Hindutva. The question of going back to Hindutva does not arise, because we have never left it, nor will we ever leave it."[98] He went on to add "as far as the BJP is considered [sic], there is no question of being apologetic about Hindutva".[99] L.K. Advani endorsed the same view: "The BJP has not abandoned, and will not abandon, its ideology [....] We remain firm and unapologetic about our espousal of Hindutva."[100] On 3 August 2004 the BJP, while explaining the '10 Point Conclusion Document' produced after four days of deliberations in Goa, the vice-president of the party and spokesperson Mukhtar Abbas Naqvi stated that Nationalism is another word for Hindutva.[101]

Praful Bidwai says that the BJP is an extremist party with a sectarian agenda and is a dark force of historic proportions. It is diabolically manipulative. BJP is not only just a political party but also a *movement* around religious, social and political issues.[102] In fact during the national executive meeting of the BJP held in Mumbai from 22–24 June 2004 the party was declared as part of a movement. It said: "We are a PARTY THAT IS AN INTEGRAL PART OF A MOVEMENT [sic]."[103] Obviously, the movement is, as everyone knows, for the creation of a Hindu *rashtra* out of secular and pluralistic India, for it was said: "What is this talk of a Hindu Rashtra in the next two years? *India has always been a Hindu Rashtra*."[104] The tallest leader of the BJP – Vajpajee – is uncompromisingly committed to this movement.

An Artificially Created Larger-Than-Life Image of Vajpayee

The BJP consistently projected a larger-than-life image of Vajpayee to the Indian masses through its propaganda for gaining political mileage. For the BJP, Vajpayee has been their trump card for winning elections. This was especially manifested during the general elections of 2004. The BJP ran a two-month long campaign projecting Vajpayee as the party's biggest asset and pointing out the absence of a similar tall leader in the opposition camp. The question which the BJP leaders frequently asked was: 'Who could match the towering personality of Vajpayee?' In their perception, the general elections of 2004 hinged on 'Vajpayee versus a question mark' – a reference to the opposition party's inability to present a candidate of the 'stature' of Vajpayee for prime ministership. Their exaggerated propaganda even presented him as one having all the qualities of Plato's 'philosopher king' and Kautilya's (Chanakya's) *Rajarshi* (wise and righteous king).[105]

During the elections of 2004 Vajpayee's photograph was printed on almost every page of the BJP manifesto. In the "Vision Document 2004" (a 48 page booklet) the BJP showed that the party's unique selling point in the elections was the person of Vajpayee, who was projected as the embodiment of India's best political traditions. The Document contained photographs of Vajpayee taken during the last 52 years. They projected him as a nationally accepted leader. During an interview, Arun Jaitley, one of the key strategists of the BJP for the 2004 general elections, said: "The basis of our optimism is that popular choice is restricted. That is, the NDA under Vajpayee versus we don't know. There is no alliance, no leader, no common minimum programme, no performance, and no capacity on the other side".[106]

The BJP ran a high-tech campaign transmitting Vajpayee's appeal to the electorate through telecommunication channels. Anyone could dial the BJP phone-in-service number '3030 1000' and hear a message from Vajpayee, his rendition of a poem, campaign songs of the BJP and audio recordings of some of the achievements of the NDA government. By dialling '3030 100' callers could also participate in a slogan contest and the caller who sends the best slogan would get a special gift from the Prime Minister Vajpayee.[107] We give below some extracts from the BJP propaganda aimed at creating a larger-than-life image of their leader:

> "Today, Shri Atal Bihari Vajpayee is the tallest, most popular and most respected leader among all sections of the Indian society, including the minorities."[108]
>
> "Few nations have had the good fortune to be led by a man of Mr Vajpayee's calibre. This is the moment to pay tribute to a giant [....] If he has not been able to fulfil the unfinished tasks of nation building he had himself laid out, it is because he was not given the time."[109]
>
> "India with Atalji at [sic, as] the Prime Minister is today one of the most important poles in world politics."[110]

"he [Vajpayee] is clearly the front-runner. Not only this, his stature has grown and the grand old man is seen as the biggest political brand. Sachin Tendulkar of politics."[111]

"Mr. Vajpayee [...] has proved to be a true Rajarshi [wise and righteous king] as envisioned by Kautilya."[112]

"he [Jawaharlal Nehru] was undoubtedly a true democrat, patriot and a visionary and so is Mr.Vajpayee."[113]

"[Vajpayee is] the Statesman India Adores and the World Admires."[114]

"speaking in a region of the sub-continent where the Vedas and Upanishads were formulated, Atalji spoke like a Vedic sage."[115]

"With courage of conviction, Mr.Vajpayee traced the contour of a dream few before him had dared to: India among the best, India better than the best, India Shining."[116]

"In this election [of 2004], there are only three issues: Development, development, development. Vajpayee, Vajpayee, Vajpayee. India, India, India."[117]

"Mr. Vajpayee rose above his ideological anchor. He built from scratch. He started with a bang: Pokhran II [nuclear test, 1998] told the world that India was no pushover on the global stage. With that first act of bold national assertion, he would come to be feted at the high table of the world's great powers."[118]

"Watching on Doordarshan [Indian TV] Prime Minister Atal Bihari Vajpayee addressing the 12th SAARC Summit at Islamabad in January 4, 2004, one felt it was not a politician or a diplomat, but a statesman who looks far ahead towards the future."[119]

Praful Bidwai observes that the BJP 'Vision Document 2004' of 48 pages had no fewer than 54 of his pictures similar to a long series of photographs accompanying the hundreds of newspaper and television advertisements used for the 'India Shining' campaign and promotional material showering praise upon Vajpayee. The advertisement had a definite pattern. Vajpayee's face was everywhere. In the BJP campaign he invariably stood taller than ordinary mortals. The BJP thus glorified Vajpayee as a superman, a kindly demigod, a miracle worker, a visionary and a statesman in whose hands lay the destiny of India.[120] Thus the "Vision Document 2004" took the personality cult to new heights. But such sycophancy about an individual is only slightly less crude than the personality cult about Hitler and Mussolini, or Stalin and Kim-II Sung. The BJP's publicity material has the same fawning, adoring attitude to Vajpayee as Nazi sympathiser Leni Riefenstahl's films on Hitler.[121] He was even depicted as the Father of the (New) Nation – as if he were on par with Jawaharlal Nehru or Mahatma Gandhi.[122]

As a culmination to BJPs larger-than-life image-building of Vajpayee, the June 2004 issue of the *BJP Today* stated: "Even in defeat [in the general elections of 2004), he [Vajpayee] will go down in history as arguably India's best and indisputably the most visionary Prime Minister".[123] It may be recalled that in Adolf Hitler's Germany the Nazi propaganda did the same. It projected a larger-than-life image of Hitler and presented him as the charismatic saviour of the German people. This was an important aspect of Nazi propaganda.[124]

However, it can well be stated that outside the BJP media none saw anything striking in Vajpayee apart form being a shrewd politician who has grown old in wearing the masks of moderation and secularism and a notorious specialist in speaking with a fork-tongue. Bidwai assesses Vajpayee as follows: "A mediocre leader with a shallow comprehension of global and national developments."[125] The BJP propaganda was obviously a desperate attempt to create a titan out of a pigmy in order to capture political power in New Delhi.

Ally of the Fascist Shiv Sena

Vajpayee betrayed his anti-secularism and communalism when he allied with Shiv Sena[126] which is described as a fascist, militant and parochial organisation. In its party manifesto it is stated: "We are Hindustanis and, therefore, Hindu is the belief of our party. We love Hinduism more than we love ourselves."[127] After the demolition of the Babri mosque Bal Thackeray said that if his 'boys' (Shiv Sainiks) had done it, he was proud of them.[128]

During the past four decades Shiv Sena has evolved into a militant, fundamentalist and nationalist organisation whose leader never fails to use any opportunity to attack minority communities, especially the Muslims. It has projected itself as an organisation anxious to protect the Hindu interests. Sena has the reputation of being prone to incite violence. This has been focused in several crimes. Often it uses violence to attain its goals. Shiv Sena earned notoriety in the 1960s and 1970s when it attacked South Indian and Gujarati establishments in Mumbai. It gained further strength after it broke the Left-led trade union movement in the textile industry of Mumbai. In 1992-1993 it became more crime prone by its involvement in the post-Babri mosque riots in which about a thousand people were killed, mostly Muslims.[129] It was held responsible for violence against the Biharis who came to Mumbai to give the Railway Recruitment Board examinations. It gained notoriety for its attacks on north Indian fishermen.[130]

In 1984 Shiv Sena aligned with the BJP over the Ram temple issue and soon they became political allies. The Shiv Sena *shakhas* (branches) are of great help for the BJP to reach out to the masses. Today the Sena believes that it is the upholder of Hindutva. In fact, Bal Thackeray likes to call himself the *Hindu Hriday Samrat* ('Emperor of Hindu Hearts'). While the BJP needs the Shiv Sena, given its consistent electoral performance in the Konkan belt and in Mumbai, the Sena needs to use the BJP's platform of Hindutva.[131]

In the 1999 general elections, of the 48 Lok Sabha seats in Maharashtra, the Shiv Sena-BJP combine won 28, of which the Shiv Sena secured 15. The Sena held important posts in the Vajpayee government, the most prominent one being the position of Lok Sabha speaker by M.M. Joshi. In the 2004 elections the Sena put up candidates not only in Maharashtra but also in the neighbouring states: three constituencies in Northern Karnataka, two in Goa and one in Dadra and Nagar Haveli. During the Shiv Sena-BJP election campaign in March 2004, Bal Thackeray said: "The Shiv Sena will not allow India-Pakistan cricket matches in the country if Pakistan continues to encourage cross-border terrorism."[132]

Perhaps, Laloo Prasad Yadav has correctly assessed the true identity of the BJP when he said: "The BJP is a communal party. But it is just the *mukhouta* (mask) and the real forces behind it are the RSS, the VHP and the Shiv Sena."[133]

Defender of Narendra Modi a 'Modern Day Nero'

Narendra Modi is the symbol of Hindutva consolidation in the recent times. After the spectacular election victory of the BJP in Gujarat–127 seats in the 182-member assembly – under his leadership in Gujarat in December 2002, Vajpayee told *Dainik*

Bhaskar that the Gujarat elections will help the nation understand secularism in the proper perspective. Gujarat has released new energies, which must be skilfully used to help the party preserve the values of Hindu life.[134] On the day of the swearing in ceremony Modi went over to the special enclosure to seek the blessing of Vajpayee, Advani, Joshi and other party leaders, by touching their feet[135] – an obvious sign of the support and confidence which Modi enjoys from the senior BJP leaders.

Modi is not just another BJP leader or Gujarat Chief Minister. Today, for the public, he is the organiser of the Gujarat pogrom 2002.[136] Ashok Singhal, of the VHP said: "Godhra happened on February 27 [2002] and the next day, 50 lakh Hindus were in the streets. We were successful in our experiment of raising Hindu consciousness, which will be repeated all over the country now".[137]

The extent and magnitude of the crime committed in Gujarat during the post-Godhra incidents in 2002 is unimaginable. Reports show how rape, especially gang rape, and defiling and mutilation of the female body were central planks of the violence in Gujarat. Thousands of Muslim women suffered horrific forms of bestiality when they were raped to the shouts of *har har Mahadev* and 'Go to Pakistan', 'Why are you in Hindustan?' The cutting off of women's breasts, the splitting open of their bellies, the spearing and burning of their foetuses were virtually ubiquitous in Gujarat.[138] Studies have shown that the violence committed in Gujarat fits the legal criteria of Article 2 of Genocide Convention.[139]

Muslims complain that Vajpayee as Prime Minister of India said nothing and did nothing when Muslims were being killed in Gujarat in 2002, let alone removing Narendra Modi, the Chief Minister of the State.[140] Praful Bidwai argues that the only real proof of genuine regret on the part of Vajpayee would have been to dismiss Narendra Modi. Instead, Vajpayee addressed several election meetings with him.[141] He did not hesitate to lavish praise on Modi for bringing 'peace and prosperity' to Gujarat and asked other States to 'take a lesson' in turning themselves into 'investment destinations' like Gujarat. He then asked the people of Gujarat to forgive and forget the past. This statement demolished any hope that the BJP's central leadership would exercise restraining or sobering influence on Modi, remind him of his constitutional duty and promote the cause of justice for the victims. Modi himself continued to brand maliciously all human rights-defenders as 'five-star activists' and 'pseudo-secularists' bent on trying to tarnish the image of Gujarat.[142] *The Times of India* wrote about Vajpayee: "A leopard, they say, cannot change its spots. But in India we have long been prepared to believe otherwise. A case-point is that of prime minister Atal Bihari Vajpayee [....] Mr Vajpayee gave the discredited chief minister a virtual clean chit even as he sanctified the post-Godhra carnage in Gujarat as an inevitable reaction."[143]

Vajpayee never showed serious concern in rehabilitating the victims of the Gujarat pogrom. He did not show any real sympathy for them. All that he did was to pay lip service like a seasoned politician. Addressing the BJP parliamentary party meeting on 17 December 2002, Vajpayee stated, defending Modi: "We are being asked whether we will adopt the Gujarat formula elsewhere. I ask them. 'Will they repeat Godhra as well? [...] It saddens me that not many from the Muslim community are stepping forward to say they are repentant for Godhra."[144] After the Godhra incident, Vajpayee during his speech in Goa said: "Wherever there are Muslims, they do not want to live with others (who practise different faiths). Instead of living peacefully, they want to preach and propagate their religion by creating fear and terror in the minds of people."[145] This was a species of 'negative campaigning' against opponents, a tactic which the Nazis in Germany used very effectively.

About Vajpayee, Seema Mustafa says that if the former Prime Minister is wedded to secularism, as he so often wants everybody to believe, he should have asked Narendra Modi to toe the line set out in the Constitution of India.[146] But Vajpayee used Narendra Modi in the election campaigns of the BJP during the state assembly elections of 2003 and the general elections of 2004. In fact, during the Assembly elections of 2003 Narendra Modi was drafted as a star campaigner of the BJP in all the four states of Madhya Pradesh, Rajasthan, Chattisgarh and Delhi, and was expected to address some 40 election meetings. On several occasions during public meetings Vajpayee and Modi shared the dais. Vajpayee needed agents or instruments to accomplish his mission. Narendra Modi was one such to fulfil the criteria needed.

Narendra Modi is one of the BJP leaders most dreaded by the minority groups and secularists of India. The appeal of the Gujarat government against the transfer of case to the Maharashtra court was dismissed in 2004. While doing so the Supreme Court of India came down heavily on the Gujarat government. In a historic verdict it called the leaders of the Narendra Modi-led Gujarat government 'modern day Neros' who looked elsewhere when innocent children and helpless women were burning, and were probably deliberating how the perpetrators of the crime can be saved or protected.[147] Millions of Indians and many human rights activists both in India and outside rejoiced when the Supreme Court of India defended the victims of the Gujarat pogrom and castigated Modi by calling him 'a Modern day Nero'. But Vajpayee disgraced himself and brought ignominy to his high office by supporting Modi.[148] "Vajpayee will go down in history as the *defender* of the 'modern-day Nero' of Gujarat."

'Life-long' Association with Hardliner L.K. Advani

Lal Krishna Advani is a Hindutva hardliner, a staunch votary of Hindu nationalism and the icon of communal politics in India. The concept of secularism is alien to him and he openly mixes religion with politics. He is adept in Adolf Hitler's Nazi methods,[149] while being greatly influenced by V.D. Savarkar's *Hindutva* in shaping his concept of Hindu nationalism.

Advani is one of the faces of aggressive Hindutva in the BJP. His roots too, as is the case with Vajpayee, goes back to the RSS and the Jana Sangh. Commemorating the 100th anniversary of the birth of Keshav Baliram Hedgewar – the founder of the RSS – Advani declared: "We will march ahead in co-operation with those who support the cause [of Ram] and without bothering about the opposition from some quarters."[150]

Advani controls the BJP. It was in 1995, on the eve of the 1996 general elections, that Advani conceded the crown of Prime Ministership to Vajpayee, who is generally considered the mask (*mukhota*) of moderation, who could be trusted to do the Sangh Parivar's bidding while deploying rhetoric to project a liberal image.[151]

Advani was the most powerful person in the BJP-led NDA government Vajpayee headed as Prime Minister. Vajpayee appointed Advani to two coveted posts in his government, namely, that of the Deputy Prime Minister and the Home Minister. On 5 April 2004 Vajpayee said in Lucknow's Ambedkar Park that he became the Prime Minister in 1999 *because* it was Advani who wanted him to become so.[152] After the defeat in the general elections of 2004 Vajpayee was elected Chairman of the Parliamentary Party.

Education Ministers' Conference in New Delhi, Vajpayee reiterated that human resources development is the most critical area in nation-building because the development of a nation will depend on the education of her citizens.[165] To look after this important department, Vajpayee appointed none other than the RSS trained Hindutva hardliner Murli Manohar Joshi, a former professor of physics at the Allahabad University. During the 2004 general elections some advertisements carried larger than life pictures of Murli Manohar Joshi and Vajpayee together.

BJP's educational policy ever since the party came to power was dictated by an obsession to introduce obscure and strange Hindu doctrines and ideologies in the academic curricula of the country. Joshi had commendable success in carrying out the BJP agenda of saffronisation of education. It was during Vajpayee's rule that saffronisation of education received a flip in the name of the so-called preservation and propagation of Indian culture and values – which for him meant Hindu culture and Hindu values. Lauding Joshi's efforts at saffronisation of education Vajpayee said: "[I] strongly endorse the change in [NCERT] textbook curriculum effected by Dr Joshi,"[166] "I have seen that the Opposition has launched an attack on Dr Joshi, accusing him of saffronising the education system. Saffron is the colour of performing *yajna* and sacrifice. So, we encourage the colour."[167]

Tampering with the educational system, curricula and textbooks of India is in the blood of the RRS – an old strategy of the RSS in order to indoctrinate the masses with its nationalist and sectarian ideology. In the course of its history Dayanand Anglo Vedic schools and colleges (Arya Samaj-affiliated educational institutions),[168] Banaras Hindu University (BHU),[169] Vidhya Bharati,[170] and Saraswati Mandirs[171] (RSS-affiliated schools), etc., were established in order to better co-ordinate this task. Where Krishna Kumar writes: "The BJP continues to pursue its hegemonic agenda in educational and cultural spheres with the help of the RSS, as well as a variety of quasi-cultural organisations and fellowships composed primarily of unemployed or self-employed youth."[172]

Due to Vajpayees's Arya Samaj and RSS training he knows better than anyone else the importance of education in indoctrinating the masses, especially the young generation. For this purpose he deliberately chose Dr Murli Manohar Joshi to pursue and implement the Sangh Parivar agenda of indoctrination of the young minds in Hindu cultural nationalism, just as Hitler chose Dr Joseph Goebbels for a similar purpose.

Defender of Tainted Ministers in the Cabinet

Vajpayee as Prime Minister of India inducted into his council of ministers many 'tainted' persons and some of them held vital portfolios in his government. For example, L.K. Advani held the important offices of the Deputy Prime Minister and of the Home Minister; Murli Manohar Joshi that of the Human Resource Development; George Fernandes that of Defence. Uma Bharati was initially a Minister of State in the HRD ministry and later Minister for Coal and Mines. They functioned as cabinet ministers while facing accusations of serious wrongdoing. Advani, Joshi and Uma Bharati, for instance, faced two charges each in two courts for delivering inflammatory speeches prior to the demolition of the Babri mosque on 6 December 1992, and for criminal conspiracy to demolish the mosque in the beginning of 1990.[173] The three leaders were charged by the trial court under Section 153-A of the Indian Penal Code for their complicity in the demolition of the Babri mosque. Section 153-A makes promoting enmity between different groups on the basis of religion, race, place of birth, residence and language an offence.[174] Advani had no compunction in continuing as Deputy Prime Minster and Home Minister despite facing serious charges in court, and like him, other ministers did the same. In spite of the overwhelming evidences against these ministers and many demands from the public to remove them from the Council of Ministers, Vajpayee persisted in his stout resistance from removing them out of his cabinet. In addition, Uma Bharati had a case pending in the High Court of Hubli, Karnataka, since 1994 for defiance of the court.[175] In spite of this Vajpayee 'rewarded' Uma Bharati with the Chief Ministership of his own home State of Madhya Pradesh.

George Fernandes as Defence Minister faced charges of serious corruption relating to defence purchases which was exposed by the news portal Tehelka.[176] Dilip Singh Judeo was another person in the Vajpayee's cabinet charged with serious malpractices. He was caught on camera accepting a huge sum from an unidentified person in lieu of certain ministerial favours.[177] He was also notorious for his aggressive re-conversion (*shuddhi*) activities. To this we need to add that Vajpayee and his government defended Jayalalita as the Chief

Minister of Tamil Nadu, and Narendra Modi the Chief Minister of Gujarat while they were accused of serious crimes. D. Raja, the Communist Party of India's national secretary states: "in principle no tainted person should be made a Minister. 'But what about Jayalalitha and Narendra Modi, who have been indicted by the Supreme Court in serious cases? Are they not tainted and are they not continuing in office as Chief Ministers? Is not the BJP defending them?."[178] Yet, paradoxically, Vajpayee declared: "Any person, howsoever influential, and any organisation howsoever strong, will be dealt with according to the law for any activity violative [sic] of the law;"[179] "if anyone from our party [BJP] is found indulging in corruption, he is expelled."[180]

Blatant inconsistency in ethical principles was evident in Vajpayee's reaction to the United Progressive Alliance (UPA) government which came to power in 2004 with Dr Manmohan Singh as Prime Minister. Vajpayee endorsed and actively participated in the agitations organised by the opposition party demanding the removal of the 'tainted' ministers in the UPA government. He refused to admit that his own cabinet ministers had not been 'eminent moral beings', and had conveniently forgotten to clean his own front yard. In June 2004 both the houses of parliament adjourned after the opposition, the National Democratic Alliance (NDA), disrupted proceedings demanding the sacking of 'tainted' ministers in the UPA government. The paradox is that the protest against the 'tainted Ministers' (Laloo Prasad Yadav, Muhammad Taslimuddin, Jai Prakash Yadav, Shibu Soren, M.A. Fatmi, Premchand Gupta) in the Manmohan Singh government was led by NDA leaders like L.K. Advani and George Fernandes,[181] the very persons who were themselves considered by the public as seriously 'tainted'.

An Adept in Doublespeak

Doublespeak is an art which Vajpayee seems to have cultivated since his younger days and developed to perfection during his long political career. Being a seasoned politician his talks are calculated and opportunistic and he makes sure that he does not depart from his Sangh Parivar ideology.

K.N. Panikkar commenting on Vajpayee's notorious 'talent' for doublespeak observes that wherever attempts were made to disturb the *status quo* at Ayodhya, he expressed his anguish, but soon gave the impression that such acts were inspired by the legitimate aspirations of the Hindus and thus justified what he had earlier disapproved.[182] Vajpayee insisted that building the temple at Ayodhya is the essential test of patriotism which lies in devotion to Ram.[183] While releasing the agenda of BJP-led National Democratic Alliance in New Delhi on 8 April 2004 he said: "we have not forgotten our promises and Ayodhya still plays a dominant role in our agenda."[184] He even maintained that with the demolition of the Babri mosque a symbol of national shame had been erased.[185] But the same Vajpayee said during an election campaign that demolishing the mosque was a Himalayan blunder which ruined everything.[186] Again the same Vajpayee stated in an interview in May 2004: "Ram Temple or Hindutva are not election issues for us [BJP]."[187]

When Vajpayee visited Gujarat after the notorious Godhra and post-Godhra incidents of 2002 his rhetoric and doublespeak did not fail him. He said: "With what face, I do not know, will I go abroad after all has happened here."[188] He spoke of it on television as a 'black mark on the nation's forehead' which had 'lowered India's standard in the world'.[189] But a week later, at the BJP's national executive meeting in Goa on 12 April 2002 Vajpayee revealed his real identity. He argued that wherever Muslims are, there is always trouble. He then asked who started the Godhra incident of 2002? The answer was obvious to him and the BJP that it was the Muslim community that had started it. He said: "had the Sabarmati Express train incident been condemned, the subsequent violence could have been avoided."[190] Vajpayee stunned the world by defending and justifying the post-Godhra carnage.

Vajpayee in his usual poetic rhetoric declared: "We are absolutely clear on the Gujarat communal strife. We will not spare anybody, and no criminal involved in the violence would be allowed to go scot-free, whatever his reach. The country belongs to people of all religions, ethnic and linguistic group. My government will ensure their protection."[191]

A.G. Noorani observes that the victims of post-Godhra were taunted, not consoled, still less succoured by Vajpayee's words. In addition, the Muslim community was condemned *en bloc* globally, for he said: "Wherever there are Muslims, they do not want to live with others. Instead of living peacefully, they want to preach and propagate their religion by creating fear and terror in the minds of others."[192] "Islamic fundamentalists are spreading terror and intimidation. This is [the] opposite [of] the culture of Hinduism."[193] When some of the Al Qaeda activists in Singapore were arrested, Vajpayee said: "Wherever Muslims live in large numbers, the rulers apprehend that Islam could take an aggressive turn."[194] The same Vajpayee also praised Islam as a peace-loving tolerant religion.[195]

The violence in Gujarat of 2002 persisted for over six weeks. On 17 December 2002 Vajpayee spoke at the BJP's parliamentary party meeting thus: "Why didn't many people of the Muslim community condemn the Godhra incident? Even today there is no repentance. There had not been much opposition from the minority community after the Godhra carnage."[196] He was all praise for Narendra Modi for the 'good work' he had done. He sang a different tune only after the electoral debacle of the BJP in May 2004 and wanted Modi to be removed as Chief Minister of Gujarat. Vajpayee said in an interview to a T.V. channel at Manali, Himachal Pradesh, where he had gone for a holiday, that Gujarat riots was one of the causes of BJP's defeat in the elections and that Narendra Modi's removal from the government was one of the options that would be discussed at the Mumbai meeting of the national executive of the BJP.[197]

Two years after the Gujarat riots, on the eve of the general elections of 2004 Vajpayee pleaded for forgiveness from their Muslim victims, who were yet to be rehabilitated. He said: "One who forgives is a greater person than one who seeks forgiveness."[198] Equally belated was his promise that 'those guilty will be punished'. Vajpayee knew very well that the Gujarat government headed by Narendra Modi was responsible for launching persecutions and that he had absolutely no intention of punishing the guilty. This led A.G. Noorani to ask why should one make promises and play with people's emotions? Besides, a plea for forgiveness is an admission of wrong-doing and guilt.[199]

Retired Colonel M.J. Shamsi who is associated with the Nadwatul Ulema in Lucknow, a major centre for Islamic studies in India, says: "In Goa he says Muslims should trust the BJP, then in Mumbai he says Muslims themselves do not live in peace and harmony. He says one thing today and another tomorrow."[200]

In January 2004 in Delhi, Vajpayee came out with trenchant criticism against the vandalism of the Bhandarkar Oriental Research Institute (BORI), Pune, by the front organisation of his electoral allies ostensibly in retribution for the denigration of the Maratha icon Shivaji in a book that was partly researched there. On the election campaign trail in Maharashtra in March the same Vajpayee changed his views and fully declared his endorsement of the state government's ban on the book. He added that the central government was willing to do all that was necessary to avenge the insult inflicted upon the Maratha sense of honour.[201]

The double talks of Vajpayee were heard also on other occasions. For instance, he said: "We believe in the concept of *Sarva Dharma Sambhav* ('all religions are equal')."[202] He publicly said in Teheran on 11 April 2001: "We do not consider any religion foreign to us. For nearly a thousand years, Islam, has been part and parcel of our national life."[203] He also stated that in Teheran that since his youth Moharrum processions made a profound impression on him – a secret which, says A.G Noorani, Vajpayee had successfully concealed in India for long years.[204] But it was the same Vajpayee who also said: "'We' [Hindus] are different from and superior to the 'later arrivals'; we were secular even in the early days when Muslims and Christians were not here. We have *allowed* them to do their prayers and follow their religion."[205] These words came from the Prime Minister of a democratic country. For Vajpayee 'we' means the Hindus and 'they' denotes the Muslims and the Christians who are not eligible to be true Indian citizens but live in India only because of the magnanimity and tolerance of the Hindus.

Vajpayee's post-election statements in June 2004 were provoked by the shock of unexpected electoral defeat and loss of power. He was keen that Narendra Modi be removed from being the Chief Minister of Gujarat on the ground that his handling of the Godhra incidents in Gujarat was a key factor for the defeat of the BJP. But Noorani argues that the thought of Modi's dismissal was inspired by *politics, not ethics*. If Modi is ever removed from being the Chief Minister of Gujarat, it will not be because he performed as a Nero in 2002 but because he failed to perform as a hero in 2004 general elections.[206] But paradoxically Vajpayee had also said to the members of the BJP Parliamentary party on 1 June 2004: "Gujarat or the Modi factor had nothing to do with this [general election 2004] verdict."[207]

In the 1980s BJP campaigned against the appeasement of Muslims by the so-called 'pseudo-secular' parties and acquired national prominence and credibility among the middle class.[208] But during the 2004 elections Vajpayee himself wooed the Muslims with promises. He offered 2,00,000 jobs for Urdu teachers and handsome grants for Madrasas.[209] BJP also claimed that their leader Vajpayee does not believe in political opportunism.[210]

However, it is to be noted that, as Bidwai observes, the abject manner in which Vajpayee solicited Muslim votes lacks grace and decency. He had not once repudiated the BJP's communal ideology or demonstrated that he was truly sorry for the violence unleashed against Muslims in the past years, especially in Gujarat. The only proof of genuine regret would have been to dismiss Narendra Modi which never happened. Instead, Vajpayee addressed election meetings with him. His appeal for Muslim votes not only reeked of sanctimonious dishonesty but also downright duplicity in resorting to cheap tricks to confuse Muslims.[211]

In mid-April 2004 on the eve of the general elections 2004 Vajpayee said that there are no serious ideological differences between the BJP and the Samajwadi Party (SP) and that the two could even form an alliance. The objective of the ploy was to draw Muslims away from the Samajwadi Party, hitherto the BJP's strongest opponent.[212]

It has been rightly observed by J. Kattoor that a leopard cannot shed its spots and a dog cannot get its tail straightened. Even so Vajpayee cannot give up his habit of double talk.[213] F. Arackal says: "Vajpayee is a master of 'Double-Talk', [...] 50 years of political experience has not taught him 'straight talk'."[214] Because of this doublespeak Vajpayee has often been called a mask by many, including K.N. Govindhacharya, one of BJP's notable leaders.[215] On 18 April 1998 during the 'Motion of Confidence' Mulaym Singh Yadav said: "I never doubted your [Vajpayee's] wisdom and understanding. My only regret is that you have been labelled a mask."[216] He then added: "The day you throw away this mask, we shall stop opposing you."[217]

Did Vajpayee with his doublespeak deserve to lead the nation as Prime Minister which has as its motto *satyameva jayate* ('truth alone triumphs')? There is much truth in Praful Bidwai's description of the BJP as a political party that is diabolically manipulative with a sectarian agenda and mired deeply in duplicity, deception and outright dishonesty,[218] and Vajpayee was the founder president of such a party and had led it from the front for decades and became the Prime Minister of India on its strength. Swami Agnivesh said on the eve of the general elections of 2004: "I would contest the coming

Lok Sabha elections against the Prime Minister [Vajpayee] from Lucknow or support a candidate who was capable of defeating him. My main objective is that Vajpayee should be defeated."[219]

Politics of Expediency

Sangh Parivar always needed one or more enemies in order to consolidate its aggressive Hindu community. After the electoral success of Narendra Modi in Gujarat, in December 2002, the BJP party's national executive at its meeting on 23rd of the same month in New Delhi, described the Gujarat verdict as an endorsement of the party's commitment to cultural nationalism. Venkaiah Naidu the then president of the BJP even spoke about replicating the Gujarat experiment in Sates going for elections in 2003, but soon backtracked and clarified that he only referred to repeating the party's experience of ensuring a cohesive campaign.[220]

It is certain that Gujarat pogrom of 2002 would not have happened if the BJP regime in Delhi had not signalled to its followers that they would not be called to account if they persecuted members of any minority group. Persecution of the Christians was started in an organised way in Gujarat already from 1997, the one State where the BJP has on its own a stable majority, and spread to the Adivasi areas of Orissa. In Gujarat it began with attacks on Christians in the Dangs district in 1998, as soon as the BJP–led government came to power in Delhi. On 8 October Gujarat's Director-General of Police C.P. Singh said authoritatively: "One thing was clear in the pattern of incidents. It was the activities of the Vishwa Hindu Parishad and Bajrang Dal who were taking the law into their own hands, which posed a serious danger to peace in Gujarat."[221] The then archbishop of Delhi Alan de Lastic noted later on 22 November that attacks on Christians had increased ever since the BJP government came to power. On 4 December around 23 million Christians across India observed a protest.

By August 2000 attacks on Christians had spread to many parts of the country: Uttar Pradesh, Haryana, Punjab, Madhya Pradesh, Andhra Pradesh, Karnataka, Tamil Nadu, Goa, etc.[222] Vajpayee as Prime minister watched, probably with contentment, that the Hindutva lab was successfully operative and producing results. Through the use of propaganda and official pronouncements of responsible people in Vajpayee's government dismissed the crimes and atrocities committed against the minority groups as sporadic normal criminal acts that have nothing to do with the ideology of Hindutva or religious fanaticism. Whenever nothing worked they simply blamed it on the ISI of Pakistan. However, during the 2004 election campaign, among the achievements of the BJP-led NDA government it was claimed that there was a significant reduction in communal and caste violence in the past five years compared to previous years.[223]

In the wake of the attacks against minorities like Christians and Muslims by Hindutva outfits, Vajpayee as Prime Minister of India declared that there is need for a debate on conversion[224] which re-echoed in L.K. Advani's call for a debate on secularism. According to Sumit Sarkar, Vajpayee's suggestion for a 'national debate' on conversion was not a liberal proposal put forward by a good man fallen among unfortunate associates but part of a well-thought out strategy of the Sangh Parivar.[225] Vajpayee as the Delhi 'director of the Hindutva lab' forgot altogether Article 25 (1) of the Fundamental Rights which allows all persons as equally entitled to freedom of conscience and the right to profess, practice and propagate religion.[226] Sarkar observes that propagation makes no sense at all without the possibility of convincing others of the validity of one's religious beliefs and rituals.[227]

According to Sarkar what is new in the national scenario is that for a couple of years after coming to power of the BJP in Delhi and prior to the Gujarat genocide of 2002, Christians appeared to have displaced Muslims as primary target of Hindu nationalist organisations.[228]

Politics of expediency of Vajpayee is too evident to go unnoticed. This was a clever strategy propagated and practised by the Nazis under Hitler. Hitler wrote in his *Mein Kampf*: "The problem of the inner organisation of the movement is not one of principle but of expediency."[229] Narendra Modi was supported by BJP leadership during the Gujarat pogrom 2002. It was only on 4 April 2002 that Vajpayee went to Gujarat, about six weeks after the killings broke out. In the meantime he had promoted his poems on MTV and had two holidays in the hills. This is a clear proof that the Vajpayee government had connived with the Modi government to test the Hindutva agenda. It is worth recalling a report about how Mrs. Indira Gandhi responded to the 1969 riots in Gujarat. She was in Nagaland when she received the news about the grim situation in

Gujarat. Instead of returning to New Delhi she flew straight to Ahmedabad.[230]

Jawaharlal Nehru, the first Prime Minister of India has spelt out clearly the duties of a Prime Minister when he said: "The Prime Minister's role, should be, an important role. He is not only a figurehead but a person who should be more responsible than anyone else for the general trend of policy and for the co-ordination of the work of various departments [....] in the type of democratic set-up we have adopted, the Prime Minister is supposed to play an outstanding role."[231]

The Supreme Court verdict in the Best Bakery case in 2004 said that the modern day Neros were looking elsewhere when Best Bakery and innocent children and helpless women were burning. The court's use of the plural 'Neros' is significant. The 'Neros' were not only in Gujarat but also in Delhi and elsewhere. Asghar Ali Engineer says: "It would be wrong to say that only Narendra Modi was guilty of the Gujarat carnage of 2002; Vajpayee's BJP-led NDA at the Centre was equally responsible for it."[232]

No electoral campaign touched such low level of decency and public morality as that of the BJP in the 2004 general elections. The aggressiveness of the BJP was clearly manifested in the campaign of calumny, abuse and defamation it launched against its opponents. Crude and vulgar tactics were employed by Vajpayee's supporters to win the favour of the masses. The language and demeanour of Narendra Modi, Sushma Swaraj, Uma Bharati, Vinay Katiyar, Pramod Mahajan and others, received no reprimand from Vajpayee or the national leadership of the BJP. Praful Bidwai observes that the aim was to exploit xenophobic prejudices. The vile fashion in which the party and its members targeted Sonia Gandhi and her children Rahul and Priyanka is the best example of it. It allowed Modi to call Sonia Gandhi a 'Jersey cow' and Rahul a 'hybrid calf'. This he said in the attentive presence of L.K. Advani, Vajpayee's Deputy. K.N. Panikkar observes that even Atal Bihari Vajpayee the then Prime Minister who is hailed as a statesman chose to keep quiet. He had nothing to say about the uncultured behaviour of his party members. But then Vajpayee himself had resorted to puns to demean his opponents for which he was popular.[233] For example, he said about Sonia Gandhi: "She is a woman and that too a foreign woman."[234] Yet BJP claims that Vajpayee, like Nehru, never made any personal attack on any politician despite all provocations.[235]

On the eve of the general elections of 2004 several publications by the BJP denigrated Sonia Gandhi. For example, a booklet published by a certain Kanayalal M. Talreja, with the approval of Vajpayee, L.K. Advani and Venkaiah Naidu, the BJP president, stated: "Unlike the Congress, headed by imported, raw, novice, *Videshi Dynastic Bahu*, the BJP is guided by experienced, honest and dedicated team of tried, tested and trusted leadership;"[236] "It is a matter of irony, anguish and astonishment that the Congressmen project novice, raw Sonia, whose only qualification for the post of prime ministership is that she is *Bahu* (imported) [sic] of Nehru family. Bharat is not her fatherland or motherland, but mother-in-law-land. She is alien to Bharatiya culture, civilisation and traditions. [....] Unlike Shri Atal Bihari Vajpayee, who is highly competent to deliver extempore speech eloquently, she is too novice to speak a few sentences even, nor can she read properly with correct pronunciation the speech written for her in Roman script."[237]

BJP Today, the mouth piece of the BJP said about Sonia Gandhi: "Senora [sic] Sonia and her children, due to their foreign ancestry and half-Italian genes can have little love and respect for Indian Culture and Tradition or Hindutva;"[238] "If Senora [sic] Sonia wins over India's Atalji, I can guarantee that the whole white west will back her unashamedly."[239] Bidwai argues that the hysterical anti-'foreigner' campaign which is similar to the ethnic chauvinist parties such as the Nazis in Hitler's Germany, the Likud in Sharon's Israel, the British National Party in the U.K. or Jean-Marie Le Pen's National Front in France.[240]

Scholars say that the Nazis were notorious exponents of what is called 'negative campaigning'.[241] Use of undignified language against the opponents was a vile technique widely used and perfected by the Nazis. Maligning the opponents, ridiculing and humiliating them was part of what was called the *Schwarz-Weiß-Technique* (Black-White-Technique) of Joseph Goebbels. Goebbels consistently argued that the purpose of propaganda is success at any price (*Erfolg um jeden Preis*). He stated that none should say that a particular propaganda is brutal or row or ordinary. According to him propaganda should never be decent or soft or humble or gentle. It should challenge the opponent, make him confused and turn him into a laughing stock for the people.[242] The Sangh Parivar seems to have followed a similar strategy against its opponents during the general elections of 2004.

After the Godhra events Vajpayee rejected the plea to ban the VHP and the Bajrang Dal though there were serious reasons to do it.[243] Instead he blamed the media for exaggerating the reports and asked them to play a constructive role. In other words, Vajpayee conveniently 'looked the other way', for any action against these organisations would have invited wrath from the Sangh Parivar and it would even meant the end of his Prime Ministership. But we may recall that the Narasimha Rao government did impose a ban on the RSS and the Bajrang Dal after the demolition of the Babri Mosque in 1992.

Hindutva lab was extended to Madhya Pradesh in a big way ever since Uma Bharati became the Chief Minister of the state in 2003. Bharati's fetish for Hindutva was obvious right from the day she was sworn-in in the presence of saffron-clad *sadhus*. A journalist said in April 2004: "It is a fact that Bajrang Dal and VHP people have become very aggressive ever since Uma Bharati became Chief Minister."[244] Purnima S. Tripathi, after narrating a number of incidents involving the high handedness of the Bajrang Dal, VHP and Durga Vahini in the State of Madhya Pradesh asks: "Is Madhya Pradesh becoming yet another laboratory of the Hindutva forces? This streak of intolerance, as opposed to the benign tolerance of Hinduism, is more in evidence now than ever before among the votaries of Hindutva."[245] It may be remembered that in choosing Uma Bharati as the chief ministerial candidate of Madhya Pradesh, his home state, Vajpayee had a special say.

The 'Big Lies' of Vajpayee and His Government

The concept of 'Big Lie' developed by the Nazis was often utilised by many Hindutva ideologues in order to gain political mileage. Hitler argued that success is the only rule of judgement whereby we can decide whether an undertaking was right or wrong.[246] Vajpayee was an opportunist and as occasion demanded he tactfully used the concept of the 'Big Lie' for political ends. We give below some statements from Vajpayee, which may be classified as 'Big Lies':

> "We [BJP] are not communal. We don't discriminate on the basis of caste and religion."[247]

"I don't indulge in chalaki (cunning) with anyone. I don't let down people. I don't indulge in ustadgiri (roughly translated, crookedness)."[248]

"the BJP had always believed in fair play with allies and it had never indulged in un-principled alliance in order to grab power."[249]

"Let me make it clear that all this is part of the Left's Goebbelsian propaganda – I am a moderate, the party [BJP] is not; I am secular, the party is not."[250]

"Minorities are safe and have faced no discrimination under the NDA Government."[251]

"Secularism means that there will not be any discrimination on the basis of religion or caste or community. It also means that there would be no state religion and no state-sponsored practice of worship."[252]

"All citizens of this country, particularly these belonging to smaller communities, must be protected. They should be our special concern. The increasing intolerance in the country signifies a dangerous trend."[253]

"Wherever any incidents [of violence against minorities] have taken place, the culprits have been arrested and their cases are in courts. Gujarat is also included in this."[254]

"if anyone from our party [BJP] is found indulging in corruption, he is expelled."[255]

"Our [BJP-led] Government is determined to ensure security for every citizen, create confidence among minorities and strengthen the law and order machinery."[256]

In 2004 the Vajpayee government led a pan-India campaign before the general elections using the tactic of the 'Big Lie'. But in the elections the people of India rejected Vajpayee and his government. One of the main reasons for the electoral debacle was the 'Big Lies' propagated by the BJP epitomised in such slogans as 'Indian Shining', 'Feel Good', 'Irreducible India', 'Super Power India', etc.

The 'India Shining' campaign mocked the deprivations of the large section of the Indian masses that suffer from acute poverty, hunger, malnutrition, illiteracy, deplorable health care facilities, and conveniently forgot about the livelihood issues of the people. It opened up a huge credibility gap between the Vajpayee government and the Indian masses. In 2003 Vajpayee endorsed quotas for upper caste 'poor' with elections in the State of Rajasthan in mind.[257] People of India discovered that the Vajpayee government stood for the rich and the upper middle class and the upper castes of Hindu society and that India was shining only for the privileged few.

The hyperbolic claims about India's economic performance was also a Big Lie. For example, the human development report of the United Nations Development Project (UNDP) released in July 2002 ranked India as the largest democracy in South Asia. But she was placed 124th in the Human Development Index (HDI), and the lack of progress was largely due to lack of development in health, education and other social sectors. However, in the same report Sri Lanka was ranked 89th and China 96th. Again, India had 23 per cent of the population suffering from under-nourishment. Both China and Pakistan fared better with nine per cent and 18 per cent respectively.[258] The Human Development Report published in 2003 placed India further below as the 127th in the Human Development Index in the comity of 175 nations.[259] According to a statistics published in 2004, India had half of the world's illiterates – over 350 million! One wonders in what sense was India shining during the BJP-led NDA government!

The paradox of 'Indian shining' and 'Feel good' was also evident when thousands of poor women braved the cruel April heat of North India on 12 April 2004 for a free sari worth Rs 50 at the most, and ultimately 25 persons (22 women and three children) paid it with their lives. This happened in Vajpayee's own constituency.

Therefore, anyone with a little common sense can conclude that under Vajpayee's rule there was hardly anything to feel good about, and India was not shining for the vast majority of Indians. Hence, the vocal statement of the Vajpayee government 'India first' is to be re-read as 'Hindus first', and the propaganda of 'super power India' is to be understood as 'super power of the Sangh Parivar'.

Vajpayee's Prime Ministership as RSS Rule

Sangh Parivar is the umbrella term for the RSS-affiliated Hindutva groups and organisations. The Parivar first tasted political power as Jana Sangh and then as BJP. History tells us that the real origin of the BJP is traced back to the formation of the RSS in 1925 and its politicisation with the formation of the Jana Sangh in 1951.[260] The

BJP rule has been described as fascist because the goal of Vajpayee and his political party is same as that of the RSS: i.e. to make India a Hindu nation.

According to A.G. Noorani, Vajpayee is a typical product of the Sangh Parivar. He did not acquire political power and become Prime Minister in order to dilute its ideology or foil its programme. He himself held out no such promise.[261] On 18 April 1999 Vajpayee said: "But I do submit that I have never aspired for anything other than to serve the country honestly.[262] (Here one needs to read 'country' to mean Hindu *rashtra*). In fact, he had no other agenda than that of the Sangh Parivar, namely, to establish the Hindu *rashtra* based on the concepts of one nation (Hindu *rashtra*), one culture (Sanskrit), one people (Aryan), one language (Hindi) and one religion (Hinduism).

In 1998 BJP won 180 seats in the twelfth Lok Sabha and together with its allies it had 250 seats. On 19 March 1998 Vajpayee was sworn in as Prime Minister and the RSS claimed its due credit for the victory of the BJP.[263] Consequently, many with RSS background and training were inducted into the government as cabinet ministers and into the administrative sectors of vital importance.

Today, many of the outstanding BJP leaders have a Sangh Parivar background. For example, BJP stalwarts like Vajpayee, L.K. Advani and Murli Manohar Joshi were RSS cadres. K.R. Malkani had close relations with the RSS; Vijaya Raje Scindia was associated with Jan Sangh; Sundar Singh Bhandari and K.L. Sharma had RSS-Jana Sangh connections.[264] Outstanding young leaders of the BJP like, Jagdish Prasad Mathur, Pramod Mahajan, Kedarnath Sahani and Kushabhau Thakre have RSS-Jana Sangh association; K.N. Govindacharya has RSS-ABVP background; Arun Jaitley, Sushil Modi and Narendra Modi and Gopinath Munde and many others like them have come from the ranks of the RSS or ABVP prior to their joining the BJP.[265] Dilip Singh Judeo became an RSS full-timer in 1992.[266]

Everyone knows that important support groups and front organisations of the BJP include members of the Sangh Parivar like, the RSS, the Bharat Mazdoor Sangh (launched in 1955 as an RSS-affiliated trade union), the Akhil Bharatiya Vidyarthi Parishad (an RSS-affiliated students' organisation founded by Balraj Madhok in 1948),[267] Vidya Bharati and Seva Bharati (both RSS-run educational organisations), the Vanavasi Kalyan Ashram (started in 1952 with the support of the RSS to cater to the tribal people), the

Bharatiya Kisan Sangh (Indian Farmers Union) and Rashtriya Sevika Samiti (National Women Workers Council; both RSS-affiliated organisations), Vishva Hindu Parishad and Bajrang Dal (the militant wing of the VHP founded in 1984).[268]

Hitler's Nazi party also created a host of ancillary organisations, including National Socialist Leagues for teachers, doctors, students, civil servants, farmers, youth and women. It also had its own street fighting force called the *Sturmabteilungen* (*SA*. 'Stromtroopers')[269] which has a parallel in Bajrang Dal.

Sudheendra Kulkarni, who is himself an RSS-influenced person states the following about the functioning of the Vajpayee government: "For six years I was in the Vajpayee administration, in the Prime Minister's Office to be precise, [....] I know many RSS-nurtured and RSS-influenced persons who were, like me, inducted into the administration or appointed to statutory bodies and Constitutional posts."[270]

The RSS organisational principle has always been following one leader. It was clearly manifested in the way BJP prepared for the elections in 2004. Before the general elections of 2004, the BJP had openly expressed its dependence on the RSS. The inevitability of this dependence was formally accepted on March 2004 at a special meeting of the BJP and the RSS leaders at Vajpayee's residence.[271] The party relied on the RSS wherever it was weak. Prior to the general elections of 2004 thousands of RSS workers went from door to door explaining why Vajpayee should be re-elected even as over 100 'men with a mission', all RSS-affiliated professionals in various fields, gathered inputs and redefined the campaign strategy at the party's central media cell. The RSS workers also campaigned in Muslim areas with great passion.[272]

In 2002 Advani passionately declared that the bond between the Vajpayee regime and the RSS is based on ideology and moral principles and that it was unbreakable.[273] In January 2004 Vajpayee said that there are no fundamental differences between the RSS and the BJP, though the opinions of individuals may differ.[274] Then he went on to state: "I am the Prime Minister today but may not remain tomorrow. But I was a swayamsevak yesterday and will remain one till my death."[275] During the national executive meeting of the BJP held in Mumbai from 22-24 June 2004 it was said: "We have reached where we have reached because of the dedicated efforts of lakhs of workers and well-wishers of our IDEOLOGICAL PARIVAR [sic].

They have laboured hard to put us in our present position. They have done so with a certain emotional attachment to the BJP."[276] When the RSS called for a 'swadeshi church' for Christians after the model of China, and declared that unless the minorities earn the goodwill of the majority there can be no guarantee of their rights, Vajpayee, as Prime Minister, did not react or come to the defence of the minorities, although the statements had dangerous implications for the secularist and pluralist principles enshrined in the Indian Constitutions.[277] After the electoral debacle of 2004, on 27 July 2004 Vajpayee, L.K. Advani and Venkaiah Naidu, the then president of the BJP, went to the RSS office to meet the RSS leaders.[278] In the revamp that was made in the organisation of the BJP after this meeting, many full-time RSS *pracharaks* were made BJP regional secretaries.[279]

Vajpayee's tenure as Prime Minister of India was a BJP, VHP. RSS, Shiv Sena, Bajrang Dal combined rule supported by all the other members of the Sangh Parivar. But the RSS was his ideological anchor in all major policies and decisions of his government. It gave substance, vision, direction and support to his functioning. Whenever he gave the semblance of deviating from the RSS ideology, the organisation effectively intervened and asked him to toe the line. In 2002 the RSS forced Vajpayee to make Advani the Deputy Prime Minister.[280] In April 2005 in a widely televised interview K.S. Sudarshan, the RSS chief, suggested that Vajpayee and Advani step down from leadership and make way for the younger generation.[281] It was again a reassertion of the authority of the RSS over the BJP's leadership. Jaffrelot observes that although apolitism is part of the propaganda of the RSS, the movement is in fact eminently political.[282]

The Terrorism Research Centre (TRC) of the United States of America mentioned the RSS in its list of terrorist organisations of 2004 operating in India.[283] The RSS is also an organisation that was banned a number of times by the Government of India for its militant, extremist and communal activities. It is such an organisation with its dubious credentials and dangerous ideology that has taught Vajpayee discipline and given him an ideology to live by. It has also given him political power and shown him the path he and his government should take and provided him with helpers and supports to realise it. Thus it has been observed that four years after it won power at the Centre, the BJP had come completely under the

RSS' direct control and Vajpayee's government was expected to keep the RSS informed of all major policy decisions on the domestic and international front.[284] Asghar Ali Engineer maintains that Vajpayee is basically committed to the RSS ideology, which is rigid and sectarian and hostile to Muslims and other religious minorities. He also proved himself to be as much an RSS *pracharak* as Narendra Modi, though of a crypto variety rather than an open one – Narendra Modi.[285]

Vajpayee always defended the RSS. For example, on 27 May 1996 he openly defended the RSS in the Indian parliament and argued that there is no justification to malign the organisation. He argued: "I am sorry to say that the names of such organisations [RSS and others] were mentioned during the course of discussion, an effort was made to drag them here, which are independent organisations engaged in nation-building activities and character-building work. I am referring to the R.S.S. [...] the kind of allegations levelled against it were not warranted."[286]

Vajpayee was fond of repeating 'the Sangh is my soul' to express his uncompromising allegiance to the RSS. If BJP alienates the RSS, it will cease to exist. In April 2005 on the occasion of the 25th anniversary of the founding of the BJP, the party president L.K. Advani reiterated the party's unambiguous relationship with the RSS. He affirmed: "Our inflexible stand on our association with the RSS gave us a distinct ideological identity, about which we have never been apologetic, nor will we ever be."[287] P. Kanungo says: "Vajpayee is the product of the RSS; without its ideological and organisational support he would have been a nobody. Thus, both the RSS and Vajpayee need each other and supplement each other."[288]

Was Vajpayee an Informer to the British?

During the pre-independence era of India, Golwalkar, the RSS chief, kept himself aloof from anti-British struggle. The RSS as an organisation neither joined the Civil Disobedience of 1940 nor the Quit India Movement of 1942. The Sangh Parivar scrupulously kept itself within the law and refrained from taking any part in the disturbances that broke out in 1942. All the same a few RSS workers participated in the 1942 movement in their individual capacity. Leeladhar Bajpai, a freedom fighter, alleges that during the Quit

India Movement, Atal Bihari Vajpayee made a 'confession' to the British police on the basis of which Bajpai was jailed for five years. Bajpai reportedly took out a procession at Bateshwar (Vajpayee's village) in Agra district on 27 August 1942 and hoisted the Congress flag on two government buildings one of which was the Forest Department office. Vajpayee and his brother were part of the procession. Though the procession was non-violent, the British police attempted to create a 'false' story that they had damaged the wall of the Forest Department building. In his statement to the police, Vajpayee reportedly said that he neither caused any damage nor rendered any assistance in demolishing the government building. However, naming Leeladhar Bajpai and a certain Mahuan, Vajpayee told the British police that they had delivered a speech in the Bateshwar bazar and persuaded the people to break the forest laws, that when about 200 people went to the forest office he and his brother stayed back, that he did not know the names of any other person except Mahuan and Kakua (Leeladhar Bajpai) who were there and that it appeared to him that bricks were falling but he did not know who was demolishing the wall.[289] At any rate, there is a serious allegation that Vajpayee was an informer to the British.[290] Reacting to this incident Laloo Prasad Yadav said: "Vajpayee was an approver in the case involving freedom fighters in Gwalior in 1942. His statement before the Magistrate at that time led to a whole lot of people being sent to prison. Such a person is the Prime Minister."[291]

The Non-Existent Vajpayee Mystique

One of the aims of BJP's participation in government was to enable the Sangh Parivar to pursue its project of creating a Hindu *rashtra*. What was expected of the BJP was to use the government authority and machinery to ensure its construction and to create the necessary cultural and ideological structures through government channels. BJP wanted to remember Vajpayee as the *father* of their Hindu nation. It projected him as one who provided a dream leadership to the country for six years and deserved at least five more to complete the 'gigantic' tasks he had undertaken.[292] M.V. Kamath, an RSS ideologue and columnist in the RSS weekly *Organiser*, said eulogising Vajpayee that he had become a father figure respected by one and all who had dreamt dreams but in his case the dreams were becoming a reality.[293] The Overseas Friends of the BJP (OFBJP) also created a cult around Vajpayee as a great scholar, poet, statesman, visionary, charismatic leader, skilful, trusted and admired leader.[294] But the BJP's 'dream leadership of Vajpayee', Kamath's 'father figure', and the 'superman-image' created by the OFBJP will have very few takers among people who know the truth about the real identity of Vajpayee.

On the eve of the general elections of 2004 there was an aggressive campaign in Lucknow even though there was no doubt about Vajpayee's victory. But if the mascot of the BJP fails to win by a large enough margin, it would affect the party's image. The meetings addressed by Vajpayee and other top leaders did not attract as big crowds as the party leaders had expected. Commenting on this fact Praful Bidwai observes that the BJP's star campaigner, and its publicly most acceptable asset, Vajpayee, had turned out to be a hollow leader, and even a poor crowd-puller, especially in States like Uttar Pradesh, Bihar and Maharashtra. His vicious rhetoric against the policies of Jawaharlal Nehru, his persistent personal attacks on the Congress president Sonia Gandhi and her children had also eroded his stature.[295]

Vajpayee was also a victim of xenophobia. In 2004 two days after the publication of the 'Vision Document 2004' of the BJP, he called for a 'national debate whether a foreigner can occupy a high office' – reference to the question of course was the Congress president Sonia Gandhi's foreign origin. But the same Vajpayee had earlier stated in an interview with Tavleen Singh that Sonia Gandhi is an Indian citizen and that her origin would not be an issue in election.[296]

Praful Bidwai, like many others, has demolished the puffed up image of Vajpayee. He argues that the election result of May 2004 proved the non-existent Vajpayee-mystique which was supposed to charm the voters from north to south and east to west. Not even the managerial politics liberally utilised could save the BJP and their effort to sell brands and images did not work. They tried to present Vajpayee as a mascot, BJP's most recognisable symbol, principal campaigner, its source of inspiration, the supreme leader and its everything. Using the power of the media they tried to convince the masses that he is in the same league as Jawaharlal Nehru or Indira Gandhi and Rajiv Gandhi at their respectable peaks. But in reality Vajpayee turned out to be something different. Even in popularity he was never in the same league as Nehru. In Lucknow he demonstrated tremendous nervousness and started begging for Muslim votes in an undignified way[297] – though on an earlier occasion in 2002 he had threatened the Muslims publicly that his party was capable of wining in the Uttar Pradesh Assembly elections even if the Muslims voted against it.[298] In April 2004 his campaign resorted to outright bribery in the form of distribution of saris. This programme, on the campaign-manager Laljit Tandon's birthday, led to a stampede killing 25 persons.[299] The sari-stampede convinced the public that the person who is the BJP's tallest claimant to the top office of the Prime Minister might only be a pretender who has to bribe the poor to get their votes.[300]

Author and social activist Arundhati Roy says: "While Gujarat burned our Prime Minister was on MTV promoting his new poems [….] It took him more than a month – and two vacations in the hills – to make it to Gujarat;"[301] "the Prime Minister of Secular, Democratic India, A.B. Vajpayee, made history. He became the first Indian Prime Minister to cross the threshold and publicly unveil an unconscionable bigotry against Muslims, which even George Bush, and Donald Rumsfeld would be embarrassed to own up to. 'Wherever Muslims are', he said, 'they do not want to live peacefully'."[302] In February 2003 Vajpayee said: "I prefer to die rather than eat beef."[303] His concern was beef and not to bring justice to Gujarat.

Bidwai has identified two things that have damaged Vajpayee the most: his demonstration of a deep personal insecurity about his own constituency and his desperate wooing of the Muslims vote.[304] Statistics show that in Lucknow, in the general elections of 2004, only 35.4 per cent of the electorate bothered to cast their vote for the tallest leader of the BJP[305] as against 50.9 per cent in 1991, 52.24 in 1996, 57.82 in 1998 and 48.11 in 1999.[306] Vajpayee addressed rallies covering 41 parliamentary segments and the party won only 18 seats. Despite his presence in Uttar Pradesh with his seat secured in Lucknow, the party won only 10 seats. The party's projection of Vajpayee's magic of a statesman did not cut much ice with the voters.[307] Yet the BJP kept repeating: "Shri Atalji has been in the saddle for six consecutive years, but his popularity and stature have continued to grow year after year."[308] The low polling rate of 35.4 in 2004 is probably unprecedented in a senior politician's constituency, leave alone a candidate for prime ministership. Bidwai's analysis of Vajpayee concludes by stating that he turned out to be a very pedestrian politician.[309]

After the electoral defeat of 2004 it was a vastly diminished Vajpayee who emerged from the Mumbai session of the BJP executive in June 2004. If reports were to be believed he even thought of quitting active politics.

Vajpayee as a Hindutva Hardliner

K.N. Panikkar observes that, for Vajpayee, the demolition of the Babri mosque at Ayodhya on 6 December 1992 was an expression of national sentiment. He was reluctant to condemn the Gujarat pogrom of 2002. These unambiguously demonstrate his commitment to Hindutva.[310] Sumit Sarkar notes that it is not at all accidental that the so-called mild face of the BJP, namely, Vajpayee, had recourse to a ploy when he visited Gujarat just after the burning of churches in December 1998. On that occasion he called for a 'national debate' on conversion, thus adroitly hinting that Christians are ultimately responsible for their own woes,[311] and that too, in spite of the fact that the Director-General of the Gujarat Police had declared categorically on 6 December 1998 that charges of forced inter-religious marriages and conversions by Christian missionaries in the Dangs Adivasi belt of Gujarat were baseless, and the real 'serious danger to peace' was coming rather from the Vishva Hindu Parishad and the Bajrang Dal activists.[312]

It has been observed that Vajpayee was keen that the BJP's chief ministerial candidates in the three States of Madhya Pradesh, Rajasthan and Chattisgarh for 2003 elections should be Hindutva zealots. The fielding of fiery Hindutva icons like the saffron-clad Uma Bharati and Narendra Modi as campaign leaders also conveyed an unambiguous message of Vajpayee's hardcore Hindutva moorings.[313] N. Das argues that when Vajpayee was the Prime Minister of India he brought Dilip Singh Judeo, a Hindutva hardliner, to Delhi to give him a profile and some administrative experience. However, the only experience Judeo had was his missionary basing and involvement in *shuddhi* or re-conversion movement in Chattisgarh and Orissa. It was a great qualification as far as Vajpayee and his party were concerned. Das argues that the day is not far off when Dara Singh, the prime accused in the murder of the Stains' in Orissa in 1999, may be projected as the Orissa Chief Minister aspirant by the party.[314]

In 2003 when Vajpayee reshuffled the cabinet he included the BJP Member of Parliament Swami Chinmayanand from Jaunpur, Uttar Pradesh, as Minister of State for Home. Swami Chinmayanand had figured prominently in Advani's Rath Yatra as it travelled through Uttar Pradesh in 1990. He was a founder-member of the Ramjanmabhoomi Mukti Yaga Samiti that was set up in 1984 to lead the movement for a Ram temple. He continues to be on a VHP committee that seeks to facilitate the construction of a temple at the disputed site of the Babri mosque in Ayodhya. It may be remembered that it was L.K. Advani who wanted to give the VHP a say in the running of his ministry, which is responsible for the maintenance of internal security. This step, according to critics, has also cast a shadow on the Vajpayee's government and its objectivity in dealing with communal matters and signalled the return of hardline Hindutva.[315]

One of the major projects of Hindu nationalism is to militarise Hinduism. Since decades the RSS has been systematically working in order to achieve this goal. It has been reported that during the 13-day government of Vajpayee in 1996, his ministry had already decided on nuclear testing. However, it may be remembered that already in the early 1940s, V.D. Savarkar one of the major Hindutva ideologues, had demanded a Hinduisation of India and militarisation of Hinduism.[316] On 26 February 1966, just before his death Savarkar called upon the Indian government to immediately equip India with nuclear weapons and missiles. In 1951 Jana Sangh too had openly proclaimed the need for India to go nuclear. Thus the aggressive mind-set of Vajpayee which was visibly manifested in the Pokhran nuclear test of 1998, has its roots in Savarkar, Jana Sangh and above all in his RSS training. But there is another side to the nuclear test. As Gurcharan Das observes, national pride is the result of performance and does not come from testing nuclear bombs or bashing Muslims or Christians.[317] He adds that he was not thrilled by the Pokhran nuclear test. He would have been prouder if instead the government had announced that India's poverty had come down to twenty per cent, or literacy had risen to eighty per cent or that we had achieved eight per cent GDP growth.[318]

None can deny the consistency of Vajpayee's profound commitment to Hindutva. He upholds Hindu cultural nationalism as any RSS *pracharak.* On 5 November 1995 he said in Mumbai that India's unity rests on its roots in Hinduism and nationalism, and secularism was never mentioned in the Indian Constitution until 1976.[319] He remains a crafty politician, a hardliner and a mask-wearer for whom politics and not ethics or humanity that matters. A.G. Noorani observes that it took the Sangh Parivar long to own up V.D. Savarkar. The Jan Sangh never spoke of him or of Hindutva from 1951-1977. The BJP, formed in 1980, took up Hindutva only in 1990 and Savarkar in 2000, through Atal Bihari Vajpayee.[320]

Vajpayee had declared in a speech at Staten Island (USA) that RSS is his soul and that he would always remain a *swayamsevak*. He also promised to his wealthy NRI supporters 'the India of their dreams', if given a two-thirds majority.[321] In New York on 9 September 2000 at a Sangh Parivar meeting he said: "if the electorate give us a clear two-thirds majority, we will build India of our dreams"[322] – the Hindu *rashtra*. On 6 February 2004 this was exactly what Vajpayee asked from the people of India. He gave a call to the people of India to provide a two-thirds majority in Parliament to complete his 'unfinished' task.[323] On 8 February 2004 during the election campaign, Vajpayee said at Ayodhya that he needed five more years in order to fulfil his promise to build the Ram temple at Ayodhya.[324] When Adolf Hitler came to power he asked the Germans for four years to execute his plans. He said: "*Alles, was ich verlange, sind vier Jahre*"[325] ('all that I demand is four years')' "*Deutsches Volk gib us die Zeit von vier Jahren – dann richte und urtile uber uns*" ('German people, give us a time of four years, then judge us').[326] Vajpayee was asking for something similar from the Indians.

Vajpayee is Bharatiya Janata party's mask of moderation. The RSS presented him to the masses as an epitome of justice and upholder of human norms and values. Even R. Venkatraman, the former President of India, joined the Sangh Parivar to endorse Vajpayee as a moderate. He said: "Atalji is a moderate, following the middle path on every issue. On religious issues, he is no hardliner."[327] Unfortunately, even the former President of India misread the character of Vajpayee. During the April-May 2004 elections BJP also carefully projected the Brahmin identity of Vajpayee, especially in Uttar Pradesh.[328]

Vajpayee's rule was essentially an effort to enforce the Hindutva ideology by stages through political manoeuvring. Noorani reiterates: "not once did he [Vajpayee] depart from the Sangh's credo or its policy; whether on the Babri Masjid, Hindutva or on the 'communal riots' from 1967 to this day. Not once did he express any sympathy for the Muslims; *not once*."[329] Swami Agnivesh observes: "I had considered Vajpayee a liberal but his real face came to light after the Gujarat pogrom as he did not condemn violence."[330] Today, Vajpayee's alleged humanity, morality and integrity as a senior political leader is seriously suspect. Hence, we are left with some disturbing questions like, whether he deserved to occupy the exalted office of the Prime Minister of India? Whether it is worth lauding him as a statesman of world standing? And whether he deserved the awards of the 'best parliamentarian' and *Padma Vibhushan*? Perhaps, as a nation, we were mesmerised and beguiled by the propaganda and the 'Big Lies' about the 'mystique' of Vajpayee.

The secular and pluralistic ethos of India demand that we denounce Hindutva hardliners like Atal Bihari Vajpayee. The rhetoric of him being a moderate is far from true. He is neither a moderate nor secular but a hardliner with an aggressive, sectarian, communal and nationalist agenda. He is at best the shrewdest 'politician' – with all the viciousness and villainy which often accompany this word – the Sangh Parivar has so far produced. Noorani observes that it was on the eve of the 1996 general elections that Advani conceded the crown to Vajpayee who could be trusted to do the Sangh Parivar's bidding while deploying rhetoric to project a liberal image.[331] But in reality Vajpayee is a hardcore, well trained Hindutva tactician who wears the mask of moderation. At heart he is a Sangh Parivar's man, an Arya Samaj, RSS and Jan Sangh-trained BJP's mask of liberalism. Sometimes people not very familiar with the political philosophy consider Vajpayee as a moderate and Advani as a hardliner. But in reality the two do not represent, as Jaffrelot opines, two opposed groups or even ideological tendencies.[332] Hence, if anyone considers Vajpayee as a moderate, the reason for it is to be sought in the ignorance of facts.

Hindu nationalists came to power for 13 days in May 1996 and more durably in March 1998. Had the BJP and its allies won the 2004 general elections it would have meant the death of secular and pluralistic India and the birth of the Hindu *rashtra* with Vajpayee at its helm.

Vajpayee as the Quintessence of Arya Samaj, RSS, Jan Sangh and BJP

The BJP media describe Vajpayee as a quintessential Indian who will take India to the pinnacle of glory.[333] But from what has been discussed above, Vajpayee deserves to be considered as the quintessence of Arya Samaj, RSS, Jana Sangh and BJP. In other words, the personal identity of Vajpayee is that his ideology is same as that of these four communal, fundamentalist and nationalist organisations. He never claimed to be secular in the sense of separating religion from politics. Basically, Vajpayee's political agenda is same as theirs. His carefully cultivated 'soft' image is meant to promote a personality cult around him with a view to gain political power. Hence to consider Atal Bihari Vajpayee as a 'moderate' is to mistake the mask for the man and to be mislead by the 'Big Lies' of his party.

Conclusion

All that we have discussed above is of decisive importance in order to assess the real identity of Vajpayee. He has deep-seated prejudices against the minorities of India like the Muslims, Christians and the Left parties. He has not diluted the Hindutva ideology at any time in his political career. He did not make any such promise to anyone in the country either. To the Sangh Parivar he simply says: "Get me a [two-thirds] majority in our own right and I'll carry out your programme fully."[334] Political analysts say that if the BJP and its allies had come to power in the general elections of April-May 2004, Vajpayee would not have remained prime minister for five years but would have paved the way for other Hindutva hardliners like L.K. Advani or Murli Manohar Joshi. But the results of the general elections rejected Vajpayee because it was a mandate for secular forces. The defeat was also a proof that Vajpayee was discovered as a mask-wearer by the Indian masses, that in the final analysis the simple people are cleverer than those who govern them. Here we are reminded of a great saying which Joseph Goebbels was fond of repeating: "*Das Volk ist am Ende immer noch klüger als seine Regierung.*"[335] ('In the end the people are always cleverer than their government').

Vajpayee ruled India as its Prime Minster for the sake of the goals of the Sangh Parivar. To be fair to him it must be admitted that at times he was a voice of moderation and sanity. But in general his political life was guided by ethical relativism and expediency, and spoke a language of ambivalence and equivocation. He proved to be a common politician in handling the Gujarat pogrom, using casuistry as a shelter against his failure to take the steps a truly upright Prime Minister would have taken. The Centre's inaction was eloquently wilful. K.R. Narayanan, the former President of India, authoritatively stated that there was in fact a *conspiracy* involving the state and Central governments behind the Gujarat riots. In an interview to the Malayalam monthly *Manava Sanskriti* he said: "There was a governmental and administrative support for the communal riots in Gujarat. I gave several letters to Prime Minister Vajpayee in this regard on this issue. I met him personally and talked to him directly. But Vajpayee did not do anything effective. I requested him to send the Army to Gujarat and suppress the riots. The Centre had the constitutional responsibility and powers to send the military if the state government asked. The military was sent, but they were not given powers to shoot."[336] The so-called 'success' of Vajpayee as a political leader and Prime Minister of India consisted not in meeting the real needs of the people of India but in pushing forward the agenda of creating a Hindu *rashtra* out of India and in colouring many of the government institutions and administrative bodies in the country in saffron with the hope that some day he will be honoured as the *father* of the Hindu *rashtra*.

Notes

1. See S.K. Dass (ed.), *Atal Bihari Vajpayee*, 11-12; C. Jaffrelot, *The Hindu Nationalist Movement*, 131.
2. See "Atal Bihari Vajpayee in His own Words", 1024; See also C. Jaffrelot, *The Hindu Nationalist Movement in India*, 131. Arya Samaj was a Hindu organisation with right-wing leanings. It was founded by Swami Dayananda Saraswati (1824-1883), a Gujarati, in 1875.
3. See C. Baxter, *The Jana Sangh*, 78.
4. According to Bidwai, *Panchayajna* is a propaganda organ of the RSS. Its editors are appointed not on account of their journalistic talents but on their political loyalty to the Sangh Parivar and the ability to articulate its positions. For instance, Vajpayee edited *Panchayajna* for years in political apprenticeship of the Jana Sangh. See P. BIDWAI, "Sanskrit and *Sanskriti* as Weapons", 33-34.
5. See A.B. Vajpayee, *Four Decades in Parliament*, vol. 1, *falp*.
6. See A.B. Vajpayee, *Four Decades in Parliament*, vol. 1, *flap*. See also S.K. Dass (ed.), *Atal Bihari Vajpayee*, 12.

7. See A.B. Vajpayee, *Four Decades in Parliament*, vol. 1, *flap*; S.K. Dass (ed.), *Atal Bihari Vajpayee*, 11-12.
8. See S.K. Dass (ed.), *Atal Bihari Vajpayee*, 11-12. The BJP made a coalition consisting of 24 political parties and they had a total of 299 seats out of 543. The BJP alone won 183 seats. See W. Röhrich, *Die Macht der Religionen*, 155.
9. For a list of them see S.K. Dass (ed.), *Atal Bihari Vajpayee*, 12.
10. On 11 December 1995 the Supreme Court of India 'defined' Hindutva as 'a way of life' so that it may not be equated with Hindu religious fundamentalism but as a synonym for 'Indianisation'. See T.J.S. George, *The Enquire Dictionary*, 229.
11. "This is the First Election", 6.
12. V. Venkatesan, "A Secular Veneer", 37.
13. See V. Venkatesan, "A Secular Veneer", 37.
14. Critics say that this statement inadvertently refuted the decade-long campaign of the BJP that secularism as practised by successive Congress (I) Governments at the Centre and in the States since independence was not genuine. See V. Venkatesan, "A Secular Veneer", 37.
15. A.B. Vajpayee, *Decisive Days*, 325.
16. "Lack of Proper Political Conduct of MLAs", 11.
17. It is to be noted that it is only towards the end of the 1980s and early 1990s that Shiv Sena grouped itself with Hindu nationalist groups. See C. SIX, *Hindu Nationalismus und Globalisierung*, 66.
18. See M. Ruthven, *Fundamentalism*, 171.
19. A.B. Vajpayee, *Decisive Days*, 67.
20. See A.B. Vajpayee, *Decisive Days*, 67; C. Jaffrelot, *The Hindu Nationalist Movement*, 131.
21. Krishna Kumar, a leading analyst of Hindu nationalism in India, observes that the DAV schools provided education to children in the line with the syllabus and examination pattern of the State system but in an ethos featuring Vedic rituals and a yearning for the revival of India's ancient glory. This latter feature expresses a specific view of history in which the conquests of India by the Mughals and the English are seen as causes of India's cultural and moral decline. Large pictures of medieval heroes like Rana Pratap and Shivaji and modern ones who symbolise Hindu revival are commonly used in DAV schools to decorate assembly halls and corridors. In this regard, at least, it is difficult to distinguish a DAV school from a school affiliated with the RSS. See K. Kumar, "Hindu Revivalism", 551.

22. See T.J.S. George, *The Enquire Dictionary*, 31. This idea is systematically presented in Dayananda Saraswati's controversial work *Satyartha Prakash*. In addition to this, the work also demonstrated his intolerance towards all non-Vedic religions and philosophies such as the Carvacas, Buddhists, Jains, Muslims and Christians, including popular Hinduism. See D. Saraswati, *Satyartha Prakash*, 1956.
23. See T.J.S. George, *The Enquire Dictionary*, 31.
24. See K. Kumar, "Hindu Revivalism", 539.
25. L.L. Rai, *The Arya Samaj*, 161.
26. L.K. Advani, *People Betrayed*, 97.
27. C.F. Andrews as cited in L.L. RAI, *The Arya Samaj*, 171.
28. See K. Elst, *Decolonising*, 14, 105.
29. See K. Elst, *Decolonising*, 109.
30. See K. Elst, *Decolonising*, 113.
31. See K. Elst, *Decolonising*, 111.
32. See K. Kumar, "Hindu Revivalism", 539.
33. See K. Elst, *Decolonising*, 111.
34. All India Hindu Mahasabha was a Hindu political movement that came into existence in 1913 (some sources say in 1915). Over the years it developed a stridency of its own in retaliation to the apparent growth of Muslim strength under British patronage which they interpreted as appeasement of Muslims. In 1937 the leadership of Hindu Mahasabha passed to Vinayak Damodar Savarkar, a firebrand nationalist. He turned the Hindu Mahasabha into an uncompromising opponent of the minority religions in India and remained its president till 1948. Thereafter the organisation 'withered away' but the ideology espoused found renewed strength through the RSS. See T.J.S. George, *The Enquire Dictionary*, 228.
35. See M. Ruthven, *Fundamentalism*, 171.
36. See M.G. Chitkara, *Rashtriya Swayamsevak Sangh*, 56.
37. See W.K. Andersen and S.D. Damle, *The Brotherhood in Saffron*, 5-6.
38. See S. Sarkar, *Beyond Nationalist Frames*, 200 and footnote 7.
39. *Hitlerjugend* (Hitler Youth) consisted of boys from 18-25 years old. There were also organisations for boys of 6-10 years and 10-14 years (the latter group was called *Jungvolk*). These organisations gave Nazi education for boys and created a 'pure race' of Nazi men well indoctrinated in the Nazi ideology. *Bund Deutscher Mädel* (The League of German Girls) was a youth organisation for girls. See B.R. Lewis; *Hitler Youth*, 23, 37, 39.
40. See F. McDonough, *Hitler and the Rise of the Nazi Party*, 70-71, 121.

41. See A.B. Vajpayee, *Decisive Days*, 67. Vajpayee joined the Student Federation of India in his college days. It was an organisation affiliated to the Communist Party. See ibid.
42. See A.B. Vajpayee, *Decisive Days*, 67.
43. See F.B. Ahmed, "Poet Prime Minister Turns 78", 9.
44. See A. Kulkarni, *The Advent of Advan*, 4.
45. See P. Kanungo, *RSS Tryst with Politics*, 185.
46. Golwalkar says: "The ancient tradition of *Gurudakshina* that the Sangh has followed is also in keeping with this spirit. Once a year on the auspicious Guru *Poonrima* day, every Swayamsevak worships the sacred *Guru*, the *Bhagawa Dhwaj*, and offers his *dakshina* (offering of money)". M.S. Golwalkar, *Bunch of Thoughts*, 413.
47. See L.K. Advani, *People Betrayed*, 97.
48. See A.B. Vajpayee, *Decisive Days*, 333-335.
49. See P. Kumar, "Stop Criticising RSS", 10.
50. See K. Kumar, "Hindu Revivalism", 545.
51. See W.K. Andersen and S.D. Damle, *The Brotherhood in Saffron*, 48.
52. See M.G. Chitkara, *Rashtriya Swayamsevak Sangh*, xii.
53. I quote the exact words of M.S. Golwalkar, the greatly revered RSS leader: "the foreign races in Hindustan [India] must either adopt the Hindu culture and language, must learn to respect and hold in reverence Hindu religion, must entertain no idea but those of the glorification of the Hindu race and culture [...] or may stay in the country, wholly subordinated to the Hindu Nation, claiming nothing, deserving no privileges, far less any preferential treatment – not even citizen's rights". M.S. Golwalkar, *We or Our Nationhood Defined*, 47-48.
54. P. Bidwai, "For Justice in Gujarat", 122.
55. See K. Singh, *The End of India*, 11-12.
56. See K. Kumar, "Hindu Revivalism", 537.
57. See C. Baxter, *The Jana Sangh*, 84.
58. See C. Baxter, *The Jana* Sangh, 86.
59. See C. Baxter, *The Jana Sangh*, 149.
60. See C. Baxter, *The Jana Sangh*, 6. The founder of the Jana Sangh, Shyama Prasad Mukherjee replaced V.D. Savarkar for a time when the latter declined to be the president of the Hindu Mahasabha Sabha on health grounds at the Amritsar session in 1943. See ibid., 21.
61. See C. Baxter, *The Jana Sangh*, 31, 32.
62. C. Jaffrelot, *The Hindu Nationalist Movement*, 117.

63. See A.B. Vajpayee, *Decisive Days*, 67.
64. See C. Jaffrelot, *The Hindu Nationalist Movement*, 122.
65. See C. Jaffrelot, *The Hindu Nationalist Movement*, 123.
66. See C. Jaffrelot, *The Hindu Nationalist Movement*, 132.
67. See C. Jaffrelot, *The Hindu Nationalist Movement*, 114.
68. See C. Jaffrelot, *The Hindu Nationalist Movement*, 164.
69. See C. Baxter, *The Jana Sangh*, 144.
70. See C. Jaffrelot, *The Hindu Nationalist Movement*, 168.
71. See C. Jaffrelot, *The Hindu Nationalist Movement*, 204.
72. See C. Jaffrelot, *The Hindu Nationalist Movement*, 205.
73. See A.B. Vajpayee, *Decisive Days*, 2-3.
74. See C. Jaffrelot, *The Hindu Nationalist Movement*, 234, 239.
75. See C. Jaffrelot, *The Hindu Nationalist Movement*, 244.
76. See F. McDonough, *Hitler and the Rise of the Nazi Party*, 74.
77. See P.C. Swain, *Bharatiya Janata Party*, 65.
78. See S. Sarkar, *Beyond Nationalist Frames*, 238. It is worth recalling that the Niyogi Committee report (1956) was far from objective. The Committee consisted of six members with Dr. Bhavani Shankar Niyogi as Chairperson, and its Secretary, the only official representative of the government, all others being non-officials. The only Christian member of the Committee was, a certain K.C. George from Kerala, who had many grievances against the foreign missionaries and had often attacked them publicly in the press. Thus the Committee gave the appearance of having a Christian representative among its members. Dr. Niyogi himself was a man deeply prejudiced against the foreign missionaries. See *The Niyogi Committee Report A Critical Appraisal*, 9, 13. See also *Vindicated by Time*, 30. C. Jaffrelot observes that the Niyogi Committee report took a view close to that of the Hindu nationalists. See C. Jaffrelot, *The Hindu Nationalist Movement*, 164.
79. Insurgency in itself has nothing to do with religious minorities. Here it may be remembered, for instance, that the ULFA of Assam is predominantly Hindus which is the religion of the majority in India.
80. See S. Sarkar, *Beyond Nationalist Frames*, 238.
81. See A.B. Vajpayee, *Decisive Days*, 9.
82. *Statesman*, 12 December 1951 as cited in C. Baxter, *The Jana Sangh*, 91.
83. See V.S. Naipaul, *India: A Wounded Civilisation*, 114.
84. See C. Baxter, *The Jana Sangh*, 36.
85. See P.C. Swain, *Bharatiya Janata Party*, 60.

86. See C. Baxter, *The Jana Sangh*, 2-3.
87. L.K. Advani, "National Security in Jeopardy", 17.
88. C. Jaffrelot, *The Hindu Nationalist Movement*, 315.
89. See C. Jaffrelot, *The Hindu Nationalist Movement*, 315-316.
90. See "BJP Seeks Superpower Status for India", 24.
91. L.K. Advani, "National Security in Jeopardy", 17.
92. See C. Jaffrelot, *The Hindu Nationalist Movement*, 375.
93. See C. Jaffrelot, *The Hindu Nationalist Movement*, 376.
94. It is to be remembered that the Ayodhya temple issue is a very complicated one as the place Ayodhya is sacred to the Jains, Buddhists, Muslims and Hindus. The Jains consider it as the birth place of the first, second, fourth and fifth *Tirthankaras* ('Ford-makers') for the Buddhists it is one of the oldest places mentioned in their mythology; the Muslims believe that the tomb of Noah is close to the Babri mosque; and for the Hindus it is the birth place of Ram. See C. SIX, *Hindu Nationalismus und Globalisierung*, 88.
95. See C. Jaffrelot, *The Hindu Nationalist Movement*, 376.
96. See C. Jaffrelot, *The Hindu Nationalist Movement*, 320.
97. See C. Jaffrelot, *The Hindu Nationalist Movement*, 411-414.
98. "Back to the Basics", 7.
99. "Back to the Basics", 8.
100. "We shall Return – Advaniji", 15-16.
101. See "Nationalism is another Word for Hindutva", 11.
102. See P. Bidwai, "More than Just a Wake-up Call", 124.
103. "Lack of Proper Political Conduct", 13. (Block letters in the original)
104. A.G. Noorani, "The BJP-RSS Equation", 50.
105. See B.R. Mishra, "Won Won't Let You Go", 18.
106. "The BJP has Evolved", 32.
107. See "'3030 1000' – BJP's Phone in Service", 25.
108. "BJP's Minority Development Convention", 23.
109. "Standing Ovation", 23.
110. A. Ghose, "Stability and Development", 7.
111. "This is the First Election", 4.
112. "The 'King, the 'Prince' and Shri Vajpayee", 22.
113. B.R. Mishra, "Won Won't Let You Go", 17.
114. "BJP Succeeded in Unleashing Potential of India", 7.
115. "The Statesman Speaks", 3.
116. "Standing Ovation", 23.

117. "BJP Succeeded in Unleashing Potential of India", 8.
118. "Standing Ovation", 23.
119. "The Statesman Speaks", 3.
120. See P. Bidwai, "'Vision' and Vitriol", 127.
121. See P. Bidwai, "'Vision' and Vitriol", 127.
122. See P. Bidwai, "'Vision' and Vitriol", 127.
123. "Standing Ovation", 23.
124. See F. McDonough, *Hitler and the Rise of the Nazi Party*, 74.
125. P. Bidwai, "The BJP's 'Plan B'?", 110.
126. Shiv Sena ('Army of Shivaji') was founded by Bal Thackeray in 1966 and is essentially a pro-Hindu but an anti-Brahmin party. See K. Elst, *Decolonising*, 196. Thackeray in his younger days had briefly joined the RSS to leave it soon. See ibid.
127. www.shivsena.org as cited in K. Elst, *Decolonising*, 197.
128. See K. Elst, *Decolonising*, 200.
129. See A. Katakam, "Polarised State", 125.
130. See A. Katakam, "Muscle Power and Parochial Projects", 13.
131. See L. Bavadam, "The Son Rises", 50.
132. A. Katakam, "Muscle Power and Parochial Projects", 12.
133. "Lathis against Trishuls", 6.
134. See P. Bidwai, "A Long haul for Secularists", 107.
135. See A. Kumar, "Modi Promises", 5.
136. See P. Bidwai, "More than Just a Wake-up Call", 123.
137. P. Bidwai, "For Justice in Gujarat", 122.
138. See P. Bidwai, "For Justice in Gujarat", 122.
139. See P. Bidwai, "For Justice in Gujarat", 122.
140. See P.S. Tripathi, "Strategic Voting", 12.
141. See P. Bidwai, "A Tilting of the Scales", 107.
142. See P. Bidwai, "For Justice in Gujarat", 121.
143. "Unmasked Truth", 229.
144. P. Chawla, "And Beyond", 31.
145. T. Setalvad, "Godhra Revisited", 8.
146. See S. Mustafa, "Far from Home", 8.
147. See A.G. Noorani, "Modi and His Visa", 48.
148. See P. Bidwai, "But who Lit the Fire?", 92.
149. See L.K. Advani, *A Prisoner's Scarp Book* (2002). In several parts of his book Advani discusses fascism of Europe, especially Nazism of Hitler.

150. *Organiser*, 30 October 1988, 13, as cited in C. Jaffrelot, *The Hindu Nationalist Movement*, 382.
151. A.G. Noorani," Hindutva, not Hinduism", 122.
152. See "I Became the Prime Minister because of Advaniji", 25.
153. See "We will not be allowed to Sit", 17.
154. See "I have Come here to Felicitate Advaniji", 9.
155. "No Alternative to BJP", 12.
156. A.B. Vajpayee, *Decisive Days*, 300.
157. See "This is the First Election", 5.
158. See V. Ramakrishna, "A Rough Ride Ahead", 25.
159. See J.C. Fest, *The Face of the Third Reich*, 288-289.
160. M. Domarus, *Hitler Reden*, vol.1, 338.
161. See C. Jaffrelot, *The Hindu Nationalist Movement*, 376.
162. See A.G. Noorani, "A Man of the Parivar", 98.
163. C. Jaffrelot, *The Hindu Nationalist Movement*, 382.
164. F. Langour, "Anschleichen Tarnen Melden". 400.
165. See A.B. Vajpayee, *Decisive Days*, 267.
166. "Dr. Joshi Integral Modern Education", 18.
167. "Dr. Joshi Integral Modern Education", 18.
168. For a detailed account of the nature, purpose, history and functioning of the Anglo Vedic schools and colleges See K. Kumar, "Hindu Revivalism", 540-541, 550-551.
169. Though the effort to found the Banaras Hindu University was started in 1905, it was materialised only in 1915. Behind this initiative was Madan Mohan Malavya. The institution contributed much to Hindu revivalism especially through its syllabi, textbooks and teacher education. M.S. Golwalkar who became the RSS chief after Hedgewar, was a student of this institution from 1924-1928 and a teacher there from 1930 to 1933. See K. Kumar, "Hindu Revivalism", 541.
170. It is an umbrella term for many RSS-affiliated schools. Such schools are run as part of a chain governed by a voluntary body registered under the Societies Act in each State. Some are run as purely private schools affiliated to the appropriate voluntary organisation in each State. An All-India amalgamating body called Vidya Bharati was set up by the RSS leadership in 1977 to provide an organisational umbrella to these schools. The need for such an umbrella body was caused by the state of Emergency imposed by Indira Gandhi in 1975. See K. Kumar, "Hindu Revivalism", 551.

171. Saraswati Mandirs literally means 'Saraswati temples', Saraswati being the Goddess of learning. Many RSS affiliated schools especially in the Hindi speaking areas of India are now commonly known by this name. See K. Kumar, "Hindu Revivalism", 551.
172. K. Kumar, "Hindu Revivalism", 555.
173. See A.G. Noorani, 'How Advani Went Scot-Free", 47.
174. See V. Venkatesan, "Tainted Credibility", 127.
175. See B. Putra, "Hubris at Hubli", 19-20.
176. See B. Putra, "Punish the Collaborators", 17.
177. See V. Venkatesan, "Tainted Credibility", 127.
178. D. Raja as cited in V. Venkatesan, "Tainted Credibility", 128.
179. A.B. Vajpayee, *Decisive Days*, 103.
180. "Proper Use of Resources not Made – Atalji", 11.
181. See "NDA Protest Against Tainted Ministers", 9-11.
182. See K.N. Panikkar, "Down, but not Out", 123.
183. See P.C. Swain, *Bharatiya Janata Party*, 245.
184. A. Raja, "NDA Agenda: Promise of a Developed India", 1.
185. See *Sunday* 27 December 1992-2 January 1993, as cited in P. Kanungo, *RSS Tryst with Politics*, 207, 221 note 120.
186. See K. Elst, *Decolonising*, 201.
187. "This is the First Election", 7.
188. A.G. Noorani, "The Man Behind the Image", 7.
189. See A.G. Noorani, "The Man Behind the Image", 7.
190. A.G. Noorani, "The Man Behind the Image", 8.
191. *Hindustan Times*, 22 April 2002, as cited in *The Gujarat Pogrom*, 3.
192. A.G. Noorani, "The Man Behind the Image", 7.
193. A.G. Noorani, "The Man Behind the Image", 7.
194. A.G. Noorani, "The Man Behind the Image", 7.
195. See F.B. Ahmed "Poet Prime Minister Turns 78", 9.
196. *Telegraph* December 18, 2002 ad cited in A.G. Noorani, "The Man Behind the Image", 9.
197. See S. Khosla, "No Mudslinging, Please", 2.
198. A.G. Noorani, "The Man Behind the Image", 5.
199. See A.G. Noorani, "The Man Behind the Image", 5.
200. P.S. Tripathi, "Strategic Voting", 12.
201. See S. Muralidharan, "Bankrupt Campaign", 5.
202. A.B. Vajpayee, *Decisive Days*, 78.

203. A.G. Noorani, "The Man Behind the Image", 8.
204. See A.G. Noorani, "The BJP-RSS Equation", 48.
205. A.G. Noorani, "The Man Behind the Image", 7.
206. See A.G. Noorani, "The Man Behind the Image", 5.
207. "Atalji Rules out Modi Factor for NDA's Defeat", 12.
208. See P. Bidwai, "A Tilting of the Scales?", 107.
209. See B. Puri, "BJP's Problems and Prospects", 124.
210. See "Expectations from a Visionary PM", 20.
211. See P. Bidwai, "A Tilting of the Scales?", 107.
212. See P. Bidwai, "A Tilting of the Scales?", 107.
213. See J. Kattoor, "Big Joke or Joker?", 11.
214. F. Arackal, "Double Talk", 42.
215. See "I am still Active in Politics", 32.
216. A.B. Vajpayee, *Decisive Days*, 300.
217. A.B. Vajpayee, *Decisive Days*, 300.
218. See P. Bidwai, "More than Just a Wake-up Call", 124.
219. Swami Agnivesh, "Agnivesh Vs PM?", 45.
220. See V. Venkatesan, "Winning without Hindutva?", 11.
221. A.G. Noorani, "The Man Behind the Image", 6.
222. See S. Sarkar, *Beyond Nationalist Frames*, 215.
223. See *Achievements of NDA Government*, 6.
224. See S.N. Bhaumik, "Hawk Flock", 28. Surprisingly even Swami Agnivesh, a well-known champion of many progressive causes welcomed Vajpayee's call for a national debate. See S. Sarkar, *Beyond Nationalist Frames*, 218.
225. See S. Sarkar, *Beyond Nationalist Frames*, 238-239.
226. Art 25 (1) states: "Subject to public order, morality and health and to the other provisions of this Part, all persons are equally entitled to freedom of conscience and the right freely to profess, practice and propagate religion". *The Constitution of India*, 61.
227. See S. Sarkar, *Beyond Nationalist Frames*, 218. Sarkar adds that a Supreme Court judge defied common sense by declaring that the right to propagate does not include the right to convert. See ibid.
228. See S. Sarkar, *Beyond Nationalist Frames*, 215.
229. A. Hitler, *Mein Kampf*, 290.
230. See V. Thampu, "No, Prime Minister", 126.
231. S. Gopal and U. Iyengar (eds.), *The Essential Writings of Jawaharlal Nehru*, Vol. 2, 53.

232. A.A. Engineer, "Secularism's Victory", 7.
233. See K.N. Panikkar, "Down, but not Out", 122.
234. A.G. Noorani, "The Real Vajpayee", *Hindustan Times*, 30 April 2002.
235. See B.R. Mishra, "Won Won't Let You Go", 17.
236. K.M. Talreja, *Triumphant March*, 8.
237. K.M. Talreja, *Triumphant March*, 75.
238. B. Ghose, "Senora Sonia vs. India's Atalji", 27.
239. B. Ghose, "Senora Sonia vs. India's Atalji", 27.
240. See P. Bidwai, "'Vision' and Vitriol", 128.
241. See F. McDonough, *Hitler and the Rise of the Nazi Party*, 74.
242. See E.K. Bramsted, "Fanatisch und Bedingungslos", 474.
243. It is surprising that even the UPA government which came to power on 2004 on a secular mandate has not considered the banning of aggressive, communal and fundamentalist Hindutva outfits like the RSS, VHP, Bajrang Dal, Shiv Sena and the like.
244. P.S. Tripathi, "A Law unto Itself", 42.
245. P.S. Tripathi, "A Law unto Itself", 42.
246. See A. Hitler, *Mein Kampf*, 377.
247. "Proper Use of Resources not Made – Atalji", 11.
248. "This is the First Election without any Tension", 6.
249. "I have Come here to Felicitate Advaniji", 9.
250. A.G. Noorani, "A Man of the Parivar", 98; ID., "The Man behind the Image", 4.
251. "BJP's Minority Development Convention", 23.
252. A.B. Vajpayee, *Decisive Days*, 78.
253. A.B. Vajpayee, *Decisive Days*, 103.
254. A.B. Vajpayee, *Decisive Days*, 103.
255. "Proper use of Resources not Made – Atalji", 11.
256. A.B. Vajpayee, *Decisive Days*, 103.
257. See R. Parihar – R. Desphpande, "Forward March", 24.
258. See "Men, Muscle and Money", 2.
259. See "India Slips on Human Development Index", 1.
260. See P.C. Swain, *Bharatiya Janata Party*, 68.
261. See A.G. Noorani, "The Man Behind the Image", 4.
262. A.B. Vajpayee, *Decisive Days*, 290.
263. See P. Kanungo, *RSS Tryst with Politics*, 233. The RSS reiterated that the victory was the result of the clear-cut ideology of Hindutva, the

hard work of many disciplined, devoted and dedicated RSS workers and the leaders of proven merit in the BJP. See ibid.

264. See P.C. Swain, *Bharatiya Janata Party,* 110-113. K.R. Malkani was instrumental in formulating the BJP party stance on socio-economic issues and in recruiting intellectuals; Vijaya Raje Scindia was a Hindutva-hardliner committed to Hindu *rashtra* and she worked for widening the base of the party; Sundar Singh Bhandari played a significant role in the formulation of the party constitution; K.L. Sharma headed the party working group and recommended to revive Jana Sangh ideology. See ibid.
265. See P.C. Swain, *Bharatiya Janata Party,* 88, 113-117. Sushma Swaraj may be the only one in the high level leadership of the BJP who does not seem to have an RSS-Jana Sangh background. See ibid., 115.
266. See S. Sarkar, *Beyond Nationalist Frames,* 240.
267. See P.C. Swain, *Bharatiya Janata Party,* 86-88. RSS leader P. Sudarshan, outstanding BJP leaders like Murli Manohar Joshi, K.N. Govindacharya, Arun Jaitley, Narendra Modi, Vinay Katiyar and so on have received political training in ABVP.
268. See P.C. Swain, *Bharatiya Janata Party,* 88-89.
269. See F. McDonough, *Hitler and the Rise of the Nazi Party,* 69-70. *Sturmabteilungen* (*SA*) or the 'Stromtroopers' was founded in 1921 as a private army of the Nazi party, led by Ernst Roehm. The members of *SA* had a romantic allegiance to Hitler as leader. Between 1929 and 1933 the membership of the SA grew from 30,000 to 425,000. Most of them were young men between the ages of 18 and 25. The *SA* offered an outlet for many delinquent young men to channel their anti-social and violent proclivities against political opponents. See ibid., 70, 122.
270. S. Kulkarni, "Victim of the Juju Syndrome", 14.
271. See P. Bidwai, "The BJP's Second Mascot", 120.
272. See P.S. Tripathi, "The Blitz in Lucknow", 6.
273. See *The Hindu,* 21 March 2002.
274. See C.P. Bhambhri, "Parivar Versus Dynasty", *The Pioneer,* 17 January 2004.
275. C.P. Bhambhri, "Parivar Versus Dynasty", *The Pioneer,* 17 January 2004.
276. "Lack of Proper Political Conduct", 12.
277. See *The Hindu,* 21 March 2002.
278. See "Vajpayee Visits RSS Headquarters", 3.
279. See "RSS 'Prachraks'made BJP Regional Secretaries", 11.
280. See P. Bidwai, "Convulsions in the Parivar", 115-116.

281. See V. Ramakrishnan, "Battles Within", 7.
282. See C. Jaffrelot, *The Hindu Nationalist Movement*, 62.
283. See M.C. Menon, "RSS in US Terror List", 23.
284. See A.G. Noorani, "The BJP-RSS Equation", 49-50.
285. See A.A. Engineer, Introduction to "The Gujarat Carnage", 23.
286. A.B. Vajpayee, *Decisive Days*, 333.
287. "BJP Destined to be Stronger for a Stronger India", 13.
288. P. Kanungo, *RSS Tryst with Politics*, 264.
289. See Leeladhar's press statement in *The Hindu*, 19 September 1999, as cited in P. Kanungo, *RSS Tryst with Politics*, 52, 65-66 note 86. Some observe that Vajpayee was barely 16 at the time of the incident and had joined the RSS only in 1941, hardly few months before this incident. Hence his disposition may also be interpreted as a simple statement of facts, not necessarily part of a planned strategy. ibid., 66, note 87.
290. See I.K. Shukla, "Informer of '42'", 29-30.
291. "Lathis against Trishuls", 6.
292. See C. Mitra, "Why", 21.
293. See M.V. Kamath, "Five Years of Vajpayee Rule", 6.
294. "Overseas Friends of BJP", 24.
295. See P. Bidwai, "A Tilting of the Scales?", 106.
296. See T. Singh, *Lollipop Street*, 104.
297. See P. Bidwai, "Liberation at Last!", 126.
298. See A.G. Noorani, "The BJP-RSS Equation", 49.
299. See P. Bidwai, "A Tilting of the Scales?", 106-107.
300. See P. Bidwai, "Liberation at Last!", 126.
301. A. Roy, "Democracy: Who's She when She's at Home?", 116.
302. A. Roy, "Democracy: Who's She when She's at Home?",122.
303. P. Kumar – D. Kumar, "I Prefer to Die rather than Eat Beef", 9.
304. See P. Bidwai, "A Tilting of the Scales?", 106.
305. See P. Bidwai, "Liberation at Last!", 126.
306. See P.S. Tripathi, The Blitz in Lucknow", 6.
307. "Fatal Factor", 9.
308. "No Alternative to BJP", 12.
309. See P. Bidwai, "Liberation at Last!", 126.
310. See K.N. Panikkar, "In the Name of Nationalism", 5.
311. See S. Sarkar, *Beyond Nationalist Frames*, 217.

312. See S. Sarkar, *Beyond Nationalist Frames*, 217 footnote 6.
313. See P. Bidwai, "More than Just a Wake-up Call", 123.
314. See N. Das, "Ministry Re-scuffle", 16.
315. See V. Venkatesan, "BJP As Big Brother", 31.
316. For example, on 25 May 1941, on the eve of his 59th birthday Savarkar declared: "Hinduise All Politics & Militarise Hinduism". V.D. Savarkar, *Historic Statements*, 1.
317. See G. Das, *The Elephant Paradigm*, 247.
318. See G. Das, *The Elephant Paradigm*, 283.
319. See A.G. Noorani, "A Man of the Parivar", 98.
320. See A.G. Noorani, "Savarkar and Gandhi", 36.
321. See S. Sarkar, *Beyond Nationalist Frames*, 261-262; A.A. Engineer, Introduction to "The Gujarat Carnage", 23.
322. A.G. Noorani, "Lessons from History", 125.
323. See "Atalji Seeks Two-Thirds Majority in Lok Sabha", 5.
324. See A.G. Noorani, "Lessons from History", 125.
325. See M. Domarus, *Hiter Reden*, vol. 1, 199.
326. "Gib mir Vier Jahre Zeit Nationalsozialistischc Bilanz 1937", 532.
327. "Atalji one of the Ablest Prime Ministers of India", 8. The former president R. Venkatraman is a Hindutva sympathiser and is often found in the company of the members of the Sangh Parivar. See for example, "Coalition Politics – A Challenge", 20.
328. See V. Ramakrishnan, "The Battle for U.P", 5.
329. A.G. Noorani, "The Man Behind the Image", 4.
330. SWAMI Agnivesh, "Agnivesh Vs PM?", 45.
331. See A.G. Noorani," Hindutva, not Hinduism", 122.
332. See C. Jaffrelot, *The Hindu Nationalist Movement*, 376.
333. See *BJP Today*, 1-15 May 2004, cover page.
334. A.G. Noorani, "The Man Behind the Image", 10.
335. J. Goebbels, *Goebbels Reden*, Vol. 1, 83.
336. See A.G. Noorani, "Modi and His Visa", 48.

II

Lal Krishna Advani

His Strategies and Stratagems in Politicising Hindu Religion

Lal Krishna Advani was born on 8 November 1927 at Karachi (now Pakistan). His father was Kishinchand D. Advani and mother was Gyani Devi Mirchandani.[1] He was educated at St. Patrick's High School, Karachi founded by the Irish Christian Missionaries, Dayaram Godumal National College, Hyderabad (Pakistan) and Government Law College, Mumbai. In 1947 he was Secretary of the Rashtriya Swayamsevak Sangh of the Karachi branch. In the same year he also became an RSS *pracharak* and head of the city's intellectual cell (*Boudhik Pramukh*),[2] he joined the Jana Sangh in 1951; from 1952 to 1957, he was Joint Secretary of Bharatiya Jana Sangh in Rajasthan; from 1958 to 1963 General Secretary of the Jana Sangh; from 1965 to 1967 Vice-President of the Jana Sangh, Delhi; from 1973 to 1975 All India President of the Jana Sangh; in 1977 General Secretary of the Janata Party; from 1977 to 1979 Union Cabinet Minister for Information and Broadcasting;[3] from 1980 to 1986 General Secretary of the Bharatiya Janata Party. He was the only one to become the president of the BJP for three terms: from 1986 to 1991, from 1993 to 1998 and from 2004 to 2005.[4] From 1989 to 1991 Advani was the leader of the BJP parliamentary party in Lok Sabha.[5] He was the Union Cabinet Minister for Home Affairs in the Atal Bihari Vajpayee government in 1998-1999 and from 1999-2004. On 1 July 2002 he was appointed Deputy Prime Minister, retaining at the same time the Home Ministry, an office he held till 2004. During the emergency declared by Indira Gandhi, Advani was detained under Maintenance of Internal Security Act (MISA) from June 1975 to January 1977.

Advani's RSS Background

The RSS is an inseparable part of Advani. Eminent historian, K.N. Panikkar, describes him as the most committed *swayam sevak.*[6] Advani himself admits: "In my case, more than my family, it was my earlier association with the RSS that played a major role in shaping my personality and giving me a sense of commitment to a world outside myself."[7] Advani joined the RSS in 1942. In 1943 M.S. Golwalkar, the RSS *sarsangchalak,* visited Sindh. During his itinerary he stayed at Hyderabad for two days where Advani was a student and member of the RSS branch there. The meeting with Golwalkar changed Advani's life.[8] In May 1944 he underwent the first year programme of the Officers' Training Course (OTC) at Indore, meant for the future RSS leaders. Back from Indore he experienced a welcome change in his personality now moulded for an active, meaningful role in the RSS. Soon he was appointed a *Bal-Shikshak* (children's instructor) involved in training the youth.[9] In 1945 he underwent a similar training at Ahmedabad, but at a higher level, both intellectually and physically, after which he was made *Mukhya Shikshak* (chief instructor) of a branch.[10] The third and the final training – a forty-day course – was held at Nagpur in 1946, the camp which is generally called 'the Hindu Nation in Miniature form'.[11]

From January 1947 onwards Advani was an RSS *pracharak* and Secretary of the RSS, Karachi branch with special responsibility to indoctrinate the members of the organisation.[12] He organised the work of the RSS in Alwar, Bharatpur, Kota, Bundi and Jhalawar from 1947 to 1951. When Mahatma Gandhi was assassinated on 30 January 1948, the RSS was banned by the Government of India. On 9 February 1948 Advani was arrested, since he was an RSS functionary, along with eleven others under Section 3 (1) of the Public Safety Act. However, he was released on 16 March 1948 while the ban on the RSS remained in force.[13] For a time Advani, like many other RSS leaders, lived in hideouts. During that period he was also engaged in many underground activities.[14]

In 1977 when the Bharatiya Janata Party formed the government in New Delhi the RSS approved the merger of the Bharatiya Jana Sangh in this new party. Advani was among the three of its *swayamsevaks* from the Jana Sangh that got cabinet births.[15]

Advani worked for *Organiser*, the RSS weekly in English, for several years. His association with this weekly dates back to early 1950s when he was contributing to "Rajasthan Newsletter". In 1959 he joined the weekly as an assistant editor[16] and in 1961 he was its acting editor. At one time Advani wrote three columns in the *Organiser* under three pen-names, namely "Cine Notes", "Periscope" and "Delhi Diary".[17] Christophe Jaffrelot says: "That he [Advani] was imbued with the doctrines of Hindu nationalism was clearly evident in his articles."[18]

About his relationship with the RSS Advani says:

> "I had my training in public conduct, in patriotism, from the R.S.S. It is my *alma mater* to me, and I am proud of it."[19]

> "As far as I am aware, there is no other voluntary organisation in the country with such a large band of dedicated, selfless cadres and with enormous capacity for constructive work. I feel proud that I am associated with it. No amount of calumny is going to make me disown it."[20]

In his *Prisoner's Scrap-Book* Advani wrote:

> "On the institutional plane, if there is one organisation in the country which has made the maximum contribution towards character building and discipline, it is the Rashtriya Swayamsevak Sangh. Literally millions of young men have imbibed their basic grounding in patriotism, integrity and discipline from this body."[21]

Advani's *People Betrayed* has several sections in defence of the RSS.[22] He says:

> "A number of myths exist about the R.S.S. They need to be consciously demolished."[23]

> "I feel concerned about the R.S.S. and its image because I am personally associated with the R.S.S."[24]

> "There was increasing awareness in the country that the image of a rabid, neo-fascist, sectarian organisation which had been planted in the minds by many years of partisan propaganda had nothing with the reality of the R.S.S."[25]

In October 2004, during the BJP executive meeting, Advani said in his presidential speech:

> "I take my inspiration from the selfless patriotism of the Rashtriya Swayamsevak Sangh. Together they have given me the strength and the courage to undertake difficult journeys."[26]

Advani also admitted that the party's 2004 defeat was largely due to its neglect of the RSS ideology.

Atmaram Kulkarni in his biography of Advani titled *The Advent of Advani* affirms: "Advani installed *Hindutva* at the central-stage changing the face of Indian polity beyond recognition and pushing the adversaries of *Hindu Rashtra* [Hindu Nation] on the defensive. He symbolises the emerging India. For him no honour in the world is greater than his membership of the RSS. He remains as ever a true *swayamsevak* in the service of *Bharat Mata* [Mother India]."[27]

In July 2002 Advani was appointed Deputy Prime Minister by Vajpayee, and the RSS leadership was particularly happy with the appointment.[28] There were speculations that the appointment was the result of the pressure imposed on Vajpayee by the RSS. K.N. Panikkar opines that if the BJP-led NDA had come to power in the general elections of 2004, Advani would have been the choice of the RSS for the post of the Prime Minister over the vacillating Vajpayee.[29] All these indicate that Advani's ideological upbringing is deeply rooted in the RSS. Christophe Jaffrelot calls Advani 'the incarnation of RSS ideology'.[30] Advani even argued that the history of 20th and 21st centuries will be incomplete without the history of the RSS.[31]

Advani has publicly acknowledged the mutual relationship that exists between the BJP and the RSS. During the National Executive of the BJP in Chennai in 2005 Advani in his presidential address reiterated: "Both the organisations [BJP and RSS] have benefited immensely from this relationship and together they have succeeded in bringing our ideology of cultural nationalism to the centre stage in India's public life".[32]

Advani's Jana Sangh Background

When Shyama Prasad Mukherjee (1901-1953) founded the Jana Sangh in 1951,[33] Advani became its Rajasthan State Secretary and held that office till 1957 until he moved to Delhi to become the Delhi

Jana Sangh Secretary and during this period he was also the Secretary to the Jana Sangh parliamentary group. In 1973 he was elected President of the Jana Sangh.

Jana Sangh was a political party with strong right-wing tendencies. It was in reality the political wing of the RSS committed to Hindutva ideology prior to the founding of the Bharatiya Janata Party. It envisaged India as Hindu *rashtra,* promoted the ban on cow slaughter and waged a relentless war against the minorities, especially the Muslims. The party was also avowedly opposed to Christian missionaries. C. Rajeswara Rao wrote in 1969: "The Jana Sangh is the public face of the RSS. It supplies leaders and cadres to the Jana Sangh. It controls the Jana Sangh from behind. All the top leaders of the Jana Sangh [...] are all known RSS men;"[34] "Jana Sangh is out and out a Hindu communal reactionary organisation acting as the mass base of the RSS."[35] Thus Advani has inherited a hard-liner identity from his ideological parents, namely, the RSS and the Jana Sangh.

Advani in Bharatiya Janata Party

On 5 April 1980 the erstwhile Bharatiya Jana Sangh announced the formation of a new party, the Bharatiya Janata Party.[36] For the next six years Advani held the post of the General Secretary of this party. In 1986 he became its All India President, an office which he held until January 1991. He was elected president of the same party again from 1993 to 1998. From 2004 to December 2005 Advani was once again the all India president of the BJP. As the BJP leader Advani maintained his close links with the RSS. It is his conviction that the party is good only because of its association with the RSS.[37]

Advani is widely believed to be responsible for the BJP's dramatic political success, the man under whose leadership the party acquired a prominent place in national politics within a very short time. His journey across the country in 1990 atop a motorised chariot as part of his *Rath Yatra,* galvanised an entire generation of Hindus and drew millions of adherents to the party. A.G. Noorani says: "After Atal Bihari Vajpayee's inglorious innings as party president [from 1980-1986], it was Advani who steered the BJP to success, *albeit* by recourse to unworthy tactics."[38] There is an interesting parallel between how Hitler led DAP to success and Advani the BJP party. Hitler's entry into politics in 1919 gave a new life to

DAP mainly due to his organisational abilities and massive propaganda. It is said that within a matter of weeks Hitler transformed the DAP from a German lounge bar ranting club into a noisy local nationalist party, fond of creating public outcry.[39]

Thus in essence the *Ram Rath Yatra* of Advani in 1990 was meant to mobilise the Hindu masses and politicise Hindu religion in view of capturing political power in Delhi. However, the *yatra* had all the marks of a religious procession: the Toyota van made to look like a chariot, saffron flags, sounding of auspicious conches, the symbol *OM*, the shouts of *Jai Shri Ram* by crowds, the choice of the location to start (Somnath where the famous Hindu temple was repeatedly destroyed by the Muslim invaders but rebuilt again) and end the *yatra* (Ayodhya, the alleged birth place of Lord Ram), women holding bright pots filled with auspicious water from the nearby rivers over their heads, etc. It has been argued that Advani's *Rath Yatra* was a success largely due to the age-old devotion for Ram across the length and breadth of India.[40]

When the Narasimha Rao government introduced in Parliament two bills, the 80th Constitution Amendment Bill and the Representation of People (Amendment) Bill with the dual purpose of banning religion from public life Advani said: "We strongly object to religion being translated as dharma [...] for the average Indian, irrespective of whether he is a Hindu, or a Muslim or a Christian, his respective religion is for him an inspiration for righteous conduct. By austing (sic) religion from politics, we will only be weakening the moral base of public life [...] politics should be cleansed of adharma, not dharma. It should be rid of corruption and criminalisation, not of probity and integrity."[41] Advani soon took out the *Janadesh Yatra* to combat what he called the 'draconian religion bills'. Four *yatras* began on 1 September 1993, the birth anniversary of Swami Vivekananda from the four corners of the country. Advani led the *yatra* from Mysore, Bhairon Singh Shekhawat from Jammu, Murli Manohar Joshi from Porbandar and Kalyan Singh from Calcutta. It travelled through 14 states and two Union Territories.[42] Advani maintained that by ousting religion from politics we will only be weakening the moral base of public life. Politics should be cleansed of *adharma* (unrighteousness) and not *dharma* (righteousness, morality).[43]

The rise of the BJP to power is rightly attributed to his deft handling and manoeuvring of Hindu sentiments. He is recognised as the architect of the BJP's rise to power. With him as the leader BJP heralded the Hindu ethos of India. This radical transformation in the character of the BJP endeared the party to the RSS. In fact Balasaheb Deoras, the *sarsangchalak* changed his earlier position and stated: "May be, among political parties, the BJP is closer to the RSS."[44] During Advani's leadership BJP entered into electoral alliance with Shiv Sena, a Hindu-centric force like the BJP. He even claimed that the BJP is really the chosen instrument of the divine to take the country out of the present problems and to lofty all-round achievements.[45] In 2004 it was Advani who recommended to Vajpayee to dissolve the parliament eight months before the completion of his government's tenure and opt for early election.

Advani is involved in several court cases, most of them relating to his infamous *rath yatra* which led to dozens of communal riots across the length and breadth of the country in which hundreds of people were involved, most of them from the minority communities.[46] Advani's third term as the president of the BJP from 2004 to 2005 is generally seen as being lacklustre. The party is in complete disarray under his leadership with the second-line leaders making public display of their differences and indiscipline.[47]

Advani's Concept of Hindutva

Advani describes Hindutva as a 'way of life'. It also means cultural nationalism which is the typical Indian way of thinking and decision-making.[48] He argues that cultural nationalism is the reality of India and it may be called by different names such as *Bharatiyata* or Indianness or Hindutva, and for Advani these terms have no real difference in meaning.[49] He further maintains that Hindu represents the nation and not one sect or community, and Indian and Hindu are synonymous with India.[50] Lord Ram is the national symbol and the source of cultural renaissance and unity.[51] He described the VHP's Ayodhya movement as a stroke of genius.[52]

Basically Advani's concept of Hindutva is same as that of the RSS which wants to create a monolithic Hindu *rashtra* with Hindu culture as its foundation. K.N. Panikkar observes that Advani has been Hindutva's hard face for decades. In the past he has not deviated even a wee bit from the ideology of the RSS. He was in fact the main RSS voice in the BJP. He was not troubled by qualms of conscience in any of the activities of the Sangh Parivar. Repeatedly he celebrated the fall of the Babri mosque and defended and supported Narendra Modi in Gujarat who is 'held responsible' for the 2002 Gujarat pogrom.[53]

Major Ideological Influences on Advani

V.D. Savarkar (1883-1966)

Advani's 'contact' with Vinayak Damodar Savarkar and his ideology of Hindutva goes back to his youth. As a teenager in Karachi Advani was given Savarkar's book *1857 First War of Independence* that was bought by his friend for a princely sum of Rs 27.00 from a bookshop in Lahore that dealt in proscribed literature. While in Bombay Advani wanted to visit just one place, namely, Savarkar Sadan and his meeting with Savarkar was an unforgettable experience that remained with him forever.[54]

In the early days of the RSS the members of the Hindu Mahasabha greatly helped the organisation. In fact, B.S. Moonje, a senior Hindu Mahasabha leader, is considered as an early mentor of Hedgewar, the founder of the RSS. In his visits to Karachi, Moonje took it upon himself to explain the mission of the RSS to the Hindus living there. Equally helpful were the several visits of V.D. Savarkar to Sindh as the President of the All India Hindu Mahasabha in 1940.[55] It has been argued that Advani's whole pubic life has been true to the teachings of Savarkar. He has pursued the latter's brand of politics relentlessly, and his anti-Muslims stand and the popularisation of the expression 'pseudo-secularists' are some expressions of it.[56] Aiyar calls Advani an acolyte of Savarkar.[57]

Savarkar has been for a long time *veer* ('brave hero') Savarkar in the RSS folklore and in the school textbooks sponsored by them. Edwin Bryant says that Savarkar's *Hindutva* is still considered a seminal text by the Hindu nationalist groups such as the RSS.[58] A few years ago, the RSS made an attempt – though it was not successful – to have his statue erected in Marseilles, France, to commemorate his 'anti-British' stand in the early 1920s. More recently, the former BJP-led government in New Delhi had the audacity to propose his name for the *Bharat Ratna* ('Jewel of India') award – the highest civilian award! In September 2001, a film was produced on Savarkar projecting him as a great freedom fighter. On

4 May 2002 the Port Blair Airport, in the Andamans was re-named after him – '*Veer* Savarkar Airport'![59] Speaking on the occasion the then Home Minister L.K. Advani openly admitted his intellectual debt to Savarkar and his work titled *Hindutva Who is a Hindu.* Advani said: "today, Hindutva is considered an offensive word. But we must remember that the pioneers of Hindutva like Veer Savarkar and RSS founder Hedgewar kindled fierce, nationalistic spirit that contributed to India's liberation."[60] On 26 February 2003 when Advani was the Deputy Prime Minister and the Home Minister, the BJP-led NDA government got the President of India A.P.J. Abdul Kalam to unveil the portrait of Savarkar in the Central Hall of Parliament in New Delhi.[61] In early 2004 the same government commissioned to set up a plaque dedicated to Savarkar on the *Swatantra Jyoti* ('Freedom Torch') monument in the cellular jail of Andamans.[62] But when this plaque of Savarkar was removed and replaced with that of Mahatma Gandhi in 2004 at the behest of Mani Shankar Aiyar, the Petroleum Minister, Advani was hurt and he called upon the Prime Minister Manmohan Singh to restore Savarkar plaque,[63] which of course the Prime Minister did not comply with.

Savarkar wrote *Hindutva* in 1923.[64] The primary aim of his book was to reconstruct and mobilise the Indian Hindus through a process of Hindu identity-building based on exclusivism, xenophobia, violence, aggression and the ethics of 'end justifies the means'. He built the foundation for this on the rudimentary evidences of prejudice and conflict and by concocting false propaganda against the minorities. He said: "To us Hindus, Hindustan and India mean one and the same thing;"[65] "Mohammadens and Christian communities possess all the essential qualifications of Hindutva but one and all that is that they do not look upon India as their holyland;"[66] "Their holyland is far off in Arabia and Palestine. [...] their names and their outlook smack of foreign origin. Their love is divided."[67] As President of the Hindu Mahasabha, he exhorted the Hindus to reconvert the Christians and carry on the *shuddhi* movement.[68]

Savarkar had strong links with some of the Nazis of his time. For example, the influence of Savitri Devi,[69] the 'Hitler's Priestess' on the Hindu Mahasabha is an established fact.[70] Savarkar's oft-repeated slogan was 'Hinduise all politics and militarise Hinduism'.[71] He aimed at establishing a Hindu *rashtra* in India and he passionately appealed to the communal instincts of the Hindus. He argued that *Hindustan Hinduoṇka* (India belongs to the Hindus).[72] He said: "Dravidians or Aryans [...] Hindus first and everything else next."[73] According to him, the Hindus are a nation by themselves because of their religious, cultural, racial and historical affinities and geographical unity and these bind them together to form a homogenous nation. Such were the ideas that Advani inherited from his ideological mentor, Savarkar.

M.S. Golwalkar (1906-1973)

Advani joined the RSS in 1942. In 1943 M.S. Golwalkar (called Guruji = 'teacher') the RSS *sarsangchalak* (supreme leader) who succeeded Hedgewar visited Sindh. Advani had heard of Golwalkar from the senior RSS leaders. Golwalkar came to Hyderabad on a two-day visit. Among some two thousand fully uniformed *swayamsevaks* present on the occasion was young Advani. After this meeting, young Advani was a changed person. So transformed was he that he decided to dedicate himself to the cause of the RSS as a trained leader. He then attended the Officers' Training Course (OTC) in 1944, 1945 and 1946 at Indore, Ahmedabad and Nagpur, respectively.

Golwalkar died in 1973. Advani then as President of the Jana Sangh paid rich tribute to the late RSS leader in tears stating that Golwalkar was the Swami Vivekananda of modern times, that he was dedicated to the creation of a great India and that in patriotism and selfless service he was a source of inspiration for millions of young men.[74] Since Advani was a noted RSS leader and of its political wing the Jana Sangh for many years, it is only reasonable to conclude that he must have met Golwalkar several times and studied with greatest care his works, like, *We or Our Nationhood Defined, Bunch of Thoughts, Spotlights,* etc., and imbibed the spirit of the RSS befitting a leader. Much of Advani's negative attitude and prejudices towards the minorities of India could be traced back to Golwalkar's ideology. For instance, Golwalkar considered the Jews and Parsis of India as guests or refugees and the Muslims and Christians as invaders.[75] According to him, the religious minorities of India could become a dreadful source of disruption in the effort to create a Hindu *rashtra* in India.[76] Golwalkar argued that the Christians and Muslims of India are hostile elements within the country, internal threats to the nation and anti-nationals.[77] In his reckoning, the Communists are sworn enemy of democratic procedure.[78]

Savitri Devi (1905-1982)

Advani in his youth read *A Warning to the Hindus* by Savitri Devi[79] (1905-1982) – an ardent admirer of Adolf Hitler and Nazism and one obsessed with the superiority of the Aryan race – which made a deep impression on him. It was published by the Hindu Mission, Calcutta in 1939. Advani's biographer Atmaram Kulkarni says: "The one book, he [Advani] then read, *A Warning to the Hindu Society* [sic] made a lasting impression on him."[80]

Savitri Devi's *A Warning to the Hindus* asked the Hindus to guard themselves against western cultural imperialism. She urged them to fight back its onslaught lest their culture would one day become a thing of the past like that of the Greeks.[81] She considered Hinduism as superior to all other religions[82] and the Hindus as a nation by themselves[83] and argued that Indian Christians and Indian Muslims, being Indians, should be treated as Hindus and brought back to the Hindu fold.[84] She spoke of the Brahmins as the oldest and the finest aristocracy of pure Aryans on earth[85] and invited the Hindus to rebuild a Greater India and realise the dream of resurrecting the Aryan paganism in the West.[86] She maintained that it is through Hinduism alone that one can realise India's unity as a territory and as a civilisation[87] and affirmed that Hinduism as the only culture and civilisation for India. She said: "the only civilisation for all India is Hindu civilisation. The only culture for all India is Hindu culture. Indian national consciousness is nothing else but Hindu national consciousness."[88] It was also Devi's contention that Hinduism is the only religion which can remake India a strong glorious nation – a World power.[89] She predicted the extinction of the Hindus in Muslim majority areas in the West and in Northeast India, thus presenting Christianity and Islam as serious threats to Hindu culture and proposed the re-conversion of Indian Christians and Indian Muslims.[90] She asked the Hindus to cultivate military virtues and to become a military race[91] and acquire political power at any cost and 're-conquer' India for themselves.[92] Advani as a young man was influenced by these ideas.

A Warning to the Hindus has a foreword by G.D. Savarkar, the brother of V.D. Savarkar. G.D. Savarkar does not call Savitri Devi merely a convert to Hinduism but one who has adopted Hindutva for the rest of her life.[93]

Nicholas Gookrick-Clarke observes that by 1980s Savitri Devi had assumed the status of a cult figure herself on the neo-Nazi scene.

Her eclectic ideas deriving from Hinduism, the myth of the Aryan race, Germanophilia and adoration for Adolf Hitler supplied a new mystique for that sinister minority of Nazi apologists in various countries around the world. Following her death in 1982 her ashes were placed in a Nazi shrine at Lincoln, Rockwell's headquarters in Arlington, Virginia.[94]

European Fascism, Especially Nazism

Advani was greatly influenced by European fascism, especially Adolf Hitler and his vicious Nazi ideology. Khushwant Singh says that when L.K. Advani was imprisoned during the Emergency declared by Indira Gandhi in 1975, he spent his time studying the Nazi dictator's techniques.[95] In October 1975 Advani published a booklet entitled *A Tale of Two Emergencies* comparing Indira Gandhi's emergency to Adolf Hitler's Third Reich.[96] April 1976 saw the appearance of another booklet from Advani titled *Anatomy of Fascism* which basically dealt with the fascism of Hitler with some references to other fascists of Europe like Mussolini of Italy and Franco of Spain.[97]

Khushwant Singh argues that from Advani's subsequent career it is evident that he imbibed more from studying the Nazi dictator's techniques to gain credibility among the masses than Mrs. Gandhi who probably never read anything on fascism. Hitler realised the importance of targeting the Jews, the religious and racial minorities to focus the hatred of the majority. For Advani, the task of finding such a community in India was not too difficult? – the Muslims. It suited him to cash in on the historic resentment against the Muslims. His *Rath Yatra* of 1990 from Somnath to Ayodhya was designed to achieve precisely that goal.[98]

Hitler's *Mein Kampf*

Adolf Hitler's *Mein Kampf* ('My Struggle') contains his political strategy. It was written by Hitler and published in two volumes in 1925 and 1926, respectively. The original title of the work was "Four and a Half Years of Battle Against Lies, Stupidity and Cowardice: Account Settled". But being too long-winded it was rejected by Max Amann, Hitler's publishing manager. *Mein Kampf* is partly his autobiography, partly ideological tract and partly blueprint of Hitler's political action. The book is a very important source for understanding the essence of Nazi ideology, Hitler's worldview, the techniques of Nazi propaganda, the plan for destroying Marxism and eliminating Jews from German society, the concept of a future National Socialist State, etc.[99]

Advani's prison diary which was published as *A Prisoner's Scrap-Book* in 1978 and republished 24 years later in 2002, has frequent references to Hitler's *Mein Kampf.* He quotes elaborately and consistently from it to compare Nazism with, what he called, the 'draconian laws' Indira Gandhi had imposed on the nation.

Advani's *The People Betrayed* also shows his familiarity with Nazism.[100] Advani has read not only Hitler's *Mein Kampf* but also several works on Hitler that reveal his personality, psychology, political strategy, philosophy and techniques, such as *The Mind of Adolf Hitler* by Walter C. Langer,[101] *The Rise and Fall of the Third Reich* by William Shirer,[102] etc. All these clearly indicate the extent of the influence of European Fascism, especially Nazism on Advani.

Importance of Propaganda

The concept of propaganda of Hindutva has close affinity with the methods of the European fascists, especially the Nazis. It is a well known fact that the objectives and aims of fascism are largely irrational. Since it would be impossible for fascism to win the masses through rational arguments, its propaganda must necessarily be deflected from discursive thinking. It must be oriented psychologically and has to mobilise irrational, unconscious regressive processes.

Advani seems to have learned the importance of propaganda from his study of Nazism. In his *The People Betrayed* Advani states, quoting Hitler: "Analysts of Nazi propaganda techniques are all agreed that one of the cardinal principles of their strategy ....was: there.... there must always be an enemy for the people to be able to identify as the cause of all their problems; all propaganda must be keyed to ensuring that hatred against this enemy does not sag. The Bolsheviks and the Jews were favourite hate-objects of Nazi propaganda."[103] In *A Prisoner's Scrap-Book* Advani says: "In Nazi Germany, fascism in action developed two other distinctive characteristics: firstly, adoption of propaganda as a key instrument of state policy; and secondly, the systematic development of a demonology to keep the masses in a mood of perpetual tension and hysteria."[104]

Advani observes that Hitler frankly spelt out his own concept of the use to which propaganda would be put. Through clever and constant application of propaganda people could be made to see paradise as hell, and hell as paradise.[105] Advani goes on to say that the Information & Broadcasting Ministry (designed under the Nazis, as the Ministry of Popular Enlightenment and Propaganda) was, for Hitler a pivotal branch of the government. Hitler entrusted the portfolio to one of his closest confidants, Paul Josef Goebbels, whose name has now became synonymous with high-voltage mendacious propaganda.[106] Hence it is not difficult to see that Advani has received much inspiration from the Nazis in envisaging his own techniques of propaganda. Knowing fully well the power, importance and role of propaganda Advani chose the key ministry of Information and Broadcasting under the Morarji Desai government from 1977-1979.

Demonising the Opponent

Another method of the Nazis was 'demonising' the opponent. Nazi Germany under Hitler systematically developed the technique of 'demonology' in order to keep the masses in a mood of perpetual tension and hysteria. Advani has a deep knowledge of this strategy gained from his meticulous study of Hitler and Nazism. He writes in his *A Prisoner's Scarp Book:* "The second thrust of Hitler's regime was creation of a demonology to whip up mass passions to justify its own perpetuation. Thus, for the German masses, the Jewish community was painted as a diabolical ogre responsible for all their sufferings and misery. Legal suppression of this community, and later, even its extermination, was projected as not only legitimate but even imperative in the national interest."[107] Advani adds: "A fascist, [...] looks upon political opponents as enemies of the country, and, so, undeserving of any political freedom."[108]

Referring to Hitler's technique of demonising the opponent Advani states that spreading 'big lies' is also a species of this strategy because, as Hitler says, people will believe a 'big lie' sooner than a little one and if one repeats it frequently people will sooner or later believe it.[109] Quoting Hitler, Advani writes in his *A Prisoners Scrap-Book*: "Propaganda must not serve the truth, especially not insofar as it might bring out something favourable to the opponent."[110]

In the present Indian scenario, the Muslims, Christians and Communists are the three major groups that are frequently maligned and demonised by the Hindutva ideologues, and Advani has always been one who has led the 'attack' from the front.

Pathological Dislike for Certain Groups of People

Hitler had a pathological hatred for certain groups of people. He argued that one should concentrate on one enemy at a time and blame him for everything that goes wrong. For him the enemies of the Third Reich were essentially the Jews, the Communists and all those who did not have the pure Aryan blood.

For Advani the enemies of the Hindu *rashtra* are the Muslims, Christians and Communists. He envisages a Hindu nation which is culturally monolithic. Hence he has no hesitation to demand that the Indian Muslims should be called 'Mohammadi Hindus', Indian Christians as 'Christian Hindus' and the Sikhs as 'Sikh Hindus'.[111]

However, those who are familiar with the history of Hindutva know that Advani was only repeating what Savarkar, Golwalkar, Savitri Devi and other leading members of the Sangh Parivar have been demanding on various occasions. For example, N.B. Khare as president of the Hindu Mahasabha declared in his presidential address in 1951: "The Hindu Mahasabha believes in militarising Hinduism and Hinduising politics. I say, *'Go a step further, and Hinduise all foreign faiths.* [....] It can, therefore, also include in its fold the four foreign-born religions which are practised in India, viz. Islam, Christianity, Zoroastrianism and Jewism. [....] *They must call themselves Hindus.* They must align themselves with the Hindu group for better or for worse, [....] They must abstain from cow-killing and beef-eating. And they must regard the 'Ancient History of India' as their own; and respect the heroes of Indian history [....] In short, these faiths must not look for their culture to Arabia, Europe, Persia or Palestine, but must adopt Bharatiya culture, which, in essence, is not different from Hindu culture."[112]

Politicisation of Hindu Religion

In India, religions play a crucial role in almost all elections, and it is an indicator that Indian politics is seldom truly secular, barring a few cases. Advani says: "there have been no elections in which 'Hindutva' has not been made an issue".[113] He emphasised the cultural unity of the country by highlighting Lord Ram as the national symbol.[114]

The *Ram Rath Yatra* is a concrete example of politicisation of Hindu religion. Some Hindu scriptures prescribe precise modes for the procession of the deity through the village streets. This was to enable people, especially those who were normally barred from visiting temples, to get a glimpse of their favourite deity. The obvious religious symbolism of the *rath yatra* found a political expression in the 1980s when political leaders used it to drum up mass support. The most famous instance was the emotional cross-country *yatra* in a modern version of the *rath* by Advani in 1990. Again, the fall of the V.P. Singh government in 1990 constituted a landmark in the history of modern India because for the first time since India's independence a government in New Delhi fell on a Hindu issue. Advani said that if they had not started the Ram Janmabhoomi movement the BJP would not have been where it is today.[115] The journey was an attempt to defeat the former Prime Minister V.P. Singh's Mandal agenda.[116] While Mandal divided the society, the Sangh Parivar believed, *rath yatra* would unite the Hindus.[117] In the long run the *rath yatra* catapulted the party into power by 1996, and more durably in 1998, making its hero Advani, the Deputy Prime Minister in the process.[118]

Rath Yatras or 'chariot processions' are also related to the concept of conquest of territory and show of strength. In 1990, the *Ram Rath Yatra* of Advani was modelled on Arjuna's chariot in the television serial of the great Hindu epic *Mahabharata*. Advani travelled in the chariot from Somnath on the west coast of Gujarat to Maharashtra, Andhra Pradesh, central India, Rajasthan, Delhi, Bihar and finally Ayodhya. The chariot was decorated with flags of the BJP and the VHP, a cut out of the sacred symbol *Om*, and a Hindi sign saying 'March on for the glory of the temple and the pride of Hindutva'. The symbolism of this triumphant pilgrimage called 'the Juggernaut of Hindutva sentiment' was like the victory over the four directions by kings and spiritual leaders of former times. About Advani's *Ram Rath Yatra* it is said: "The yatra was a tremendous success – no other effort at political mobilisation had drawn such a popular response. The yatra brought into sharp focus the contrast between 'lok shakti', as represented by the masses, and 'raj shakti', as represented by the elitist rulers in Delhi;"[119] "Shri Advani's Rath Yatra from Somnath to Ayodhya effected a sea of change in the political scene. While Mandal had divided the people, Ayodhya united the people."[120] This gives us a clue to the immense potential the *rath yatras* have in mobilising the masses of India in the name of religion.

One of the lessons which Advani had learned from Hitler was that propaganda has to confine itself to little and to repeat that eternally.[121] The harping upon building the Ram temple at Ayodhya is a typical example of it. *Mandir wahin banayenge* ('We will build the temple only there') was Advani's constant assurance to the Hindus and it became the new slogan of the Hindus[122] – obviously with Hindu votes in view.

About the *Rath Yatra* of L.K. Advani from Somnath to Ayodhya, Keonraad Elst observes: "It was much to the BJP's own surprise that Advani received a stormy [rousing?] welcome by unprecedentedly large crowds. The BJP had not been aware of the groundswell of Hindu consciousness and of the mass enthusiasm for the Ayodhya temple until it was confronted with this response."[123]

Advani's Role in the Destruction of the Babri Mosque

Advani is alleged to have given full co-operation to the destruction of the Babri mosque at Ayodhya on 6 December 1992. On 6 December around 10.30 a.m. Advani arrived at the site at the same time as Murli Manohar Joshi of the BJP. Advani, among others, addressed the *kar sevaks.* His speech was intemperate. Meanwhile some *kar sevaks* had breached the security cordon and were in a highly excited state. At 11.45 a.m. Advani reportedly announced: 'we don't need bulldozers to pull down the mosque' (meaning 'we can do it manually by removing chunks of its wall'). Then began the assault of the mosque. Advani then ensured that the demolition would continue and be completed without the intervention of central paramilitary forces stationed nearby. At 3.15 p.m. he urged the *kar sevaks* to block all entry points to Ayodhya to prevent central forces from entering and warned the armed forces not to touch the *kar sevaks.* The eight accused were present at the site for a full seven hours and there was no effort to distance themselves from the destructive and illegal actions of the day.[124]

It is a well-known fact that Advani was the person who was neck-deep involved in the demolition of the 500-year-old Babri mosque. He, along with other leading Sangh Parivar members, went all out to arouse the sentiments of people in the name of Hindu religion. Their posture and elated behaviour after the demolition conveyed everything. It has been said that photos of Advani, Joshi and Uma Bharati embracing each other are enough proof of what they felt while destroying the mosque.[125] Journalist Ms. Ruchitra Gupta observes that Advani, Joshi and Uma Bharati were sharing sweets among themselves and hugging each other. Advani was advising the *kar sevaks* to lie down on the ground so that the security forces would not approach Ayodhya.[126]

According to A.G. Noorani, the Rae Bareli court verdict in the Ayodhya case discharging the then Deputy Prime Minister Advani on 19 September 2003, went against the weight of the entire evidence and violated the law as declared by the Supreme Court.[127] In his reckoning it was a gross miscarriage of justice. The CBI had filed a charge sheet in court against Advani and other accused on 5 October 1993, charging them with conspiring to demolish the mosque. Two courts found that a *prima facie* case on this charge did exist – Special Judicial Magistrate Mahipal Sirohi on 27 August 1994, while committing the accused to the Sessions Court, and the Additional Sessions Judge, Lucknow, Jugdish Prasad Srivastava, on 9 September 1997, while framing the charges.[128] The Sessions Judge concluded that the accused were involved in criminal conspiracy to demolish the disputed structure of Ramjanmabhoomi/Babri mosque and that the plot was hatched by the accused persons in the beginning of 1990 and was completed on 6 December 1992.[129]

Advani, along with Joshi and Uma Bharati faced two charges in two courts – delivering inflammatory speeches on 6 December 1992 prior to the demolition, and hatching a conspiracy to demolish the mosque from 1990.[130] Investigations revealed that on 5 December 1992 a secret meeting was held at the residence of Vinay Katiyar which was attended by L.K. Advani and others. A certain R.N. Das, one of the priests at the site where the idols were placed inside the mosque before its demolition, told the media that he was a witness in a meeting held by Advani and others on the night of 5 December 1992. It has also been observed that at each stage Advani's role was narrated in detail.[131]

The prosecution, in this case the CBI, had accused Advani and seven others[132] of instigating a mob of *kar sevaks* into attacking the Babri mosque. The main charges against Advani were the following: promoting religious enmity between different groups; imputations and assertions prejudicial to national integration; rioting; unlawful assembly and statements leading to public mischief. However, after the Rae Bareli court verdict on 19 September 2003 the CBI was accused of deliberately weakening the case against Advani.[133]

Bidwai argues that the Rae Bareli court's discharge of L.K. Advani in the Ayodhya demolition case is a mockery of justice. According to him what is downright outrageous is that Advani, who was the most important leader of the anti-Babri movement in the late 1980s, and who conducted the infamous Somnath-Ayodhya *rath yatra* of 1990 and played a direct, preponderant role in the events leading to 6 December 1992 had been let off the hook and the magistrate had erred in exonerating.[134]

It has been remarked that the waywardness of India's police and justice delivery system has few parallels when it comes to punishing communal offences and hate-crimes. The Rae Bareli court framed charges against eight persons but discharged the Deputy Prime Minister L.K. Advani. But Advani was the man who spearheaded, planned and ideologically inspired the raucous agitation that led to the razing of the mosque on 6 December 1992. Thus the perpetrators of one of the worst hate-crimes in India's history – who pulled down a monument which had become a symbol of cultural pluralism – will not even stand trial for destroying a mosque and exploiting communal hatred.[135]

Praveen Swami notes that a *Frontline* investigation of the Liberhan Commission's correspondence reveals that the Central Bureau of Investigation's decision not to appeal against Deputy Prime Minister Advani's discharge from trial is part of a larger offensive to hide the truth about the demolition of the Babri mosque.[136] Bidwai argues that independent investigations have come up with overwhelming evidence of Advani's *pivotal role* in the process and events that led to the demolition, including the happening of 6 December 1992. The Citizens' Tribunal on Ayodhya, comprising Justice O. Chinnappa Reddy, D.A. Desai and D.S. Tewari documented Advani's role at length in its *Report of the Inquiry Commission* (July 1993) and in the *Judgement and Recommendations* (December 1993).[137] The intention to raze the mosque was repeatedly and unambiguously stressed by Sangh Parivar on a number of occasions. The very purpose of the *rath yatra* was to kindle 'Hindu pride' and 'get even' with history – of 'conquest and humiliation' of the Hindus by 'foreigners'. The Inquiry Commission recorded detailed testimony of eyewitnesses to show that plans for 6 December 1992 were launched by the BJP, VHP and Bajrang Dal. By 2 November 1992, some 90,000 *kar sevaks* had gathered at Ayodhya. By 3 December they numbered 150,000. On 5 December Advani addressed a public meeting in Lucknow and was to go to Varanasi, reaching Ayodhya/Faizahabad on 5 December. He, however, altered his plans so as to reach Faizahabad to join an all-important closed-door meeting at Vinay Katiyar's house where the ultimate, detailed plans for the 6 December 1992 were finalised.[138] But the paradox of it is that when all these things were happening before the full public view, the Congress-led Narasimha Rao government closed one eye and shut the other and did nothing tangible to prevent the destruction of the Babri mosque. Hence the questions to be asked is, are not also some Congress leaders partisans to the events of the 6 December 1992?

The 6 December 1992 events were videographed and photographed by numerous journalists both Indian and foreign, and above all by the Intelligence Bureau which reportedly has nine hours of tapes. Yet the Sangh Parivar launched a misinformation campaign which claims that Advani did his best to restrain the *kar sevaks* and shed tears at the demolition.[139]

The Rae Bareli court order of 2003 took most people by surprise. Special Judge V.K. Singh absolved Advani of all charges of participating in an unlawful assembly, inciting a mob to violence and breaching communal harmony.[140]

In the light of the above Bidwai says: "The Rae Bareli order is odious."[141] Purnima S. Tripathi notes, quoting a BJP leader: "The perception in the party [BJP] is that Advani has misused the government machinery to gain relief. Even if one more person was acquitted along with him, the impression would have been different.[....] He was the one who initiated the temple movement and brought it to the State (Uttar Pradesh), as a consequence of which the Babri Masjid was demolished."[142]

About Advani it was said that the man who had led the Ramjanmabhumi movement, which culminated in one of the most notorious acts of vandalism in contemporary Indian history, was let off the legal hook by Rae Bareli special court judge V.K. Singh.[143] But a bigger crisis confronts the BJP and the Sangh Parivar over the issue of how Advani *alone* got off the hook.[144] Kapil Sibal said: "Advani will have to examine his conscience and ask whether it is fair that those who followed him should be charged while he should get off scot-free."[145]

The Mumbai-based *Midday* dated 12 January 2002 quoted Advani's estranged London-based lawyer daughter-in-law Gauri

Advani telling the Liberhan Commission that Advani plotted with Vinay Katiyar, in her presence, the demolition of Ayodhya mosque. Gauri, daughter of a journalist, got married to Lal Krishna Advani's son Jayant in October 1991. Right from November 1989 till her wedding she had worked as special assistant with Advani and was looking after the New Delhi constituency from where he had contested and won the election. Gauri also requested in her application that she be made a witness before the Commission to bring out the truth about the demolition.[146]

Kay Abey observes that Advani told the Liberhan Commission probing the Babri mosque demolition that the day the mosque was demolished was the saddest day in his life. But for those who heard his speeches when he rode the Toyota *rath* in 1990, or read his speeches it was a very surprising statement. For journalists who were in Ayodhya when the Babri mosque was demolished, it was all the more puzzling. Wasn't he the man who started all this? Was he not the one who showed no remorse when riots followed his *rath*. Did he not order *kar sevaks* to block the road to Faizalabad when the demolition was in progress? Wasn't he the man who ate sweets and was hugging and getting hugged at the dais in Ayodhya when the domes fell?[147]

Advani has consistently described the anti-Babri agitation as a 'national' movement for Hindu self-assertion. He has boldly stated that Ayodhya integrated the nation and that Hindu nationalism is an issue of national pride.[148] But a question has been put to Advani and his colleagues: if Ayodhya is so central to the pride of the Hindus, why the Babri mosque had not been raised earlier by them, including in 1977-1979, when they were part of the Janata government?[149]

According to Mani Shankar Aiyar, the Babri mosque fell because the communalist in Advani proved far stronger than the constitutionalist.[150] But Advani never accepted the blame for the destruction of Babri mosque. It is a strategic rule of Hitler's technique that *one should never admit a fault or wrong, and never accept blame*, and Advani was very much aware of this Nazi method, as is evident from his *A Prisoner's Scrap-Book.*[151] Tavleen Singh had the same experience with Advani. She found it very difficult to make him admit a mistake. She says: "It was impossible to get him to admit to any blame or guilt".[152]

The Ayodhya issue has been called Advani's Achilles' heel.[153] Fortunately, in July 2005 the court case against Advani has been taken up once again.[154] It will at least appease the sense of justice of the common people which was so grossly violated when Advani was allowed to go scot-free by the Rae Bareli court order of 2003.

Gurcharan Das commenting on the destruction of the Babri mosque says: "On 6 December 1992, a screaming mob tore down an unused mosque. The Babri Masjid in Ayodhya, Hindu fanatics claimed, had been built on the birthplace of the god Rama. Ordinary, peace-loving Indians of all persuasions were aghast. It was an un-Indian thing to do. Our ethos is pluralistic;"[155] "the demolition of the mosque looked suspiciously like political posturing – a grab for power."[156]

Rath Yatras with Multiple Vicious Motives

Advani has been a 'man on the wheels' ever since he assumed the leadership of the BJP. His first *yatra* was the *Ram Rath Yatra* in 1990 in support of the demand for the construction of a Ram temple at Ayodhya. The second important one was the *Swarna Jayanti Yatra* in 1997 to commemorate the golden jubilee of India's Independence and to popularise the BJP's resolve to transform *swaraj* (self-governance) into *su-raj* (good governance).[157] Advani announced his third major *yatra*, the *Bharat Uday Yatra*, on 3 March 2004 in New Delhi on the eve of the general elections. On 6 April 2006 he took out the 35-day *Bharat Suraksha Yatra* spanning some 6000 km covering ten states. He described the purpose of it as to highlight the threat to India's security.[158]

Advani's Somnath *rath yatra* in 1990 inflicted an indelible scar on the Indian civilisation. Through this *yatra* he infused life into the dormant movement for the construction of the Ram janmabhumi temple, alleged to have been demolished by Mir Baqui, a general of Mughal emperor, in order to construct a mosque in its place.

K.N. Panikkar says that the *rath yatra* led by Advani from Somnath to Ayodhya, which eventually made the demolition of the mosque possible, was a defining moment in the history of contemporary India, as it inflicted a deep scar on Indian civilisation. It was the most powerful religious mobilisation witnessed in contemporary times and one which earned the BJP considerable political dividends. Consequently Advani was hailed as the leader who realised Hindu aspirations and thus paved the way for the political success of the BJP.[159] Political analysts say that after the defeat of the BJP in the general elections of 2004 Advani was re-inducted as the BJP president with the expectation that he would as before, re-energise the party.

Advani's *rath yatras* had multiple motives some of which were vicious and went straight against the very secular, democratic and culturally pluralistic fabric of India. Some of the motivations behind Advani organising the *rath yatras* are enumerated below.

Yatras to Provoke Non-Hindus

Advani organised the *rath yatras* in order to unite Hindus and to help the BJP politics by provoking the non-Hindus. Whenever there was a *rath yatra* it left its trail of destruction in many places in India. His Somnath-Ayodhya *Ram Rath Yatra* sparked violence in 26 places that it passed through.[160] Aiyar observes that what Advani's *rath yatra* did was to unleash across the country the lumpen elements of organised communalism into mainstream polities.[161] About his *Bharat Uday Yatra* of 2004, the CPI (M) Polit Bureau apprehended that the *yatra* would vitiate the atmosphere. It argued that under the cover of an election campaign the BJP leadership was once again seeking to arouse communal passions in the garb of a resurgent nationalism.[162]

The *Bharat Uday Yatra* was primarily a political *yatra* to mobilise support for the NDA. As Advani said: "I have decided to conduct my election campaign in the form of a nation-wide *yatra*. It will be called Bharat Uday Yatra, which aptly captures the emerging reality and the strengthening resolve of a resurgent India."[163] The *rath* (an improvised Swaraj Mazda bus[164]) took Advani for a 7,800 km journey. He spoke to *Organiser* in an interview: "This yatra is directly related to an election. The special message of the yatra is the BJP's vision for the future as well as the NDA's agenda for the next five years and to seek a decisive mandate for their realisation."[165]

It is to be noted that the BJP came to the centre stage of Indian politics after a number of *yatras* organised by Advani. Advani talked of an intrinsic link between the *Bharat Uday Yatra* and his two previous *yatras*. He said; "There is a common conceptual and emotional thread of resurgent nationalism that runs through all of them."[166]

Yatras to Arouse Hindu Sentiments

In 1990 Advani covered nearly 10,000 km in a vehicle designed to look like a *rath* with the Hindu sign *Om* and the BJP election symbol, the lotus etched on it. The *rath yatra* began on 25 September and ended on 30 October 1990. During the *rath yatra* at Ahmedabad a young member of Bajrang Dal applied to Advani's forehead a *tilak* with his own blood.[167] At Jetpur in Gujarat 101 Kshatriya youths offered Advani a bowl containing their blood. The slogans raised were highly inflammatory: 'When the Hindus have arisen, the mullahs have fled the country'; 'Muslims have two places – Pakistan or the graveyard'.[168]

During the *Ram Rath Yatra* Advani was presented with a *dharma dhwaja* by the priest of Somnath temple before he started his *dharma yudha* (holy war). For the people the decorated *rath* was a temple. They greeted with folded hands, touched the tyres and took the sand below it placing it on their forehead. Women danced and performed *arati*. At every place the most common offering was traditional weapons: arrows, dices, maces, swords, *trishuls,* and *kirpans.*[169] Talveen Singh tells us that in Delhi people dressed up as Shiva and as characters from the *Ramayana* and *Mahabharata*. They had knots of uncombed hair piled on their heads, snakes wound around their necks, and wore saffron robes with Sri Ram printed on them in maroon. It was a return to orthodoxy and religious conservatism of the most frightening kind.[170] Advani was arrested at the fag end of his journey in Bihar by Laloo Prasad Yadav the then Chief Minister of the State.[171]

All the *yatras* of Advani were organised around Hindu religious motifs. For example, during the *Bharat Uday Yatra* of 2004 when the Swaraj-Mazda bus was flagged off from Delhi on the way to Kanyakumari, there were loud chants of 'Jai Sri Ram'. Worse, Dilip Singh Judeo, of cash-on-camera notoriety, who had used the same vehicle earlier to Hindutva's nefarious ends – for his campaign against the alleged conversions to Christianity in the tribal areas of Chattisgarh before the assembly Elections in the state in December 2003 – ensured auspicious luck for it by smashing 101 coconuts and also by sacrificing a goat.[172] Commenting on the *yatra* Praveen Togadia said: "Politics cannot be fought, nor reported on, by ignoring religious appeal, by scoffing at Hindu sentiments."[173]

Way back in 1954 Nehru said: "The Hindu communal organisations are definitely aggressive and they can play on the religious or other feelings of the majority community."[174] The situation has not receded an inch in India even after half a century. The *yatras* organised by the BJP are burning examples confirm this fact.

Yatras for Communal Polarisation

The *rath yatra* is basically a Sangh Parivar strategy for communal polarisation of the Indian society. Jawaharlal Nehru described communalism as a narrow group mentality basing itself on a religious community that is concerned with political power and patronage for the interested group.[175] Advani's *rath yatra* of 1990, for instance, was not the unilateral decision of the BJP. It was a carefully designed strategy of the RSS. The *yatra* was a concerted effort of all the leading members of the RSS family. Bhaorao Deoras, brother of Balsaheb and a master political strategist of the RSS, reportedly spent two weeks in Delhi co-ordinating Advani's *rath yatra* plans.[176]

The VHP organised three major *yatras* with the slogan of 'Pilgrimage for Unity' (*Ekatmata Yatra*) between mid-November and mid-December 1983, for the whole of India: from Haridwar in the foothills of Himalayas to Rameshwaram in Tamil Nadu; from Pashupatinath in Nepal to Kanyakumari; and from Gangasagar in West Bengal to Somnath in Gujarat. All these *yatras* intersected at Nagpur, the RSS headquarters.[177] According to the VHP the month long campaign mobilised sixty million people and covered 85,000 km. The route of the *yatras* were so planned that they touched maximum number of Hindu shrines and religious places. The chariots of the VHP carried a huge portrait of Mother India and urns containing Ganga water throughout the journey. During the campaign, religious books, portraits of Bharat Mata, badges and stickers depicting 'Om', yogasana charts and pictures of great personalities of Hinduism were sold through stalls set up along the route. Thus the VHP used a lot of Hindu religious paraphernalia and sacred symbols to create a community consciousness among the Hindus.[178]

Yatras are organised also abroad. In 1999, after the BJP came to lead the coalition government in New Delhi, a *yatra* was taken out to 10 cities of the Unites States of America. It was named the *Dharma Prasar Yatra* and was described as a means of 'strengthening the Hindu community. In 2001 the Hindu Leaders Forum launched (founded in the same year) a *Vishwa Dharma Prasar Yatra* touching 47 cities in 38 countries and five continents. Its press coverage was extensive.[179]

Advani described his *rath yatra* of 1990 as the 'greatest mass movement' in independent India.[180] The *yatra* obviously brought together various sections of the Hindus closer to the ideology of Hindutva. It widened the gulf between the Hindus and the Muslims. Commenting on Advani's *rath yatras* Bidwai says: "BJP [...] is integrally connected to Hindutva through communalism and a certain belligerent form of nationalism, which find a distilled expression in the Advani rath campaign and the profound deception that lies at its core."[181] Tavleen Singh observes that the soldiers of Hindutva saw Advani's *rath yatra* as a sanction to finally attack the Muslims.[182] People who had never before shown any antipathy to Muslims were suddenly talking a new language. Advani had poisoned the air.[183]

P. Kanungo says: "Advani might have succeeded in using the Hindus, but he certainly divided the nation by igniting anti-Muslim hysteria among the Hindus."[184] What V.P. Singh says is very much applicable to Advani. "Their Hindutva is just this: consolidate the Hindu society as a vote bank and in this you use hatred as the main element."[185]

Yatras with Political Motifs

Savitri Devi's book *A Warning to the Hindus*, which made a deep impression on Advani, repeatedly asked the Hindus to acquire political power at any cost. She argued that the Hindus should organise themselves and conquer India for themselves.[186] Savarkar demanded the same from the Hindus. His oft-repeated slogan was 'Hinduise all politics and militarise Hinduism'.

The fundamental motive of the *rath yatras* of Advani was political. The BJP symbol prominently displayed on the *raths* made the political intentions clear. Though Advani was shrewd enough to call his *yatras* as means for promoting national unity and 'genuine' nationalism in the country, the political intentions were evident from the contexts, especially from his criticism of what he called 'pseudo-secularism' of the Congress governments, minority-bashing, anti-Pakistan discourses and the claim that India is a Hindu *rashtra*.

The *Bharat Uday Yatra* of 2004 was clearly meant to galvanise BJP and especially RSS cadres in areas where the BJP was weak. According to the media reports, of the 121 constituencies it covered, the BJP had planned to contest about 100 constituencies (of a national total of 350). However, most of them were not its strongholds. Hence, it needed all the support it could get there – no matter what the cost, including greater dependence on RSS cadres. The inevitability of this dependence was formally accepted on March 2004 at a special meeting of the BJP and RSS leaders at Vajpayee's residence.[187]

All the major *yatras* in which Advani was involved, such as, the *Ram Rath Yatra, Suraj Yatra, Swarna Jayanti Yatra, Bharat Uday Yatra* and *Bharat Suraksha Yatra,* had strong political motifs. Advani's example was emulated by BJP stalwarts in most of the states before the assembly elections. One may recall here the *Gujarat Gaurav Yatra* of Narendra Modi in 2002, *Parivarthan Yatra* of Uma Bharati in Madhya Pradesh in 2003, the *Samkalp Yatra* of Vasundhara Raje Scindia in Rajasthan in 2003, to mention a few.

Yatras for Personal Promotion

Advani's *yatras* had the sinister aim of promoting himself which became very evident in his *Bharat Uday Yatra* of 2004 and *Bharat Suraksha Yatra* of 2006. According to Bidwai the *yatra* had a three-fold purpose: (a) to project Advani not just as the BJP's number two campaigner, but as a leader of great stature in his own right, independently of Vajpayee; (b) to stress the continuity between Advani's present venture and the original *yatra* of 1990 and remind the party that it is he who built up the BJP's strength from a pathetic two seats in the Lok Sabha first to 86 and then on to three-digit number. The key to this was Advani's strategy of mobilisation around the Ayodhya temple issue and the *Ram Rath Yatra;* (c) to launch Advani, not merely as the BJP's organisational boss but as someone who would quickly take over from Vajpayee as the leader of its parliamentary wing.[188]

But according to Bidwai there was a huge deception involved in it – a sinister design. The BJP had until then run its election campaign on an exclusively Vajpayee-centric basis to fully exploit his (largely deceptive) image of a 'moderate', 'soft', 'liberal', 'reasonable' and widely acceptable leader. But with Advani's *yatra* a new twist was given to the campaign; the pro-Vajpayee voter would have unwittingly ended up voting Advani to the country's top job if the NDA had returned to power in 2004. The BJP was aware that Advani always had an embarrassingly poor public image. According to the ORG-MARG opinion poll published in *India Today,* 9 February 2004,

Advani's acceptance rating as potential Prime Minister was an abysmal two per cent, even lower than that of Mulayam Singh Yadav. According to an *Outlook* poll, the two per cent put Advani on a par with Mayawati. Hence Bidwai's speculation was that the BJP was trying to convert Vajpayee's popularity (47%) advantage factor to install the two per cent rating Advani in power.[189]

Critics opine that the sinister design of personal promotion was clearly manifested in his organising the *Bharat Uday Yatra* in 2004. It also revealed his ability to occupy the top post of Prime Minister. It has been pointed out that it was Advani who forced Vajpayee to opt for early elections in 2004.

Rath Yatra: An Imitation of Hitler's Technique

Rath Yatras may have religious connections. Initially in 1990 on the occasion of the *Ram Rath Yatra* Advani had planned to travel by Jeep and avoid a *rath* (chariot) as he thought that the idea of a chariot was archaic suited for N.T. Rama Rao, an ex-hero of mythological movies but not for him. But later Pramod Mahajan prevailed upon him and Advani consented.[190] As far as Advani was concerned *Rath Yatra* was essentially a political means to mobilise the masses in favour of the BJP using Hindu religion.

Advani's concept of *rath yatra* is largely an inspiration from Hitler. Hitler's rise to power in Germany had much to do with his mass contact programmes carried out especially through his extended tours on motor vehicles. For example, in March 1932 he undertook a whirlwind tour of Germany on a motor vehicle (*Kraftwagan*) lasting for eleven days. It was basically an election tour (*Whalreise*) in which he addressed some 500,000 persons and met with many journalists, and propagated his ideas of National Socialism. At the end of the election tour the NSDAP[191] papers proudly declared: 'tomorrow Hitler will be German President (*Reichspräsident*)'. The election result which was announced on 13 March 1932 registered a spectacular victory for Hitler's party which emerged as the second largest in the country with 11.3 million votes as against the 6.4 million votes it had secured in the previous election.[192] In less than a year later, in January 1933, Hitler became the undisputed leader of Germany, thus ushering in the notorious era of Nazi dictatorship.

In the past Advani has undertaken – either alone or in collaboration with others – several *rath yatras,* such as, the *Ram Rath Yatra*

(1990), the *Janadesh Yatra* (1993), the *Suraj Yatra* (1996), the *Swarna Jayanti Yatra* (1997), the *Bharat Uday Yatra* (2004), *Bharat Suraksha Yatra* (2006), traversing the length and breadth of India in order to mobilise public opinion in favour of the BJP, and to indoctrinate the masses with ideas of Hindu cultural nationalism. For example, explaining the purpose of the *Suraj Yatra* Advani said, among other things: "Through this Suraj Yatra we will take the BJP's message of Suraksha, Shuchita, Samarasta and Swadeshi, and its ideology of cultural nationalism (Hindutva) to the people."[193] About the objective of *Swarna Jayanti Yatra* he stated: "Projecting 'Cultural Nationalism' as India's true national identity and the dynamo for our national renaissance".[194]

Advani's study of Hitler's technique made him realise that the masses are 'feminine' acting on the feeling and sentiment rather than reasoning and that whatever one tells them should be addressed to the dullest ignorant among them in order to reach and convince the broadest possible audience.[195] The repeated *rath yatra* is based on a strategic rule of propaganda used by Hitler who maintained that one should *never allow the public to cool off.*

Advani as Promoter of Communalism

Communalism means the dominance of one religious community.[196] Advani is an ardent promoter of Hindu communalism. He is a symbol of communal polarisation of India which is detrimental to the secular credentials of the nation. For Advani the Indian Muslims and Christians are foreigners. They are culturally and politically non-Indians. Like his ideological ancestors – Savitri Devi, V.D. Savarkar and M.S. Golwalkar – he views them as elements hostile to the creation of a Hindu nation in India.

Pakistan is central to the communal agenda of the Sangh Parivar. Sangh Parivar has listed some 1000 temples allegedly demolished by Muslim rulers.[197] The communal agenda is to reclaim these temples and thus to avenge the insult inflicted on Hindus by Muslim invaders. On 19 November 1990 at Ayodhya, revealing his communal passion Advani stated: "No government in India could survive if it continued its anti-Hindu posture and showed disrespect to Shri Ram."[198]

Ever since Advani first took over as the president of the BJP in 1986, the BJP intensified its anti-minority campaign by accusing the government of promoting 'minoritism'. He summed up 'minoritism' as the promotion of a minority complex among the minorities which, according to him, serves neither national interest not even minority interest. He branded the secularism of the Congress governments of the past as 'pseudo-secularism'.[199]

In 1993 when Advani once again assumed the reigns of the BJP he pledged to usher in *Ram Rajya* and asked the BJP workers to emulate the thousands of dedicated RSS activists who have been working selflessly for it.[200] It is said that to Advani the happiest moment in his life was 30 October 1990 when the BBC announced that thousands of *kar sevaks* had swarmed into Ayodhya and successfully performed *kar seva*. The news gave him a sense of exhilaration which he had never experienced in his life.[201] He always defended the demolition of the Babri mosque with the exception of his opportunistic statement on certain occasions that the day of demolition of the mosque was the 'saddest day' in his life.[202]

Advani's communal politics was frequently manifested during his tenure as Union Home Minister of India, especially during the days of the Gujarat pogrom of 2002. Many are convinced that the Central government connived with the State Government of Gujarat headed by Narendra Modi of the BJP to carry out the atrocities against the Muslim community of the state. As the Union Home Minister of India, Advani did not do anything to stop the spread of violence, but allowed it to continue for several weeks.

Again it was during Advani's tenure as Home Minister that many crimes against the Indian Christian community took place in Assam, Bihar, Chattisgarh, Gujarat, Haryana, Jharkhand, Karnataka, Kerala, Madhya Pradesh, Maharashtra, Orissa, Rajasthan, Tamil Nadu, Uttar Pradesh, and many other parts of India.

When Graham Staines and his two sons were burnt alive by Dara Singh's Bajrang Dal in Orissa in January 1999, Advani was the first to give the Bajrang Dal a clean chit. He took it upon himself to defend the fanatic outfit on national television.[203] He also dismissed other cases of anti-Christian violence in the country as isolated incidents.[204]

When Advani visited the USA and UK in 2002 he was greeted with vociferous protests by Indian groups. In Washington several groups under the banner of 'Coalition to Support Democracy and Pluralism in India' submitted a letter to American authorities asking them not to hold dialogue with Advani as he was guilty of orchestrating communal violence against India's minorities as well as gross violation of human rights. Protest placards were displayed which proclaimed 'Advani is India's Hitler'. In London, a determined protest was held at a reception hosted by NRI businessmen for Advani. The protest was called by the South Asia Solidarity Group and supported by several anti-war, anti-communal, Asian women's and worker's groups. Protesters held banners and placards and shouted slogans such as 'We remember Gujarat Genocide – L.K. Advani has to Go', 'L.K. Advani, we say – Don't sell India to Bush and Blair"; 'No Indian Troops in Iraq', etc. The protesters distributed leaflets and their slogans penetrated the venue, forcing the chief guest Advani to sneak in through the back door under a heavy police escort.[205] Even Tony Blair reportedly told Advani that there were 2,500 asylum seekers from India, a number which would be 'expected from a dictatorship, not from a democratic country like India'.[206]

Several organisations grouped under the banner of the 'Coalition to Support Democracy and Pluralism in India' wrote to senior Bush administration officials that they were not 'comfortable' with the fact that it was conducting talks 'with people like Advani'. The letter pointed out that Advani was 'directly responsible for criminal activities against religious minorities and gross violation of human rights'. Relatives of the victims of the Gujarat riots and Indian-Americans staged a token demonstration outside the Indian embassy in Washington on 10 June 2003 against Advani's visit.[207]

Praful Bidwai argues that during the visit of Advani to Pakistan in June 2005 he seemed to have had a larger, more pernicious purpose in portraying Jinnah the way he did. He 'normalised' the use of ethno-religious mobilisation as a valid political strategy even to achieve the goal of creating a nation in which all citizens enjoy equal rights. This, Bidwai argues, amounts to sanctifying communalism.[208] Years ago Jawaharlal Nehru succinctly stated what is implied in communalism. He said: "It is, in fact, a negation of nationalism and of the national state."[209]

The Case of Tainted Ministers: Hypocrisy in Practice

As soon as the Congress-led UPA government came to power in Delhi in 2004, Advani and others in his party raised the question of the so-called 'tainted ministers' and boycotted the parliamentary procedure for several days. But little did Advani realise that he was the Home Minister when the Ayodhya case involving criminal charges were pending against him and a number of others holding ministerial posts. Advani in fact set the tradition of charge-sheeted ministers continuing in office. Had Advani set the precedent of resigning from the Home Minister's post after being charge-sheeted in the Babri Masjid demolition, probably no subsequent government would have had the courage to induct charge-sheeted ministers. In a letter to Advani, Wasim Ahmed, the Congress leader said: "You were personally the pioneer in setting the tradition of charge-sheeted ministers continuing to hold office. I think you will introspect and clarify your position."[210]

Hitler wrote in his *Mein Kampf* that success was the sole earthly judge of right and wrong, and Advani was familiar with this type of ethics[211] from his assiduous study of the Nazi techniques.

Advani's New Found Love for 'Secularism': A Political Ploy?

Advani, ever since his visit to Pakistan in June 2005, has projected himself as a 'secularist'. During that visit he openly declared Muhammad Ali Jinnah as a secularist, which created furore in India, especially among the RSS and the VHP. VHP's general secretary Praveen Togadia called Advani a traitor. He said: "Mr. Jinnah was a traitor, is a traitor and will remain a traitor and a person glorifying him is also a traitor."[212] Another VHP leader said that he and his associates would not accept Advani as a Hindutva leader any more. He even demanded an apology from Advani to the Hindus of the country and relinquishing of his political office.[213] K.S. Sudarshan, the RSS chief endorsed the opinion of the VHP. Quoting a Sanskrit *sloka* and translating it into Hindi he said that just as a prostitute changes her clothes and appearance, a politician changes his stand.[214]

In the wake of an upheaval in the Sangh Parivar, Advani resigned as president of the BJP only to take back the resignation after four days. In a Marathi-language daily the RSS ideologue and former spokesperson M.G. Vaidya stated plainly that the BJP leadership should have accepted Advani's resignation.[215] There was also indications that long before the journey of Advani to Pakistan the RSS had decided to make moves to remove Advani from the top organisational position of the Sangh Parivar's political arm (BJP) as early as March 2005. It appears that the decision was taken by the Akhila Bharatiya Prathinidhi Sabha (National General Council) of the RSS in Mangalore between 11-13 March 2005. But even prior to that the RSS had considered in their closed door sessions the removal of Advani. For example, the RSS national executive at Haridwar in November 2004 which was followed by a series of high-level closed-door sessions in different parts of the country. The argument of these meetings was that the BJP had lost its ideological moorings over the past few years. A section of the RSS delegates at the Haridwar conclave even came up with a proposal to abandon the BJP to start a new party firmly committed to the Hindutva ideology. According to Sangh Parivar insiders, through these deliberations it was decided not to float a new party but to set the BJP's course right by concrete and authoritative interventions. In actual fact it meant the RSS would bring about a leadership change in the BJP by installing leaders more amenable to its cause.[216] For long Advani has been the favourite of the RSS among the BJP leaders. But since 2004 that perception has undergone a significant change. According to the RSS, Advani is also peddling for power at the cost of larger Hindutva goals and objectives.[217] In all likelihood Advani knew the determination of the RSS to remove him from the leadership of the BJP. But in all probability his pronouncements in Pakistan about Jinnah's secular vision was motivated by an effort to create a controversy and build up a moderate, secular image acceptable to the partners of the NDA.[218]

Many political analysts hold the view that Advani's pronouncement about the secularism of Jinnah is to be seen as a *political ploy*. He realised that time was not suitable for an aggressive pursuit of Hindutva agenda in India. In his view the BJP should wait for the collapse of the Congress-led United Progressive Alliance government at the Centre, strengthen the NDA by roping in more regional allies and come back to power. The VHP leaders also said that Advani was of the view that the Left parties would become the rallying point for non-Congress, non-BJP parties if the BJP did not adopt the above strategy.[219]

Advani's entire political career is marked by a relentless attack on secularism. He propagated the notion of pseudo-secularism. He led the *rath yatra* to Ayodhya which appealed to the religious sentiments of the Hindus and which was translated into votes.

Political analysts ask the question how can Advani who has a life-time commitment to anti-secularism and Hindu cultural nationalism be trusted with his claim of a change of heart just because he has made a pronouncement in favour of secularism while visiting a *foreign country*? Perhaps his statement was a species of doublespeak in which politicians are so adept. Some think that his tribute to Jinnah in Pakistan was too fantastic a leap for a man who made a career of recreating and reselling the Hindutva of Savarkar. Others consider it as a shortcut to power and the Prime Minister's office, or an aberration, a 'momentary lapse' induced by the emotion of revisiting the land of his birth and youth.[220]

Neena Vyas argues that Advani's views on 'secularism' cannot be gauged from a single speech made in the Constituent Assembly of Pakistan. His communal politics of 50 to 60 years cannot be overlooked because in Pakistan he chose to describe the demolition of the Babri mosque on 6 December 1992, as the 'saddest day' of his life. Soon one can expect Advani to proclaim loudly his *swayamsevak* credentials.[221]

Pronouncements in Pakistan, an Attempt to Project a Liberal Image?

Since some time Advani has been making frantic efforts to soften his stand on Hindu cultural nationalism and to project himself as moderate. In November 2002 he said in Parliament as Deputy Prime Minister that India could never be a Hindu nation for which the VHP accused him of pseudo-secularism.[222] Advani may try his best to project the image of being a liberal. But the problem is, will he be accepted by all, especially the RSS?

The ideological position of Advani with regard to Jinnah's 'secularism' manifested in some of his statements in Pakistan in June 2005, signalled a departure from his previous views and was once again an attempt to project a new liberal image for him and the party. His pronouncements in Pakistan ran counter to the fundamental tenets of the Sangh Parivar which Advani himself had helped to evolve, propagate and establish. He also expressed his regret over the demolition of the Babri mosque of which he is generally considered as the chief instigator. As on some earlier occasions he said that the day of the demolition was the saddest day in his life. K.N. Panikkar commenting on this incident remarked that it sounded like a confession and an apology addressed to the Islamic world.[223] But everyone familiar with contemporary Indian history knows that for the Sangh Parivar the demolition of the Babri mosque was not a matter of regret but a religious and patriotic act, one which redeemed the Hindu national pride and self-esteem. For the Sangh Parivar, Advani had destroyed the self-esteem, which the Hindu had redeemed by the demolition of the mosque.[224]

It appears that with his pronouncements in Pakistan, Advani had hoped to initiate a debate about the history of politics in the subcontinent and about Hindutva's approach to it. But the RSS shut out such a possibility by insisting that the Parivar's existing understanding of Jinnah and his politics which led to the partition of the country and the killing of thousands of innocent people is not open to debate. The RSS also held that Advani's visit to Pakistan undermined the ideology and practice of the Sangh Parivar and his commitment to the Hindu cause became so suspect that he was termed a traitor.[225] Even Murli Manohar Joshi and Yashwant Sinha, both outstanding leaders of the BJP argued that Advani's statement in Pakistan about Jinnah had diluted the Hindutva ideology. The VHP and the RSS were so enraged that they demanded and obtained his resignation as the BJP party president in December 2005, six months after the incident. Advani had to retrace from his Pakistan stance in order to retain his post.[226]

The opposition to Advani's new 'stand' by the RSS and other important members of the Sangh Parivar once again confirms that BJP is the political wing of the RSS and that it has the right to dictate to the party. K.N. Panikkar affirms that the RSS's reassertion of authority within the Sangh Parivar has serious implications for the future of the country. He asks if the 'Iron Man' (Advani) could be humbled in this manner, what about the lesser mortals in the party? For the assertion by the RSS means that the BJP is likely to move towards a more fundamentalist and obscurantist politics.[227]

Appeal to Secularism, A New Game Plan of the BJP?

Bidwai argues that the issues which Advani raised in Pakistan in June 2005 went to the very heart of the ideological premises on which the Sangh Parivar is founded. These premises are Islamophobia, distrust of Muslims, hatred for Pakistan as India's inveterate enemy and an aggressive assertion of the Hindutva identity.[228] Advani had gone to Jinnah's mausoleum and described him as a 'great man' and 'a rare individual' who 'created 'history'. Hence he justified his visit as a way of paying respectful homage' to Jinnah. But it was considered by he RSS as something simply sacrilegious.[229] Although Advani's speech to the Karachi Council on Foreign Relations, Economic Affairs and Law on 5 June 2005 did not explicitly describe Jinnah as 'secular', it praised him for advocating on 11 August 1947 the 'equality of all citizens in the eyes of the State and freedom of faith for all citizens which 'what we call in India a secular or a non-theocratic state'.[230]

Political analysts say that Advani's pronouncements in Pakistan were miscalculated and it precipitated a fresh crisis in the BJP. It aggravated the ideological and organisational crisis of the Sangh Parivar and created new divisions. In addition, his use of the obsolete instrument – Jinnah – to make a last attempt at a change of strategy or image makeover as a moderate and secularist belied the claim that he is an extraordinarily shrewd, tactful leader who keeps his fingers on the pulse of his own party, if not the people.[231]

According to K.N. Panikkar, given the influence of caste-based parties in different regions of the country, the steady increase in the following of the Left parties and the new found energy and enthusiasm of the Congress under Sonia Gandhi, a section within the BJP realised that Hindutva was not likely to shine in the future to the extent necessary to regain power. Hence, it preferred a revisionist policy that would appeal to a larger section of the population. Advani's pronouncements in Pakistan were a precursor to this possible change of track. Unfortunately it misfired because it was premature and without adequate preparation.[232]

One wonders what prompted Advani to question an RSS-BJP orthodoxy? Was it an attempt to make the BJP more autonomous of the RSS and the VHP or was it part of a larger game plan to bring about a change in the BJP's strategy for electoral gain?

Advani learned a major lesson from the BJP's rout in the 2004 elections: religo-political mobilisation has reached a plateau; the BJP cannot regain power by relying on that strategy – even if it revives the Ayodhya temple campaign.[233] The *rath yatra* has lost its magic touch to rouse the sentiments of the masses. Hence we have sufficient reasons to conclude that Advani's 'discourse on Jinnah's secularism' in Pakistan was probably part of a larger game plan for BJP's own survival.

Advani as a Hindutva Hardliner

Advani is an acknowledged Hindutva hardliner in the BJP. This attribute endeared him to the members of the Sangh Parivar like the RSS, VHP and Shiv Sena. It was because of his hardline stand that VHP leader Ashok Singhal demanded in 2003 that Vajpayee must quit and hand over everything to Advani.[234] Advani's *Bharat Uday Yatra* was an attempt to legitimise him as Vajpayee's 'natural' successor and mobilise RSS support for the BJP's election campaign. This led Bidwai to state on the eve of the general elections of 2004 that those who vote for the BJP's 'moderate' Vajpayee version could end up putting Advani, the hardliner, in the top seat.[235]

As a Hindutva hardliner Advani's priorities are: to legislate on the building of the Ram temple at Ayodhya, ban on cow slaughter, prevention of religious conversion from Hinduism, re-conversion of Indian Muslims and Indian Christians to Hinduism, replacement of the minority commission with human rights commission, enforcement of the Uniform Civil Code, and creation of a Hindu *rashtra*.

Advani always nurtured a pathological dislike for Muslims. He had an aversion for Pakistan especially because it is a Muslim country. In fact, it was Advani who said on 30 November 2002 that 'let there be a fourth war with Pakistan'.[236]

Advani seems to have a dislike for everything non-Hindu. For instance, he said that there is nothing more unfortunate on the national flag than the Ashoka Chakra adorning it, which according to him symbolised Buddhism. But this is Advani's distorted concept of the Ashoka Chakra which symbolises peace rather than a religion.[237]

In 2004 BJP raised the foreign origin issue of the Congress President Sonia Gandhi. But it was a tactical, insincere and opportunist move on the eve of the general elections. However, the Congress put Advani on the defensive by reminding him of the absurdity of taking the 'foreign origin' issue to the extreme because having born and brought up in his youth in Karachi, Advani's own roots are deep in Pakistan. In fact while in Pakistan in June 2005 Advani wrote in a visitor's book "I do feel sentimental while I am in Pakistan […] I am somewhat at a loss to articulate the totality of my feelings and thoughts"[238] – a natural feeling of nostalgia for the land of his birth and early upbringing.

Hence one would do well to dismiss as part of a political game Advani's display of moderation in recent years, his new found so-called love for secularism and his concern for minorities, especially the Muslims.

Advani's 'Sincere Commitment to Vicious Causes'

Secularist and political thinker Mani Shankar Aiyar once called Advani a man with 'sincere commitment to a vicious cause'.[239] The vicious cause to which Advani is committed is the creation of a monolithic Hindu *rashtra* out of the multi-cultural, multi-religious and ethnically plural India, which is in essence the agenda of the Sangh Parivar. On several occasions Advani has argued: "it [India] has been a Hindu Rashtra all along. Nationalism in this country is rooted in the Hindu ethos;" "Majority of the people in this country are Hindus. Hinduism collectively represents the culture and the basic ethos of this country." This claim is not an iota different from that of K.S. Sudarshan, the RSS chief or Ashok Singhal and Praveen Togadia of the VHP or Bal Thackeray of the Shiv Sena – all of whom are acknowledged Hindutva hardliners.

Advani clearly demonstrated his anti-Muslim attitude when he 'participated' in the demolition of the Babri mosque at Ayodhya on 6 December 1992. He remained unflinching in his support to Narendra Modi, the symbol of the post-Godhra violence. He rescued the latter from dissidents clamouring for his removal. When in August 2005, Madan Lal Khurana, a respected senior BJP leader wrote to Advani demanding the removal of Narendra Modi as the Chief Minister of Gujarat, disciplinary action came for the former within hours of writing the letter.[240] A.G. Noorani commenting on the Gujarat pogrom of 2002 says that two persons qualify pre-eminently for the description of being 'modern day Neros' Chief Minister of Gujarat Narendra Modi and the then Union Home Minister L.K. Advani as they had alike the responsibility to protect the killers.[241]

In December 1990 BBC 'Radio 4' announced Advani as the 'Man of Year' for propagating the Hindu cause. But later it was withdrawn alleging that the popularity poll favouring Advani was rigged.[242]

In 1999 Advani's picture was hanging in the rogue's gallery of the Simon Wiesenthal Centre's Tolerance Museum, Los Angeles, for a few months, in the company of Saddam Hussein and Idi Amin[243] – an indication of how the world at large envisages him, his ideology and his activities.

In 2005 there was an allegation that Advani conspired to assassinate Muhammad Ali Jinnah before he migrated to India, which of course he dismissed as totally baseless.[244]

Is Advani BJP's Prime Minister-in-Waiting?

There is hardly any politician without ambitions for power. Atmaram Kulkarni, a biographer of Advani, wrote in 1995: "If BJP comes to power at the Centre, it looks certain that L.K. Advani would be the Prime Minister as he alone has been widely considered as the right candidate for the post."[245] A book published on Advani in 2002 titled *Today's Iron Man Life and Times of Lal Krishna Advani* presented him as the Prime Minister-in-waiting and interpreted his appointment as the Deputy Prime Minister by Vajpayee as a prelude to succeeding him. It said: "Now, as the new Deputy Prime Minister of India, he is on the way towards the premiership of the largest democracy in the world."[246] In 2003 Advani visited the United States and made a world-wind tour of four major cites: Washington, Los Angeles, Chicago and New York and met with various organisations of the NRIs. Many took him as the Prime Minister-in-waiting including the Bush administration.[247] When asked what would happen if for some reason Vajpayee left office, Advani said: "I happen to be Deputy Prime Minister. That in itself indicates what he (Vajpayee) is thinking."[248] To the question whether he as a 'hard-liner' would be acceptable as a leader to all sections of people Advani said that he is what he is and that he does not regret it being so.[249]

Ever since Venkaiah Naidu replaced Jana Krishnamurthy as the BJP party president, Advani has held undiluted hegemony over the party apparatus. His followers did their utmost to bolster his image. In June 2003 Venkaiah Naidu declared that the BJP has two great leaders, the *vikas-purush* (developmental man) Vajpayee and *loh-purush* (iron man) Advani.[250] According to Bidwai the most obvious landmark in Advani's ascendancy was the creation of a new office of the Deputy Prime Minister by Vajpayee in July 2002. Advani by then had already consolidated his hold on the party apparatus. Most of the 'bright sparks' in the BJP's second-rank leadership from Venkaiah Naidu and Pramod Mahajan to Arun Jaitley, Sushma Swaraj and Rajnath Singh, indeed even Kalyan Singh were his 'finds' or proteges.[251]

Many political analysts argue that Advani's appointment as Deputy Prime Minister was done in order to soothe his impatience to become the Prime Minister.[252] It was because of the planned succession of Vajpayee by Advani that there was an urge to building up new liberal image for Advani in the BJP circles. On the eve of the general elections of 2004 Advani took special care to cultivate a 'soft' and 'moderate' image. This was especially evident in his wooing the Muslims by this 'friendly' and inclusive attitude towards them.

According to Bidwai, Advani's *rath yatra* on the eve of the general elections of 2004 was an attempt to legitimise him as Vajpayee's 'natural' successor.[253] A.G. Noorani, writing on the eve of the general elections of 2004, argued that the BJP's real candidate for the Prime Minister's office is Advani, not Vajpayee. He warned Indians that even if the BJP romps home in the general elections as head of another NDA coalition, Vajpayee will relinquish the post in favour of Advani.[254]

If Advani ever becomes the Prime Minister of India, it will, in all likelihood, ring alarm bells for India's secularism, cultural pluralism, democracy, religious tolerance and civilised life. Muslims and Christians of India will reel under Sangh Parivar's persecution. India will witness another phase of aggressive, militant and ruthless propagation of the Hindutva ideology and imposition of the narrow-minded Hindu cultural nationalism, and perhaps also of the realisation of a Hindu *rashtra* in India, the ultimate dream of the Sangh Parivar. However, reading the political signs of the times we may be assured that the danger of Advani becoming the Prime Minister of India is now quite remote, though it cannot be ruled out completely as the Indian politics is full of surprises.

Conclusion

Lal Krishna Advani can rightly be described as the symbol of Hindu communalism and politicisation of Hindu religion in contemporary India.[255] Tavleen Singh calls him a 'fascist monster' and the man personally responsible for using religion and communal hatred to build the political base of the BJP.[256] Mani Shankar Aiyar has compared him to the Muslim hardliner Maulana Fazlur Rahman of

Pakistan and finds nothing to choose between them.[257] Advani is a quintessential Hindutva ideologue possessed with the imagination and commitment to translate theory into practice. He has understood, more than anyone else, the potential of Hindu religion for mass mobilisation, and has successfully manipulated the same with rich political dividends for about two decades. Atmaram Kulkarni, Advani's biographer rightly opines that Advani legitimised the Hindu ethos and rejuvenated the nation as never before through the biggest ever mass movement in post-independence Indian history.[258] Vidya Subrahmanyam observes that it is inconceivable that anyone else could have harnessed Savarkar's Hindutva for votes better than Advani.[259]

But times have changed. We are no more in the 1980s or 1990s. BJP under Advani's third tenure as President, could not maintain its original discipline or ideological strength. It was like an old cart drawn by an old horse. The former BJP President Venkaiah Naidu often referred to Advani as *loh purush* (iron man). But today Advani is, as Ravi Shankar Kapoor prefers to call him, a 'rusted iron man'.[260] (It may be recalled that under Hitler, Hermann Göring, the second powerful man of the NSDAP government was also called the 'iron man' and at times 'iron knight').[261] Today, the very identity of the BJP is in grave crisis. Advani's attempt to lend it a secular tinge in order to save it from sinking could not change its natural 'colour', which is 'communal', 'sectarian' and 'fundamentalist'.

Notes

1. See *Today's 'Iron Man'*, 11-12; A. Kulkarni, *The Advent of Advani*, 18-21. It may be noted that though the author of this book claims that his account of Advani is 'an authentic critical biography' it is very much pro-BJP, pro-Advani and pro-Hindutva.
2. A. Kulkarni, *The Advent of Advani*, 32.
3. He introduced two innovations: a daily recitation from Tulasidas' *Ramcharitamanas* on All India Radio (which still continues) and recitation on Tuesdays of the *Hanuman Chalisa* (discontinued when Indira Gandhi returned to power in 1980). See K. Elst, *Decolonising*, 167.
4. See V. Ramakrishnan, "A Rough Ride Ahead", 24.

5. See "Ideologue Dossier", 40; http://pib.myiris.com/profile/article.php3?fl=b9416
6. See K.N. Panikkar, *Before the Night Falls,* xv.
7. A. Kulkarni, *The Advent of Advani,* 228.
8. See A. Kulkarni, *The Advent of Advani,* 24.
9. See A. Kulkarni, *The Advent of Advani,* 25.
10. See A. Kulkarni, *The Advent of Advan,* 26, 31.
11. See A. Kulkarni, *The Advent of Advani,* 28-29. The expression "Hindu Rashra in a miniature form" was first used by K.B. Hedgewar, the founder of the RSS at Nagpur in 1940 during an Officers' Training Camp. See C.P. Bhishikar, *Shri Guruji Pioneer of a New Era,* 1.
12. See A. Kulkarni, *The Advent of Advani,* 32-33.
13. See A. Kulkarni, *The Advent of Advani,* 43.
14. A. Kulkarni, *The Advent of Advani,* 45-46.
15. See P. Kanungo, *RSS Tryst with Politics,* 185.
16. See A. Kulkarni, *The Advent of Advani,* 69. *Organiser,* which is the mouthpiece of the RSS, was started on 3 July 1947 with A.R. Nair as its editor and Bharat Prakashan Trust as its publisher. See ibid., 70.
17. See A. Kulkarni, *The Advent of Advani,* 70.
18. C. Jaffrelot, *The Hindu Nationalist Movement,* 237.
19. L.K. Advani, *People Betrayed,* Delhi 1979, 96.
20. L.K. Advani, *People Betrayed,* Delhi 1979, 96.
21. L.K. Advani, *A Prisoner's Scrap-Book,* 150.
22. For example see chapter VIII of L.K. Advani, *People Betrayed,* 80-102.
23. L.K. Advani, *People Betrayed,* 100.
24. L.K. Advani, *People Betrayed,* 100.
25. L.K. Advani, *People Betrayed,* 81.
26. L.K. Advani, "Let us Re-dedicate Ourselves", 17:
27. A. Kulkarni, *The Advent of Advani,* 255.
28. See http://www.rediff.com/news/2002/jun/29adv.htm
29. See K.N. Panikkar, "The Sangh Strikes", 20.
30. See C. Jaffrelot, *The Hindu Nationalist Movement,* 237.
31. See P. Kumar, "Stop Criticising RSS", 10.
32. L.K. Advani, "National Security in Jeopardy" 17.
33. See L.K. Advani, *A Prisoner's Scrap-Book,* 151; S.P. Mukherjee, *Leaves from a Diary,* 240.
34. C.R. Rao, *RSS and Jana Sangh,* 3.
35. C.R. Rao, *RSS and Jana Sangh* 3.

36. See A. Kulkarni, *The Advent of Advani*, 151.
37. See A. Kulkarni, *The Advent of Advani*, 228.
38. A.G. Noorani," Hindutva, not Hinduism", 122.
39. See F. McDonough, *Hitler and the Rise of the Nazi Party*, 40.
40. A. Kulkarni, *The Advent of Advani*, 241.
41. *Today's 'Iron Man' Life*, 54.
42. See *Today's 'Iron Man'*, 2002, 54-55.
43. See *Today's 'Iron Man'*, 42.
44. A. Kulkarni, *The Advent of Advani*, 169.
45. See A.G. Noorani, "The BJP-RSS Equation", 52.
46. J. Dayal, "Will CBI ever Catch Advani?", 12.
47. See V. Venkatesan, "Image and Reality", 14.
48. See *Today's 'Iron Man'*, 29-30.
49. See *Today's 'Iron Man'*, 63.
50. See *The Asian Age*, 20 February 2003.
51. See *Today's 'Iron Man'*, 30.
52. See *The Indian Express*, 26 November 2002.
53. See K.N. Panikkar, "The Sangh Strikes", 20.
54. See B.K. Punj, "Understanding Hindutva", *Pioneer*, 11 July 2002.
55. See A. Kulkarnai, *The Advent of Advani*, 5.
56. See *The Asian Age*, 20 February 2003.
57. See M.S. Aiyar, *Confessions of a Secular Fundamentalist*, 24.
58. See E. Bryant, *The Quest for the Origins of Vedic Culture*, 270.
59. See A.G. Noorani, "Savarkar and Gandhi", 34.
60. A.G. Noorani, "Savarkar and Gandhi", 36.
61. See "Kalam Unveils Savarkar Portrait", 1.
62. When the Congress-led UPA government came into power after the general elections of April-May 2004, under the order of Mani Shankar Aiyar, the Union Minister for Petroleum, the plaque carrying quotes from Savarkar was removed from *Swatantra Jyoti* and were substituted by words of Mahatma Gandhi. This of course led to a political controversy.
63. See "Advani Calls upon Manmohan Singh", 21.
64. The first edition of this book was brought out by V.V. Kelkar, Nagpur. As Savarkar was still in prison the author's name was not published. The author was simply referred to as 'A Maratha'. See "Preface by the Publisher of Second Edition", V.D. Savarkar, *Hindutva*, vi.
65. V.D. Savarkar, *Hindu Sanghatan*, 83.

66. V.D. Savarkar, *Hindutva*, 113.
67. V.D. Savarkar, *Hindutva*, 113.
68. See V.D. Savarkar, *Hindu Sanghatan*, 91.
69. See below for her biographical sketch.
70. See Trimondi, V. – Trimondi, V., *Hitler, Buddha, Krishna*, 344.
71. See V.D. Savarkar, *Historic Statements*, 1,2,76,98.
72. See V.D. Savarkar, *Hindu Sanghatan*, 116.
73. V.D. Savarkar, "Then Who is Who, Pray", 169.
74. See C.P. Bhishikar, *Shri Guruji Pioneer of a New Era*, 257.
75. See M.S. Golwalkar, *Bunch of Thoughts*, 138, 141.
76. See M.S. Golwalkar, *Bunch of Thoughts*, 158.
77. See M.S. Golwalkar, *Bunch of Thoughts*, 177-194.
78. See M.S. Golwalkar, *Bunch of Thoughts*, 195.
79. Savitri Devi's real name was Maximiani Portas. She was a French national by birth but her early sympathies were with Greece. In fact she renounced French citizenship and formally acquired Greek nationality. In the late 1920s she become an admirer of German National Socialism (Nazism) and was obsessed by the superiority of the Aryan race, first in India and then in Germany. Deeply impressed by the racial heritage of India and its caste system, she emigrated to India in the early 1930s to acquaint herself at firsthand with what she regarded as the cradle of the Aryan race. She was powerfully attracted to Hinduism, had sympathy for paganism and a confirmed aversion to Christianity. See N.G. Clarke, *Hitler's Priestess.*, 7-8. In India Devi was converted to Hinduism and was married to Asit Krishna Mukherjee, a Hindu publisher with strong Pro-German sympathies and whose editorials were unabashedly pro-Nazi. See ibid., 67. For Devi, Hinduism was the custodian of the Aryan race. According to her, Hinduism is the sole surviving example of that Indo-European paganism once common to all the Aryan nations. See ibid., 41. When Devi became politically active in the 1930s such Hindu nationalist movements as the Hindu Mahasabha and the RSS were growing in response to Muslim ascendancy. In 1937 she presented herself to Swami Satyananda, the president of the Hindu Mission in Calcutta. Satyananda shared many Hindus' admiration for Adolf Hitler on account of his Aryan mythology and the use of the swastika. He also considered Hitler as an incarnation of Vishnu. See ibid., 43-44. Devi was a scholar of high calibre. During her years in India she elaborated an extraordinary synthesis of Hindu religion and Nordic racial ideology involving the polar origin of the Aryans,

the cycle of the ages and the incarnation of the last *avatar* of Vishnu in Adolf Hitler, and all the time she nurtured an unswerving loyalty to the Nazi cause. See ibid., 4.

80. See A. Kulkarni, *The Advent of Advani,* 23.
81. See A. Kulkarni, *The Advent of Advani.* 23.
82. See S. Devi, *A Warning to the Hindus,* 44.
83. See S. Devi, *A Warning to the Hindus,* 76.
84. See S. Devi, *A Warning to the Hindus,* 86, 95, 97, 113, 122.
85. See S. Devi, *A Warning to the Hindus,* 87.
86. See S. Devi, *A Warning to the Hindus,* 150.
87. See S. Devi, *A Warning to the Hindus,* 37.
88. S. Devi, *A Warning to the Hindus,* 32.
89. See S. Devi, *A Warning to the Hindus,* 36.
90. See S. Devi, *A Warning to the Hindus,* 86,94-95, 97.
91. See S. Devi, *A Warning to the Hindus,* 131, 145.
92. See S. Devi, *A Warning to the Hindus,* 101.
93. G.D. Savarkar, "Foreword" to *A Warning to the Hindus* [1939] by S. Devi, 11.
94. N.G. Clarke, *Hitler's Priestess,* 6.
95. See K. Singh, "The Next Heir to the Throne", 2.
96. See A. Kulkarni, *The Advent of Advani,* 105. For the text of the booklet of 1975 see L.K. Advani, *A Prisoner's Scrap-Book,* 167-183.
97. For the text of the booklet of 1976 see L.K. Advani, *A Prisoner's Scrap-Book,* 211-228.
98. See K. Singh, "The Next Heir to the Throne", 2.
99. See F. McDonough, *Hitler and the Rise of the Nazi Party,* 58.
100. See L.K. Advani, *People Betrayed,* 80.
101. See L.K. Advani, *A Prisoner's Scrap-Book,* 148.
102. See L.K. Advani, *A Prisoner's Scrap-Book,* 218.
103. L.K. Advani, *People Betrayed,* 80. k
104. L.K. Advani, *A Prisoner's Scrap-Book,* 214.
105. See L.K. Advani, *A Prisoner's Scrap-Book,* 215.
106. See L.K. Advani, *A Prisoner's Scrap-Book,* 215.
107. L.K. Advani, *A Prisoner's Scrap-Book,* 215.
108. L.K. Advani, *A Prisoner's Scrap-Book,* 216-217.
109. See L.K. Advani, *A Prisoner's Scrap-Book,* 148.
110. L.K. Advani, *A Prisoner's Scrap-Book,* 220.

111. "Advani wants Muslims to identify with 'Hindutva'", *Times of India*, 30 January 1995 as cited in K. Elst, *Decolonising*, 480.
112. N.B. Khare, *Presidential Address* (1951), 8-9 (Emphasis in the original).
113. "Talks only Solution: Advani", 1.
114. *Today's 'Iron Man'*, 30.
115. See A.G. Noorani, "The BJP-RSS Equation", 48.
116. In 1979 a commission headed by B.P. Mandal was appointed by the then Prime Minister Morarji Desai to identify the backward classes, investigate their conditions and recommend measures for their social and economic advancement. By the time the Commission completed its work in December 1980, Indira Gandhi had become Prime Minister and the report was shelved. It was resurrected in 1989 when V.P. Singh become Prime Minister. In a bid to win backward class support he announced that he would implement the recommendations of the Mandal Commission which included the reservation for backward classes of 27 per cent of jobs in central government services and public sector undertakings in addition to existing quotas of reservation for Scheduled Castes and Tribes. This greatly divided the Indian society along caste lines. Widespread and violent protest demonstrations helped oust the Singh government. See T.J.S. George, *The Enquire Dictionary*, 306.
117. Rajmohan Gandhi notes that Mandir and Mandal sharpened India's religious and caste divisions. They did not exactly polarise society for there were those who supported both Mandal and Mandir, while some were uneasy with both. Some claimed that Mandal brought 'social justice' to the centre of the Indian agenda while Mandir did the same for 'Hindu sentiments'. See R. Gandhi, *Revenge and Reconciliation*, 374.
118. See *India Today*, 18 August 2003, 76.
119. *Today's 'Iron Man'*, 47.
120. *Today's 'Iron Man'*, 20.
121. See L.K. Advani, *A Prisoner's Scrap-Book*, 220.
122. See *The Indian Express*, 1 February 2004.
123. K. Elst, *Decolonising*, 174.
124. See P. Bidwai, "Between Despair and Hope", 125-126.
125. See http://www.milligazette.com/Archives/01062001/07.htm
126. See http://www.milligazette.com/Archives/01062001/07.htm
127. See A.G. Noorani, "How Advani Went Scot-Free", 47.
128. See A.G. Noorani, "How Advani Went Scot-Free", 47.
129. See A.G. Noorani, "How Advani Went Scot-Free", 47.

130. See A.G. Noorani, "How Advani Went Scot-Free", 47.
131. See A.G. Noorani, "How Advani Went Scot-Free", 48.
132. The other seven accused include the former Human Resources Development Minister Murli Manohar Joshi, the former Chief Minister of Madhya Pradesh Uma Bharati, the former Bajrang Dal leader Vinay Katiyar, VHP leaders Ashok Singhal, V.H. Dalmia, Giriraj Kishore and Sadhvi Ritambara. See R. Deshpande, "Advani's Ordeal", 27.
133. See R. Deshpande, 'Advani's Ordeal", 27. Charges against *kar sevaks* were the following: dacoity; robbery or dacoity with attempt to cause death or grievous hurt; voluntarily causing hurt to deter public servant from doing his duty; causing hurt by endangering life or personal safety of others; causing grievous hurt by endangering life or personal safety of others. See R. Deshpande, "Advani's.
134. See P. Bidwai, "Between Despair and Hope", 125.
135. See P. Bidwai, "Between Despair and Hope", 125.
136. See P. Swami, "A Campaign of Sabotage", 33.
137. See P. Bidwai, "Between Despair and Hope", 125.
138. See P. Bidwai, "Between Despair and Hope", 125.
139. See P. Bidwai, "Between Despair and Hope", 26.
140. See S. Yadev, "Face Off", 26-27.
141. See P. Bidwai, "Between Despair and Hope", 126.
142. P.S. Tripathi, "Aftershocks of a Verdict", 18.
143. See S.N. Bhaumik and S. Mukherjee, "The Big Fish Escapes", 36.
144. See S.N. Bhaumik and S. Mukherjee, "The Big Fish Escapes", 36.
145. S.N. Bhaumik – S. Mukherjee, "The Big Fish Escapes", 36.
146. See "When Advani was Unmasked", 14. See also R. Bonney, "Introduction" to J.P. Hartung, G. Hawkes and A. Bhattacharjee, *Ayodhya 1992-2003*, 9.
147. See K. Abey, "The Doctrine of Deception", 50.
148. See *Organiser*, 18 April 2004, 20.
149. See R. Gandhi, *Revenge and Reconciliation*, 375.
150. See M.S. Aiyar, *Confessions of a Secular Fundamentalist*, 89.
151. L.K. Advani, *A Prisoner's Scrap-Book*, 148.
152. See T. Singh, *Lollipop Street*, 138.
153. See T. Singh, *Lollipop Street*, 151.
154. See "Charges Framed against Advani, 1.
155. G. Das, *The Elephant Paradigm*, 74.

156. G. Das, *The Elephant Paradigm*, 75.
157. See V. Venkatesan, "Advani's Yatra and Other's Fears", 28.
158. See D. Mukerji, "Popularity Test Ride", 32; "Yatra's Aim to Highlight Threat", 12.
159. See K.N. Panikkar, "The Sangh Strikes", 21.
160. See D. Bunsha, "Organised Intolerance", 18.
161. See M.S. Aiyar, *Confessions of a Secular Fundamentalist*, 26.
162. See V. Venkatesan, "Advani's Yatra and Other's Fears", 29.
163. *Organiser*, 14 March 2004, 2.
164. The bus was fitted with many useful things. There was a hydraulic lift for Advani to address the public on the roof of the bus. There was a public address system, emergency lights and specially arranged tent fitted on the roof of the bus to give protection from the scorching sun. Mobile phone, fax, Internet and DVD were also there in the vehicle. A bed-cum-sofa was there, but night stays were at stations. Packed food had been arranged for refreshments in the daytime. *Organiser*, 14 March 2004, 2.
165. D.K. Rath, "Mission Mandate", 1.
166. *Organiser*, 14 March 2004, 2.
167. Y. Ambroise, "Hindutva's Real Agenda", 49; K.N. Panikkar, *Before the Night Falls*, 32.
168. See P. Kanungo, *RSS Tryst with Politics*, 203. See also K.N. Panikkar, *Before the Night Falls*, 32.
169. See *Organiser* 14 October 1990, as cited in P. Kanungo, *RSS Tryst with Politics*, 203, 220 note 102.
170. See T. Singh, *Lollipop Street*, 137.
171. See R. Gandhi, *Revenge and Reconciliation*, 375.
172. See P. Bidwai, "The BJP's Second Mascot", 120.
173. P. Togadia, "Final Warning", 35.
174. S. Gopal and U. Iyengar (eds.), *The Essential Writings of Jawaharlal Nehru*, vol.1, 190.
175. See J. Nehru, *The Discovery of India*, 420.
176. Reported in *India Today*, 15 October 1990, as cited in P. Kanungo, *RSS Tryst with Politics*, 202, 220 note 98.
177. See P. Kanungo, *RSS Tryst with Politics*, 193.
178. See P. Kanungo, *RSS Tryst with Politics*, 194.
179. See A. Rajgopal, "Non-Resident Nationalism", 128.
180. See P. Kanungo, *RSS Tryst with Politics*, 204.

181. P. Bidwai, "The BJP's Second Mascot", 120.
182. See T. Singh, *Lollipop Street*, 136.
183. See T. Singh, *Lollipop Street*, 137.
184. P. Kanungo, *RSS Tryst with Politics*, 203.
185. V.P. Singh, "Hindus are Next", 32.
186. See S. Devi, *A Warning to the Hindus*, 101.
187. See P. Bidwai, "The BJP's Second Mascot", 120.
188. See P. Bidwai, "The BJP's Second Mascot", 119.
189. P. Bidwai, "The BJP's Second Mascot", 119.
190. See A. Kulkarni, *The Advent of Advani*, 188-189.
191. *Nationalsozialistische Deutsche Arbeiterpartei* (The National Socialist German Worker's Party).
192. See M. Domarus, *Hitler Reden*, vol.1, 97-98.
193. *Today's 'Iron Man'*, 58.
194. *Today's 'Iron Man'*, 63.
195. See L.K. Advani, *A Prisoner's Scrap-Book*, 86.
196. See S. Gopal and U. Iyengar (eds.), *The Essential Writings of Jawaharlal Nehru*, vol.1, 192.
197. See S.R. Goel, *Hindu Temples What Happened to Them*, 2 vols. (1993,1998)
198. A. Kulkarni, *The Advent of Advani*, 203.
199. See P. Kanungo, *RSS Tryst with Politics*, 198-199.
200. See A. Kulkarni, *The Advent of Advani*, 221.
201. See A. Kulkarni, *The Advent of Advani*, 233.
202. For instance, his statement to this effect in Pakistan in June 2005. See "Advani Regrets Babri Masjid Demolition", 12.
203. See T. Singh, *Lollipop* Street, 154-155.
204. See J. Dayal, "Will CBI ever Catch Advani?", 13.
205. See http://www.cpiml.org/liberation/year_2003/july/commentary 2_advani.htm
206. See http://www.cpiml.org/liberation/year_2003/july/commentary 2_advani.htm
207. See J. Cherian, "Advani's Crusade", 25.
208. See P. Bidwai, "Jinnah's Ghost Haunts the Parivar", 115.
209. S. Gopal and U. Iyengar (eds.), *The Essential Writings of Jawaharlal Nehru*, vol. 1, 192.
210. http://www.hindustantimes.com/news/5922_808914,001500-2200000057.htm

211. See L.K. Advani, *The Prisoner's Scrap-Book*, 66.
212. "Ban, Excise, Punish, Gag", 28.
213. See V. Ramakrishnan, "Battles Within", 6.
214. See V. Ramakrishnan, "Battles Within", 6.
215. See V. Ramakrishnan, "Battles Within", 6.
216. See V. Ramakrishnan, "Battles Within", 6-7.
217. See V. Ramakrishnan, "Battles Within", 7.
218. See V. Ramakrishnan, "Battles Within", 7.
219. See V. Ramakrishnan, "Battles Within", 7.
220. See V. Subrahmanyam, "Lal Krishna Advani's War with the *Parivar*", 10.
221. See N. Vyas, "No Change in the Advani Persona", 11.
222. See V. Venkatesan, "Image and Reality", 14.
223. See K.N. Panikkar, "The Sangh Strikes", 21.
224. See K.N. Panikkar, "The Sangh Strikes", 21.
225. See K.N. Panikkar, "The Sangh Strikes", 20.
226. See K.N. Panikkar, "The Sangh Strikes", 20.
227. See K.N. Panikkar, "The Sangh Strikes", 22.
228. See P. Bidwai, "Jinnah's Ghost Haunts the Parivar", 114.
229. See P. Bidwai, "Jinnah's Ghost Haunts the Parivar", 114.
230. See P. Bidwai, "Jinnah's Ghost Haunts the Parivar", 114.
231. See P. Bidwai, "Jinnah's Ghost Haunts the Parivar", 114-115.
232. See K.N. Panikkar, "The Sangh Strikes", 22.
233. See P. Bidwai, "Jinnah's Ghost Haunts the Parivar", 114.
234. See *Outlook*, 21 July 2003, 21.
235. See P. Bidwai, "The BJP's Second Mascot", 119.
236. See A.G. Noorani, "The Man behind the Image", 5.
237. See V. Venkatesan, "A Secular Veneer", 38-39.
238. See P. Bidwai, "Jinnah's Ghost Haunts the Parivar", 114.
239. See M.S. Aiyar, *The Telegraph*, 9 March 2004, 9.
240. See "BJP Suspends Khurana", 1.
241. See A.G. Noorani, "Modi and His Visa", 50.
242. See A. Kulkarni, *The Advent of* Advani, 238-239.
243. See K. Elst, *Decolonising*, 5 footnote 7.
244. See "Advani Regrets Babri Masjid Demolition", 12.
245. See A. Kulkarni, *The Advent of Advani*, 248.
246. *Today's 'Iron Man'*, 5.

247. J. Cherian, "Advani's Crusade", 25.
248. http://timesofindia.indiatimes.com/articleshow/27950.cms
249. See http://timesofindia.indiatimes.com/articleshow/27950.cms
250. See P. Bidwai, "The BJP's Second Mascot", 119.
251. See P. Bidwai, "The BJP's Second Mascot", 119.
252. It was in 1995, on the eve of the 1996 general elections that Advani conceded the crown to Vajpayee; the *mukhota* (mask) who could be trusted to do the parivar's bidding while deploying rhetoric to project a liberal image.
253. See P. Bidwai, "The BJP's Second Mascot", 119.
254. A.G. Noorani," Hindutva, not Hinduism", 122.
255. Paradoxically, it has been alleged by Gauri Advani, the estranged daughter-in-law of L.K. Advani, that Advani and his family follow the Sikh religion and that despite being a follower of the Sikh faith Advani was using Hinduism to mobilise the Hindu votes. See www.gsbkerala.com/gotra.htm as cited in J.P. Hartung, G. Hawkes and A. Bhattacharjee, *Ayodhya 1992-2003*, 10, footnote 11, 10.
256. See T. Singh, *Lollipop Street*, 135.
257. See M.S. Aiyar, "BJP and the Hindu State", *The Indian Express*, 26 November 2002.
258. See A. Kulkarni, *The Advent of Advani*, xi-xii.
259. See V. Subrahmanyam, "Lal Krishna Advani's War with the *Parivar*", 10.
260. See R.S. Kapoor, *Failing the Promise*, 43.
261. See J.C. Fest, *The Face of the Third Reich*, 115-116.

III

Murli Manohar Joshi's Saffronisation of Indian Education and Cultural Institutions

Murli Manohar Joshi, the son of Manmohan Joshi and Chandrawati Joshi, was born on 5 January 1934 in Delhi. He received his early education at Hindu High School, Chandur, and completed his higher education from Meerut College and Allahabad University. Specialising in Spectroscopy he was awarded Ph.D by the Allahabad University. In 1994 he retired as Head of the Physics Department of the same university after 37 years of service. Even during his nearly five decades of political career, Joshi pursued his academic life. During the emergency declared by Indira Gandhi in 1975 he underwent imprisonment for 19 months under Maintenance of Internal Security Act (MISA). He has published two books in Hindi: *Vikalp* (The Alternative) and *Pragya Pravah* (The Continuing Wisdom), besides some 100 research papers in scientific journals. He has addressed several conferences such as, the European Hindu Conference at Frankfurt, Germany (1991); the Global Vision 2000 International Conference in U.S.A. (1993); the International Youth Conference at Chicago (1993) to mark the 100th Anniversary of Swami Vivekananda's address to the World Parliament of Religions; the International Seminar on Science and Religion held in Washington (1993); the Vishwa Hindu Mahasangh Conference at Varanasi (1993); the Hindu Conference in Durban, South Africa (1995), etc. He has delivered lectures on various aspects of Indian

Philosophy and science in different countries. In an advertisement by the Indian Institute of Information Technology, Allahabad, a Deemed University, on the occasion of the inauguration of its campus, the following was said of Joshi eulogising him: "Man of education, eminent scientist, sharp thinker and architect of future technology of the nation".[1]

Joshi was elected to the Lok Sabha in 1977, 1996, 1998 and 1999 but lost in 2004. In 1996 under the BJP-led Atal Bihari Vajpayee government, which lasted for 13 days, he was the Union Cabinet Minister of Home Affairs. In 1998 he was Union Cabinet Minister for Human Resource Development (HRD) and Science and Technology. From 1999 to 2004 he held charge of three ministries: Minister for Human Resources Development, Science and Technology and Ocean Development.[2]

Joshi is essentially a convinced and committed Hindutva ideologue with hardliner tendencies. For him Hindutva means 'national consciousness'.[3] It is all inclusive and accepts traditions that flow out of Indian civilisation.[4] Joshi is married to Tarla Joshi and they have two daughters.

Ideological Influences on Joshi

The ideological influences on Joshi are of wide range. Swami Vivekananda (1863-1902) was a thinker who left a lasting impression on Joshi's concept of Hindu nationalism. However, it is to be remembered that ideologically Swami Vivekananda had a 'double face', one of universalism and toleration, and another of Hindu nationalism, absolutism of Advaita Vedanta and consequently intoleration of other faiths, especially Islam and Christianity.[5]

Another person who left a lasting influence on Joshi was Bal Gangadhar Tilak (1856-1920), the author of *Gita Rahasya* ('The Secret of the *Gita*').[6] Though he was an eminent freedom fighter, Tilak was a militant Hindu nationalist who advocated a warrior morality, upheld the philosophy of 'end justifies the means' and rationalised violence and proposed it as a higher duty.[7]

Another thinker who left an indelible mark on Joshi was Aurobindo Ghose (1872-1950). Aurobindo's early writings and activities were characterised by aggressiveness, extremism and Hindu nationalism.[8] For him nationalism was religion.[9] He argued that *ahimsa* (non-violence) cannot be the virtue of the Kshatriya.[10] In fact he asked the Hindus to cultivate 'aggressive virtues' and to engage in 'courageous attack'.[11]

The great RSS leaders and ideologues like M.S. Golwalkar (1906-1973), Deendayal Upadhyaya[12] and Rajendra Singh[13] also played a major role in shaping Joshi's ideology. Golwalkar's political and religious philosophy was centred around the concept of India as a Hindu *rashtra* (nation). It was founded on the principle of *one nation* (Hindu), *one culture* (Sanskrit) and *one religion* (Hinduism). This necessarily implied a negation of cultural and religious pluralism and true secularism. In fact, Golwalkar openly declared that the Muslims, Christians and Communists of India are internal threats to the nation.[14] He also took inspiration from Adolf Hitler's ideology of National Socialism, especially with regard to the racial factor in the Hindu *rashtra*[15] and radically rejected the concept of a multi-ethnic nation.[16] Thus it is not difficult to perceive that Joshi is a convinced and committed Hindu nationalist *par excellence* with an unambiguous hard-liner identity. In fact Koenraad Elst, who is himself a pro-Hindutva scholar, has observed that Joshi is an 'acknowledged hard-liner'.[17]

The RSS Roots of Joshi

Joshi is essentially a person formed and shaped by the RSS and is a trusted confidant of the Sangh Parivar. He joined the RSS in 1944, at the age of ten. In 1949 he became a member of the Akhil Bharatiya Vidyarthi Parishad (ABVP).[18] From 1953 to 1956 he was elected General Secretary of the ABVP of the Uttar Pradesh unit and All India General Secretary of the ABVP. He was also an RSS *pracharak*. As the HRD minister in the BJP-led NDA government in New Delhi (1998, 1999-2004) it was his keen interest to implement the RSS project of saffronising the Indian educational system and cultural institutions in view of creating a new generation of Indians rooted in the ideology of Hindu cultural nationalism with its accompanying anti-secularist, anti-pluralistic, anti-democratic, anti-minority and communalist overtones.

Joshi in Bharatiya Jana Sangh

Joshi had close contact with Deen Dayal Upadhyaya, one of the founder members of the Bharatiya Jana Sangh. He invited the latter to lecture to the students of his college and accompanied him in some of his journeys.[19] In 1957 Joshi officially joined the Bharatiya Jana Sangh. In the same year he became the organising secretary of the party of the Allahabad unit. From 1967 to 1975, he was the zonal organising secretary of the BJS in Uttar Pradesh.

Joshi in Bharatiya Janata Party

Joshi represents a generation of Bharatiya Janata Party leaders that stand midway between older generation like A.B. Vajpayee and L.K Advani and the young generation in the BJP. While Vajpayee and Advani emerged through the ranks of the Jan Sangh, Joshi came to the leadership position, especially through the RSS/ABVP ranks.

Joshi was the founder General Secretary of the BJP in 1980. In February 1991 the BJP changed president and Joshi replaced Advani[20] and held that post till 1993. When he took charge as party president he decided to embark on a *yatra*. Thus he took out a 47-day *Ekata Yatra* which was flagged off from Kanyakumari on 11 December 1991 and was concluded at Srinagar on 26 January 1992 with the hoisting of the national flag at Lal Chowk. During the campaign he attacked Article 370 of the Indian Constitution and asked the people to reflect seriously on the dangers faced by the Indian nation. Kanyakumari revives memories of Swami Vivekananda, one of his ideological mentors, who passionately espoused the cause of cultural nationalism and restored pride in being a Hindu.[21] The *yatra* of Joshi drew attention to the situation of the 'martyred' Hindus in the State of Kashmir. It also served a purpose by keeping the anti-Muslim propaganda alive. The march contributed to the building up of pressure that eventfully led to the destruction of the Babri mosque at Ayodhya on 6 December 1992.[22]

Joshi is considered as a hardliner in the BJP because he takes a militant, aggressive and orthodox Hindu chauvinistic approach to socio-political issues. This added to his popularity among the RSS and the VHP. His critics argue that he is noted for his Machiavellian manoeuvres and coercive tactics.[23] However, Joshi seems to have a lot of enemies within the BJP. It is a fact that when he resigned from the Union Cabinet in 2003 as he was charge-sheeted in the destruction of the Babri mosque at Ayodhya, hardly any of the senior BJP leaders called on him.[24] In December 2005 when Advani stepped down as the president of the BJP, a significant section of the

RSS did favour Joshi to the post. But the negotiations between the RSS and the BJP highlighted the point that the former HRD minister would not be acceptable to the second generation leadership of the BJP as a whole, especially due to his 'overbearing style of functioning'.[25]

Joshi and the Ayodhya Movement

Joshi was very closely associated with the Ayodhya movement and his alleged active involvement in the destruction of the Babri mosque is taken as a fact by most people. He argued: "The mosque is a sign of slavery. An independent India will not accept it."[26] India's noted journalist Khushwant Singh writes: "Everyone in the world who watched the event [of the destruction of the Babri mosque on 6 December 1992] on television saw who was seated on the dais, *goondas* armed with pick-axes hacking the domes of the mosque; heard the exultant cries of victory when it came down; Uma Bharati embracing Murli Manohar Joshi, with the prime perpetrator of the crime L.K. Advani and Kalyan Singh looking on."[27] Joshi was arrested on 8 December 1992 and detained at Mata Tila, Uttar Pradesh along with Advani and Ashok Singhal for his alleged involvement in the demolishing of the Babri mosque. A second arrest was made in December 1993. But Joshi was discharged in the Ayodhya case by the controversial Rae Bareli court verdict of 19 September 2003, which is seen by many as a gross miscarriage of justice. Commenting on his acquittal A.G. Noorani said that the Rae Bareli court verdict in the Ayodhya case discharging the then HRD minister Joshi was against the weight of the entire evidence and violates the law as declared by the Supreme Court.[28]

Saffronisation of Indian Education

Joshi's educational policy is generally given the appellation 'saffronisation of education'. In many aspects it has similarities with Hitler's educational policies known in common parlance as *Die Nazifizierung des Schulwesens* ('The Nazification of the School materials or syllabi').[29] It has always been the conviction of the RSS and its affiliated organisations that the Indian educational system was imposed upon the country by the British colonisers more with the aim of anglicising the Indians in order to make them an army of clerks to run their administration than to enlighten them and make them agents of progress. Hence they demanded a drastic change in the entire educational system, and suggested an alternative system of education – the so-called *Bharatiya* education – that best suited their ideology with an emphasis on character building, Indian culture, discipline, patriotic pride, love of mother tongue, devotion to Indian values of life and virtues.

India's school system primarily uses government recommended textbooks. Hence a major agenda of the Sangh Parivar is to 'saffronise' education by influencing all premier institutions dealing with school, university and advanced research. During the last fifteen years or so the Sangh Parivar adopted many aggressive strategies to advance and reinforce its appeal to the Indian masses and the young generation, and one major area where this was keenly felt was the strategic field of education. Since 1989, the RSS founder K.B. Hedgewar's birth centenary, the RSS has massively expanded its service and education networks across India. Parallel organisations have been started abroad that have a key aim of raising funds for RSS and VHP projects in India – especially for *Sewa Bharati, Vanavasi Kalyan Ashram, Vidhya Bharati* and *Ekal Vidyalayas*. Two important international funding organisations of the Sangh Parivar are the US-based India Development and Relief Fund (IDRF) and Sewa International UK.[30]

The access to political power by the Hindu nationalists in recent decades in several State governments and in New Delhi considerably benefited the RSS and its affiliated organisations to execute their plan. As member of the Sangh Parivar, the saffronisation of education was one of the major ventures of the BJP-led government in New Delhi, and Joshi was the chosen instrument of the Sangh Parivar to execute this vital task, and the ministry of Human Resource Development was the most important forum for Joshi to realise his vision.

Education was an important priority issue for the BJP-led government. When the party assumed power in New Delhi in March 1998, keen observers detected a special focus on two ministries, namely, the Human Resource Development and Information and Broadcasting. These are the two ministries which are of pivotal importance in any kind of ideological indoctrination. The induction of Joshi as Cabinet Minister in charge of Human Resource Development with Uma Bharati as Minister of State – two known hardliners in the BJP – was read by political observers as a signal that the new government was fully cognisant of the importance of the portfolio to implement its hidden agenda in education. It was their task to intervene, enhance, promote and expand the Sangh Parivar agenda in education already in operation since decades especially through the *Vidhya Bharati* chain of educational institutions through a core curriculum dealing with Hindu religion and culture. Joshi without delay got into action and called for a conference of state education ministers and secretaries in New Delhi from 22 to 24 October 1998. 'Indianise', 'nationalise' and 'spiritualise' education were the watchwords of the meet. Incidentally, during the meet, participants were asked to sing the *Saraswati Vandana*, the hymn to a Hindu Goddess, which sparked protest from many participants.

It is argued that Joshi who is a committed RSS ideologue used his official position to patronise and promote the Sangh Parivar ideals in education with great zeal and aggressiveness. In February 2004 the RSS weekly *Organiser* reported with pride the achievements of Joshi. It said: "Vajpayee Government has quite a few Ministers who have made a lasting impact on the course of history. Union Human Resources Development Minister Dr Murli Manohar Joshi is one of them".[31] Political analysts point out that what resulted as a consequence of his saffronisation programme was not mere Hindu revivalism but growth of communalism, anti-secularism and intolerance towards minority groups. The educational reforms carried out by the BJP government in recent years clearly show this.

Saffronisation of education is essentially an RSS agenda. Since its inception in 1925 the RSS is engaged in constructing a more abiding influence in society and on the young minds through the activities of cultural, educational, social and institutional network. The RSS leadership, beginning with Hedgewar and Golwalkar, had identified this as an important component of their Hindutva philosophy. The latter spoke in unambiguous terms about the importance of re-vamping the entire Indian education along the RSS ideology. He said: "Without dilating upon this aspect, suffice it to say that the whole system of education seems to need a complete change."[32] In the 1950s, Shyama Prakash Mukherjee, the founder of the Jana Sangh, spoke of the importance of what he called a 'comprehensive national system of education', which in essence also catered to the Hindutva ideology.[33] Thus the business of running educational institutions by the RSS has a political, ideological and social agenda as its foundation. According to the organisation's own assessment, as reflected in publications such as *RSS: A Vision in Action* and *Lakshya Ek, Karya Anek* ('One Goal, Several Enterprises'), efforts in this direction have spread far and wide over the last 50 years.[34]

Saffronisation of School Education

The effort of the RSS to saffronise education has a long history. Since 1942 the RSS has been promoting their schools with great zeal. Initially it concentrated in Uttar Pradesh, Bihar, Andhra Pradesh and a few other states. An all India body called *Vidya Bharati Akhil Bharatiya Shiksha Sansthan* – usually known as *Vidya Bharati* – was set up in 1978 to provide an organisational umbrella to these schools. However, with the BJP – the political wing of the organisation – coming to power in a number of states in the 1990s, it massively expanded its educational network across India. *Vidya Bharati* runs an estimated 14,000 to 19,000 RSS schools. The cluster of RSS educational activities include the one-teacher schools (*Ekal Vidyalayas*) run by the VHP, *Vidya Bharati, Sewa Bharati* and the *Vanavasi Kalyan Ashram*. There is also a nation-wide network of RSS pre-primary, primary and secondary schools, colleges, technical institutions and Hindutva teachers' bodies. Each of these organisations is linked to RSS strategic aims. RSS schools are typically called: *Saraswati Vidya Mandirs* (RSS schools, which can also include residential schools), *Saraswati Shishu Mandirs* (RSS primary schools), *Shishu Vatikas* (pre-primary schools for indoctrination), *Sanskar Kendras* (ideological indoctrination centres and activities, often one-teacher schools operating in rural, tribal or slum areas), *Ekal Vidyalayas* (or *Ekalavyas*), Vivekananda Kendras/Vidyalayas,[35] etc.

Significantly, the state and regional-level governing bodies of RSS educational institutions do not always go by the name of *Vidhya Bharati*. They have a host of other local names, such as *Bharatiya Vidya Niketan, Gyan Vidyalaya, Saraswati Bal Vidyalaya, Sewa Dham Vidya Mandirs*. For example, there is a range of RSS *gurukulas* run by the Karnataka-based Hindu *Seva Pratishthan* and the *Jana Seva Vidya Kendra*. The governing bodies in Delhi, where the RSS and the BJP have a significant political presence, flaunt the title *Hindu Shiksha Samiti*; Punjab has *Sarvhitkari Shiksha Samiti* (Education Council for

Universal Benefit); Orissa has *Shiksha Vikas Samiti* (Education Development Council) and Haryana has *Hindu Shiksha Samiti*; in the Jharkhand region of Bihar the *Vidya Bharati* governing body is called *Vananchal Shiksha Samiti*.[36] *Samarath Shiksha Samiti* is another organisation with numerous educational institutions. Of considerable significance in recent years has been the importance attached by the RSS to the non-formal one-teacher schools (*Ekal Vidyalayas*) in tribal and border areas.

Vidhya Bharati

Vidya Bharati is the leading organisation of the RSS in the area of education and runs thousands of schools. IDRF funds have been given to many schools affiliated with *Vidhya Bharati*. The course material used in the *Vidhya Bharati* schools throughout the country is the same. As already stated, the schools themselves are known by a variety of names. They use different names depending on the socio-political situation in each State.

First *Saraswati Shishu Mandir* ('Temple of the Goddess Saraswati dedicated to the children') was established in 1952. It was inspired by some RSS workers to take up education of children as a mission of their life. The first school was set up at Gorakhpur (Uttar Pradesh). They named the school *Saraswati Shishu Mandir*. It may be recalled here that prior to the *Saraswati Shishu Mandir*, Gita school was established at Kurukshetra (present-day Haryana) in 1946 by M.S. Golwalkar. As the number of schools increased, a state-level *Shishu Shiksha Prabandh Samiti* was formed to co-ordinate their activities.[37]

In 1978 the *Vidhya Bharati* Akhil Bharatiya Shiksha Sansthan or simply Vidya Bharari was founded,[38] and all the state-level boards were affiliated to it. *Vidhya Bharati's* growth has been phenomenal. In 1978 it managed only 500 schools and just over 20,000 students. But towards the end of 1991 the organisation claimed that their educational network covered the whole of India except a few States of the Northeast India and it consisted of about 4,000 schools, 36,000 teachers and over one million students. By 1998 it was regarded as the largest NGO in education, running some 13,000 institutions which employ about 71,000 teachers and educate nearly 1,70,000 students. It had 8,145 primary schools, 2,800 high and senior secondary schools, 2,000 single-teacher schools, 40 colleges, 15 teacher training colleges and seven technical institutions.[39]

According to the statistics of January 2003, *Vidhya Bharati* had over 21,000 schools, 1,07,000 teachers and about 25,00,000 students.[40] In addition to this the RSS has been spearheading its educational network also by establishing *Shishu Niketans* and *Vanavasi Kalyan Kendras* as Friends of Tribal Society (FTS).[41] It is reported that the RSS today runs about 60,000 schools in different parts of the country under different denominations.[42] All these are schools launched to provide a highly ideological education. *Vidhya Bharati* also has a research centre called Vidhya Bharati Central Educational Research Institute with its headquarters in Lucknow.[43]

In the schools of the *Vidhya Bharati* network, apart from the academic content of the instruction there is a 'core curriculum' comprising six subjects: (a) physical education, (b) yoga, (c) music, (d) Sanskrit, (e) moral and spiritual education, and (f) *sanskriti gyan* (knowledge of culture). It is through this core curriculum that the Hindutva agenda is transmitted to the young generation. The core curriculum seeks to pass off as historical truth many scientifically unverified claims and myths. For example, it teaches that the site where the Babri mosque stood at Ayodhya is the birthplace of Ram; it argues for a ban on cow-slaughter and claims that protecting the cow is important since 'it is the mother of all beings and the abode of gods'[44] and a symbol of cultural sanctity and national oneness'.[45]

Most of the *acharyas* (teachers) of the *Vidhya Bharati* schools are RSS *swayamsevaks,* properly trained in the ideology of the Hindu *rashtra.*[46] The classroom is an ideal place to teach the RSS viewpoints on culture and history. A periodic examination called *Sanskriti Gyan Pariksha* is conducted among the students belonging to Class IV to XII to assess their knowledge of Indian history and culture.[47] Besides classroom teaching where culture and history are taught, the ideology is also conveyed through co-curricular activities and publications, including children's magazines. The children sing the prayers and songs steeped in devotion to the Hindu *rashtra.* Assemblies and stage performances organised on Hindu festivals are another example of ideologically relevant activities. Occasionally an activist of the Sangh Parivar addresses them, further cementing their ideological belief. The virtual absence of non-Hindu children in these activities adds to the collective sense of a distinct self-identity, which these activities evoke in RSS schools. Thus arousing a sense of collective Hindu identity may be seen as the basic philosophy of education in these schools.[48]

Parent's education programme is an essential part of *Vidhya Bharati* activity. It is carried out through personal contacts with the families by the school teachers, meetings of parents in schools and distribution of suitable literature to families, specially prepared by *Vidhya Bharati*. In Gujarat, for example, the programme is called 'Home, the first School'. Another feature of the *Vidhya Bharati* institutions is the family style of informal relationship between teacher and students which tries to recapture the *gurukul* style of education of ancient India.[49]

In 1969 the RSS formed the *Bharatiya Shikshan Mandal* (BSM), essentially an organisation of teachers belonging to the RSS, which focussed its attention on evolving a *Bharatiya* content (Indian content).[50] According to an RSS publication, the BSM's objective was to infuse a *Bharatiya* content to the educational system; it even drew up syllabi for Classes I to X on moral education and tried to get acceptance from state and Union governments.[51]

A large number of *Vidhya Bharati* schools are in states where the BJP is in power. In the State of Madhya Pradesh *Vidhya Bharati* functions parallel to the State Government Educational Board and is permitted to incorporate any change in the school curricula.[52] Again, the State Education Boards of Uttar Pradesh, Madhya Pradesh and Rajasthan have been forced to change the school syllabi to give the RSS a free hand. The history textbooks have been re-written in such a way that the Hindutva viewpoints are projected. For instance, the chapter on freedom movement refers to the RSS and its founder Hedgewar in a way to provide respectability and to legitimise the role of the Hindu communal organisations and its leaders.[53]

V. Ramakrishnan, writing in 1998, observed that *Vidhya Bharati* schools operate even in Kerala, where the political influence of the RSS and the BJP is not as significant as in many other States of India. The first *Vidhya Bharati* school in the State, the *Vyasa Vidya Peetam,* was established in Kallekkadu in Palakkad district. The organisation has since then established its presence in all the 14 districts in the State, and in 1998 it had 174 schools. Of these, 120 are *Saraswati Shishu Vidyalayas,* imparting education only up to Class IV. The rest, called *Bharatiya Vidya Niketans,* have up to Classes VII or XII. Seven schools in Malappuram, Kozhikode, Kannur, Palakkad and Ernakulam districts which have a sizable population of Muslims or Christians follow the CBSE syllabus with English as the medium of instruction. The rest follow the state syllabus up to Class IV and the medium of instruction is Malayalam. About 90 per cent of the teachers are women; all teachers are required to undergo a five-month 'special training' in Indian tradition and culture and the 'Hindu way of education' at the *Bharatiya Vidya Niketan's Adhyapaka Prasikshana Kendram*, at the *Vyasa Vidya Peetam* campus in Palakkad. The Sangh Parivar considers this as essential because it is alleged that a majority of graduate teachers who pass out of mainstream education courses are convent-educated or otherwise not properly acquainted with the Hindu way of life. Classes in all these institutions start with invoking Saraswati, the Hindu Goddess of learning. As elsewhere, the Sangh Parivar has focussed its attention on the backward areas of the state and places inhabited by tribal communities. The *Vidya Niketan* schools and *Saraswati Vidyalayas* employ nearly 1,300 teachers; the main organisers of the schools are the RSS *pracharaks* committed to the Hindutva ideology.[54]

In Tamil Nadu alone about 150 schools are functioning under the guidance of the *Vidhya Bharati.* Of these 24 are Hindu *Vidyalayas* run by the VHP – generally called *Vishwa Hindu Vidya Kendra.* Other schools are under the control of many organisations, including the Vivekananda Educational Society and Vivekananda Educational Trust, both based in Chennai. There has been a substantial increase in the number of schools run by these institutions during the past years. Most of these schools cater to middle class families. Over 17,000 students of the schools run by the Vivekananda Educational Society are trained in music, dance, yoga, physical exercise and related disciplines. Besides, Hindi, Tamil and English, Sanskrit is made a compulsory fourth language. In the name of moral instruction they are taught Hindu epics and the Puranas. Before the public examinations the students are taken to a temple nearby and placed at the feet of the deities, invoking their blessings. All students irrespective of their religion are compelled to participate in this ritual. Teachers and students are expected to attend camps in the name of refresher courses. At a certain stage students are taken to the Vivekananda Kendra in Kanyakumari for a 21-day camp organised on the lines of a *shakha* of the RSS. This camp is believed to serve the purpose of recruiting cadets for the RSS. One significant development with regard to the *Vidhya Bharati* schools in recent years is that they have been increasingly using textbooks prepared by the NCERT.[55]

Ramakrishnan observes that in Tamil Nadu all *Vidhya Bharati* schools typically have a prayer hall with idols of Hindu deities such as Lakshmi, Saraswati and Ganesh. Religious festivals like Krishna Jayanti, Vinayaka Chaturthi, Deepavali and Pongal – and even the anniversary of Chatrapati Shivaji's coronation, which has now come to acquire quasi-religious symbolism – are celebrated. These schools observe Teachers' Day not on September 5, the birth anniversary of Dr S. Radhakrishnan, but on 25 July, which is claimed to be the birth anniversary of the sage Vyasa. They observe Children's Day not on November 14, Jawaharlal Nehru's birth anniversary, but on Krishna Jayanti. In the Vivekananda schools a lesson on the life of the RSS ideologue Golwalkar is a prescribed reading material in Tamil for students of Class VII.[56]

Orissa is another state where the RSS has established a network of educational institutions. The *Saraswati Shishu Mandir* network is popular in urban and semi-urban areas because of the perception among some sections of society that these schools offer a higher standard of education than government-run schools and charge lower fees than most other private schools. The method of indoctrination in Hindutva ideology is identical to that adopted in most other states. Teachers are advised to visit the parents of the students once a month. The Oriya-language weekly publication of the RSS, *Rashtra Deepa,* is mailed to all the parents. Affiliation to the state education board is a crucial aspect which gives to these schools a popular appeal, and the curriculum followed therefore conforms to the one prescribed by the state board. The core of the ideological programme is therefore carried out through extra-curricular activities.[57]

Since 1980 *Vidhya Bharati* concentrated its effort to start a chain of schools in Northeast India. By 1998 it had 171 schools in Assam, 5 in Manipur, 3 in Tripura, 1 in Meghalaya and 6 in Arunachal Pradesh.[58]

The Assam *Shishu Shiksha Samiti* is a *Vidhya Bharati* unit in Northeast India. It began its work in 1979 with the foundation of a school called *Shankardev Shishu Niketan*. In the same year a *Bal Vidya Mandir* was started in Manipur. The Samiti's work grew steadily during the first 12 years and during that period 29 schools were founded. But from 1993 to 2004 the number of schools grew up to 455, excluding the 115 single-teacher schools. In 1991 Samiti's schools were established in Meghalaya while work in Arunachal

Pradesh began in 1994, Nagaland in 1995, Tripura in 1999 and Mizoram in 2002. In 2004 the Samiti had more than 1,100 schools in the North-eastern states of which 700 were in Assam alone.[59]

According to critics much of the publications of *Vidhya Bharati* are meant to teach prejudice against non-Hindus. Some years ago the NCERT's National Steering Committee on textbook evaluation found that the RSS-run *Vidhya Bharati* schools are purposely being used for the dissemination of blatantly communal ideas in a series called *Sanskriti Gyan* (knowledge of culture).[60] The Committee found that the *Vidhya Bharati* schools prescribed for their pupils a series of booklets under the general titles of *Sanskriti Jnan Pareeksha* (Cultural Knowledge Examination) and *Sanskriti Jnan Pareekhsa Prasnottari* (Cultural Knowledge Examination Questions and Answers). These consist of a series of questions and their answers, which are provided in a manner that makes the rigour of original thinking superfluous. Students are required to learn by rote the contents, as the NCERT envisages it. However, the kind of 'cultural knowledge' these booklets impart are found to be of questionable nature: For example, it is stated that the Ram Janmabhoomi was 'invaded' no fewer than 77 times between A.D. 1528 and A.D. 1914, that 3.5 lakh 'devotees laid down their lives in defending this holy site in that span of time', that 2 November 1990, when an attempt by Hindutva hordes to mount an assault on the Babri mosque was repulsed by the police, would go down as a 'black day' in India's history[61] and so on.

In a section on world religions, the *Vidhya Bharati* books resort to outright communal propaganda and falsification of history. It claims that India was partitioned on account of the conspiratorial policies of the followers of Christianity and that Christian missionaries are even today engaged in fostering anti-national tendencies in Nagaland, Meghalaya, Arunachal Pradesh, Bihar, Kerala and other regions of the country.[62]

Sanskar Kendras

Since it was not possible for *Vidhya Bharati* to keep on opening more and more schools, a nation-wide plan was drawn up to initiate a large number of *Sanskar Kendras* – single teacher schools for imparting Hindu cultural education. *Vidhya Bharati* emphatically requested all schools to operate at least one *Sanskar Kendra*.[63]

Sanskar Kendra was launched in 1988-1989 as a component of the memorial campaigns organised during the birth centenary celebrations of Hedgewar, the founder of the RSS. Today there are over 2000 *Sanskar Kendras* in the country.[64] These centres conduct informal activities for imparting literacy, health-education, self-reliance, *sanskriti,* (culture), love for the country and social harmony. Special efforts are made to contact and educate the children who are unable to attend formal schools due to family circumstances or non-availability of such schools near their localities. Then there are children who attend formal schools but remain below standard due to adverse family circumstances. An effort is made to provide specific coaching to such children to bring them up to the required standard of their classes. Songs, story telling, games, role-acting, etc. are the major activities for children's development and *sanskar* learning.[65]

The children of the *Vidhya Bharati* schools, indoctrinated with the ideology of the Hindu *rashtra* are supposed to spread their knowledge to the children of the nearby slums and villages through the sanskar kendras. However, at present, these centres have been operating primarily in the remote and tribal areas where very few schools exist. Also, about 500 such centres are functioning in the urban slum areas. These extension centres have been set up with two aims: first, education is to be imparted to those children who are unable to attend the school; secondly, these children will be taught 'noble virtues' by exposing them to the Hindu culture and tradition through songs, stories and ceremonies.[66]

Sanskar Kendras are organised in four different kinds of localities: in the backward and slum localities of cities, in comparatively affluent localities of cities where children usually go to the so-called convent or English medium schools. These children, it is alleged, are generally ignorant or ill-informed about *Bharatiya sanskriti* (Indian culture). *Vidhya Bharati* also organises *Sanskar Kendras* for children in rural areas and *vanavasi* regions. Along with education and *sanskar* training of children, efforts are also made to contact their parents, guardians and other members of their families. Through various informal activities efforts are made to create awareness among people for a healthy, cultured life both for individuals and society.[67]

Sewa Bharti

Sewa Bharati, as RSS associated institution is also engaged in educational activities, especially in promoting literacy among the masses.

For example, in February 2006 it organised a massive literacy drive in Delhi to mark the birth centenary of M.S. Golwalkar. Some 1200 volunteers dedicated one hour a day to work as teachers to teach people reading and writing.[68]

Vanavasi Kalyan Ashram

The *Vanavasi Kalyan Ashram* (VKA) was founded at Jashpur in Madhya Pradesh in December 1952 by Ramakant Keshav alias Balasaheb Deshpande in consultation with M.S. Golwalkar of the RSS. Its main purpose was to stop conversion of tribals to Christianity.[69] In 1977 it was renamed All India Vanavasi Kalyan Ashram.[70] Sewa International UK, Sewa International India, India Development and Relief Fund USA, are some of its leading funding agencies.

Persuading the tribals to go back to their so-called roots in Hindu culture, the RSS had first set-up Vanvasi Kalyan Ashrams in some 32 districts in central India covering more than 32,000 villages and nearly 70,000 families.[71] Over the years VKA has expanded its activities in practically every state of India. In 2004 VKA reached 43,000 *vanavasi* villages of India, and out of the total of 467 *vanavasi* communities living in 301 districts, the VKA was working among 431 communities in 260 *vanavasi* districts.[72] In addition, the VKA also operates in all major cities and in 43 other non-Adivasi districts. It proposes to reach each of the remaining *vanavasi* districts in the coming years. The VKA operates in such fields as health, education, social organisation, economic development as well as carrying out numerous casual/need-based programmes. But one of the major areas of its attention is the field of education with the aim of countering the influence of Christian missionaries.[73] Special camps are organised for *vanavasi* students of Northeast India staying in hostels in various parts of the county. In the different hostels 'patriotic educations' meaning Hindu education is imparted to them.[74]

RSS service and education networks cover a range of activities and groups, but the main focus is *Adivasi* and *Dalit* groups. Key areas of activity include border territories, areas such as Northeast India and those that have significant Christian communities, Christian-run schools or Christian missionary influence.[75] Buoyed by the success of the network established by them, as reflected in the result of the assembly elections of 2003, in 2004 the VHP and the RSS decided to provide tribals with four A's – *Akshar* (education), *Anna* (foodgrains), *Arogya* (healthcare) and *Aradhanasthal* (place of worship) on the pattern of the Christian missionaries. In fact, the tribals were made to celebrate Ganesh festival, hold *Ramlila* celebrations, conduct *Geeta Paath* and use 'Ram Ram' to greet each other.[76]

The *Vanabandhu Parishad* (Friends of the Tribal Society, FTS) was established in Calcutta in the year 1989. The main thrust of the organisation is on exposing various classes and groups of the non-*vanavasi* people to the life styles of the *vanavasis*. The FTS' main agenda is a systematic programme to Hinduise primary education especially in states like Jharkhand where Christian missionaries have been working among tribals in remote tribal areas for long. The *Vanabandhu Parishad* organises planned visits to the *vanavasi* areas for various groups of the urban people with their families. The *Vanabandhu Parishad* participates in organising human developmental and educational services in *vanavasi* areas. It is through the financial and other resources mobilised by the *Vanabandhu Parishad* that numerous *Ekalavya Vidyalayas* and health centres are being operated in the *vanavasi* areas of Bihar, Orissa, Northeastern states and West Bengal. *Rama Katha* programmes are also being conducted on a mass scale by training the tribal population. The concept of establishing branches of *Vanabandhu Parishad* in urban and metropolitan areas is catching up fast in many states. In fact, branches are already started in Ranchi and Mumbai. Other cities are expected to follow suit in the near future.[77]

Ekal Vidyalayas

Ekal Vidyalaya (single teacher schools) is an educational institution started by the VHP to indoctrinate students in remote areas in Hindu cultural nationalism, especially tribal villages. Different Sangh Parivar organisations raise funds for this project and help in the administration of these schools. Some of them are the *Bharat Kalyan Pratishthan*, Swami Vivekananda Rural Development Society, Friends of Tribal Society and the Vanavasi Kalyan Ashram – all of which are funded by the IDRF. It is claimed that this system of education is founded on the *gurukul* tradition of ancient India. Classes are held under a tree where the blackboard attached to a tree and piece of chalk are the only tools used.[78] It was started in 1999 as a unique movement in the remote tribal areas of Kerala and since then it has gathered momentum. Children are taught reading, writing, mathematics, history, science, yoga, health and hygiene, and local customs and culture. Classes are held three hours a day, six days a week. The teachers, specially trained by the foundation, are local men and women who have studied up to Class VIII or X. They are paid an honorarium of about rupees five hundred a month and are deeply committed to the Hindutva ideology. Bolstered by its exceptional growth – 10,000 schools in four years – Sangh Parivar aims at 100,000 *Ekal Vidyalayas* in Tribal India by 2011.[79] The movement received wide support from state and central governments during the BJP-led NDA government. According to a statistics published in 2004 in *Organiser*, Ekal Vidyalayas are running in Rajasthan, Orissa, Madhya Pradesh, Chattisgarh, Maharashtra, Bihar, Jharkhand, Karnataka, Tamil Nadu, Kerala and Northeastern states.[80] According to the statistics of April 2005 there were 14,108 *Ekal Vidyalyas* with 4,37,806 students.

The main agenda of *Ekal Vidyalayas* is a systematic programme to Hinduise primary education in the country. It is reported that during roll call in classrooms, students are made to respond with 'Jai Shri Ram', and only the names of Hindu Gods are used to teach English alphabets. For example, in an English booklet in Jharkhand meant for the Class-II primary students we read: A for Arjun, B for Brahma, C for Cow, D for Dhruva, G for Ganesh, H for Hanuman, J for Jambavan, M for Mahadev, O for Om, R for Ram, T for Temple, U for Uma. (Ironically, the letters 'E', 'F', 'Q', 'W', 'X' and 'Z' simply do not exist in this booklet. No names of Hindu Gods beginning with these letters are readily available!). Each day school prayers are devoted to different Hindu Gods like Shiva, Vishnu, Hanuman and others. Some of the books meant for the training of teachers of the *Ekal Vidyalayas* contain distorted historical facts. For example, a base book for teachers titled *Khele, Kude, Nache, Gaye* by a certain Rakesh Popli states that Birsa Munda studied in a missionary school, converted to Christianity. He was made to eat beef and forced to cut his tuft in hostel. He returned home upset, began worshipping *tulsi*, wore sacred thread, roamed in forests, struggled against Christian missionaries, landlords and British government. He was later arrested and slowly poisoned in jail. Popli's book also contains a series of rhymes on cow, Ram-Sita and other Gods of Hinduism. *Ekal Vidyalaya* teachers also participate in direct actions to promote the Hindutva ideology of the Sangh Parivar.[81]

While the stated purpose of the *Ekal Vidyalyas* is eradication of illiteracy in remote areas, the schools are heavily involved in spreading Hindutva education with a focus on stopping conversions to Christianity and encouraging re-conversions to Hinduism. The VHP advances the doctrine that Indian society is in grave danger from Christianity, and hence it is necessary to counter the moves of missionaries to 'save' the nation. The Sangh Parivar believes that the *Ekal Vidyalayas* can best counter the designs of the Christian missionaries because they impart education based on Hindu culture.[82] It has been observed for instance that the *Ekal Vidyalayas* in Orissa are indulging in hatemongering and perpetrating hatred against Christians by assiduously building up hate zones.[83] In 2000, the state VHP vice-president and chief of publicity Ganga Prasad Yadav said: "Our people are being targeted by the missionaries [...]. The Catholic Church has found the need to create four dioceses – Ranchi, Khunti, Simdega and Gumla, out of the earlier one Ranchi diocese. The sole intention is to convert more and more people. We have information that they want to construct one church in every village. We have accepted the challenge. Our fight will continue till conversions, fuelled by foreign funding, come to an end."[84]

The Sangh Parivar, as it spreads a network of institutions in tribal India – has been on the internet, soliciting funds worldwide. The *Ekal Vidyalaya* group recently roped in the Zee Television media group to help it sell its appeal for funds for what it says is its Vivekananda inspired pedagogy.

In 2005 the Human Resources Development Ministry under the UPA government stopped grants to *Ekal Vidyalayas*. The decision was the result of study, which revealed that the FTS which was provided huge financial assistance by the erstwhile BJP-led NDA government since 1999-2000 under the 'Innovative and Experimental Education Component of the Education Guarantee Scheme and Alternative & Innovative Education' was 'misusing' the funds and using the grants for creating communal disharmony among the religious groups and creating a political cadre.

Sarva Shiksha Abhiyan

The 93rd Constitutional Amendment Bill was passed in the Indian Parliament in November 2001 with the view to make free and compulsory education available for all children between the ages of

6 and 14.[85] On the face of it Joshi launched the *Sarva Shiksha Abhiyan* (SSA, Education for all Campaign).

One of the most ambitious schemes of the BJP-led NDA government was to put all the 19.2 crore children in 11 lakh habitations by the year-end of 2003. In 2003 the HRD ministry decided to take 2,38 crore children then in farms, sweat shops and dingy homes and put them in schools across the nation to be educated by some four lakh freshly appointed teachers. Detailed plans were demanded from each of the districts of the country and for the setting up of a separate machinery for its implementation. (It may be recalled that the former Prime Minister of India, Rajiv Gandhi's pet scheme, 'Operation Blackboard', which began in 1986-1987 lasted for 10 years).[86] It was also planned that all children between the ages 6 and 11 are to be in school by the end of 2003 and all children are to be in school by 2007, and all these children are to pass Class VIII by 2010.[87]

SSA was the pet project of Joshi, the then HRD minister, and was an ambitious programme as a reply to the stigma of illiteracy in India – about 350 million people which is nearly half of the world's illiterates.[88] While the initiative in itself is laudable, it was not free from the Hindutva ideology filtered into the classrooms in subtle ways, through the kind of textbooks used, teachers appointed and the attention given to the teaching of Hindu culture. In addition, critics of this project observe that the scheme may have been visionary, but the goals were only a virtual reality. Even the most optimistic educationists called it an impossible target to achieve. Some have called it a 'paper scheme'. One of the major problems the scheme faced was finance. The poor quality of education also was seriously criticised. Sanjive Kaura of the National Alliance for Fundamental Right to Education (NAFRE) argued that the education being given to 10 crore children in government schools is highly suspect. About 30 per cent of the schools are a single room and single teacher set-up; another 20 per cent have only two teachers and only 9 per cent have toilets for girl children.[89] Though the former Prime Minister Vajpayee had announced free education for all girl children in 1998, the scheme was scrapped because of the special focus on the girl child in SSA. Yet the Union Cabinet again announced a Rs 1000 crore National Programme for the Education of Girl Children (spread over four years) in 2,200 educationally backward blocks and slums.

The present Congress-led UPA government has given considerable emphasis to SSA and has hailed it as a major agent in the universalisation of education in the country. It has also allotted more funds for the project. Currently it is correcting the distortions in the CBSE and NCERT textbooks done under the guidance of Joshi and his HRD ministry.[90] However, the UNESCO Global Monitoring Report asserts that India is one of the 40-odd countries not likely to meet most of the education for all goals even by 2015.[91]

Brahmin Schools

In January 2002 an announcement appeared in the media which said that the BJP-led NDA government had decided to open special Brahmin schools supposedly for the popularisation of the Vedas. Through the good offices of a central minister, the UNESCO was persuaded to provide Rs 5 crore for his scheme. Under this project 15 Brahmin schools are to be opened in different parts of the country. To encourage meritorious Brahmin students, 120 students in each school would be given a scholarship of Rs 2,000 per month while 10 other students would be given Rs 1,000 per month. These schools, to be called *Gurukul Ved Pathshalas* would impart education through oral tradition. The rationale behind the founding of these schools is believed to be to counter the religious education being imparted through the Islamic *madrasas*.[92] It also aims to reshape the curriculum to serve Brahmin interests against those of often illiterate lower castes.

Change of School Textbooks

Under Joshi's direction the NCERT, which is the apex central government body in charge of textbooks went in a big way to 'saffronise' Indian education. Consequently, the saffronisation of education has deeply affected the primary and secondary education in the country. Bidwai says that within barely three years of coming to power in a coalition in New Delhi, the BJP had so purposefully pushed through many changes in the fields of education, especially school education, social science research and culture.[93]

The NCERT and its National Curriculum Framework (NCF) were subject to controversy during the tenure of the BJP-led NDA government and after. The document, brought out by the NCERT, under the aegis of the HRD ministry headed by Joshi was aimed ostensibly at reducing the burden of learning on children. But what it did was to recommend a rewriting of social science textbooks, primarily history. The 'rectification' process, driven by the zeal of Hindu cultural nationalism, saw the virtual withdrawal of history textbooks authored by widely acclaimed historians for the simple reason that they were not ideologically compatible with the views of the Sangh Parivar.[94]

The first set of new history textbooks that it brought out in 2002 was criticised by historians, teachers, other academicians, concerned citizens and the press throughout the country for their blatant communal distortions and utter disregard of certain elementary historical facts.[95] In 2003 it brought out some more history textbooks as part of its new series and these also have been assault on history. In fact, new dimensions have been added to the assault.[96] For example, the textbook conveniently *forgot* to mention that Mahatma Gandhi was assassinated by Nathuram Godse. It was alleged that the NCERT school textbooks deliberately concealed the murder of Gandhi from the present generation of school students because he was formerly a member of the RSS.[97] The reason for the omission was that the Sangh Parivar wanted to present Godse as a Hindu revolutionary and a hero.[98] When the issue was raised they treated it as a minor mistake and reinstalled it. In 2001 the former NDA government had also arbitrarily removed the Preamble to the Constitution from all NCERT textbooks.[99] Some of the textbooks 'glorified' Adolf Hitler as a nationalist and as a man who stood for socialism and nationalism. But the textbooks were silent about the cold-blooded massacre of Jews and others under his regime.[100] Those who reviewed some of the history books for school children allege that Hitler is a hero in the NCERT textbooks.[101] In fact, as a reaction to Joshi's educational policies the Education Ministers of 16 states walked out of the General Council Meeting of the NCERT on 26 May 2002.[102] On 18 October 2004, Arjun Singh, the present HRD Minister in the Congress-led UPA government said that in the land of the Mahatma, Hitler and Nathuram Godse are being idolised instead of the 'saint' from Sabarmati.[103]

The new textbooks written by academicians appointed by the NCERT came under fire also for plagiarism, factual errors and distortion of facts. Scholars say, for instance, that *Modern India*, the NCERT's history textbook for Class XII, copied major portions from historian R.C. Majumdar's classic *History and Culture of the Indian People* who was pronounced for his pro-Hindutva bias. Similarly,

Ancient India reproduced entire paragraphs from Romila Thapar's *History of India*. Many of the textbooks are replete with incorrect statements about places, dates and events. They also seem to have taken care to suppress certain unpleasant and inconvenient facts.[104] Some of the textbooks also clearly projected Hindutva's gender bias.[105]

Chitra Srinivas who has over 25 years of experience of teaching history and who attended the five-day review workshop organised in January 2002 by the NCERT for the class X textbooks states: "Gandhiji's assassination finds no mention, nor do the roles of the RSS and the Hindu Mahasabha during riots and partition. Also omitted is V.D. Savarkar's reference to Hindus as a separate nation;"[106] "Thanks to the strong ideological slant, our Freedom Movement looks as if it was a religious struggle against Christian missionaries and Muslim communalists."[107]

In July 2003 Saradindu Mukherji came out openly arguing that there was a conspiracy in writing the Class XII textbook. He said: "Thanks to media pressure and the news that three authors were clandestinely writing the text for *Contemporary World* assigned to me originally."[108]

In spite of this, J.S. Rajput the former NCERT director lauded the new textbooks. For instance, he described the textbook for Class XII on contemporary world history as 'a marvel of 21st century scholarship'. But later it was discovered that the authors had plagiarised almost word for word from *World Civilisations: Their History and Culture* (1955) by eminent American historians Edward McNall Burns, Philip Lee Ralph, Robert W. Lerner and Standish Meacham.[109]

Chief Minister of Delhi, Sheila Dikshit said: "You should read some of the errors pointed out by the Indian History Congress in the new NCERT books. The children deserve better."[110] She added: "You can't have books that promote hatred towards one community, books that divide the nation."[111]

Vivekananda Kendra Vidyalayas

Another institution which promotes the ideals of Hindutva is the Vivekananda Kendra movement started by Eknath Ranade in the 1970s to take Swami Vivekananda's message through various projects and service activities. It includes *Vivekananda Kendra Vidyalayas*, Rural Development Programme, Natural Resources

Development Programme, Vedic Vision Foundation, Institute of Culture, Vivekananda International, Medical & Research Foundation, etc. According to the statistics of 2003 the Kendra runs 45 schools for Vanavasi and rural children in Arunachal Pradesh, Nagaland, Assam, Andamans, Tamil Nadu and Karnataka for approximately 16,000 students. There are also hostels for Vanavasi children. Besides, 150 *balwadis*, it also runs non-formal schools for preservation of Vedic vidyas. The Vivekananda Kendra Institute of Culture, Guwahati, Assam, is established with the purpose of discovering the cultural continuity of the North-eastern states with the rest of India.

In Arunachal and Assam alone there are some 41 schools. They have earned reputation and often they are favoured over those managed by Christian missionaries. A programme for the multi-dimensional development of the Arunachali society – *Arunjyoti* – is a part of the Rural Development Project organised by the Kendra in Arunachal Pradesh.

As part of its various activities the Kendra has been bringing out a number of books and periodicals based on India's cultural ethos. The Vivekananda Kendra's periodicals include, *Yuva Bharati* (English monthly), *Vivekananda Kendra Patrika* (English thematic half yearly), *Kendra Bharati* (Hindi monthly), *Vivek Vani* (Tamil monthly), *Vivek Vichar* (Marathi four monthly), *Jagriti* (Assamese-English quarterly) and *Vivek Sudha* (Gujarati quarterly).

In 2003 Vivekananda Kendra had 169 branch-centres in 18 states of India. Character-building and Nation-building are envisaged as the principal aims of the *Kendras*. In an advertisement seeking volunteers for the *kendras* we read: "To make India a mighty, strong, prosperous, developed nation. Through Kendra's Man-making, Nation-building programmes".[112] Obviously by 'nation' what is meant is 'Hindu nation'. It also encourages education research for students, which includes development of the physical, mental, emotional, intellectual and spiritual personality. The Kendra also tries to awaken the civic sense, patriotism and spirituality of the younger generation.

Vivekananda schools are under the control of many organisations, including the Vivekananda Educational Society and the Vivekananda Educational Trust activities based on the ideas and values taught by *Sanatana Dharma*. ('Eternal religion/law'). These include education for the tribal children of Assam, Arunachal

Pradesh, Mizoram, Nagaland, Manipur and Andaman and Nicobar Islands; rural development projects in Tamil Nadu, Andhra Pradesh, Madhya Bharat, etc.[113] There are three *satras* in Majuli. A *satra* is a very ancient monastery-like school of sorts. In these *satras* young children are taught ancient dance, drama and music to keep the rich heritage of the area alive for posterity.[114] During the BJP-led NDA rule, on 22 February 2004, foundation was laid for the Vivekananda Kendra International, a new global-level institute, in New Delhi.[115]

Ramakrishna Mission Schools

Another institution through which the ideological agenda of Hindutva is imparted to the young generation is the Ramakrishna mission schools. Since its establishment in 1897, the Mission has been running thousands of institutions for formal and non-formal education. These include orphanages, students' homes, a Blind Boys' Academy, non-formal and adult education centres, self-employment training centres, agricultural research institutes, cattle farming institutes, technical schools, polytechnics, community polytechnics, computer training centres, language schools, libraries, librarianship training centres, hospitals and institutes for training nurses, teachers' training institutes, post-graduate medical research institutes, Veda Vidyalaya, and countless formal schools and colleges. The Mission also runs schools and hostels for tribal boys and girls in Arunachal, Assam, Madhya Pradesh, Meghalaya, Orissa and other remote parts of the country. The Ramakrishna Mission aims at man-making and character-building education. Vivekananda argued that religion should be the core of our education system as it helps one to attain real manhood.[116] Mani Shankar Aiyar observes that the Rama Krishna Mission is the most widespread, most influential and most effective of the missions operating in India. It also extends its activities beyond the frontiers of India to America, Europe and elsewhere.[117]

Saffronised Contents of School Education

Way back in 1990 the NCERT conducted an evaluation of school textbooks, including those prescribed for the *Vidhya Bharati* schools in the country. It made the alarming diagnosis that many of the *Vidhya Bharati* textbooks were designed to promote communalism and religious fanaticism in the name of inculcating knowledge of Indian culture in the young generation.[118]

The RSS is opposed to the so-called 'colonial educational heritage left behind by Lord Macaulay' and aims to replace it with a system based exclusively on Hindu values. It is to be noted that in the RSS parlance the school is called *mandir* and the teachers are called *acharyas* – thus the RSS gives a Hindu touch to the nomenclatures. All these schools have a prayer hall with idols of Hindu deities: these schools observe, as already mentioned, Teachers' Day on the birth anniversary of the sage Vyasa, and Children's day on Krishna Jayanti (birthday of Lord Krishna). The aim of these schools is said to be 'character building'. The theme of education is represented in the daily prayers: *jag-sir mor banaye Bharat* ('let India be the pride of the world').[119]

In the 1990s the BJP government introduced Vedic Mathematics in the state of Uttar Pradesh. In the same state moral classes were introduced in schools headed by RSS *pracharaks* and students were to respond to the roll call saying '*Vande Mataram*' instead of *upasthit* (present) or 'yes sir'. *Vande Mataram* was presented as the national hymn[120] and singing of it was made compulsory. *Vidhya Bharati's* projection of the map of India included Nepal, Pakistan, Bangladesh and parts of Myanmar – the RSS dream of *Akhand Bharat* (undivided India). The Indian Ocean was introduced as *Hindu Mahasagar* and the Arabian Sea as *Sindhu Mahasagar*. The writings of Deendayal Upadhyaya and contributions by RSS ideologues like Rajendra Singh and K.S. Sudarshan discussing science and environment, respectively, also entered school textbooks.[121] *Vidhya Bharati* periodically organises for its students all India level *Sanskriti gyan* (knowledge of culture) quiz, Vedic Mathematics quiz, paper-reading contest on Vedic science, etc.[122]

In the state of Goa the BJP-led government under the leadership of the former Chief Minister Manohar Parikkar had a hidden agenda to saffronise education according to the directives of the RSS. From the beginning the government under the leadership of the Chief Minister began restructuring the education system on a large scale. First the RSS took control of the 20-member Goa school Education Advisory Board of the government by appointing as its head Subhash Bhaskar Velingkar, the RSS general secretary. Later the Education Department issued a circular that some 50 schools that lacked the minimum number of students would be amalgamated. Suddenly in an arbitrary decision all the 50 schools were handed over to organisations such as temple organisations,

Mahila Mandals and other similar organisations. The hidden agenda was to handover these schools to organisations that are associated with the RSS. Further, 'surplus teachers' were recruited ostensibly to make the syllabus fall in line with the rest of the country. But it was argued that the recruitment was a pre-conceived agenda to saffronise education in the state. A delegation of the NCERT team visited the state to clear the decks for a change in the content of the syllabus with saffron content.[123]

Sanskriti Gyan (knowledge of culture) texts are taught in *Vidya Bharati* schools and *Shishu Mandirs*. These and similar texts are made compulsory for all schools to teach. The students are tested on dubious 'facts' such as the following:

> 'Ram Janmaabhoomi is the birthplace of Ram'.
>
> 'Iran was first settled by Indians (Aryans)'.
>
> 'Homer adapted Valmiki's *Ramayana* into an epic called *Iliad'*.
>
> 'Greek philosophers like Herodotus and Aristophanes were influenced by the Vedas'.
>
> 'The cow is the mother of us all, in whose body Gods are believed to reside'.
>
> 'The Ayurveda is the finest medical system of the world, and it naturally evolved in India'.
>
> 'Jesus Christ roamed the Himalayas and drew his ideas from Hinduism', etc.[124]

The *Sanskar Saurab* series presents, among other things, that *sati* (widow burning) is a Rajput tradition that one should be proud of;[125] Bharat exists and has culture, learning, civilisation, religion, good deeds as long as the Hindu *jat* survives and remains dominant.[126]

The Hindu beliefs are characterised as a *Dharma* (religion) while Sikhism, Christianity, Islam are described as sects.[127] 'The cow, Ganga, *gayatri mantra* and *Gita* are revered by all equally; all believe in rebirth and *karma* and everyone equally pays respect to *sadhus* and *sanyasis*.[128] In the same book the cultural symbols are identified as and confined to the lotus, *gayatri mantra, Natraj, Ganga, Gita,* sun, swastika, etc.[129] The first human being was born in Tibet, originally a part of Bharat (India).[130]

In the *Akhil Bharatiya Sanskriti Gyan Pariksha Prashnotri* we read 'that the real name of Lucknow is Laxmanpuri and it was made into a habitation by Laxman.[131]

The SAHMAT statement of 2001 observed that Open School textbooks already written, approved and paid for have been abandoned but not published because it has been found out that an association of secular historians had framed the syllabi for them. Many non-formal education centres and continuing education programmes are run by sympathisers of the Sangh Parivar. Many literacy centres and rural libraries established in the past years under National Literacy Mission for adult education have RSS influenced textbooks. There has been large transfer of government funds for education along Hindutva lines in the BJP ruled states to RSS affiliated organisations.[132] Even the Kendriya Vidyalayas were not spared from the Sangh Parivar's ideological education which follows the CBSE syllabus prepared by the NCERT. In June 2004 the RSS weekly *Organiser* said: "The credit for the remarkable improvement in results goes to the staff as well as the hard work of the former HRD Minister, Murli Manohar Joshi, who brought major changes in school curriculum, cannot be ignored."[133]

Distorted Version of Indian History

Hindu nationalists have envisaged history as the most effective vehicle for indoctrination of minds. Thus they have tried to tamper with educational curriculum. As early as 1939 M.S. Golwalkar, the RSS ideologue, had exhorted his followers to 're-write our history ourselves'.[134] Thus, one of the strategies employed by the Hindutva historians was to be selective in the presentation of history. They also did not hesitate to project fictions and myths as facts. In their eagerness to establish itself within the discipline of history they adopted certain unethical measures such as 'deletion', 're-writing', 'concealing', 'falsifying' and 'inventing' Indian history along Hindu nationalist lines.

Initially *Vidhya Bharti* developed curricula for four subjects: Physical exercise (including *Yoga*), music, Sanskrit and cultural knowledge. But the RSS always eyed on the subject of Indian history. In its view the textbooks give the 'Communist' rather than the 'Hindu' viewpoint. In the Sangh Parivar parlance the Communists are people with extra-territorial loyalties.[135] Therefore, they need to be rewritten and reinterpreted afresh. The opportunity came with the rule of the Janata Party at the centre in 1977. Morarji Desai the then Prime Minister, under the RSS influence made an attempt to withdraw those textbooks whose 'controversial and biased material' would lead their readers to acquire a prejudiced view of history.[136] Attempts were also made to control institutions like the Indian Council of Historical Research (ICHR), Indian Council of Social Science Research (ICSSR), the National Council for Educational Research and Training (NCERT), the Indira Gandhi National Centre for the Arts (IGNCA), National Book Trust (NBT), University Grants Commission (UGC) and so on.[137] Though the short Janata experiment aborted the RSS plan, it never gave it up. During early 1990s with the patronage of the BJP governments of states like Uttar Pradesh, Rajasthan, Himachal Pradesh and Madhya Pradesh the *Vidhya Bharati* not only expanded in terms of numbers, but also was granted autonomy to frame the syllabi for lower classes and conduct examinations.[138]

Under Joshi's direction the re-writing of Indian history along nationalist lines was accomplished through a virtual takeover of important academic and cultural institutions like, ICHR, ICSSR, NCERT, IGNCA, National Book Trust, UGC, etc. They also replaced eminent historians and scholars of prestigious institutions with persons of lesser repute and those known for their bias in favour of a particular interpretation of history. In addition, the national and other museums had many galleries renamed and descriptive placards re-written along Hindutva lines. The new Harappan Civilisation Gallery at the National Museum in Delhi today projects the Hindutva reinterpretation of this culture as Vedic against accepted archaeological evidence and scholarship.[139] In the Indian Council of Historical Research topics for study and research included 'Indus Saraswati Civilisation', 'Archaeology and Tradition', etc. The Archaeological Survey of India was preoccupied with funding excavations and publications to prove that the Aryans were the original inhabitants of India, that Indian civilisation is essentially Aryan,[140] and that Ayodhya is the *exact* birth place of Ram where the Babri mosque once stood. The re-written history books depict Rama and Krishna not as mythological, but historical, figures. Portions of them exclude Islam and Sikhism from the list of major religions, and present medieval wars between different kings as 'national' wars fought by Hindus against Muslims. In short they depict Hinduism as the 'essence' of Indian culture and other religions as 'alien' or 'invading' faiths.

The Hindutva ideologues present Indian culture as the 'mother' of all civilisations, and argue that everything noble and good in the world has come from India. They glorify history through falsehood and distortion, presenting ancient India as the world's 'master' civilisation and culture, denying the contributions of other great civilisations. A typical example of such a claim is an article published in 2004 in *Organiser*, the RSS weekly, by a certain R. Brahmachari. Some of his blatant claims are the following: The Greek civilisation which is the fountainhead of today's Western wisdom and personalities like Aristotle, Plato, Socrates, Pythagoras, etc. were influenced by Indian thought, and the father of Western wisdom were people who migrated in large numbers from India and established colonies in Greece, Egypt, Persia, Mesopotamia, Italy, North and South America and many other places. Then he goes on to say: 'Lord Krishna became Apollo in Greece; Lord Shiva became the Greek god Zeus; the place in Greece where people from Magadh (today's Bihar) were settled was called Magadhan. After a passage of time Magadhan became Makedan or Macedan and finally Macedonia the birthplace of Alexander; a man of incomparable beauty is called Alokasunder in Sanskrit and after passage of time, this Alokasunder became Alexander in Greece; the immigrants from Ayodhya were called Ayodhan (people of Ayodhya) in Greece. Later on this Ayodhan became Ionan and the nearby sea was named the Ionian Sea; the word Europe was derived from Sanskrit *surupa*; the epics *Illiad* and *Odyssey* are nothing but imitations of *Ramayana*; the Sanskrit word Arya became Aristo in Greece and from this Aristo names like Aristotle, Aristarcus and English words like aristocrat, aristocracy, etc. have been derived; Socrates was a corrupt of Sukracharya or Sukra. In Sanskrit *vidyapith* stands for a seat of learning and Vidyapith-guru stands for the teacher or *acharya*. In Greece this Vidyapith-guru became pith-guru which after a passage of time became Pithgoras, and from Pithgoras the English Pythagoras was derived. The author of the article then concludes by saying that the Greek civilisation was in fact a creation of Kshatriya immigrants from India. Hence it can safely be said that India is also the mother of civilisation, which is now known as Greek civilisation.[141]

In 2002 the NCERT published some new textbooks on history which marked the completion of an important academic and political chapter in contemporary India: *India and the World: Social Sciences Books* for Class VI; *Ancient India* for Class XI and *Contemporary India* for Class IX. The justification for introducing new textbooks was sought on two grounds. First, there was the argument about upgradation of the outdated knowledge in old textbooks. The reason why they needed replacement, and not revision, was their inherent biases, 'leftist' and other. But certain portions of these books were found to be so objectionable on other grounds that the NCERT ordered their immediate deletion. The deletions were carried out in early 2002. In Ancient Indian History the deletions included: (a) reference to beef-eating and cattle sacrifice; (b) a critical evaluation of the Puranic and the epic traditions in the light of archaeological and epigraphic testimony, with regard to the antiquity of the Ayodhya and the origin of Krishna worship in Mathura; (c) the exposition of Brahmanical hostility towards Ashoka despite his policy of religious tolerance; (d) the exploitive and ideological aspects of the caste system; and (e) the entire early life of Vardhamana Mahavira. In Medieval Indian History the target was the allegedly dishonourable discussion on the execution of Guru Tegh Bahadur. In Modern Indian History a one-line reference to the plundering activities of the Jat rulers of Bharatpur was thought noxious enough to be removed.[142]

The school curriculum, as we saw in the case of *Vidhya Bharati,* promotes mythology as history where 'Lord Ram, the blue-skinned warrior-king of Hindu lore, lived 886,000 years ago', a conclusion based on 'ancient texts and astrology'. Further, Ram is described as 'the source of inspiration for Indian culture" and a Hindu golden era is constructed as one that dates back to the time of the Indus Valley Civilisation of the third millennium B.C. Furthermore, the students are also fed the Sangh Parivar propaganda about its campaigns. A certain Sengupta records the contents of a quiz for eighth graders as follows: "[it] tests their knowledge of the continuing campaign to build a Hindu temple in Ayodhya, the mythical birthplace of Ram, where Hindu militants razed a 16th-century mosque in 1992. Students are grilled on everything from the date on which the temple reconstruction movement began to the names of those killed by the police."[143]

Thus scholarly interpretation of history has been dismissed in the saffron syllabus. Pernicious attempts to twist facts in textbooks and brainwash children were evident. In the 64th session of the Indian History Congress (IHC) in Mysore, December 2003, it reacted to ideological pressure that it had been under since some years. It published *History in the New NCERT Textbook: A Report and an Index of Errors* in 2003 which listed the errors, distortions and biases that inform a recent set of textbooks brought out by the NCERT.[144] Irfan Habib in his keynote address said that if a school child grows up thinking that men are superior to women, that his religion is better than all others, that his caste is superior to others, that property is everything that counts, would such a person be able to make use of the scientific education that he received?[145]

A film on Goa liberation produced by the Department of Education while the former BJP Chief Minister Parikkar was in charge and which was supposed to educate school students was accused of a lot of distortion of history by a group of Goa freedom fighters. They have argued that some of the scenes were highly objectionable and would have terrible implications for the communal harmony in the state and polarisation of Goa's society into Hindu and Christian.[146]

Several Brahmin scribes have over the millennia been engaged in a wilful distortion and concealment of historical facts and have consistently tried to erase the memory of the past that has not been to their taste. Hindutva historians present Indian history as a homogenous whole and define it as a uniform, monolithic, Hindu religious community functioning as the centre of Indian history. It is also a history of the Hindu elites and the upper castes where the lower castes play only a marginal role. In their history the Muslim emperor Akbar the Great was intolerant, India's freedom struggle is almost entirely a Hindu undertaking, etc. Hindutva historians also took care to present a communal history of India where the Hindus continuously confront the Muslims, Christians and the other minorities.

Most historians have expressed their deep concern about the fate of ongoing historical research and teaching with saffronisation in view. They were surprised that the BJP-led NDA government did not seem to be interested in any kind of historical work but was keen on destroying genuine historical research.[147] Agathon (447-401 B.C.) said that even God cannot change the past.[148] But Sangh Parivar wanted to do it.

Irfan Habib says that like any branch of knowledge, the essential requirement of History is the pursuit of truth. This requires one to collect and sift evidence critically. Bias, whether religious, racial, regional or national, or any other must be avoided. It is, therefore, important to realise that what the Central government agencies and the Sangh Parivar are now projecting as the history of

India is not anything that professional historians of any repute could regard as legitimate.[149]

It is worth mentioning here that the primary concern of the Nazi scholars and researchers, especially that of the *NS-Geisteswissenschaft* was to prove that the Aryan race is the superior race and that it was responsible for all worthwhile civilisation and cultural progresses in any part of the world – be it in Europe, North Africa, China, Near-East, India, South and North America. Archaeology (germanised as *Spatenwissenschft*) played a crucial role in 'establishing' this central doctrine of the Nazis. Hitler even sent out archaeological expeditions to various parts of the world to give 'foundation' for this pet theory.[150] In India a similar trend has seen in the effort of the Sangh Parivar historians to re-write Indian history. The insistence on doing archaeology at the site where the Babri mosque once stood is also to be seen as an imitation of Hitler's preoccupation with archaeology to prove his version of truth.

Communalisation of Education

Since the BJP take over of the government in New Delhi and several states in India, value education, moral science, patriotism and nationalism become synonymous with Hindu cultural nationalism and Hindu religion with token representation of other religions. The emphasis on the religious interpretation of history is a reflection of a general shift from a secular perspective to a religious orientation.

The Hindutva ideologues emphasise integral humanism. But what is propagated as integral humanism is in reality Hindu communalism. Deen Dayal Upadhyaya to whom the Hindutva version of integral humanism is attributed was a frontline Jan Sangh leader.

In the textbooks of Class V for *Shishu Mandir* schools we read: "Lakhs of foreigners came during these thousands of years but they all suffered humiliating defeat [...] Mughals, Pathans and Christians are today some of these people."[151]

The idea of M.S. Golwalkar opposing the pluralistic nature of Indian culture is presented in some of the textbooks of *Sanskar Saurab* series. It says, for example, 'we are one, our culture is one, our tradition is one, our life-current is one, and we have but one history';[152] 'the Muslim butchers are the killers of cows and the Hindus who killed them are to be venerated, their only fault being that they did it while they were asleep';[153] 'the worldview, thought, values and behaviour of the Hindus is most superior in this world';[154] 'in our lives we should accept only the *swadeshi* religion, *swadeshi* culture and *swadeshi* goods, celebrate our birthdays according to the Indian tradition and for the defence of the country it would not be a crime to buy MIGs from Russia'.[155]

Ekal Vidyalayas which are primarily based in tribal areas have the goal of bringing the tribals into the Hindu fold. *Vanavasi Kalyan Ashram* works mainly for Hinduising the tribals, and Dilip Singh Judeo is the patron of operation *ghar vapasi* ('home-coming', re-conversion) drive of the *Vanavasi Kalyan Ashram*. The *Saraswati Vidya Mandirs* impart 'Hindu' education to children. The Sangh Parivar's efforts to recast Adivasis as *vanavasis* is a critical component of their ideological project. Their project of 'Hindu *rashtra'* rests on a claim of Hindus being indigenous to India and any other claimants to that slot, as Adivasis are, fundamentally challenges their project of a Hindu nation.

One of the strategies of imparting cultural nationalism is by promoting Hindu non-Governmental Organisations (NGOs). Thus small organisations have mushroomed everywhere in the area of development, labour, education, culture and health sectors. These NGOs are able to secure grants from abroad and from the Central and state governments. The *Vanavasi Kalyan Ashram* is largely supported by non-resident Indian community in the West.

Sewa Dham is also one of the educational organisations of the Sangh Parivar funded by the IDRF. The level of distortion of facts propagated by it drew attention from the *New York Times*. An article by Somini Sengupta who visited the *Sewa Dham* school, New Delhi, concludes: "Education is a centrepiece of the Hindu revivalist campaign, which is natural, considering its cause: to build a Hindu nation out of what is officially a secular country with rights accorded to religious minorities."[156]

The Bharatiya Education Society is an RSS School in Rajasthan. It elevates mythology to the status of history and subtly promotes communalism in the educational curriculum. A Christian Science Monitor describes education in this school as follows: "Students get a large dose of 'Hindutva' values – teachings that argue for the pre-eminence of India's 5,000-year-old civilisation. Girls learn that Hindu females are at their best as mothers."[157] Thus education clearly is a critical component in the Sangh Parivar's efforts to build a Hindu *rashtra* and the IDRF contributes significantly to the creation of infrastructure and promotion of a curriculum that can help attain their goal.[158]

It has been observed that the new history textbooks of the NCERT (2002) written in conformity with its own saffronised National Curriculum Framework of School Education, are replete with factual errors, falsehoods and bias. According to critics the textbooks *India and the World* for Class VI, *Ancient India* for Class XI, *Medieval India* for Class XI, *Contemporary India* for Class IX reveal a shocking lack of awareness of basic historical facts and the language is riddled with grammatical errors, spelling mistakes and inappropriate expressions and they all present history with a strong chauvinistic and communal bias. According to the saffronised *Ancient India* textbook, India is the original homeland of the Aryans, Indus Valley civilisation is Vedic, Hinduism is the most advanced of all religions, the caste system was initially good and rigidities crept in later, women in ancient India were held in high esteem and had equal inheritance rights as men.[159]

The *Mediaeval India* textbook is imbued with anti-Muslim prejudice. Muslims who are 'foreigners' brought nothing to India but bloodshed, violence and the practice of temple destruction.[160] In order to malign Islam, in Maharashtra, in a textbook recommended for third year B.A., the students of history are told in a chapter on Mahmud Ghaznavi: "it [Islam] has been a curse for the people outside Arab world because wherever the Islamic hordes went, they not only conquered the countries, but killed millions of people and plundered their homes and places of worship and destroyed their homes, and above all their artworks."[161] The author then concludes by saying: "Why these atrocities? Because Islam teaches only atrocities. Have not Islamic invaders done so wherever they had gone, be that India or Africa or Europe?."[162]

The *Contemporary India* textbook portrays 'Muslim separatism' as the best while Hindu communalism is ignored and Hindu Mahasabha leaders are idolised as patriots. The great Indian social reform movement is ignored, Jawaharlal Nehru is either ignored or presented in an unfavourable light and the communists are vilified. Critics consider this single textbook as perhaps the most damaging of all.[163]

In the textbook for Class IX of the Gujarat Board there is a chapter titled 'Problems of the Country and their Solutions'. One of the sub-headings given in the text is titled 'Minority Community' which labels the Muslims, Parsis and Christians as foreigners. It also states that in some states the Hindus are a minority. We read in the textbook: "But apart from the Muslims, even the Christians, Parsees and other foreigners are also recognised as the minority communities. In most of the states the Hindus are in minority and Muslims, Christians and Sikhs are in majority in these [...] states."[164] The same text also selectively denigrates the Catholic priesthood of the middle ages. But similar exacting criticism is not accorded to the Brahmin religious hierarchy in India which is not free from monetary exploitation and sexual harassment of the weaker sections of society even today.[165] In the Social Sciences textbook for Class IX we read:

> The priests of the Catholic Church had accumulated plenty of wealth through unjust taxes, illegal fees, ownership of large tracts of land, selling miracles and indulgences. They spent this money on worldly pleasures and immoral behaviour.[166]
>
> The Pope who was the head of the Roman Catholic Church was himself a big landlord. The Church received sumptuous gifts of land from the king as well as the lords. Thus the Church had amassed great wealth. The Pope, archbishop [sic], bishops and other priests lost their heads, forgot their duties and lived a life of luxury and sensual pleasures.[167]

K.N. Panikkar says that the rewriting of history by the Sangh Parivar undertaken with the connivance and collaboration of the government, is essentially an attempt at communal mythification, which lends ideological support and legitimacy to the politics of cultural nationalism.[168] Habib says: "If the BJP is to have its way, we would soon be competing with Pakistan in framing the utmost possible parochial view of the past. Just as Buddhism and Guru Nanak are in effect excluded from the cultural legacy of Pakistan, Islam and Kabir will soon be marched out of heritage."[169] During the debate on the non-confidence motion in Lok Sabha in 2003, Sonia Gandhi said concerning rewriting school curricula by the BJP-led government: "Obscurantism is being thrust upon us, heroes of the freedom movement are being denigrated and excluded and in their place those with dubious credentials are being celebrated."[170] According to Arjun Dev, retired head of the department of social sciences at NCERT, the Hindutva re-writing of history is 'communalisation of history'.[171]

Saffronisation of Higher Education

Under Joshi's leadership higher education in India underwent many revolutionary changes, and inspired by *swadeshi* ideas and Hindu cultural nationalism the alterations in the syllabi were made under the auspices of the UGC. The UGC also insisted that all universities and institutions under them be subjected to the recognition of the National Accreditation Assessment Council (NAAC). But it was feared that such a standardisation would undermine the autonomy of the universities and thus facilitate the introduction of a Hindu national curriculum.[172] Attempts were also made to unify and integrate the different varsities functioning under the UGC with a 'uniform' syllabus that subtly cater to the Hindu nationalist ideology.[173] It was also alleged of the appointments of Vice-chancellors of universities were mostly made under ideological grounds.

Joshi who was under the *swadeshi* spell showed an obvious bias towards Western scholarship and tools of research. For example, in August 2003 in Kochi, Kerala, a three-day seminar was organised by the *Bharatiya Vichara Kendra* in co-ordination with the UGC, NAAC and all the universities of Kerala, for research scholars, guides and representatives of major research institutions. The HRD minister Joshi speaking at the valedictory session called upon the researchers to shun Western approach to research. He urged the scholars to know more about India's contribution to knowledge in the world, which was thousands of years old, whereas Western research, he argued, was hardly 300-400 years old.[174] The critics accused the seminar as part of the agenda of Sangh Parivar to saffronise education and research sector.

Introduction of Vedic Astrology in Universities

Since some years UGC has been working to introduce courses on Vedic studies, Vedic Astrology, Palmistry and Hindu rituals. The issue of introducing courses in Vedic Astrology (*Jyotir Vigyan*) in universities seems to have been first mooted on 16 July 2000. UGC constituted a nine member 'expert' committee on 14 August 2000 to study the case. On the basis of its recommendations it was decided on 25 January 2001 to introduce the subject and approved a set of guidelines for the new course. On 23 February 2001 proposals were invited from universities for setting up of departments of Astrology with 5 May 2001 as the deadline. On 13 June 2001 the 'expert' committee examined the proposals received from 41 universities of 16 states and recommended the creation of independent departments in 20 select universities. On 27 June 2001 the Commission approved the recommendation of the 'expert' committee and on 21 July 2001 the decision was communicated to the concerned universities.[175] Thus in 2001 UGC decided to introduce Astrology courses leading to under-graduate and post-graduate degrees. Reports say that cash incentives were offered to universities to start the courses. Meera Nanda says: "Under the kindly patronage of the state, Hindutva's wedge strategy is working wonders. Astrology is flourishing as an academic subject in public and private colleges and universities, and is being put to use in predicting natural disasters."[176]

Ever since the UGC concurred with HRD Minister Joshi's proposal to introduce courses in Vedic Astrology a debate was initiated in academic circles. According to London *Financial Times* more than 100 scientists and 300 political and social scientists protested by writing to the government.[177] In August 2001 some 200 scientists opposed the UGC's proposal to introduce Astrology, *Vastu Shastra*, etc. in universities.[178] Special leave petition challenging the decision and seeking to restrain the UGC from starting these courses had been filed by Pushpa M. Bhargava, an eminent biologist and former Director of the Centre for Cellular and Molecular Biology, Hyderabad, K. Subhash Chandra Reddy, former Head of the Department of Political Science at Osmania University and Chandana Chakrabarti, a writer and a consultant. But the Supreme Court verdict came exactly three years after the UGC accepted the proposal of as many as 20 universities for starting new departments of astrology. This was a serious blow to the efforts of the scientific community and rational minded people who have been relentlessly campaigning against the pernicious move. Some even argue that the language of the Supreme Court judgment actually betrayed an undercurrent of sympathy for Astrology.[179]

Introduction of Vedic Astrology as a subject of study in universities by UGC is a setback to the efforts to promote scientific temper in society and runs counter to the secular foundations of the Constitution. Some argue that a course in Vedic Astrology cannot be termed as a course of scientific study as Astrology has never been regarded as a science as it lacked the basic attributes and tenets of science. Introduction of astrology in the curriculum would erode and negate Article 51A of the Indian Constitutions, which entrusts a fundamental duty upon the citizens of the country to develop a scientific temper, humanism and spirit of enquiry and reform.[180]

Some argue that teaching Vedic Astrology amounted to saffronising education and imposing Hindu values in higher education, which violates the secular credentials inherent in the Constitution. The very term 'Vedic' in Vedic Astrology implies that the subject has the Hindu religion as its basis.[181] The money expected to be spent on each university for promoting irrational disciplines like Astrology would run into several million rupees while other programmes, especially primary education, are deprived of funds.[182]

A research done over a period of 45 years in the West by Canadian professor of Psychology Ivan Kellty and one-time Australian astrologer Dr Geoffrey Dean, with over 2,000 persons and published in one of the issues of the *Journal of Consciousness* attempts to prove that Astrology is just guesswork.[183]

In October 2003 *India Today* reported a typical case of astrological fallacy. Naina Dholakia, a 49 year old woman died while chopping cabbage. A sudden heart attack was the cause of it. It happened two days after the astrologer she had been consulting for the past 18 years reassured her that she had a long, healthy and uncomplicated life ahead, that her son would soon get married and her daughter would win a prestigious award. None of it happened.[184] In spite of the dubious nature of Astrology as a science the then UGC Chairman Hari Gautam defended the decision to introduce Astrology. He argued that if astrological predictions go wrong, doctors go wrong with their diagnosis too.[185]

Scientific truths are universal and are not dependent on the whims and fancies of individuals whereas the practice of astrology in different parts of the world is varied. Astrology does not use the accepted scientific methods of inquiry. In fact, it has been conclusively demonstrated by well-designed investigations that astrological predictions are no better than random chance coincidences. Vedic Astrology cannot be termed as a subject of scientific study as astrology has never been supported by any research conducted according to stringent scientific procedure[186] and the scientific world dismisses it as a superstitious practice. For any sensible person, star and planetary movements are not something that can be linked with the fortunes and misfortunes in an individual's or a nation's or the world's existence.[187] There is no cause and effect relationship between the change in star patterns and the vicissitudes of human fortunes. Human persons make or mar their destiny through the exercise of their reason and free will. But the crux of the matter is not whether astrology is right or wrong but whether it should be allowed to influence national and personal consciousness to the extent it does.[188] Hence it has been said: "The decision of Dr Joshi to institutionalise the study of *Jyotish Sastra* in Indian Universities is foolish. This will only encourage our upcoming generations to be dogmatic, obscurantist, and backward."[189]

Heinrich Himmler, the director of the *Schutzstafel* (SS) under the Nazi regime and the one who was directly responsible for the genocide under Hitler was a firm believer in astrology, magic, hypnotism, spiritism, telepathy and other forms of occult. The historian Michael Kater has described Himmler as a prisoner of horoscope and astrology and he allowed himself to be advised by many astrologers and often compared their opinions.[190] He also engaged the researchers to 'prove' the scientific nature of the occult practices.[191]

Introduction of Vastu Sastra Courses

Vastu Sastra is another subject that has figured in the educational programme that has attracted governmental grants for research and education. *Vastu Sastra* is the ancient Indian science of architecture based on the Vedas and is an integral part of Vedic Astrology and Vedic Mathematics. It is based on the philosophy that where one lives can influence ones happiness, wealth, health, and prosperity. *Vastu Sastra* deals with rules, regulations, directions which the builders and architects are expected to follow in order to overcome the alleged negative influences. It teaches that improper construction or renovation of houses or buildings can adversely affect ones life and future. Thus *Vastu Shastra* takes into consideration, for instance, the astrological placement of the Sun, Earth, and other planets during the actual construction, where the building site is located, the shape of the site, the shape of the proposed building, the direction the structure will face, the location of gates, entry doors, room doors, windows, the general design of the building, etc.

But in reality *Vastu Sastra* is a combination of a bit of 'science', lot of fiction and much superstition. Today enlightened people go to a professional architect or a civil engineer than to an expert in *Vastu*

Sastra in matters regarding buildings and constructions. Professional architects know that a good building needs a solid foundation, strong walls, a proper structural balance with the right weight and pressure distribution, proper plumbing, electricity, air light, etc. It is also true that people can live in buildings where everything is totally wrong according to *Vastu Sastra* and yet enjoy peace, prosperity, fame and wealth than those who live in 'good *Vastu*' houses. In addition, any reasonable person will agree that mind power, human potentialities and divine help are definitely greater than *Vastu* power. Hence any adherence to *Vastu Sastra* is a sign that we are governed by unscientific principles, outdated technologies and superstitious beliefs and that we are backward looking in architectural and technological matters. Hence there is no denying the fact that obscurantist practices like *Vastu Sastra* can do havoc on the educational framework at all levels, to say the least.

Introduction of Karmakanda Courses

Under Joshi's direction efforts were made to impart Hindu religious character to education system by incorporating in the curricula subjects traditionally associated with Hindu religious practices. The most glaring example of this tendency is the promotion of a course called *Karmakanda* that would produce certified priests for conducting Hindu rituals. Today some select universities in India have a department of *Karmakanda* with the objective of producing a trained group of young scholars with proficiency in Vedic rituals and other related subjects, and they had been provided with extra funds for such courses.[192] For example, a three-month training course – a *Karma Kand Kriya* course – for students aspiring to become Hindu priests is being offered by the Uttar Pradesh Sanskrit Sansthan.[193] A fifteen-day long *Grama Kovil Poojarigal Peraval* (Village Temple Priests' Forum) is being conducted in Tamil Nadu for the backward and depressed classes.[194] But according to K.N. Panikkar, *Karmakanda* is unacademic and undesirable and is likely to encourage inward looking, closed minds and intellectual backwardness.[195] Praful Bidwai observes that the UGC is busy trying to make India the world's intellectual backwater and a morass of obscurantism via Vedic Astrology and *karmakand* courses.[196] It may be recalled that Himmler who belonged to the notorious Nazi regime also made efforts to develop special rites and rituals for the new SS Religion.[197]

Promotion of Vedic 'Sciences'

It is generally agreed that the Vedic Science movement began in 1893 when Swami Vivekananda addressed the World Parliament of Religions in Chicago. In his discourse he sought to present Hinduism not only as a fulfilment of all other religions, but also as a fulfilment of all of science.[198] Vivekananda was followed by Aurobindo Ghose.[199] The writings of 19th and 20th centuries, especially the writings of Dayananda Saraswati and Sarvepalli Radhakrishnan, are replete with celebration of Hinduism as a 'scientific' religion.[200] Today the scientific version of Hinduism has found its way to the West through the numerous *ashrams* and Yoga centres set up, most prominently by Maharishi Mahesh Yogi and others like him.[201]

The obsession with finding all kinds of obscure Hindu doctrines had been dictating the official education policy of the BJP ever since it came to power in New Delhi. In 2001 Joshi in his capacity as HRD minister organised the Indian Science Congress in New Delhi. In July 2004 the RSS Weekly *Organiser* announced that the first World Congress on Vedic Sciences would be held in Bangalore between 9 and 13 August 2004 under the banner of *Vijnana Bharati,* an all-India body of various *swadeshi* science movements active in different parts of the country. It was stated that the purpose of the Congress was to bring together scholars from different walks of life for the first time to explore the scientific basis of the content of the Vedas. About 40 foreign delegates were to present papers in the Congress and they were to come from such countries as America, Thailand, China, Canada, Mexico, Sri Lanka, England, Kenya, West Indies, etc. The main objective of the Congress was to inform the world that the Vedas are an eternal source of science and also to present the Indian worldview on science. The Congress was to be organised by the *Vivekananda Yoga Anushandhan Samsthan* (a Deemed University). Over 252 scientists and scholars were expected to present papers on different subjects contained in the Vedas in the Congress representing 42 universities of India and abroad.[202]

Meera Nanda argues that all the numerous celebrations of 'Vedas as science' follow a similar intellectual strategy of finding analogies and equivalence. All invoke extremely speculative theories from modern cosmology, quantum mechanics, vitalistic theories of biology and parapsychology and other sciences. They read back these sciences into Sanskrit texts chosen at will, and their meaning decided by the whim of the interpreter, and claim that the entities and processes mentioned in Sanskrit texts are 'like' or 'the same thing as' or 'another word for' the ideas expressed in modern cosmology, quantum physics or biology. Thus, according to Nanda, there is a bit of a Brahman here and a bit of quantum mechanics there, the two treated as interchangeable. A close examination of it reveals that the terms are scientific, but the content is religious and there is no regard for consistency either of scientific concepts or of religious ideas. The only idea that gives this whole mish-mash any coherence is the great anxiety to preserve and protect Hinduism from a rational critique and demystification.[203] It is argued that Vedic science is motivated by Hindu cultural chauvinism, and by teaching Vedic Hinduism as 'science' India can portray the country as 'secular' and 'modern', a model of sobriety and responsibility in contrast with those obscurantist Islamic fundamentalists who insist on keeping science out of their *madrasas.*[204]

Obsession with Obscurant Topics

Under Joshi's leadership many obscurant topics also found their way into the field of science. About eighteen subjects mentioned in the *Chandogya Upanishad* have been incorporated into the school/college curricula by Joshi's HRD ministry – for example, subjects such as Vedic Mathematics, Astronomy and Palmistry,[205] 'miraculous effects of *agnihom,*[206] etc. There was also a widespread tendency to 'target' those centres of higher education that did not agree with the Sangh Parivar agenda of saffronisation of education.[207]

The Ministry of Defence was sponsoring research and development of weapons and devices with magical powers mentioned in the ancient epics; the Health Ministry was investing in research, development and sale of cow urine, sold as a cure for all ailments from the Acquired Immune Deficiency Syndrome (AIDS) to tuberculosis (TB). Faith-healing and priest-craft were other 'sciences' receiving public and private funding. Miracles and superstitions of all kinds had the blessings of influential public figures, including elected Members of Parliament.[208] There were also experiments with cow's urine claiming that the Indian cow's urine is chemically very different from that of other cows. A senior BJP leader claimed that the experiment had an answer to India's malnutrition problems – cow's urine along with a glass of cow's milk'.[209] Under the BJP government it was decided to introduce compulsory courses on patriotism in the state universities and science and professional colleges.[210]

In some places there had been stiff resistance to Joshi's educational policies. For instance, when the UGC's suggestion to start courses in Vedic Astrology and Vedic Mathematics came up for implementation, representatives of the Madurai University Teachers Association in the various university bodies protested against the move and stopped it. In the University of Madras, an M.A. degree course in *Natya* (Dance and Theatre) was sought to be introduced with the blessings of Sangh Parivar experts. At a meeting of the Academic Council the proposal was opposed on the grounds that the project had no scientific basis and contained retrograde features in the name of incorporating the learning advantages of the centuries of *guru-shishya parampara* (the ancient tradition of education founded on teacher-student relationship) along with research and training methodologies of modern education. The Vice-chancellor had to shelve the proposal pending detailed discussion.[211]

Vedic Mathematics, Vedic Astrology, Vedic Astronomy are now being taught in 30 universities as a full Master's Course, all supposedly created 4000 years ago.[212] Many right minded persons in India think that Joshi's attempt to introduce Astrology, *Vastu sastra, Karmakanda* and *Paurohitya* (rituals to be followed by Hindu priests), and so on as subjects in the University syllabus was an absurd move. The best Indian scientists have decried the wisdom behind this move as the promotion of such an unscientific field of study will only contribute to obscurantism and superstition. Some academics feel that the introduction of obscurant subjects will only make India a laughing stock in the eyes of the world. If subjects of the kind mentioned above are introduced in university curricula there is nothing to stop India from becoming, as T.N. Seshan says, a non-achieving society.[213] Tavleen Singh notes: "Murli Manohar Joshi is a lousy education minister. [....] Mr. Joshi would not have wasted time on stupidities like introducing 'Indian values', astrology and similar wacky ideas."[214]

Concept of Compulsory Military Training

The concept of military training is an essential aspect of fascist training of the youth. During the period of Italian fascism Benito

Mussolini had his own highly organised military schools and colleges. Hitler also had well organised military institutions.

The compulsory military training is basically an agenda of the RSS.[215] In 1926 Hedgewar introduced for the members of the RSS a uniform consisting of khaki shorts and khaki (later white) shirts and black forage caps. The company of *Swayamsevaks* observed strict discipline symbolised by the detailed code of regulations for the daily assembly and dismissal of the company. On some occasions, such as the festival of *Dasahara,* they marched in-step through streets holding their *lathis* (bamboo staves) to demonstrate the strength of the movement.[216] The paramilitary style extended also to sports and weapons training with the *lathi,* sword, javelin and dagger.[217]

In February 2003 the HRD ministry's department of secondary and higher education was seriously considering ways and means of introducing compulsory military training and social service and making the national curriculum attuned to the concept of cultural nationalism. The aforesaid task force was asked to submit a report within six months so that – according to an HRD ministry's official – the 'secondary education is made more relevant to our times, needs and aspirations and help keep pace with the global demands'.[218]

In 2003 the then BJP President Venkaiah Naidu proposed the idea of compulsory military training for the youth.[219] Naidu's proposal was not anything new. Hindu militancy has been closely linked to the notion of military schools. B.S. Moonje was a Hindutva ideologue who believed in fascist ideology and its organisational strategies. He was the first Hindu nationalist who was in direct contact with the fascist regime of Benito Mussolini of Italy and while in Italy he visited several military schools of the Italian fascist leader.[220] On his return he started immediately to work for the foundation of his Bhonsla military school and for the militant re-organisation of Hindu society. He also publicly admitted that his idea of reorganising Hindu society militarily was inspired by the military training schools of England, France, Germany and Italy.[221]

V.D. Savarkar, had envisaged compulsory military training for the Hindu youth.[222] Savarkar's militancy is evident in many of his statements. For example, he said that in order to forestall and counteract the Islamic peril India must raise a mighty force exclusively constituted by the Hindus, must open arms and ammunition factories exclusively manned by the Hindus and mobilise everything on a war scale.[223] When released from prison Savarkar toured

India extensively and tried to spread the message of militarisation through public and private meetings.[224] The neo-Nazi, Savitri Devi, who is hailed as 'the Hitler's priestess', also repeatedly argued for the making Hindus a military race with military virtues.[225]

A unique feature of Maharashtra is its 'military' schools. They are run primarily by RSS members and such schools have been around since the time the RSS came into existence in the 1920s.[226] Today, in general, members of the RSS, Bajrang Dal,[227] Shiv Sena,[228] Durga Vahini[229] and so on receive a paramilitary style of training. The Vishva Hindu Parishad offers a training course to women of 15 to 35 years of age called *Durga Vahini* which consists of, among other things, wielding of *lathi* (bamboo staff) and small firearms.[230]

Imposition of Sanskrit

Hindutva presents Sanskrit as the only language capable of fostering cultural unity of India giving insight into the Indian culture. Hence it was proposed to make it compulsory in many sectors of Indian education. The RSS always insisted that it is the *rashtra bhasha* (national language) *par excellence*.[231] Thus saffronisation of education is manifested also in the insistence on a revival of Sanskrit learning. Savarkar described the Sanskrit language as the richest and the most cultured of the ancient languages of the world, the holiest tongue of tongues and the mother of the majority of mother tongues.[232] He insisted that Sanskrit language must be an indispensable constituent of the classical course for the Hindu youths.[233] Golwalkar considered Sanskrit as one of the greatest cementing factors of Indian national life and affirmed the importance of learning it.[234] Under Joshi's guidance the HRD ministry was to make Sanskrit learning obligatory for students from Class III to Class X[235] and promote it in various university departments. He even claimed that Sanskrit is the most highly acknowledged international language.[236] Joshi as HRD minister, following the long standing prejudice of the RSS against English language argued that medium of education should be the national language, regional language or one's mother tongue so that the child does not have to work twice as hard at grasping the language and then the subject.

Since more then two decades *Sanskrit Bharati* is India's reputed organisation engaged in teaching Sanskrit through simple means. The organisation is best known for its innovative ways of teaching

Sanskrit.[237] 'Speak Sanskrit Movement', 'Ten-day Sanskrit conversation camps', 'Correspondence courses in Sanskrit', Internet websites, etc. were some of the innovative programmes for the teaching and propagation of Sanskrit.[238]

Under Joshi's guidance the government did much to popularise not only conversational Sanskrit for the masses but also the study of it in schools and universities. During his tenure in office the entire year 2000 A.D. was observed as Sanskrit year and organised programmes to encourage Sanskrit studies at all levels and introduced complete education in Sanskrit institutions. In Andhra Pradesh, free Sanskrit postal tuition is being conducted by VHP and about 20,000 students are benefiting from it. Camps are being organised for teaching Sanskrit as a spoken language and a special curriculum has been designed to teach Sanskrit so that students are able to speak and talk in Sanskrit in 10 days' time.[239] In Gujarat, where the language is compulsory, the Sanskrit teachers are regularly sent to the RSS-run skill development centre.[240] In 2004 the *Rashtriya Sanskrit Sansthan* based in New Delhi started 35 informal centres in Uttaranchal for evening Sanskrit classes for the common people.[241] The *Sanskrit Samvardhan Kendra,* under the aegis of *Sanskrit Bharati,* Gujarat, organised a four-day Sanskrit learning camp in Ahmedabad in August 2004.[242]

Samvadshala is a unique experiment in the field of Sanskrit education. Situated in the Mandoli village on the outskirts of Delhi *Samvadshala* is a joint project of Sanskrit Bharati and Badri Bhagat Devi Mandir Society to train people to teach and speak Sanskrit. It is a 14-day intensive residential programme in teaching Sanskrit using the most modern methods and aids. The 108th batch of *Samvadshala* had their course from 15-30 November 2004. With the 107th batch it had trained over 3000 persons over a period of five years.[243] In the same year Sanskrit training camps are organised also in the USA by Sanskrit Bharati.[244]

When Joshi was the HRD minister there was also a move to introduce besides Sanskrit, the heritage of the Vedas and Upanishads also in the curricula from the primary to the higher level, including vocational stream. This was severely opposed for favouring Hindu culture, and had to be abandoned.[245]

According to Bidwai compulsory Sanskrit proposal is gravely and intrinsically, flawed. Joshi's claim that it is 'well established that Sanskrit is the most highly acclaimed international language', and that it is the 'mother' of all Indian languages embodying what is highest in Indian culture, is to be seen in a certain context.[246] But in reality, as any competent historian of ancient India can tells us, Sanskrit is not the 'mother' of all Indian languages. Each of these evolved through complex, non-linear interaction and exchange between a number of ethnic groups, cultures and linguistic entities. Nor was it the language of common people, which in its plurality was Prakrit with many versions, scripts and dialects. Sanskrit was once the language of India's ruling elites. Access to Sanskrit scriptures was jealously controlled by Brahmins and barred to the plebeian castes, as stipulated by the *Laws of Manu*.[247]

Joshi made Sanskrit compulsory for Class X to XII which meant that teaching it from Class VII onwards, if not earlier.[248] Bidwai argues that a Dalit or OBC child is at a fundamentally disadvantage vis-à-vis Sanskrit. Cramming declensions and complex rules of grammar is less a function of intelligence than memory. The quality time or attention this demands from parents or tutors is normally unavailable to underdeveloped pupils. Hence compulsory Sanskrit will act as a harmful social filter, protecting the elite privileges and eroding social opportunities available to the underprivileged.[249] Hence according to Bidwai, Joshi's promotion of 'spiritualism' as the core of Indian culture and his plan to make Sanskrit compulsory for Classes X to XII are part of Hindutva's elitist, partisan agenda to favour further the already privileged.[250]

Today in India some 30 million people learn Sanskrit at school level. In India alone there are nine Sanskrit universities exclusively teaching Sanskrit and 120 universities offer graduate and post-graduate Sanskrit courses. In USA some 15 universities have various levels of Sanskrit courses and at the world level there are some 300 universities that offer Sanskrit courses.[251]

In 2004 the RSS weekly *Organiser* published the real motive behind for promoting Sanskrit. It said: "Use of Sanskrit will make Hinduism strong, dynamic, youthful and vibrant. All our scriptures will be available to one and all without any language barrier".[252]

Saffronisation of Cultural and Academic Institutions

Joshi as the head of the HRD ministry succeeded to a great extent in denuding the cultural, scientific, technological and research institutions of their academic character and making them centres of communal divide and Hindu cultural nationalism. Institutions like the University Grants Commission (UGC), National Council of Educational Research and Training (NCERT), Indian Council of Social Science Research (ICSSR), Indian Council of Historical Research (ICHR), and so on became establishments for the dissemination of the Hindutva ideology. For example, once considered an invincible Left bastion, the Jawaharlal Nehru University (JNU), New Delhi, has come a long way with the rising saffron activities, deepening further the roots of Hindutva in the campus. In March 2003 it had five *shakhas*.[253] The Shyama Prasad Mukherjee Documentation Centre established in honour of the founder of the Jana Sangh within the ICSSR has been given huge funds; the entire campus of JNU City Centre has been changed to 'Shyama Prasad Mukherjee Gateway of Social Sciences'.[254] The ICSSR also established a new Deen Dayal Upadhyaya Centre for Social Welfare.[255] The HRD Ministry and many other bodies frequently organised seminars on 'spirituality and science', 'consciousness', 'technology', Vedanta,' 'Cultural Heritage', 'patriotism', etc., all at public expenses.[256] Often they were used as a forum for the propagation of Hindutva ideology. Cultural festivals were funded by the government and ministers openly associated with promoting the identity of Indian culture with Brahmanism.[257] Sometimes in the process of rating films in national films awards too ideology came into play. For example, sometime back the poor mythological film *Pandavas* was awarded.[258]

In 2003 the Sri Narayana Dharma Paripalana Yogam (SNDP) invited the then Human Resources Development Minister Joshi to inaugurate its three-day convention and global meet in Kochi, Kerala. Joshi seized the occasion to announce that he would include Narayana Guru's teachings in the NCERT and CBSE syllabus and set up a national university in his name.[259] Joshi added that Sree Narayana Guru was a great inspiration to the RSS and the BJP and that he was remembered in RSS *shakhas* daily.[260] Critics argue that on close examination it became clear that the entire exercise was an effort to maintain caste distinctions in society and to utilise it for political mobilisation and not to abolish it.

It is alleged that under Joshi's guidance often highhandedness was the means used to saffronise cultural and academic institutions. For instance, the ouster of M.G.S. Narayanan as Chairman of the Indian Council of Historical Research was believed to be part of the HRD Ministry's scheme to saffronise the agenda in academia.[261]

The usurpation of the *Sahitya Akademi*, India's premier academy of letters, was another instance of saffronisation of cultural institutions. On 17 February 2003 Gopichand Narang was elected president of the Sahitya Akademi. Critics feared that with this event the BJP was to set a saffron agenda for the institution. The election showed a tussle between Hindu fundamentalists and left-leaning writers who have for long been at the helm of affairs at the *Akademi*. Narang, former vice-president of the *Akademi*, won the election by a decisive margin of 18 votes. He was accused of being propped up by the RSS to assault the autonomy of the Akademi. Pitted against him was the defender of the leftist ideology and Jnanapeeth Award winner Mahashweta Devi who has written over a hundred novels and devoted a lifetime to the cause of tribal people and other historically disadvantaged groups. The two-month long electoral battle was compounded by the then BJP president Venkaiah Naidu's letter to Culture Minister Jagmohan urging him to cleanse the various Akademies of all Leftist influence. Venkaiah Naidu's aggressive stand fuelled anxieties that the BJP might set the agenda for the Akademies (the Sahitya Akademi, the Sangeet Natak Akademi and the Lalit Kala Akademi) the same way that it appropriated cultural and educational institutions such as the Indian Council for Historical Research.[262]

Targeting Women Studies

Joshi blocked progressive strains in education by targeting women's studies. Without any regard for academic freedom, the HRD minister merged women's studies with the study of the family. For him, women and the family are never different. Thus women's study-centres across the country became women and family study-centres.[263] Critics say that this was in a sense a subtle imposition of the *Laws of Manu* concerning women and an imitation of Adolf Hitler's idea of women and family. Hitler wanted women to be essentially mothers and housewives who will bring up the pure German race.[264] According to the *Laws of Manu* a woman is valuable only as far as she is the possible begetter of a male offspring. In her childhood a woman should always be subject to her father, in youth to her husband and when he is dead to her sons.[265] Manu also demanded that, day and night women must be kept in dependence by the male members of their families.[266] The prominent RSS leader and ideologue Golwalkar spoke disparagingly of women. He said: "There is now a clamour for 'equality of women' and their 'emancipation from man's domination'! Reservation of seats in various positions of power is being claimed on the basis of their separate sex, thus adding one more 'ism' – sexism!'."[267] Women are not being treated at par with men even by many so-called emancipated Hindus residing in America. For instance, the Swaminarayana sect in America insists on separate seating of men and women at religious functions.[268] T. Pintchman observes that the representations and conceptions of female gender in Brahmanical Hinduism provide both a theology and an ideology that ultimately can be used to support the repression of women.[269] Thus it does not take much speculation to realise that Joshi's policies regarding women were arch conservative and biased.

Placement of Sangh Parivar Loyalists in Universities and Government Departments

The HRD ministry is one of the key sectors in the Central government. It is alleged that the 'experts' consulted by the former HRD ministry headed by Joshi were mostly from the 'saffron' group. When Joshi was the HRD minister almost all major academic institutions had been headed by chosen men and women with an ideological view that was sympathetic to the Sangh Parivar. According to a report published in November 2000, the head of the Indian Council of Historical Research was B.R. Grover who was close to Joshi; the National Council of Educational Research and Training had J.S. Rajput who was also an associate of Joshi; the Indian Council of Social Science Research had a veteran Sangh Parivar man and former Jawaharlal Nehru University Professor M.L. Sondhi as its head; the Chairman of the University Grants Commission, Hari Gautam, was an old Sangh Parivar sympathiser; the National Open School had a BJP man N.K. Ambasth as in-charge; the Indian Institute of Advanced Studies (IIAS) in Shimla had the Sanskrit scholar G.C. Pande who was known to have old BJP connections and another member Kirit Joshi was a member of the RSS affiliate *Ved Vidya Pratishthan*.[270] Indira Gandhi National Centre for the Arts had L.M. Singhvi as its president for ten years and was a sitting BJP M.P. The National Film Development Corporation (NFDC) was headed by Hema Malini, whose allegiance to the BJP is well-known. Kirit Joshi, President of Dharam Hinduja International Centre was appointed Chairman of the Indian Council of

Philosophical Research.[271] Several educational committees had also been constituted by Sangh Parivar adherents.[272]

The RSS is particularly grateful to Joshi for placing numerous Sangh Parivar adherents in universities and government departments. In fact, during the crisis following the Rae Bareli court verdict when Joshi submitted his resignation from office the K.S. of Sudarshan and other RSS leaders acknowledged Joshi's contribution to the saffron agenda and staunchly supported him.[273] Though today the BJP-led NDA government is not in power, the numerous Hindutva oriented bureaucrats appointed by them continue to wield power in the administrative machinery of the Indian government and carry out the RSS agenda.

Saffronisation Process Overseas

Under Joshi's leadership Hindu cultural nationalism was firmly established overseas especially in the United States of America, Canada and the United Kingdom.[274] The Sangh Parivar animates numerous student organisations, Sunday schools and community centre-based workshops for overseas Hindus in order to influence the children of all ages. Special teacher-training workshops are also organised for schools.[275]

There is an increased presence of Sangh Parivar-influenced activity in the Western universities. The foreign arms of the Sangh Parivar organise and encourage many intellectuals abroad to promote Hindutva ideology. They target specific professors whom they accuse of faulty and insulting treatment of Hindu religion and culture. The American Hindu Anti-Discrimination League is one such. There is a pro-Hindu Indian American Intellectual Forum, a New York based group, which organises seminars and studies on Hinduism and Indian culture.[276] There is also much lobbying going on for greater participation of pro-Hindu speakers at seminars and courses and for scholars. It chooses only those scholars who identify with their ideology or adopt a pro-Sangh Parivar position. Thus they ward off critique of Hinduism. Weekly bulletins, quarterly newsletters, and monthlies are published and internet websites are fully utilised for the promotion of Hindutva ideas.

Perhaps the best student organisation sponsored by the Sangh Parivar is Hindu Students' Council (HSC) established in 1990. It has over 70 Chapters and thousands of members across college campuses in the United States and Canada. It publishes a weekly bulletin across the net called 'Hindu Digest' and circulates a newsletter called *Samskar* (culture).[277] The HSC's initiative is expanding the Hindu-Rights' Presence on the internet, creating sites for each university chapters as well as organising an overreaching website for the Global Hindus.[278]

In 1993 the VHP organised an international conference in Washington D.C. called 'Global Vision 2000'.[279] In the same year the HSC organised a youth conference similar to the 'Global Vision 2000', which was attended by over 2100 youths.[280] In 1998 the first *Dharam Sansad* (Parliament of Religion) was held in USA.[281] In 1999 a *yatra* was taken out to ten cities of the US named *Dharma Prasar Yatra* to strengthen the Hindu community.[282] In 2001 the Hindu Leaders Forum was launched to provide a unified global voice for the Hindus. The Forum also launched in the same year a *Vishwa Dharma Prasar Yatra* touching 47 cities and 38 countries covering all five continents.[283]

Sangh Parivar organisations in India receive enormous financial support from the United States for their ideological nourishment in the form of minority bashing literature, websites and propaganda. In 2002 the India Development Relief Fund (IRDF) was found diverting funds to the religious conversion of tribal people.[284]

The Infinity Foundation in Princeton, New Jersey, seeks to influence student perspectives on Hindu culture by direct outreach and by volunteering for teaching-training workshop programmes in city school districts.[285] Since 2003 the *Hindu Swayamsevak Sangh* (HSS) in the USA organises *Sakhi Sammelan* for Hindu women to educate them in Hindu culture, values and heritage.[286]

In May 2003, as part of the indoctrination process of the Indians living overseas in Hindu cultural nationalism, the birthday of Nathuram Godse, who assassinated Mahatma Gandhi the Father of India, was organised by Hindu Unity (HU) which is the US based wing of the Bajrang Dal. The Hindu Mahasabha also made a call to celebrate the birthday of Nathuram Godse on 19 May 2003 and a 'send a message' to the world, it claimed, that they will fight and even die to protect the basic principles of Hinduism.[287] It further denigrated Mahatma Gandhi by saying: "Gandhi was a downright pacifist, without guts and scruples. His constant preaching to his fellow Hindus, to be non-violent at all times, even in the face of aggression, paralysed the manhood of India, mentally and physically."[288]

The Hindu Right-wing's presence on the website is constantly expanding. The Sangh Parivar periodically organises conferences at different universities combining the celebration of 'cultural diversity' code for American Hindu identity with carefully selected history and philosophy lessons. Sangh Parivar in India provides the organisational resources, sends activists, programme mobilising support, and above all by co-ordinating diverse activities under the umbrella of Hindu identity.[289]

According to a study made in 2001 nearly 15 million Americans are attending Yoga centres regularly. Today Yoga has also emerged as a business in America. The number of Yoga centres is sky-rocketing, along with the number of Yoga teachers.[290] In order to take Swami Vivekananda's message abroad and also engage in 'civilisational' and religious dialogues, the *Kendra* has set up Vivekananda Kendra International, which was inaugurated by the then Prime Minister, Atal Bihari Vajpayee on 23 May 2003. When in July 2003 the first ever Global Dharma Conference was held in Edison, New Jersey, in which some 2000 people, primarily youth, from across the world participated, the then HRD minister Joshi present at the Conference urged the Indian Americans to utilise their heritage to show the world a new path.[291] In June 2005 the second International Ramayana Conference was held at Illinois, USA.[292] During the BJP rule in New Delhi there was even an ambassador-at-large for the NRIs and PIOs in the person of Bhishma K. Agnihotri, a staunch Hindutva ideologue.

The temples are one of the important places where the majority of Hindu Indian Americans meet on a regular basis, and these are reportedly controlled by Hindutva elements that actively promote their ideology. The leader of the Hindu Swayamsevak Sangh in the USA, Madan Das Devi, has observed that today almost everywhere in America there are Hindu temples, which organise various religious activities and other celebrations like Diwali, Holi, *bhajans*, study sessions on Hindu scriptures and teachings. Many of the Hindu parents prefer to send their children for special Sunday activities in the temple so that they may get exposure to many aspects of Hindu religion.[293] Youth summer camps to assist second generation Indians to learn about their culture are also used as powerful vehicles to propagate their concept of Indian culture, history, society and politics. There are many Indian Americans who believe that the USA is growing into the most influential fortress for the rallying of the forces of Hindutva after the State of Gujarat.[294]

Attempts are being made by diasporic Hindu nationalist organisations in the USA to intervene in revising lessons on India, Indian history and Hinduism in 6th grade textbooks in California State schools. In 2005 the Curriculum Commission, an advisory body to the California State Board of Education accepted 131 of the 153 revisions proposed by Hindu Education Foundation (HEF) and Vedic Foundation (VF), two groups affiliated to Hindu nationalist ideology. The edits offered by these groups were adopted amid intense lobbying and presented their views as representing those of 'all Hindus' in the diaspora. This bears testimony to the power and resources of diaspora Hindu nationalism and its organising capabilities in the United States.[295] Fortunately, the Hindutva group did not have a walkover, thanks to the vigilance and commitment of many academics involved in Indian studies all over the world. Intervention of professors Michael Witzel and Steve Farmer in the form of a letter, signed by 50 other scholars presented at a public hearing on 9 November 2005 resulted in the Board reversing its initial approval of the pro-Hindutva changes. The scholars made the important point that the corrections proposed by the Hindu Right in the USA reflect political agenda discriminatory to millions of people in India especially the minorities, 'lower' castes and women. Finally, it was agreed that the Board would allow only such changes as meet the standard of objective scholarship.[296]

In June 2003, Harsh Mander wrote after his visit to the USA: "The visit confirmed to me how closely the turbulent recent history of the dramatic rise of [Hindu] right-wing religious fundamentalism and the politics of hatred in India is related to and nourished by the Indian diaspora in the US. An influential segment of this diaspora is ideologically committed to the politics of Hindutva, and shares its irrational malevolent hostility towards minorities, and uncompromising opposition to the vision of a pluralistic, democratic India with genuinely equal citizenship for people of all faiths, caste and gender."[297]

According to Mander, there is evidence of influential political alliances with powerful sections of the American ruling political establishment, especially after the tragic events of 11 September 2001 and the wars against Afghanistan and Iraq. The media is also engaged in demonising the Muslims. All this has created an uncompromising and unprecedented divide between people of Indian origin who are born into the Hindu and Muslims faiths. This spills into even second and third generation Indian Americans and increasingly characterises social relations even in universities.[298]

Mander opines that there is a need to work with young people of Indian origin in the US, including those of second and third generations in order to strengthen their commitment to pluralism, secularism, tolerance, peace and justice. Spaces like place of worship need to be reclaimed from fundamentalist elements; young people need authentic humanistic teachings of their respective faiths. Secular avenues also need to be built to enable them to acquire an undistorted picture of what constitutes Indian culture, its pluralistic and tolerant character, and also its traditional injustices of caste and gender.[299]

It is estimated that today in Britain there are over 300,000 Hindus. The Hindu Forum of Britain claims a membership of over 270 Hindu organisations from different regions and cultural backgrounds in Britain.[300] Meera Nanda informs us that in 1996 the VHP of the United Kingdom produced a book entitled *Explaining Hindu Dharma: A Guide for Teachers* for introducing Hindu ideas and topics in the classroom at the Middle to High School level in the British schools system.[301] It portrays Vedic Aryan India as the 'cradle' of world civilisation and science and advises British teachers to introduce Hindu *dharma* as just another name for 'eternal laws of nature' first discovered by Vedic seers and subsequently confirmed by modern physics and biological sciences.[302]

In 2003 the Vishwa Hindu Parishad, UK, organised a pictorial exhibition on the life of V.D. Savarkar to mark his birth anniversary.[303] In 2005 under the auspices of Hindu Council, UK, some Hindu bodies in England were promoting Hindu education in British schools by interacting with young people between 11 to 18 yeas of age. It was also lobbying for a mechanism through the Department of Education to have multi-faith assemblies in UK schools.[304] Britain is to have the first state-funded Hindu school by 2008.[305]

In Britain, in imitation of the 'Operation Black Vote' launched by the black community the Hindus have launched an 'Operation Hindu Vote" under the banner of the Hindu Forum of Britain. They intent to send a Hindu or two to the House of Commons, for a start.[306] There are reasons to believe that it is a kind of BJP abroad or a British version of Hindu cultural nationalism. In 2004 Nanda asked a pertinent question: "If Hindu propagandists can go this far in UK, imagine their power in India, where they control the Central government and its agencies for media, education and research."[307]

In March 2000 'Agni Corporation', a registered Dutch corporation, was launched with its headquarters in Hague to fight violations of human rights against Hindus at the global level.[308] In 2003 it was reported that in Russia *gurukula* system of schools are run by International Society for Krishna Consciousness (ISKCON or Hare Krishna Movement).[309]

Hindutva has reached also South America. In 2003 Sant Murari Bapu organised a recitation of the *Ram Katha* at a famous Amazon resort known as 'The Aryan Towers' in Brazil. All the residents of this place observed vegetarianism and wore saffron shirts including the hotel resort staff, during the course of Hindu festivals.[310]

In 2000 the RSS World Camp (*Vishva Sangh Shibir*) was organised near Mumbai in which NRIs from 40 countries took part.[311] From 26 December 2005 to 1 January 2006 the *Hindu Swayamsevak Sangh* (HSS), an NRI organisation, held a seven-day world convention (*Vishva Sangh Shibir*) in Ahmedabad, Gujarat, in which some 510 delegates from 32 countries of the world participated. Among other things they alleged that there is distortion of Hinduism in textbooks abroad and errors in the World Almanac about Hinduism.[312]

Indoctrination as the Aim of Saffronisation of Education

The Sangh Parivar's educational strategy has many similarities with fascist forms of education. The Italian scholar of Indian politics Marzia Casolari tells us that B.S. Moonje, the politician close to the RSS, after meeting Benito Mussolini, the Italian fascist leader in Rome on 19 March 1931, wrote two pages in his diary where he described the keystone of the fascist system as *indoctrination* rather than education of youths.[313] Perhaps the word 'indoctrination' sums up the ultimate aim of Joshi's educational reforms. Indoctrination of the young generation has been the strategy followed by all major fascists and dictators of history. Inspired and guided by his ideological family, Joshi followed the same trodden path through his saffronisation of education from school education through university studies to advanced research.

The RSS always wanted to shape the future citizens of the Hindu nation through their system of education. As the head of the HRD ministry Joshi envisaged an educational strategy which would ensure the realisation of this agenda. Even today the popularity of this education system is soaring among the Indian middle and lower classes for various reasons. While government schools have almost become defunct and private English medium schools have become very expensive, the RSS-run schools charge a reasonable fee. Besides, as the RSS schools impart cultural values like respect for elders and learning of Hindu traditions, middle class parents feel that their children are getting an all-round education at a nominal price.[314]

Thanks to Joshi, enormous funds have been poured into implementing the Hindutva agenda, and priorities of academic and cultural institutions have been altered. Lakhs of school children are growing up with prejudice and hatred towards the minorities and in total ignorance of the pluralistic and composite heritage of the country.[315]

Joshi as an RSS ideologue was convinced that for the realisation of the Hindu *rashtra* it is imperative to invest in the education of the young. Hitler held a similar belief. He used to say: *Wer die Jugend hat, hat die Zukunft* ('The one who has the youth, has the future'). Accordingly he began a system of education in order to indoctrinate the young minds with falsehood, propaganda and hatred for communities that did not belong to the so-called superior Aryan race. Thus school textbooks and other learning materials were tailored to his project. A typical example of it can be found in a *Kinderbuch* (Children's Book) prepared by the Nazis which has a chapter entitled *Der Giftpilz* (The Poisonous Mushroom). While collecting mushrooms in the forest the mother tells her little son Franz: "*Es gibt gute Menschen. Und es gibt schlechte Menschen. Die Schlechte Menschen sind die Juden* ('There are good people and bad people. The bad people are the Jews')."[316] "*Die Juden sind schlechte Menschen. Sie sind wie Giftpilz*"[317] ('The Jews are the bad people. They are like the poisonous mushroom"). "*Wie ein einziger Giftpilz eine ganze Familie toten kann, so kann ein einziger Jude ein ganzes Dorf, eine ganze Stadt, ja sogar ein ganzes Volk vernichten*"[318] (Just as a single poisonous mushroom can kill a entire family, so also the Jews can destroy the entire village, the entire town and even an entire generation of peoples'). In the Indian context, for the Hindutva ideologues and organisations the *Giftpilz* are the Muslims, Christians, Parsis, Jews, Communists, Dalits, Tribals and other minorities.

In Nazi Germany, fascism developed several characteristics, one among them was adoption of propaganda as a key instrument of State policy. On 13 March 1933 Adolf Hitler started a new department in his government for Culture and Propaganda (*Reichsministerium für Volksaufklärung und Propaganda*) with Dr Joseph Goebbels as its head. Goebbels who considered himself as an expert in German culture was eager to accept that post. During the Third Reich of Hitler, Joseph Goebbels was described as the 'brain behind the manipulation of minds'.[319] Hitler then established another ministry for Science (*Wissenschaft*), Education (*Erziehung*) and education of people (*Volksbildung*) with Bernhard Rust as its head. Both these ministries were inventions of Hitler for the propagation of his ideology.[320]

We may argue that in the Indian context the roles of Goebbels and Rust were played by Joshi as the head of the HRD ministry. He was also the brain behind the manipulation of minds through his Hindutva oriented educational policy. Through his meticulously calculated and zealously implemented educational strategy he wanted to ensure that future generations of Indians would grow up steeped in distorted version of Indian history, ignorance, prejudice against all non-Hindu religions, cultures and peoples and hatred for all minorities. According K.N. Panikkar, under Joshi's guidance, the entire educational curriculum was given a communal orientation, history was re-written and the achievements of indigenous science was romanticised. To implement these ideas a large number of schools were set up, particularly in tribal areas. Even the funds of scientific research institutions were diverted to 'invent' and privilege the 'Hindu sciences'. The 'achievements' of the BJP government in these areas being of a high order, it would require considerable effort to undo the damage to the educational system of the country.[321] Hence he says that it is not true that the BJP has not achieved a measure of success in colouring the state institutions saffron and turning them into powerful instruments of communal discourse. The impact of their effort is quite evident in the fields of education, science and technology and culture. Simultaneously, secular values have been undermined and the secular character of public institutions has been deformed.[322]

Joshi's Saffronisation Project Essentially as an RSS Agenda

Joshi's project of saffronisation of Indian education and cultural institutions was in essence an RSS agenda. The RSS involvement in the field of education and culture is not anything new. The *Vidhya Bharati* schools existed throughout the Nehruvian era of politics, and they grew even while the RSS was banned. While in power, the BJP government in New Delhi gave more space and freedom to the RSS and its affiliated organisations to implement their curricula of Hindu cultural nationalism in education. Consequently, the RSS control over the organisational and institutional network of cultural and educational bodies increased tremendously during the BJP rule. The government resources were freely made available to the Sangh Parivar, and unrestricted freedom was given to implement the Hindutva agenda more fiercely and openly than ever before in Indian history.

According to Bidwai, Joshi as the HRD minister, made about 250 key appointments to institutions as variant as the IGNCA, UGC, ICHR and NCERT. Many RSS insiders say that he did much more than Advani to advance the Hindutva ideology. He alone among the BJP ministers appointed hardcore RSS cadres to his personal staff, and his saffronisation is far more thorough and dangerous than anything.[323] Bidwai goes on to add that Joshi was perhaps the crudest personification of bigotry to adorn the HRD ministry, and was bent on destroying every vestige of independence and secularism from the academic world. He deliberately stuffed the research institutions with RSS cadres who often lacked academic competence and even integrity. His entire agenda was to divide, split, ruthlessly push communalism as part of Hindutva's aggressive project to colonise the Indian minds with hatred and infuse poison into the educational system which would affect the whole generation of Indians.[324]

BJP, the political wing of the RSS, was asked to utilise its political privileges to radically re-mould civil society in line with RSS ideology. Accordingly, Joshi relentlessly pursued the ideal as a fanatic RSS ideologue. By using the powers of patronage he managed to ensure the collaboration of a section of the intelligentsia in this effort. Several intellectuals and cultural leaders were more than willing to act as his collaborators. The alternative education proposed by the Sangh Parivar as indigenous system was implemented by the BJP-led government. It was a system which M.S.

Golwalkar had earlier conceived as religious in character, with emphasis on tradition, discipline and military training, romanticisation of traditional knowledge, celebration of religious beliefs and emphasis on conformism.[325]

The RSS, since the time of its inception, has been attempting to construct a Hindu identity and homogenise the Hindus. Golwalkar gave a decisive thrust to the agenda of homogenisation when he created the Sangh Parivar to attract and assimilate different identities into the framework of Hindu *rashtra*. But the actual credit goes to Balasaheb Deoras for giving a dynamic orientation to the RSS project of homogenisation. Deoras was intelligent enough to sense that the Dalits, the tribals and the women were getting conscious of their socio-political rights and looking for self-expression. He had the foresight to see their immense political potential as vote banks. Hence he argued that all these sections needed to be carefully integrated, assimilated and homogenised for the success of the RSS mission.[326] The *Ekal Vidyalayas* set up and manned by the RSS and the VHP and the sanskritisation of Dalits and tribal worship practices have played a major role in bringing these marginalised groups under the umbrella of Hinduism.

The RSS was always opposed to the educational system in India and considered it a vestige from the colonial era. It wanted an educational system based exclusively on the principles of Hindutva. It opposes English as medium of instruction and views the special permission granted to the minorities for the sustenance of educational institutions as a tacit act of discrimination against the Hindu religion. With the BJP assuming power in New Delhi in the late 1990s the RSS made sure that the key portfolio of education remained with a proven Hindutva ideologue, and Joshi was assigned this ministry. His task was to complete the unfinished RSS agenda that was initiated in 1977 during the Janata Party government.[327] However, it is to be noted that saffronisation of education was already part of the agenda of the Hindu Mahasabha in the last century. In the *Hindu Mahasabha Ideals* published in 1950 we read: "The Hindu Mahasabha is fully cognisant of the short-comings of the present education and examination system, and shall set up, as soon as may be, an Education Board, [...] to prepare an education scheme more in consonance with the actual requirements and *ideological aspirations of Hindudom*."[328]

Under Joshi's guidance the educational curricula underwent major changes. In the new system value education was given importance which was perceived as a major input in the process of character building of students as well as a means for the inculcation of healthy social attitudes. Unfortunately, in practice, the value of education was restricted to Hindu religious instruction, which was a step towards inculcating not only religious but also communal view of the world.[329] One of the major compulsions for changing the content of education was the realisation of the communal objective of creating a Hindu national identity and national pride. Some of the negative effects of such a system of education are a false sense of pride bordering on chauvinism which is detrimental to the pursuit of knowledge and creating a generation incapable of critically interrogating the problems of society.[330]

Scholars opine that Joshi's educational policies were primarily aimed at redefining India in religious terms, with a promotion of Hinduised history by the Sangh Parivar. The soul of Hinduisation is a religious interpretation of the past so that a communal history is created. In this new interpretation all communities other than the Hindus are identified as foreigners and therefore enemies of the nation. The efforts made to prove the indigenous origins of the Aryans is part of establishing historical legitimacy for Hindu nationhood. A concerted effort was made to create an alternate historical consciousness not only through school textbooks, research projects sponsored by the ICHR, but also through extensive distribution of pamphlets in the vernacular distributed through religious and social networks of the Sangh Parivar. As for the contents they do not make any distinction between myth and history.[331]

In the educational system proposed by the Sangh Parivar the students are frequently exhorted to look back nostalgically to an alleged glorious past when the Indians were highly cultured, enlightened, prosperous, powerful, religious-minded and tolerant. But the truth is quite different from the claim. For instance, historian Abraham Eraly reminds us that Alberuni, the great Arab scholar of the 10th century AD, left a record stating that 'Indians came to believe that there is no country but theirs, no nation like theirs, no kings like theirs, no religion like theirs, no science like theirs. They are haughty and foolishly vain. If they had travelled and mixed with other nations, they would have changed their mind, for their ancestors were not so narrow-minded.[332]

Meera Nanda argues that Hinduism is a religion which refuses to grant other faiths their distinctiveness and difference, even as it proclaims its great 'tolerance'. Hinduism's tolerance is a mere disguise for its narcissistic obsession with its own greatness.[333] In this sense Joshi's saffronisation of education is an expression of the intolerance of his ideological family towards all non-Hindu religions and cultures.

Gurcharan Das observes that ancient Indians were cruel, barbarous, mean and oppressive to the weak. But they also created masterpieces like *Mahabharata* and *Ramayana*. It is something that we cannot even imagine doing today in our more 'enlightened' age. But these great epic masterpieces belong to the ancients and that world is long gone. Hence there is no point in trying to slavishly recreate it, even if we could. Our world has science, democracy, the Internet and the prosperity engendered by rapid economic growth. The best we can do, Das argues, with our past is first to read about it with a critical eye as the source of historical materials and myths; then learn from it with a legitimate expectation that it might help us to understand ourselves better.[334]

Joshi's saffronisation of education and cultural institutions was essentially the implementation of the RSS educational project which has much similarity with that of Hitler's. In fact, Bidwai argues that a line of continuity runs from Savarkar and Mussoslini to Golwalkar and Nathuram Godse, from Hedgewar and Upadhyaya to Advani, Joshi, Vajpayee and Thackeray, from Hitler's *Schutzstaffel* to Shiv Sena.[335]

The ultimate aim of Joshi's educational policy was to create a Hindu rashtra out of India, promote the hegemony of the upper castes, maintain the divide between the majority community and the minorities, make the Hindus aggressive and war like race, indoctrinate the rising generation in Hindu cultural nationalism and maintain the gender inequality as demanded by the orthodox Hindu law. When it was opposed by the UPA government which came to power in 2004, the Sangh Parivar launched a counter offensive called the *Siksha Bachao Andolan* (Save Education Campaign)[336] and made efforts to take the campaign to grassroot level.

Conclusion

The BJP-led government in New Delhi embarked upon the controversial and partisan agenda of saffronisation of Indian education and cultural institutions with single-minded determination, and it appointed Murli Manohar Joshi as the Human Resources

Development minister to supervise and execute the sinister project. Today Joshi remains as the minister to have pushed the saffron agenda *undeterred by considerations of truth, cultural pluralism, secular and democratic principles*. This has led some political thinkers to consider him as the most unashamed voice of the Hindu-right.[337] Others argue that through the systematic process of saffronisation, communal divide, religious fundamentalism, Hindu cultural nationalism, intolerance, downplaying of scientific temper and implicit degrading of reason have come to stay in India for many years to come. Consequently, education and cultural life in India are at crossroads because their liberal and secular character and content, carefully nourished during the last fifty years, despite several vicissitudes, is now undergoing fundamental transformation. This change rather hurriedly pushed through by Joshi and his ministry is not in consonance with the guiding principles of our country. The strategies adopted by him aims at laying the foundations of a new system of education and worldview that uncritically privileges the indigenous and celebrates the religious.[338] Hence saffronisation of education and the cultural institutions of India is perhaps the worst crime that Joshi has committed against the people of India, especially the young generation. In essence his was a game plan, in connivance with the RSS, for the indoctrination of the young minds in the most dangerous, anti-national, downright sectarian and divisive agenda called Hindutva.

Notes

1. "Going over the Top", 10. This comment has been described as containing 'embarrassing epithets'. See ibid.
2. See http://www.bjp.org/leader/mmjoshi.htm
3. See "Hindutva: Consciousness of the Country", 7.
4. See *The Indian Express*, 30 December 2003.
5. For a critical study of Swami Vivekananda's concept of Hindu nationalism see J. Kuruvachira, *Hindu Nationalists of Modern India*, 45-65.
6. It is Tilak's commentary on the *Bhagavad Gita*. He claims that his commentary shows how the Hindu religious philosophy is applied to the solution of the ethical problems involved in everyday life. See B.G. Tilak, *Selected Documents*, vol. 2, 118. According to Tilak, what is

expounded in the *Gita* is not the 'path of renunciation' (*jana marga*) or the 'path of devotion' (*bhakti marga*) but the 'path of righteous action (*karmayoga*). By action (*karma*) Tilak means duty, and the duty of a *kshatriya* (warrior) is to fight. It is his *karmayoga.*

7. For a detailed exposition of B.G. Tilak's Hindu nationalist philosophy and ethics see J. Kuruvachira, *Hindu Nationalists of Modern India,* 66-112.
8. For an overview of the Hindu nationalist views of Aurobindo see Aurobindo, *India's Rebirth,* Mysore, (3rd edition 2000).
9. He argued: "...nationalism is not politics but a religion, a creed, a faith. [...] I say that it is the Sanatana Dharma which for us is nationalism". Aurobindo, *India's Rebirth,* 50.
10. Aurobindo says: "If the virtue of Ahimsa comes to the Kshatriya, if you say I will not kill, there is no one to protect the country". Aurobindo, *India's Rebirth,* 55.
11. He said: "What India needs especially at this moment is the aggressive virtues, the spirit of soaring idealism, bold creation, fearless resistance, courageous attack; of the passive tamasic spirit of inertia we have already too much." Aurobindo, *India's Rebirth,* 23; "I believe in an aggressive and expanding, not in a narrowly defensive and self-contradicting Hinduism." ibid., 131.
12. Upadhyaya joined the RSS in 1937 and abandoned his university studies (he left before completing the first year of MA in English) in order to dedicate himself entirely to the organisation he had joined. He worked for the organisation first as *pracharak* in Lakhimpur district, then as joint *prant pracharak* between 1947 and 1951, and finally as an editor, launching a weekly called *Panchjanya.* When the Jana Sangh was founded he became the secretary of the same in Uttar Pradesh. Later he became the General Secretary of the Jana Sangh and held that office till 1967. During this period he played a major role in reshaping its political philosophy and making the party a replica and auxiliary of the RSS. Many RSS ideologues describe him as the ideal *swayamsevak.* He is noted for his concept 'Integral Humanism' which provided the basic philosophy for the Jana Sangh. See C. Jaffrelot, *The Hindu Nationalist Movement,* 119, 123-124.
13. Rajendra Singh joined the RSS in 1942. He became an RSS *pracharak* in 1944, General Secretary of the RSS in 1978, and *sarsangchalak* in 1994. He holds an MSc in Physics. See C. Jaffrelot, *The Hindu Nationalist Movement,* 47,61,67,310.
14. See M.S. Golwalkar, *Bunch of Thoughts,* 177-201. Here he deals with Muslims, Christians and Communists in three different chapters with the title 'Internal Threats' in order to drive home his point.

15. Golwalkar said: "To keep up the purity of the Race and its culture, Germany shocked the world by her purging the country of the semitic Races [sic] – the Jews. Race pride at its highest has been manifested here. Germany has also shown how well-nigh [sic] impossible it is for Races and cultures, having differences going to the root, to be assimilated into one united whole, a good reason for us in Hindustan to learn and profit by". M.S. Golwalkar, *We*, 35.
16. Golwalkar argued: "the foreign races in Hindustan must either adopt the Hindu culture and language, must learn to respect and hold in reverence Hindu religion, must entertain no idea but those of the glorification of the Hindu race and culture [...] or may stay in the country, wholly subordinated to the Hindu Nation, claiming nothing, deserving no privileges, far less any preferential treatment – not even citizen's rights". M.S. Golwalkar, *We*, 47-48.
17. See K. Elst, *Decolonising*, 169.
18. Akhil Bharatiya Vidyarthi Parishad was founded in July 1948 by Madhok Balraj in Delhi with approval from the RSS in order to infiltrate student organisations. See C. Jaffrelot, *The Hindu Nation list Movement*, 126.
19. See M.M. Joshi, "My Days with Deendayalji", 30-31.
20. See P. Kanungo, *RSS Tryst with Politics*, 204.
21. See *Today's 'Iron Man'*, 50.
22. See P. Kanungo, *RSS Tryst with Politics*, 206.
23. See P.C. Swain, *Bharatiya Janata Party*, 108.
24. See "What's the Party Line?", 48.
25. See V. Ramakrishnan, "A Rough Ride Ahead", 25.
26. *India Today*, 26 December 2005, 307.
27. K. Singh, "One-eyed Justice", 10.
28. See A.G. Noorani, "How Advani Went Scot-Free", 47.
29. For the key elements of Hitler's Nazification of the school system see W. Keim, *Erziehung unter der Nazi-Diktatur*, band–1, 86-87.
30. See http://www.awaazsaw.org/ibf/appendix6.htm
31. *Organiser*, 29 February 2004, 1
32. M.S. Golwalkar, *Bunch of Thoughts*, 380.
33. See B. Madhok, *Portrait of a Martyr*, 189-201.
34. See V. Ramakrishnan, "Hindutva Institutions in Education. The Spreading Network of RSS" as cited in http://www.sacw.net/HateEducation/Ramak101198.html. (Originally published in *Frontline*, 7-20 November 1998).

35. See http://www.awaazsaw.org/ibf/appendix6.html
36. See V. Ramakrishnan, "Hindutva Institutions in Education. The Spreading Network of RSS" as cited in http://www.sacw.net/HateEducation/Ramak101198.html
37. See http://www.vidyabharati.org/aboutus.asp; H.V. Seshadri (ed.), *RSS A Vision in Action*, 276-277.
38. See M.G. Chitkara, *Rashtriya Swayamsevak Sangh*, 288.
39. See *The Week*, 15 November 1998; http://www.hvk.org/articles/1198/0005.html
40. See H. Boro, "Free Education from Western Bonds", 20.
41. See C.P. Bhambhri, "Sangh Parivar in Government", 10.
42. See K.N. Panikkar, *Before the Night Fall*, 63, 80.
43. See H.V. Seshadri (ed.), *RSS A Vision in Action*, 278.
44. See V. Ramakrishnan, "Hindutva Institutions in Education. The Spreading Network of RSS" as cited in http://www.sacw.net/HateEducation/Ramak101198.html.
45. See *RSS Resolves*, 4.
46. An RSS resolution of 1961 says, "it is necessary that we unhesitatingly recognise the Hindu character of our nation as give up notions of pseudo-secularism". *RSS Resolves*, 26.
47. See P. Kanungo, *RSS Tryst with Politics*, 168-169. An institution which promotes typical Hindu culture is *Sanskar Bharati*, which celebrates its silver jubilee in 2007. See "Sanskar Bharati to Celebrate *Sanskritik Navchetana Varsha*", 17.
48. See P. Kanungo, *RSS Tryst with Politics*, 169.
49. See H.V. Seshadri (ed.), *RSS A Vision in Action*, 279.
50. See H.V. Seshadri (ed.), *RSS A Vision in Action*, 287. *Gurukul* system was the name given to the ancient Indian method of education. *Guru* is a spiritual preceptor. In ancient India the *guru* received pupils in his own *ashram* (hermitage). The pupil (*chela* or *shishya*) gave him implicit obedience, worked for him in the household and paid him great reverence. See B. Walker, *Hindu World*, vol. 1, 419.
51. See V. Ramakrishnan, "Hindutva Institutions in Education. The Spreading Network of RSS" as cited in http://www.sacw.net/HateEducation/Ramak101198.html
52. See "The Many Children of the Sangh Parivar", 1058. For more information on saffronisation of education see also "Saffronising Goa" 1129-1134.
53. See A. Pushparajan, "A Secular Critique of Hindutva", 240.

54. See V. Ramakrishnan, "Hindutva Institutions in Education. The Spreading Network of RSS" as cited in http://www.sacw.net/HateEducation/Ramak101198.html
55. See S. Vishwanahan, "The Spread in the South", 11.
56. See V. Ramakrishnan, "Hindutva Institutions in Education. The spreading network of RSS" as cited in http://www.sacw.net/HateEducation/Ramak101198.html
57. See V. Ramakrishnan, "Hindutva Institutions in Education. The spreading network of RSS" as cited in http://www.sacw.net/HateEducation/Ramak101198.html
58. See M.G. Chitkara, *Rashtriya Swayamsevak Sangh*, 291.
59. See "Aksharadaan Abhiyan in North-east Villages", 12.
60. See "Breeding Bigotry", 126.
61. See V. Ramakrishnan, "Hindutva Institutions in Education. The spreading network of RSS" as cited in http://www.sacw.net/HateEducation/Ramak101198.html
62. See V. Ramakrishnan, "Hindutva Institutions in Education. The spreading network of RSS" as cited in http://www.sacw.net/HateEducation/Ramak101198.html
63. See http://www.vidyabharati.org/kendras.asp
64. See http://www.vidyabharati.org/kendras.asp
65. See http://www.vidyabharati.org/kendras.asp
66. See P. Kanungo, *RSS Tryst with Politics*, 169.
67. See http://www.vidyabharati.org/kendras.asp
68. See "Massive Literacy Drive by Sewa Bharati in Delhi", 17.
69. See M.G. Chitkara, *Rashtriya Swayamsevak Sangh*, 266-267; C. Jaffrelot, *The Hindu Nationalist Movement*, 322.
70. The Sangh Parivar has set up a several of organisations that focus on tribal areas. Some of the prominent ones are: *Vanavasi Kalyan Ashram, Ekal Vidyalaya, Sewa Bharati, Vivekananda Kendra, Bharat Kalyan Pratishthan*, Friends of Tribal Society, etc. Locally, the activities of RSS service organisations overlap with each other. All major RSS affiliates undertake work among 'tribal' groups, often in the same regions and districts. Similarly, one affiliate may organise events and activities which are participated in and attended by members and supporters of the other affiliates. For example, RSS one-teacher schools (*Ekal Vidyalayas* in 'tribal' areas) can be organised under the umbrella of the VHP, *Sewa Bharati, Vidhya Bharati*, the *Vanavasi Kalyan Ashram* or all of these organisations. The RSS service department (*sewa vibhag*) considers *all* the various projects of *Sewa Bharati, Vidhya*

Bharati, Rashtra Sevika Samiti, the VHP, the VHP's *Mahila Mandal*, the *Vanavasi Kalyan Ashram*, the *Bharat Vikas Parishad*, the *Akhil Bharatiya Vidyarthi Parishad*, the *Bharatiya Mazdoor Sangh* and the one-teacher schools as part of its single vision and activities. See http://www.awaazsaw.org/ibf/appendix6.html

71. See *The Times of India*, 25 April 2004.
72. See "We are there to Support them, 13.
73. http://www.vskgujarat.com/like_minded_organization/vanavasi_kalyan_ashram.html
74. See "Connecting Northeast with Rest of the Country", 17.
75. See http://www.awaazsaw.org/ibf/appendix6.html
76. See *The Times of India*, 25 April 2004.
77. See http://www.hssworld.org/seva/sevadisha/sevadisha1/vanavasi_kalyan_ashram.html
78. See "Revolutionising Literacy in Remote Rural India", 6.
79. See "VHP to Triple Its Service Projects in Vanavasi Areas", 12; "One Lakh Ekal Vidyalyas by 2011", 9.
80. See "Revolutionising Literacy in Remote Rural India", 6.
81. See M.C. Menon, "Another Blow to VHP", 20-21. There has been serious allegations of misappropriation of funds by *Ekal Vidyalayas*, FTS, SSA and other organisations. For details see ibid., 19-22.
82. *The Hindustan Times*, 29 July 2000.
83. See *The Hindu*, 20 November 2002.
84. See *The Hindustan Times:* 29 July 2000.
85. See V. Surya, "Bitter Lessons", 84.
86. See K. Bamzai, "Elementary Failure", 54.
87. See K. Bamzai, "Elementary Failure", 55.
88. Illiteracy is considered as the greatest shame of India. At the time of India's independence the literacy rate was 17 per cent. After fifty years – in 1997 – it was only 62 per cent. In 2001 it was 66 per cent. This is far from satisfactory. It is believed that if India becomes fully literate it is sure to become one of the world's most important knowledge societies. Besides, with increase in the literacy rate, India can carve out for itself a niche in the fields of Science and Technology and other creative fields. In addition, there would be rapid economic growth and poverty, malnutrition, disease and squalour will be eradicated.
89. See K. Bamzai, "Elementary Failure", 56.
90. For details see V. Surya, "Strong on Slogans", 86-87.

91. See R. Govinda, "Class Struggle", 51.
92. See S. Gatade, "Enter 'Hero Hitler!", 21-22.
93. See P. Bidwai, "Sanskrit and *Sanskriti* as Weapons", 33.
94. See T.K. Rajalakshmi, "For a Holistic Curriculum", 85.
95. For some samples of such criticism see such publications by SAHMAT as *Against Communalisation of Education*, (2001); *The Saffron Agenda in Education. An Exposé*, (2001); *Saffronised and Substandard. A Critique of the New NCERT Textbooks*, (2002); *Communalisation of Education. The Assault on History*, (2002); *Plagiarised and Communalised. More on the NCERT Textbooks* (2003).
96. See excerpts from a statement released by SAHMAT in New Delhi on 26 June 2003, as cited in *Communalism Combat*, June-July 2003, 19.
97. See S.R. Chowdhury, "The Killing of Gandhi", 9. But Gopal Godse, the younger brother of Nathuram Godse argues that the latter did not leave the RSS. See "Gopal Godse", 27. Godse later said that he had done his duty (i.e. killing of Mahatma Gandhi) like Arjuna in the *Mahabharata* whom Krishna advised to kill his own relatives because they were evil. See Godse, *Gandhihatya ani Mee*, 46, 221, as cited in A. Nandy, *Bonfire of Creeds*, 87.
98. See "Hitler, Godse Idolise, not the Mahatma", 2. Patrick Nair reports that at Nagpur the RSS have built a shrine in honour of Godse. See P. Nair, "RSS' Godse Shrine", 47.
99. See "Hitler, Godse Idolised, not the Mahatma", 2.
100. See S. Gatade, "Enter 'Hero Hitler!", 21.
101. See "Hitler, a Hero", 5. See also B.S. Parakh (ed.), *Contemporary India*, 10.
102. See *Saffronised and Substandard*, 6.
103. See "Hitler, Godse Idolised, not the Mahatma'", 2.
104. See N. Kaur, "To Undo the Damage", 21-22.
105. For descriptions of some concrete cases of deep-seated gender bias' see A. Sadgopal, "Gender and Education", 100.
106. C. Srinivas, "Textbooks Sectarian Story or History?", 20.
107. C. Srinivas, "Textbooks Sectarian Story or History?", 21.
108. S. Mukherji, "The NCERT Conspiracy", 29.
109. See *India Today*, 20 October 2003, 44; S. Bhattacharya, "NCERT: Rewriting Indian History, Xeroxing World History", 14.
110. "All Parties must Back It", 23.
111. "All Parties must Back It", 23.
112. See *Organiser*, 5 January 2003, 15.

113. http://www.hinduismtoday.com/archives/1994/6/1994-6-03.shtml
114. http://www.hinduismtoday.com/archives/2005/1-3/62-65_tradition.shtml
115. See D.K. Rath, "A Centre for Dialogue on Civilisations", 17.
116. http://www.sriramakrishna.org/education.html
117. See M. S. Aiyar, *Confessions of a Secular Fundamentalist*, 95-96.
118. See V. Ramakrishnan, "Hindutva Institutions in Education. The spreading network of RSS" as cited in http://www.sacw.net/HateEducation/Ramak101198.html
119. See P. Kanungo, *RSS Tryst with Politics*, 166.
120. For a brief history and philosophy of *Vande Mataram* see S. Bhattacharya, *Vande Mataram*, (2003). However, it may be remembered that Nehru said in 1948 that *Vande Mataram* for all its beauty and history is not as easy tune for orchestral or band rendering. It is rather plaintive and mournful and repetitive. It has not got the peculiar distinctive features which *Jana Gana Mana* has. It represents very truthfully the period of our struggle in longing and not so much the fulfilment thereof in the future. The language of *Vande Mataram* is very difficult for the average person. See S. Gopal and U. Iyengar (eds.), *The Essential Writings of Jawaharlal Nehru*, vol. 1, 706.
121. See P. Kanungo, *RSS Tryst with Politics*, 167.
122. See "Recognize Your Glorious Heritage", 9.
123. See D. de Souza, "Goa New Hindutva Lab", 26.
124. See "Communalisation of Education and Culture", 14.
125. As cited in "Communalisation of Education and Culture", 15.
126. As cited in "Communalisation of Education and Culture", 15.
127. See "Communalisation of Education and Culture", 17.
128. See "Communalisation of Education and Culture", 17.
129. See "Communalisation of Education and Culture", 17.
130. See "Communalisation of Education and Culture", 18.
131. As cited in "Communalisation of Education and Culture", 17.
132. See "Communalisation of Education and Culture", 11.
133. P. Kumar, "A Brand India School Network", 4.
134. See *Saffronised Substandard*, 7.
135. See *RSS Resolves*, 78.
136. In May 1977 the then Prime Minister Morarji Desai received an anonymous memorandum demanding the withdrawal from public circulation of four history books, of which three were intended for use in teaching: *Medieval India* by Romila Thapar, *Modern India* by

Bipin Chandra, *Freedom Struggle* by A. Tripathi, Barun De and Bipin Chandra, and *Communalism and the Writing of Indian History* by Romila Thapar, Harbans Mukhia and Bipin Chandra. The Prime Minister was willing to withdraw these books from circulation. But a confidential note leaked out to the authors of these books who protested invoking secular values. Finally, the government passed an Act in July 1978 withdrawing another school textbook, *Ancient India* by R.S. Sharma who was a target of criticism by the RSS. See C. Jaffrelot, *The Hindu Nationalist Movement in India*, 287-288.

137. See P. Kanungo, *RSS Tryst with Politics*, 166-167.
138. See P. Kanungo, *RSS Tryst with Politics*, 167.
139. See "Communalisation of Education and Culture", 12. See a report on an exhibition in the National Museum New Delhi on the Harappan Culture and how distorted and questionable the presentations were. See ibid., 18-20.
140. See "Communalisation of Education and Culture", 10-11.
141. See R. Brahmachari, "India: The Mother of Western Civilisation", 11.
142. See V.M. Jha, "A New Brand of History", 87.
143. See http://www.foil.org/newsflash/appendixg.html
144. See P. Menon, "Concerns of History", 40.
145. See P. Menon, "A Debate on Historians", 41.
146. See D. de Souza, "Goa New Hindutva Lab", 27.
147. See T.K. Rajalakshmi, "Removing an Irritant", 126.
148. See I.K. Shukla, "Gujarat was Gifted to Godse", 6.
149. See I. Habib. "The Rewriting of History by the Sangh Parivar", 39.
150. See V. Trimondi and V. Trimondi, *Hitler, Buddha, Krishna*. 35.
151. *Ithihas Gaa Raha Hai*, as cited in see "Communalisation of Education and Culture", 13-14.
152. As cited in "Communalisation of Education and Culture", 15.
153. As cited in "Communalisation of Education and Culture", 15-16.
154. As cited in "Communalisation of Education and Culture", 16.
155. As cited in "Communalisation of Education and Culture", 16.
156. http://www.foil.org/newsflash/appendixg.html
157. http://www.foil.org/newsflash/appendixg.html
158. See http://www.foil.org/newsflash/appendixg.html
159. See P. Menon, "Books of Bias and Errors", 74-75.
160. See P. Menon, "Books of Bias and Errors", 75.
161. As cited in "Demonising Christianity, Islam", 125.

162. As cited in "Demonising Christianity, Islam", 125.
163. See P. Menon, "Books of Bias and Errors", 75.
164. As cited in "Demonising Christianity, Islam", 124.
165. See "Demonising Christianity, Islam", 124.
166. As cited in "Demonising Christianity, Islam", 124.
167. As cited in "Demonising Christianity, Islam", 124.
168. See K.N. Panikkar, "Outsider as Enemy", 47.
169. I. Habib. "The Rewriting of History by the Sangh Parivar", 45.
170. P.S. Tripathi, "A Trial Run", 25.
171. See K. Sharma, "Blot on History", 43.
172. See K.N. Panikkar, "Outsider as Enemy", 55.
173. In 2002 a case study was made by the present author on the Philosophy curriculum proposed for Bachelor of Arts by the UGC for Indian universities. It was published as an article in the national weekly *Indian Currents*. See J. Kuruvachira, "The New UGC Philosophy Curriculum", 40-44. In 2005 the Orissa government ruled by the BJD–BJP was considering unifying varsities through uniform syllabus. The ABVP which is the student wing of the BJP ardently welcomed it. See "Unifying Varsities through Uniform Syllabus", 16.
174. See S. Chandrasekhar, "Shun Western Approach", 20.
175. See R. Ramachandran, "Astrology on a Pedestal", 49.
176. M. Nanda, "Postmodernism", Part I, 79.
177. S. Vasudev and N. Mishra, "It's Not in Your Stars", 87.
178. See *Saffronised Substandard*, 8.
179. See R. Ramachandran, "Astrology on a Pedestal", 48.
180. See R. Ramachandran, "Astrology on a Pedestal", 48
181. See R. Ramachandran, "Astrology on a Pedestal", 48, 50.
182. See R. Ramachandran, "Astrology on a Pedestal", 48.
183. See S. Vasudev and N. Mishra, "It's Not in Your Stars", 86. For this research which began in London in 1958, 2000 Piscean babies were selected for a medical study. The goal was to explore future health and whether proximity in birth timings translated into identical personality trains. Dean and Kelly studied more than 100 different characteristics, including occupation, anxiety levels, aggressiveness, mathematics and reading [illegible] of which, astrologers claim, can be gauged from one's birth chart or is deciphered on the basis of sun signs. The research did not find any similarities between the 'time twins'. See ibid.

184. See S. Vasudev and N. Mishra, "It's' Not in Your Stars", 86.
185. See "HRD Ministry Its Master's Voice", 131.
186. See R. Ramachandran, "Astrology on a Pedestal", 48.
187. See http://newsanalysis-intl.tripod.com/astrology.hmtl
For a good critical evaluation of astrology see also A.V. Shetty, "Vedic Astrology in Indian Universities, 66-71.
188. See S. Vasudev and N. Mishra, "Its' Not in Your Stars", 88.
189. See http://newsanalysis-intl.tripod.com/astrology.html
190. See V. Trimondi and V. Trimondi, *Hitler, Buddha Krishna*, 24-25.
191. See V. Trimondi and V. Trimondi, *Hitler, Buddha Krishna*, 36.
192. See A. Pushparajan, "A Secular Critique of Hindutva", 243; S. Vedantam, "Tamil Nadu", 11.
193. See N. Hebbar, "Caste as Priests", 20.
194. See S. Vedantam, "Tamil Nadu", 11.
195. See K.N. Panikkar, "Whither Indian Education", 28.
196. See P. Bidwai, "Sanskrit and *Sanskriti* as Weapons" 35.
197. See V. Trimondi and V. Trimondi, *Hitler, Buddha Krishna*, 36.
198. See M. Nanda, "Postmodernism", Part I, 81.
199. See M. Nanda, "Postmodernism", Part I, 81.
200. See M. Nanda, "Postmodernism", Part I, 81.
201. See M. Nanda, "Postmodernism", Part I, 81.
202. See "Exploring Scientific Basis", 12.
203. See M. Nanda, "Postmodernism", Part I, 81.
204. See M. Nanda, "Postmodernism", Part I, 79.
205. See R. Bhushan, "Joshi's Class of 2000", 22. In palmistry the element of observation is the hand, more properly the palm. It has been argued that we know that the lines on our palms are a result of the skeletal frame within our hand. For this reasons lines similar to those on our palms are also present on our soles, armpits and at all other joints. More so, such lines exist on the palms of a Gorilla or a Chimpanzee too, but none of us would claim to foretell the fortune of any simian this way. Some critics have claimed that Joshi will some day introduce doctorate on Palmistry and Parrotology where a parrot pulls out a card on which one's fortune or misfortune is written.
206. In 2004 the Bharat Vikas Parishad and Panchnad Study Centre jointly organised a seminar on Himachal Pradesh on the miraculous effects of *agnihom*. See "Seminar on Miraculous Effects of *agnihom*", 12.
207. See "Sangh Parivar Targets K.N. Panikkar", 13.

208. See M. Nanda, "Postmodernism", Part I, 79.
209. See "HRD Ministry Its Master's Voice", 132.
210. See "Communalisation of Education and Culture", 11.
211. See S. Vishwanahan, "The Spread in the South", 11.
212. See I. Habib. "The Rewriting of History by the Sangh Parivar", 41.
213. See T.N. Seshan, *A Heart Full of Burden*, 37.
214. T. Singh, "Missing the Point", 16.
215. See S. Gatade, "Enter 'Hero Hitler!", 22.
216. See C. Jaffrelot, *The Hindu Nationalist* Movement, 50-51.
217. See N. Goodrick-Clarke, *Hitler's Priestess*, 59.
218. See S. Gatade, "Enter 'Hero Hitler!", 22.
219. See "Venkaiah Naidu Proposes", 13.
220. See M. Casolari, "Hindutva's Foreign Tie-ups", 1032.
221. See M. Casolari, "Hindutva's Foreign Tie-Ups", 1032-1033,1036.
222. See V.D. Savarkar, *Hindu Sanghatan*, 194; ID., *Historic Statements*, 239. He also constantly spoke of the need to militarise Hinduism. See ibid., 1-2,4-6, 22, 42, 76, 204.
223. See V.D. Savarkar, "Problems before Hindudom", 177.
224. See J.D. Joglekar, "Veer Savarkar: Profile of a Prophet", 328.
225. See S. Devi, *A Warning to the Hindus*, 131.
226. A. Katakam, "Polarised State", 124. Personally the author is not against military training for the Indian youth but against making them ideologically dependent. Perhaps compulsory military training for youth for a period of time can make our young people tougher, better disciplined, more active, orderly, courageous and hardy. In many countries of the world military training is seen as having a positive impact on youth.
227. Since the 1980s the *Bajrang Dal* also has adopted a paramilitary style of training and functioning. See R. Joshi. "Look Delhi", 22-23.
228. The Shiv Sena was founded in Mumbai (Bombay) in 1966 by Bal Thackeray and is considered as a militant parochial organisation. See T.J.S. George, *The Enquire Dictionary*, 431. David Smith describes Thackeray thus: "Bal Thackeray, leader of the 'Army of Shivaji' (the Shiv Sena), associate of criminals, and fascist persecutor of Muslims". D. Smith, *Hinduism and Modernity*, 181. Shiv Sena is sometimes called the 'terror-organisation' of Maharashtra having its own paramilitary outfit called Siva Sainiks. See "The Shiv Sena Indicted", 20. See also C. Jaffrelot, *The Hindu Nationalist Movement*, 458-460; "The Burning of Bombay", 29-37.

229. See K.S. Kant, "Wake up from Slumber", 13.
230. See K.S. Kant, "Wake up from Slumber", 13.
231. See *RSS Resolves*, 11.
232. See V.D. Savarkar, *Hindu Sanghatan*, 142.
233. See V.D. Savarkar, *Hindu Sanghatan*, 142-143.
234. See M.S. Golwalkar, *Bunch of Thoughts*, 112-113.
235. See A. Pushparajan, "A Secular Critique of Hindutva", 241.
236. See P. Bidwai, "Sanskrit and *Sanskriti* as Weapons", 36.
237. Sanskrit Bharati, established in Karnataka in 1981, has today branches all over India and other parts of the world. The organisation is best known for its innovative Ten-Day Sanskrit Speaking Camps. More than 3.5 million people have already participated in such camps which involve a two-hour practice session daily. Besides these camps, the organisation also holds programmes to provide training to those who act as facilitators for these camps. According to a report of 2005 about 30,000 master trainers have been trained. Where 164 whole-time volunteers of Sanskrit Bharati are working all over the country and carrying out various activities aimed at making Sanskrit the spoken language of the masses in India. See "Future of India in Learning Sanskrit", 17.
238. See H.V. Seshadri (ed.), *RSS A Vision in Action*, 290-293.
239. See http://www.vhp.org/englishsite/d.Dimensions_of_VHP/aSewa/NSNS/intheserviceofpoor.html
240. See P. Bidwai, "Sanskrit and *Sanskriti* as Weapons", 36.
241. See "A Move to Revive Sanskrit", 15.
242. See "Sanskrit Training Camp in Karnavati", 13.
243. See "Making Sanskrit a Language of the Masses", 13.
244. See "Sanskrit Going Global", 12.
245. See K.N. Panikkar, "Outsider as Enemy", 55-56.
246. See P. Bidwai, "Sanskrit and *Sanskriti* as Weapons", 36.
247. See P. Bidwai, "Sanskrit and *Sanskriti* as Weapons", 37.
248. See P. Bidwai, "Sanskrit and *Sanskriti* as Weapons", 36.
249. See P. Bidwai, "Sanskrit and *Sanskriti* as Weapons", 37.
250. See P. Bidwai, "Sanskrit and *Sanskriti* as Weapons", 33.
251. See "Sanskrit Going Global", 12.
252. A.R. Keshav, "Why not make Sanskrit the Official Language?", 15.
253. See S. Swain, "Involve Entire Society in Sangh Work", 20.
254. See "Communalisation of Education and Culture", 10.

255. See "Communalisation of Education and Culture", 11.
256. See P. Bidwai, "Sanskrit and *Sanskriti* as Weapons", 36.
257. See "Communalisation of Education and Culture", 12.
258. See P. Bidwai, "Sanskrit and *Sanskriti* as Weapons", 33.
259. See "BJP Sights Chance to Get Kerala Toehold", 7.
260. See "Hindu Hopes Rise", 7.
261. See T.K. Rajalakshmi, "Removing an Irritant", 125. The tenure of the Chairman of the Indian Council of Historical Research (ICHR) would have expired only in July 2004. But the HRD ministry hastened the departure of the Council of M.G.S. Narayanan, the incumbent, seven months in advance. While away in Kozhikode in December 2003 Narayanan was informed that the government had decided to withdraw his nomination as Chairman with immediate effect. In his place an Additional Secretary of the government was appointed as a temporary measure, pending the nomination of a regular Chairman. The immediate reason was that Narayanan made known his displeasure over the manner in which the Ministry had appointed Kapil Kumar, a Professor of History, as the Member-Secretary of the Council. He had not been consulted about the appointment, although, as Chairman, he was the appointing authority and the controlling authority for the post under the rules and service regulations of the ICHR. In addition Narayanan had also taken unpopular stands especially in the context of the new NCERT textbooks. In a strongly worded letter he charged the HRD ministry with promoting a communal agenda and accused the 'Minister and his sycophants' of squandering public funds for promoting their communal schemes in the field of historical research. See ibid.
262. See A. Gopalakrishnan, "A New Head for the Akademi", 87.
263. See "His Love for another Parivar", 8.
264. For acquainting oneself with the condition of women in Hitler's Germany see C. Koonz, *Mütter im Vaterland. Fraeun in Dritten Reich* (1991).
265. See *The Laws of Manu*, 5,148.
266. See *The Laws of Manu*, 9, 2.
267. M.S. Golwalkar, *Bunch of Thoughts*, 116.
268. See S. Shukla, *India Abroad*, 74.
269. See T. Pintchman, "The Ambiguous Female", 146. See also V. Mangalwadi, *Missionary Conspiracy*, 200-204.
270. See R. Bhushan, "Joshi's Class of 2000", 22. Some new appointments took place since November 2000. See also S. Muralidharan, "The

History Project", 28-29. It has been reported that B.R. Grover defended and argued on behalf of the RSS on the Ram temple issue. His council included B.B. Lal, B.P. Sinha and K.S. Lal with similar credentials; M.L. Sondhi was a former Jan Sangh MP; G.C. Pande is a known sympathiser of the BJP and the Anand Marg; J.S. Rajput has been openly advocating the RSS emphasis on 'Indianisation', 'Spiritualisation', 'Nationalisation of school syllabus' and 'Value' education. See "Communalisation of Education and Culture", 9-10.

271. See "Communalisation of Education and Culture", 10.
272. The SAHMAT statement of 2001 says that committee for review of elementary and primary education, committee for review of the prescribed NCERT syllabus for CBSE, selection committees for appointments in NCERT and NIEPA, the advisory committee on education in Haryana, the specially constituted National Elementary Education Mission (NEEM), the Councils in ICHR and ICSSR and Grants-in-Aid Committees for adult education and so on are some examples of it. See "Communalisation of Education and Culture", 10.
273. See S. Yadev, "Face off", 29.
274. According to Ravi Kumar, there are about seven crore Hindus in about 120 countries of the world. A considerable number of them can be found in nearly 40 countries including UK, USA, Holland, Germany, Kenya, Middle East, West Indies, South Africa, Hong Kong, Singapore, Australia, New Zealand, Fiji, Nepal, Sri Lanka, Bangladesh and Pakistan. Most of the Hindu in countries like Mauritius, South Africa, Fiji, Myanmar, Malaysia, Singapore and Caribbean countries of Trinidad, Guyana and the Surinam where they were taken by British rulers almost 120 years ago as contract labourers hail from Uttar Pradesh and Tamil Nadu. See R. Kumar, "Diaspora India", 14. is said that there are some 15,000 Hindus in Russia of whom 5000 are from India and 10,000 are Hindu converts from local Russian population. See "Hindus in Russia", 9.
275. The Vishwa Hindu Parishad of America (VHPA) is the first branch of the Sangh Parivar to have been formed in the West and was registered in 1974 in New York. See A. Rajagopal, "Non-Resident Nationalism", 127.
276. See "Intellectuals' Forum for Pro-Hindu Government in India", 14.
277. See A. Rajagopal, "Non-Resident Nationalism", 129.
278. See A. Rajagopal, "Non-Resident Nationalism", 129.
279. See A. Rajagopal, "Non-Resident Nationalism", 129.
280. See A. Rajagopal, "Non-Resident Nationalism", 129.

281. See M.G. Chitkara, *Rashtriya Swayamsevak Sangh*, 301.
282. See A. Rajagopal, "Non-Resident Nationalism", 128.
283. See A. Rajagopal, "Non-Resident Nationalism", 128.
284. See A. Rajagopal, "Non-Resident Nationalism", 128.
285. See A. Rajagopal, "Non-Resident Nationalism", 128.
286. See "*Sakhi Sammelan*: A Unique Experience for Women", 17.
287. See H. Mander, "In Search of Gandhi and Godse", 104.
288. H. Mander, "In Search of Gandhi and Godse", 104.
289. See A. Rajagopal, "Non-Resident Nationalism", 129.
290. See R. Brahmachari, "Yoga Craze of the West", 14.
291. See S. Chari, "Indian Americans", 10.
292. See A. Thakur, "Ramayana in the Global Context", 20.
293. See V. Shanmuganathan, "Indians in USA", 4.
294. See H. Mander, "In Search of Gandhi and Godse", 103.
295. See http://www.countercurrents.org/comm-chatterji080106.html The changes proposed by HEF, VF, and the *ad hoc* Committee, on the basis of recommendations made by a certain Professor Shiva Bajpai, who is affiliated with the World Association for Vedic Studies, a Hindu nationalist organisation, assert a nationalistic and mythic history of India as a fact. For example, contrary to authentic scholarship, the revisions refute the migration of Aryans from Central Asia into India, posit Aryans (consequently also Hinduism) as indigenous to India, rendering mute the histories of Adivasis and their subjugation by the Hindus. The *ad hoc* Committee proposed, and the Curriculum Commission accepted, that the existing text, 'The Aryans created a caste system be replaced with: 'During Vedic times, people were divided into different social groups (*varnas*) based on their capacity to undertake a particular profession.' Such a presentation dissociates caste system from Hindu religion, and discounts and neutralises the oppressive structure and politics which the caste system constitutes. Again it projects the caste system as a fluid arrangement, not restricted by ancestry. The *ad hoc* Committee proposed, and the Curriculum Commission accepted that the current text, 'Men had many more rights than women', be replaced with: 'Men had different duties (*dharma*) as well as rights than women. Many women were among the sages to whom the Vedas were revealed.' Thus the inequality of women's rights is legitimated and presented as 'different rights' and in the process erases women's subordinated role in Hindu patriarchal society. See ibid.
296. See N. Taneja "A Saffron Assault Abroad", 77.

297. H. Mander, "In Search of Gandhi and Godse", 103.
298. See H. Mander, "In Search of Gandhi and Godse", 103.
299. See H. Mander, "In Search of Gandhi and Godse", 103-104.
300. See "A Project to Explore British Hindu Identity", 3.
301. See M.G. Chitkara, *Rashtriya Swayamsevak Sangh,* 301; M. Nanda, "Postmodernism", Part I, 78.
302. See M. Nanda, "Postmodernism", Part I, 78.
303. See "Pictorial Exhibition on Savarkar in UK", 20.
304. J.D. Lakhani, "Promoting Education the Hindu Way", 11.
305. See "A State-funded Hindu School in Britain", 7.
306. See S. Suri, "Vote's the Good News", 38-39.
307. M. Nanda, "Postmodernism", Part I, 79.
308. See P. Kumar, "Agni Fights for Hindu Interests Globally", 7.
309. See P. Sengupta, "Russians Seek Solace in Bharatiya *Gurukula*", 8.
310. See J.K. Sharma, "Brazil Resonant with Jai Shri Ram", 15.
311. See M.G. Chitkara, *Rashtriya Swayamsevak Sangh,* 302.
312. See N. Oza, "The Hindu Way", 27. For information regarding the activities of the Hindu-Right in the 1980s see H.V. Seshadri, *Hindus Abroad* (1990).
313. See M. Casolari, "Hindutva's Foreign Tie-ups", 1032-1033.
314. See P. Kanungo, *RSS Tryst with Politics,* 169.
315. See "Communalisation of Education and Culture", 9.
316. "Der Giftpilz", *Das Reich,* 209.
317. "Der Giftpilz", *Das Reich,* 209.
318. "Der Giftpilz", *Das Reich,* 209.
319. See.J.C. Fest, *The Face of the Third Reich,* 131.
320. See M. Domarus, *Hitler Reden,* vol. 1, 224.
321. See K.N. Panikkar, "Down, but not Out", 123.
322. See K.N. Panikkar, "Down, but not Out", 121.
323. See P. Bidwai, "Politics and culture as Blind Sport", 108.
324. See P. Bidwai, "Politics and culture as Blind Sport", 107.
325. See K.N. Panikkar, "Whither Indian Education", 25.
326. See P. Kanungo, *RSS Tryst with Politics,* 169-170.
327. See P. Kanungo, *RSS Tryst with Politics,* 167.
328. *Hindu Mahasabha Ideals,* 32 (Emphasis added).
329. See K.N. Panikkar, "Whither Indian Education", 26-27.
330. See K.N. Panikkar, "Whither Indian Education", 25-26.

331. See K.N. Panikkar, "Whither Indian Education", 27-28.
332. A. Eraly, "Cry Babies", 92.
333. See M. Nanda, "Postmodernism", Part I, 81.
334. G. Das, *The Elephant Paradigm*, 74.
335. See P. Bidwai, "Politics and Culture as Blind Sport", 108.
336. See D.N. Batra, "Reject Unpatriotic Textbooks", 20.
337. See M.S. Aiyar, *Confessions of a Secular Fundamentalist*, 124. (Emphasis added)
338. See K.N. Panikkar, "Whither Indian Education", 23.

IV

Arun Shourie's Anti-Christian Syndrome

A Case Study

Arun Shourie was born on 2 November 1941 in Jalandhar, Punjab, in a Saraswati Brahmin family. He was the son of a civil servant and later founder of "Common Cause" (a pubic interest juridical pressure-group) Hari Dev Shourie and Dayawanti Shourie. Arun Shourie was educated at Modern School in New Delhi and St Stephen's College, New Delhi.[1] He earned Ph.D in Economics from the University of Syracuse (USA), and later worked for the World Bank. Back in India in 1976, Shourie was to work for several leading dailies of India. He met newspaper owner Ramnath Goenka when staying at the Indian Express guesthouse in Bangalore. Goenka made him executive editor of the *Indian Express* but dismissed him a few years later. In 1982 he joined the *Times of India,* with the understanding that he would succeed Girilal Jain as editor but Jain went back on his word and had Shourie dismissed in 1983. Then Goenka took him back and Shourie made history as editor of the *Indian Express*. In late 1990 he was again sacked as the *Indian Express* editor and since then he has established himself as a syndicated columnist and independent self-publishing writer.[2]

As editor of *The Indian Express* Shourie made a name for himself by his fearless criticism of Indira Gandhi's dictatorial methods, his lucid observation of the rule of the Janata Party government headed by Morarji Desai and more generally by his crusades against falling moral standards in public life. He played a decisive role in Rajiv

Gandhi's electoral defeat in 1989 with the revelation about the Bofors arms deal.[3]

Shourie has received several national and international awards including Padma Bhushan, Magsaysay Award, Dadabhai Naoroji Award, Astor Award, International Editor of the Year Award, etc. He is marred to Anita Shourie and they have a son.[4] He has been an important person in the BJP-led NDA government in New Delhi.[5]

Shourie as journalist, politician and minister in the union cabinet of India in the BJP-led NDA government assumed the role of a hardcore Hindutva ideologue and its leading theoretician. He chose, through his writings, to target the minorities of India like the Buddhists, Christians, Muslims, Communists, secularists, Dalits and Tribals. Shourie is clearly prejudiced against the minorities of India. In 1995, in a conversion with Mani Shankar Aiyar, among other things, Shourie declared that the Semitic tradition like Judaism, early Christianity, especially 'Christianity of the Church', Islam and Marxism-Leninism are *destructive* in the extreme.[6] A look at some of his writings against them, such as, his *Indian Controversies* (1993), *A Secular Agenda* (1993), *Missionaries in India* (1994), *The World of Fatwas* (1995), *Worshipping False Gods* (1997), *Eminent Historians* (1998), *Harvesting our Souls. Missionaries their Design their Claims* (2000), *Courts and their Judgements* (2001), etc., reveal his anti-minority stand. Koenraad Elst, a leading Hindutva ideologue, says that after Ram Swarup and Sita Ram Goel started an intellectual Hindu wakening separate from the propaganda channels of the Sangh Parivar others joined in. One of them is Arun Shourie who gained fame in India as the crusading editor of *The Indian Express.*[7]

A careful examination of his writings reveal that, much of what he has written is a studied and systematic way of spreading misinformation about the minorities in order to promote and propagate Hindu cultural nationalism. But often they are characterised by intellectual flabbiness, lack of objectivity, and a one-sided presentation of facts *to a purpose*. In a country whose religious pluralism and secular fabric are constantly under serious threat, Shourie's writings are clearly provocative, and they further damage the delicate relationship that exists between religions and communities. Through his writings he has consistently exhibited a certain anti-minority syndrome.

In this chapter we shall analyse in some detail, one of his controversial books on the Christian minority in India, entitled,

Missionaries in India.' Continuities, Changes Dilemmas, New Delhi, 1994. It is hoped that this case study will make readers understand Shourie's shallow scholarship, prejudices and anti-Christian mentality.

Shourie's Accusations Against Christianity

Shourie in the book *Missionaries in India* launches virulent accusations against Christianity and Christian missionaries. His so-called presentation of 'facts' is far from objective, and his prejudices against Christianity are so potent that they continue to breed suspicion and hatred against it. The calumny which he heaps upon Christianity is part of a much wider conspiracy to spread communal disharmony in the country by painting the Christians as anti-national and Christianity as a foreign religion – a religion that has every right to be treated as totally indigenous due to its 2000 years of existence in the subcontinent! In order to substantiate our claim that Shourie is affected by an 'anti-Christian syndrome', we attempt a critical examination of some of his major accusations against Christianity as propounded in *Missionaries in India*.

Accusation: Conversion is the Central Objective of Christianity

Shourie maintains that the central objective of Christianity is conversion. He alleges: "that premise [conversion] is not incidental, it is central. Nor is it accidental, it is the keystone of Christianity of the Church [sic]";[8] "Conversions have been going on for 2000 years. They have, therefore, been proclaimed to be an essential element of Christianity, a duty of every Christian. They have become one of the principal preoccupations – in some cases, as with the evangelists, the principal business – of the Church."[9] He further argues that many of the old means continue to be used to secure converts, such as, use of paid agents to cultivate contacts, distribution of gifts to win over poor and ignorant people, provision of board and lodging to potential converts on their visits to the foothills, payment of a price for arranging conversions and for those converted, 'buying off' of village headmen so as to convert other villagers, and so on. Thus, according to Shourie, conversions have little to do with an individual's personal choice and conviction.

Shourie further claims that, in order to keep up the scale of conversions, an incredibly vast organisation has also been built-up and inexhaustible resources are expended for it.[10] To achieve its ends, Church has also access to vast networks, such as of the media, which are more potent than funds.[11] He also accuses the Church in India of being pre-occupied with numbers. He says: "In chasing numbers the missionaries, [...] became just 'vendors of goods'. And they came to adopt the usual technique of vendors: the exaggerations common on advertising wares."[12] Commenting on the method of conversions he says: "The quest for numbers has led to another trend [...] 'Charismatic proclamation'. Thousands are gathered in a large stadium or ground [...] A preacher delivers an emotional, fiery exhortation: Sin: Damnation: The End is Near; Repent in Time; Be saved by Jesus – tonight, now; Come Hither towards the stage.... Some swoon, those who could not walk, walk [sic]".[13] Shourie, says that the charismatic retreat movement at Potta (Kerala) has a similar purpose. The retreat team is also travelling and preaching outside Kerala, even abroad, and many non-Christians actively participate in it and some even ask for baptism.[14]

However, statistics show that, despite the 2000 years of the aggressive proselytisation by the Christians, as alleged by Shourie and his friends in the Sangh Parivar, the country's Christian population has remained at a paltry 2.06 per cent of the total population.[15] There is also no change in the demographic profile of India in favour of Christianity. This fact itself is sufficient to demonstrate the falsity of Shourie's accusation that the central objective of Christianity is to convert. Any informed person knows that the essence of Christianity is *not* conversion but *witness* to Jesus Christ and *loving service* to humanity. None can convert another person. It is the free act of an individual. What people generally call 'conversion' is transformation of the interior disposition of a person where no one has access except the person concerned and the Divine.

Mani Shankar Aiyar explains the same thing in 'secular' terms. He argues that the Indian Constitution grants every citizen the fundamental right to propagate one's faith. It does not confer a right to convert. But it gives every citizen the right to be converted. In other words one is free to change one's religion or abandon ones religion altogether. The citizen is not obliged to explain to any court, or to any self appointed guardian, why he has changed his religion. He has to explain that only to his conscience.[16] Aiyar further argues that most missionary work is now being undertaken by Indian nationals. They have the constitutional right (available also to foreign missionaries) to propagate their religion, a right being equally exercised by Hindu organisations such as the Ramakrishna Mission, Maharishi Mahesh Yogi and the Divine Life Mission of Swami Sivananda, among many others, who are engaged in the propagating of the Hindu religion. Thus, the issue should be considered as settled.[17]

Accusation: Christian Educational Institutions are Meant to Convert

Shourie seldom has an agreeable word for Christian educational institutions. He reiterates that the central motive of the Christian educational institutions is also to convert people to Christianity. He alleges that, when the missionaries established schools they also painted India as a land that was bereft of education, of schools, and whose people were steeped in the darkest ignorance.[18] This observation of missionaries about the Indian educational scenario, some two hundred or hundred years ago, may not have been entirely untrue, for according to statistics, the national literacy rate in India *in 1951 was just 18 per cent*! So one can imagine the deplorable literacy rate *prior to that*! An official report by the Government of India says: "At the time of Independence, India inherited an educational system which was not only quantitatively small but was also characterised by regional, gender, caste and structural imbalances. Only *14 per cent* of the population was literate."[19]

Shourie further accuses the Christians that their educational institutions did not do any good except destroy one's self-confidence and self-respect in people. He says: "Where they [Christians] educated us to our shortcomings, they completely destroyed not only self-confidence but all self-respect."[20] Using Swami Vivekananda as his mouthpiece, Shourie says: "The child is taken to school, and the first thing he learns is that his father is a fool, the second thing that his grandfather is a lunatic, the third thing that all his teachers are hypocrites, the fourth that all the sacred books are lies. By the time he is sixteen he is a mass of negation, lifeless and boneless."[21]

Anyone who is familiar with the Christian educational institutions is aware that Shourie's accusation is grossly unfair and goes against facts. It is a well-known fact that, the Hindu elite rush their children to Christian schools. It is also an undisputed fact that, in India, about 95 per cent of those who benefit from the Christian institutions are non-Christians. But the paradox is that, in spite of the so-called negative effect of the Christian institutions on a Hindu child, Arun Shourie *himself* and his family benefited from the Christian institutions. He admits: "My wife studied at the Loreto Convent at Lucknow, as did her mother and sisters; my sister studied at the Convent of Jesus and Mary at Delhi; my brother and I studied at the St. Stephen's College at Delhi."[22] Shourie also says that none tried to convert him when he was a student of St. Stephens. He notes: "My own experience would point to what you [bishop Patrick D' Souza of Varanasi] say: I studied at a college set up by Christian missionaries, no one ever tried to convert me."[23] Mani Shankar Aiyar, who was also a student of St. Stephen's, New Delhi, corroborates Shourie's view. He says: "I can testify that no one made the least attempt to harvest my soul for anyone."[24] He adds that the most remarkable contribution of the Christians missionaries to India, is in the field of school and college education and that all the top colleges in India were founded by, and are run by, Christian missions.[25]

Shourie blames Christian educational institutions for destroying Hindu self-confidence and self-respect. His crusading spirit and vituperative attacks against the Christians and other religious minorities show that he has not lost any self-confidence, though one may not be able to say the same about his self-respect!

Shourie accuses the Christian missionaries of being champions of Western learning to the detriment of Indian education. He complains: "Where they [the Christians] introduced us to a smattering of western learning, they led us to completely forget and – with no knowledge of it at all – feel ashamed of our tradition. Where they introduced modern schools, they, along with the secular British rulers, completely erased the vast network of instruction which, [...] was in place all across the country."[26] But it may be recalled here that in spite of the so-called negative influence of Western learning on a person, Shourie himself chose Western education and went abroad to do his doctoral studies in Economics at the University of Syracuse, USA.[27] In addition, he confesses that, he knows neither Sanskrit nor Pali and so he has to depend on translations. He says: "as I know neither Sanskrit nor Pali, even for reading Hindu and Buddhist scriptures I have to rely on English translations – a number of which have been done by *Christian missionaries*."[28] Unfortunately, Shourie is unaware that when he criticises the Christian missionaries and their system of education, he is segmenting the very branch on which he sits.

Accusation: The Objective of Christian Social Services is to Convert

Another accusation which Shourie launches against the Christians is that, their contribution in the area of social services and humanitarian undertakings is not incidental for these are also means to convert people to Christianity. He claims that, the Christians use occasions like drought, epidemic, economic difficulty, chronic poverty to convert. Besides, the curse of untouchability and the proposed improvement in their social status, are also used as means for conversion.[29] According to Shourie, even Mother Teresa's primary motivation was to convert, often the helpless people, to Christianity. He says: "Yet even to such saintly effort, [of Mother Teresa] what would the orthodox doctrine of the Church impart? An anxiety to save souls, and the premise is that a person in that destitute and desperate condition, in that agony, a person that close to death would be better off, that he would be 'saved' if he were to mumble a few words before breathing his last connoting a faith in Jesus."[30] Shourie seems to know nothing of the motive behind Christian humanitarian services, even though he studied in a Christian institution. But Mani Shankar Aiyar has an answer for him. He calls Mother Teresa and her missionaries 'the very symbol of selfless secularism in practice.'[31] The official position of the Church with regard to her charitable works is quite contrary to what Shourie alleges. Pope Benedict XVI says: "Charity, furthermore, cannot be used as a means of engaging in what nowadays considered proselytism [....] Those who practise charity in the Church's name will never seek to impose the Church's faith upon others."[32]

It has been observed that if there is any group in India that has no love for Mother Teresa it is the members of the Hindu right. They see her as nothing more than just another missionary who converts through 'fraud' and 'monetary inducements'. In 2003 the RSS mouthpiece *Organiser* published a vicious attack on Mother Teresa in its Diwali special issue, written by N.S. Rajaram. He alleged, among other things, that throughout her life Mother Teresa preferred the company of the rich even when they were crooks or murderers.[33] For Balbir K.Punj, one of BJP's so-called think tanks,

Mother Teresa was only a person who portrayed the city of Calcutta as an overgrown slum.[34] The RSS ideologue Adhish Kumar commenting on the beatification of Mother Teresa in October 2003 said that the beatification of Mother Teresa by the Vatican was an award for selling 50,000 Indian women as nuns to the Christian world and that under Mother Teresa India proved to be a fertile land for conversion.[35] Perhaps Prem Shankar Jha has a fitting reply for Shourie, Rajaram, Punj and Adhish Kumar and their likes. He says: "No none since Mahatma Gandhi has poured forth his or her love, caring and compassion on India's poor and needy as she [Mother Teresa] did."[36] *India Today* said: "A young Yugoslavian nun [Mother Teresa], reached Calcutta in 1928 to teach geography. She ended up teaching the world how to love the destitute."[37] Mother Teresa was described as 'another name for love' by the people of India.[38]

Shourie holds that the purpose of the medical care given by the Christian institutions is also a means to convert people. In order to illustrate this, he quotes from an outdated handbook of little importance as far as the universal Church is concerned: "To gain access to non-Christian households, counsels the *Catholic Dharma Ka Pracharak,* the preacher should know something of medicine. He will then be sought-after whenever there is some illness in the house. Once there, he should try to prevail upon the parents that he should be allowed to baptise the child as the baptism would aid the child's recovery."[39] It may be noted that Shourie provides neither the name of the author nor the year nor place of publication of the above said handbook. Hence the book could even be a product of Shourie's own imagination.

It is clear that Shourie's anti-Christian mentality has blinded him so much that he cannot see anything other than 'conversion' as the motive for every Christian activity. He would interpret even the best of services done on humanitarian grounds as an attempt to convert, provided the doer is a Christian.

In India Christians are engaged in nation building, social and humanitarian activities, probably with greater dedication, self-sacrifice and sincerity than the most adherents of major religion of India. The missionaries are engaged in such human developmental activities as: social work, medical care, education – both technical, academic and non-formal – literacy projects, care of the poor, aged, orphans, sick, downtrodden, abandoned, street children, prisoners, as well as assisting those denied of human rights, dignity and equality, uplift of the weaker sections of the society, especially, the women, Dalits and Tribals, promotion of communal harmony, inter-religious dialogue and the like. But Shourie would see none of these activities as helps towards human development. He prefers rather to interpret them as means to convert Indians to Christianity. But to label the vast sphere of Christian humanitarian activities solely as means to convert would imply a gross misinterpretation of Christianity, to say the least.

Perhaps Shourie could profit by listening to Gurcharan Das's observation about the Christians. He says: "I have seen Christians working in the remotest places, living a selfless life, and brining education and health care to the poorest. I wonder, how many religious fundamentalists of either Hindu or Muslim varieties engage in genuine charity."[40] Mani Shankar Aiyar notes that spread of Christianity in India is a story of spiritual persuasion, not of conversion at the point of the sword. It was by and large through good deeds that they propagated church's mission.[41]

Accusation: Christians Target the Weaker Sections of Society

Another accusation of Shourie is that the Christians target the weaker sections of society, like, the Tribals, the Dalits, the ignorant and the illiterate, in order to convert them. He argues that, spurred by the new 'Liberation Theology', the Church is spurring movements among the so-called Dalits, tribals and others. He adds: "Primitive tribes [...] furnish the most fruitful field for Christian missionaries;"[42] "The other special target groups has been the Harijans."[43] He also says that the Christians are targeting them when they would be most vulnerable or receptive, using not just dialogue but allurement and violence.[44]

Shourie has also some very strong words against the Dalits – who stand up for their rights and resist being trampled upon by the upper castes to which category he too belongs as a Brahmin. He says: "But many of the leaders you [Christian missionaries] have patronised by way of helping 'Dalits' speak with poison in their tongue. They advocate hatred. They have been eulogising Bhindranwale."[45] He goes on to say: "These groups may well break India, that they will eventually bring upon even those groups the consequences that Bhindranwale's terrorism – much lauded by the 'Dalit' leadership, which in turn has been much lauded by the Church – brought upon the Sikhs."[46]

When Shourie was informed by one of the participants of the Catholic Bishops' Conference of India (CBCI) during their meeting in Pune in 1994, that there is a mass of humanity in Northeast India which is crying out for fuller expression, his reply was the following: "But isn't there humanity in Delhi, to say nothing of the U.S. and U.K., which is crying to find full expression? What is the *urgency* which leads you to conclude that the people in the Northeast must be saved, that they must be enabled to find full expression this very month?."[47] The same Shourie was minister in charge of Northeast India in the union cabinet under the Vajpayee government! What did he do for the people of the Northeast?

It is to be stated that the accusation of converting the weaker sections of society is only an *excuse*. The real issue is that Christians through their educational institutions, social services and humanitarian activities, work for the uplift of the poor, the weak and the downtrodden. If these people are educated and helped to develop themselves, they will obviously demand their rights, and it can upset the carefully and cleverly constructed and preserved caste hierarchy through which the upper castes continue their centuries-old exploitation. The cry against conversion is only a ploy, a false alarm. The real motives are to dissuade Christians from working for the uplift of the oppressed and the downtrodden.

Shourie says that though Christianity does not recognise caste the system, it survives among the Christians as well.[48] Well, if caste system and untouchability still persist in Indian society – including some Christian groups – Hinduism must take the lion's share of the responsibility for it, because, it is the only religion in the world which gives religious and legal sanction to oppress human beings on the basis of their birth, and does not allow for social or religious mobility. Buddhism and Jainism protested against caste system long before Christianity came into existence. Besides, it must also be remembered that the Christian missionaries did not bring caste system to India. They have only laboured to eradicate it from the Indian society as being unworthy of human beings. In addition, Christianity has no magical formula to overcome the social evils for which today's Hinduism and its 'antecedents' are responsible.

Dignity and Justice are birthrights of every human being. They are also guaranteed by the Indian Constitution. Unfortunately, Hinduism seldom felt – even now hardly feels – the urgency to help the downtrodden, the weak and the poor. If India is largely underdeveloped, the majority religion of the country must take the greater share of the blame than other factors. It should be recalled also that, it was Christianity that offered social criticism and challenged the Indian society to social reform. The very concept of Indian renaissance of the nineteenth century and the measures adopted for overcoming such social evils as, *sati* (widow burning), child marriage, gender discrimination, untouchability and caste system, and the promotion of equality and human rights, were largely the inspiration of Christianity, Western education and Western ideas.

When we speak of the deplorable condition of the tribal population of Northeast India and elsewhere, we also need to ask what has Hinduism done in order to better their condition? Wherever possible it has only tried to perpetuate the social evils by imposing on them a religion which only sanctions them. Hence, when Shourie grudges the various forms of social services – education, health care, sanitation, economic and development works – which the Christian missionaries render to the weaker sections of the Indian society, like the Tribals and the Dalits, is he not implying that they should be denied human dignity, human rights, justice and equality? It may also be recalled that, as Gurcharan Das says: "Every rupee of this [money comes from Christian charities abroad] is spent with care and love, in contrast to the hundreds of crores wasted in the government's poverty programmes."[49]

Accusation: A Conspiracy Between the Missionaries and the British Colonisers

Another of Shourie's accusation against Christianity is that, there was a secret pact between the Christian missionaries and the British colonialists,[50] so that they consciously reinforced one another's objectives. He notes: "But it was not just that the civil servants and the missionaries shared an objective, that they shared presuppositions. They reinforced each other's work, and did so consciously, certain that in helping the other they were ensuring the fulfilment of what was their own primary responsibility."[51]

Shourie has also the audacity to say that the work of the Church was not done by the missionaries alone but that the religiously 'neutral' administrators did a good bit of it. Correspondingly, the work of the British Empire was not done by the administrators alone but the missionaries also did a good bit of it.[52] Thus, he alleges, there was a kind of a division of labour so that the missionaries and the colonialists looked upon each other as comrades working towards a common goal, namely, that of converting India to Christianity and of securing the Empire for Britain.

Shourie misinterprets the relationship that existed between the missionaries and the British colonialists. His attempt to link the missionary activity with the colonial system is hardly convincing as far as India is concerned. Perhaps, one of the best replies to Shourie's accusation is Vishal Mangalwadi's *Missionary Conspiracy: Letters to a Post-Modern Hindu* (1996). Mangalwadi's work based on several original documents of the British administration, effectively *demolishes,* among other things, Shourie's thesis that there was a sinister pact between the Christian Missionaries and the British colonisers.

First of all, it is to be noted that not all the missionaries in India were British. Several of them came from countries that openly manifested their greatest distaste for British imperialism. Besides, Englishmen in the British East India Company were not missionaries but mercenaries who came to India in search of money. Mangalwadi's well researched study shows that as far as the colonisers were concerned they were driven by five major interests: (a) individual greed to make money for the British East India Company; (b) need for a trading base for the Directors of the same Company; (c) conquest of territory for the British military heroes; (d) Indology for the British secular scholars, and (e) improvement of Hindus for the social reformers.[53] Missionary activity *did not figure* anywhere in their agenda.

There are documents which show that initially the East India Company forbade missionaries from operating in the territories they took over. Many British people did not see that the missionaries would strengthen the empire. Rather they feared that education and Christianity would be dangerous and that it would hurt the cause of the British empire.[54] It took a long time before the missionaries were allowed to operate freely.

Documents show that during the entire seventeenth century only one Indian is known to have been baptised by the chaplains of the British East India Company. Records also show that in the eighteenth century not a single British missionary was permitted to work in the British territories. The only Protestant mission that existed in India was pioneered by the Danes in the non-British territory of Tranquebar. A few German missionaries were later tolerated in some British centres because they had earned great respect from the Hindus and the Muslim kingdoms around them. In 1793, when it was discovered that William Carey (1761-1834) was travelling to India to serve as a missionary, he was transferred from the British ship and he arrived on a Danish boat, and then worked as a manager in an indigo plantation, partly in order to evade arrest. Finally, in order to work as a missionary he had to settle in the Danish territory of Serampore.[55]

The British Christians had to struggle against their government to get permit for missionaries to enter India.[56] Charles Grant started his campaign for the mission in 1786-1787. But it was only 46 years later in 1833 that the British Parliament allowed missionaries from the West to operate in India, although in 1813 a law had been passed that missions could operate in India but only under licence. Many contemporaries of William Wilberforce, T.B. Macaulay and Charles Trevelyan thought that Christians were fighting against the British interest and for the exclusive interest of India.[57]

While the Christian missions did not receive any financial aid from the Company or from the Government, until 1858 at least 26,589 Hindu temples were receiving financial support from the Company in the Bombay Presidency alone, the biggest beneficiary being the Jagannath temple at Puri. The Company also was investing huge sums in public education and for the promotion of Sanskrit, Persian and Arabic.[58]

But records show that the Hindus were willing to enlist help from the British colonisers against the Muslims. Yechury says that the urge to establish the Hindu *rashtra* drove the RSS to be a virtual ally of the British.[59] B.S. Moonje, a prominent Hindu leader and a staunch advocate of the Hindu *rashtra* and the founder of the Bhonsla Military School, wrote to the Viceroy of India on 26 September 1940 soliciting the favour of the British colonial government. We quote from the letter of Moonje now preserved in the India Office Collections (IOC) of the British Library, London, which the present author discovered while researching there. Moonje says: "Hindustan surrounded as it is on the Western and the North-Western Frontier by its traditional enemies [Muslims] of the last more than one thousand years, is the one stable factor in its choice of its allies for its permanent safety and prosperity. *It will naturally lead the Hindus to look up to Britain,* in spite of its quarrels with it for constitutional powers, however bitter at times they may be. *Thus Hindustan and Britain are allied together in unshakeable bond of union for long years to come.*"[60]

Accusation: Christians did not Participate in the Indian Independence Movement

Shourie accuses the Christians of being anti-national by not participating in the Indian independence movement.[61] He says: "For over a hundred years thus missionary activity was interwoven with, and inextricably tied up with British imperial control of India: that the missionaries – *even those of Indian origin – did not join the Independence Movement* was not an accident."[62] It is a *serious accusation* against the Indian Christian community and is a gross distortion of facts, as we shall demonstrate below. A similar view was held by the RSS ideologue M.S. Golwalkar. He said: "In general, the Christians kept themselves aloof from the freedom struggle."[63]

Felix Wilfred, an internationally renowned theologian, notes that those who look objectively at the history of the freedom struggle in India, would admit that there were several Christian missionaries who gave full support to the nationalist cause to the embarrassment and indignation of the British colonial government. Among these missionaries the more well known names are: Stanley Jones, C.F. Andrews, J.C. Winslow, Verrier Elwin, Ralph Richard Keithahn and Ernest Forrester-Paton. Some missionaries were even deported from India for their support to nationalist cause.[64]

George Thomas, a well known Church historian maintains that the Indian Christian Community played an influential role, especially in the early phase of the Indian National Congress – founded in 1885 – which was the premier instrument of political nationalism. According to him, the influence of the Christians was impressive at the various sessions of the Indian National Congress. For example, in the third annual session of the Congress in 1887, out of 607 participants at the session, 15 were Indian Christians, and among those who addressed the assembly was Madhu Sudhan Das (1848-1934, popularly known as 'Utkal Gourab'), a prominent leader from the Christian community in Orissa. The number and influence of Indian Christians continued to be impressive at the subsequent sessions of the Congress. Kali Charan Banerjee (1847-1907), a Bengali Christian regularly addressed the annual sessions of the Congress in moulding the policy of National Movement. At the Congress session of 1889, among the ten women delegates, three were Christians:

Pandita Ramabai Saraswati (1858-1922), Mrs. Triumbuck, Mrs. Nikambe.[65]

There are records of active Christian participation in the *Swaraj* Movement (1905), the Non Co-operation Movement (1920), the Civil Disobedience Movement (1930) and the 'Quit India' Movement (1942). Since the 1920s, many Christian institutions and organisations like, the All India Conference of Indian Christians, the National Christian Council of India, Christian leaders and student groups related to United Theological College (Bangalore), Serampore College (Bengal), St. Paul's College, Calcutta (Bengal), Malabar Christian College, Calicut (Kerala), the Youth Christian Council of Action (Kerala), the Student Christian Movement of India, the Indian Christian Association of Bengal, a conference of Christians in Bombay, a meeting of Christians in Palayamcotta and Tinnavelly, and the like, passed resolutions expressing complete solidarity with the freedom movement. Some of them even took part in massive demonstrations against the British colonial government.[66]

In 1973 the Government of Tamil Nadu published a list of freedom fighters of the state in three volumes under the title *Who is Who of Freedom Fighters, Tamil Nadu.* From these volumes D. Arthur Jayakumar has culled the names of 103 persons who have been positively identified as Christians.[67] Basing ourselves on Jayakumar's findings we mention below some of the outstanding Indian Christians who took part in the freedom struggle.

J.C. Kumarappa (or John Jesudason Cornelius, 1892-1960) was a veteran Congress leader. On 9 May 1929 he met Mahatma Gandhi at Sabarmati *ashram* and that resulted in their becoming close associates. He was a strong supporter of *Satyagraha,* and encouraged Christian participation in the national movement.[68] Before Mahatma Gandhi set out for the Dandy March in 1931, he encouraged Kumarappa to write regularly for his weekly *Young India* and informed him that he would be its editor after his imprisonment. Thus Kumarappa became editor of *Young India* and his fiery writings gave him one and a half years of rigorous imprisonment in 1931. But fortunately he was released after a couple of days, because of the Gandhi-Irwin Pact. He took up again the editorship of *Young India* from Mahatma Gandhi in 1932, which sent him to jail and was detained in Nasik prison for two and a half years. In 1942 he was under detention and trial for a year and a half in both Bombay and

Nagpur. During the 'Quit India Movement', he had a hand in the underground activities in Bombay along with his Congress colleagues. These secret sabotage activities led to his arrest. He was sentenced to two and a half years of rigorous imprisonment for three charges and sent to Jabalpur central jail until 1945. After his release from the prison, his health by then completely broke down, he took rest at the guesthouse of Leonard Theological College, Jabalpur.[69]

Paul Ramasamy (b.1906) was another important Christian who took part in the freedom struggle. In 1930 he joined the freedom movement during the *Salt satyagraha* days. He picketed the Bishop Herber College, Thiruchirappalli. He was arrested and sentenced to six imprisonment and was kept at Thiruchirapalli and Alipuram jails.[70]

Venkal Chakkarai (b.1880) participated in the Civil Disobedience Movement started by Mahatma Gandhi.[71] In 1930 Kanakarayan Tiruselvam Paul (1876-1931) went to England to participate in the First Round Table Conference. He decried the tendency among some Christians to keep aloof from the national movement.[72] There were many other prominent Christians who participated in the national movement either as part of the Congress or outside it.

Arthur Jayakumar says that when the Non-Co-operation Movement was started in 1920, there were Indian Christians in the whole of India who took part in it.[73] The All India Conference of Indian Christians held at Lucknow between 27-30 December 1922 made a reference to some of the Indian Christians who had suffered imprisonment as a result of their involvement in the national movement.[74] N.H. Tubbs, the principal of the Bishops College, Calcutta, wrote a confidential letter to his Mission dated 23 February 1921 stated: "A very significant feature of the last months have been the deep interest of Christian students in the national non-co-operation movement."[75] In 1930 the editor of *The Guardian* said that a number of Christian young men have joined the Civil Disobedience Movement.[76] Nirad Biswas who later became the bishop of Assam of the Church of India, Burma and Ceylon (CIBC) joined the national movement in making salt outside Calcutta in 1932.[77]

George Thomas notes that Barhmabandhab Upadhyaya (1861-1907) a 'Hindu Catholic' *sadhu* and theologian, played a leading role in the *Swadeshi* Movement. He was also one of the early leaders who enunciated the philosophy of Non-Co-operation

Movement. He edited *Sandhya,* a national journal founded in 1904, and it had a decisive influence on the masses because it was the only vernacular paper in Bengali, which boldly advocated complete Indian Nationalism. Again, a conference of leading Christians from all over India held at Ranchi in 1923 passed a resolution to give full support to the national movement. In 1930, among the 78 persons who accompanied Mahatma Gandhi during his Salt March from Sabarmati *ashram* to Dandi, there was a Christian named Thevarthundiyil Titus Titus, a young disciple of Gandhi and a member of a Christian family of Travancore. In the freedom and pro-democracy movement in Travancore in the 1930s and 1940s, Prominent Christian leaders like T.M. Varghese, A.J. John, Anne Mascarenes and Akkamma Cherian were pioneering forces.[78] Philippose Elanjikkal John (1903-1955) was another prominent member of the Travencore State Congress.[79]

Joachim Alva (1907-1979)[80] was another outstanding personality in the history of the freedom struggle. As a student leader, he was the pioneer of youth movement in India. He gave whole-hearted devotion to the national movement and gave up his lucrative job in order to dedicate himself for the freedom struggle. He was also a journalist of high calibre who vigorously advocated the concept of *swadesh* and human brotherhood, especially through his *Forum* (1943), which was a 'fighting paper' from the beginning. His editorial 'Settling the Accounts with the British' resulted in his being prosecuted for sedition in 1943.[81] Mrs. Violet Alva (1908-1969) was another personality with abiding nationalist interest. About the involvement of the Alvas in the freedom movement it has been said: "The combination of Joachim Alva and Violet Alva to the Freedom Movement is significant [....] They risked their all, but they served [the country] to the full extent of their ability which they had in plenty."[82]

M.V. Kamath, an RSS ideologue and a regular columnist in the RSS weekly, the *Organiser,* is a person with little sympathy for the Christians. Yet in his autobiography he acknowledges that several Christians took part in the freedom movement. He mentions the names of Cyprian Alvares, Joachim Alva, Marcel A.M. D'Souza as Christian freedom fighters.[83] He notes: "It is necessary to state that many Roman Catholics, whom I personally know of were very much in the freedom movement and national mainstream."[84]

Travancore received English education by foreign agencies as early as 1806. The new generation under the impact of Western civilisation came to have a broad social and political outlook. The people became independent in spirit and critical in their attitude. They also became conscious of their rights and privileges.[85] For example, the popular agitation, which came to be known as the "Travancore Memorial" or the "Malayali Memorial" of 1861, drafted and presented to the Maharaja on 11 January 1891 a demand for the political rights for the people of Travancore. The Malayali Memorial was an important landmark in the political awakening of the people in later days. The submission of the demand by the Memorial marks the awakening for the first time, of the educated sections of the State of Kerala. It reflected the political aspirations of the leading communities like, Nair, Ezhava, Nambudiri, Latin Christian, Syrian Christian and Anglo-Indian.[86]

Many Christians were associated with the Malayali Memorial and some of them presided over its public meetings. The political meetings held at North Parur, Kottayam and Trivandrum were presided over by Christians like Father Hilarion, Vicar of the Parur Church, Rt. Rev. Mar Athanasius, the Metropolitan of the Syrian Church and T.F. Lloyd, an Anglo Indian. In the conference held at Kottayam on 3 June 1891 to examine the contents of the memorial was attended by prominent Christians like Varghese Mappila and Mani Kathanar, along with leaders of various other communities.[87]

George Joseph (or Oorayil Joseph George, 1887-1938)[88] was another outstanding Christian who engaged in the freedom struggle. It has been said that the landslide in the opinion of the Indian Christian Community in favour of nationalism was very much ascribable to his dynamic leadership.[89]

George Joseph was attracted to the Home Rule Movement and given training in political organisation by Mrs. Annie Besant. In 1918 he was sent as a member of the three-party delegation to England to present the Indian case before the British public. He was one of the first batch of barristers who sacrificed their comforts to engage themselves in national work and joined the Non-Co-operation Movement and boycott of foreign cloth shops. At the bidding of Pandit Motilal Nehru he discarded his fashionable dress for the coarser homespun and associated himself as editor of the Allahabad daily *The Independent,* which used to exercise a profound influence on its readers.[90] In 1920 he courted arrest and was kept in Allahabad prison. He was subsequently sentenced to rigorous imprisonment in the course of the Non-Co-operation Movement in 1921. In 1922 Joseph was arrested for sedition and spent a year in the Lucknow district jail along with Jawaharlal Nehru, Mahadev Desai, Purushottamdas Tandon and Devdas Gandhi.[91] On his release in 1923 he was called to take up the editorship of *Young India*, Mahatma Gandhi's weekly.[92] In 1937 George Joseph was elected to the Central Legislative Assembly.[93] For a time he was also the editor of *The South Indian Mail*.[94]

George Joseph was also invited to assume the leadership of the *Satyagraha* movement. He led the *Vaikom Satyagraha* for which he was beaten and arrested and sentenced to jail. The issue was that outcaste Hindus were not allowed to enter the Shiva temple at Vaikom, in North Travancore, although non-Hindus such as Christians and Muslims were permitted.[95]

On 6 March 1938 George Joseph expired. He was one of the Keralites who had projected themselves significantly on the national political plane before the independence of India. Jawaharlal Nehru makes a reference to him in his Autobiography that of him it is said that he did not pop his tail between the hind legs but if he sowed the wind he was equally ready to reap the whirlwind.[96] It has also been observed that the Indian Christian community was drawn into the vast arena of national politics by the dynamic personality of George Joseph. He roused national consciousness and a high sense of patriotism among the Christians.[97]

C. Samuel Aaron was another prominent Christian who participated in the national movement. The active participation of the Aarons in the freedom movement began with the *Salt Satyagraha* Movement of 1930. As the *Salt Satyagrahis* of Kerala reached the village of Chombal on 16 April 1930, the local residents under the leadership of Samuel Aaron gave them a rousing reception.[98] On 21 April 1930 when the *Salt Satragrahis* led by K.Kelappan reached the village of Pariyaram near Payyannur, Mrs Gracy Aaron led the women and showered flowers and rice on them.[99] The *Satyagraha* camp at Payyannur was located on the spacious premises of the large coconut farm belonging to Samuel Aaron. He also gave the Brighter Hotel Buildings at Cannanore belonging to him for temporary use by the Congress *Satyagrahis* intent on breaking the Salt Law, from 22 May to 1 June 1930.[100] Because of the support he had given to the *Satyagrahis* he had to face prosecution and was jailed.[101] It has been observed that the participation of the Aarons in the national movement was of unique importance for the Christian community in South India.

Among the leading Christian women leaders who took part in the freedom struggle, mention may be made of Mrs. George Joseph,[102] Mrs. Gracy Aaron,[103] Mrs Margaret Pavamani,[104] Miss Mary Thomas[105] and Miss Matilda Kalten.[106]

The rise of modern journalism in Kerala also gave a great impetus to the growth of political consciousness. The press became an important medium through which the Western ideas of freedom and democracy began to spread among the members of the middle class and gradually among the masses. Christian journalistic publications such as *Rajya Samacharam* (from 1847), *Paschimodayam* (from 1847), *Paschima Taraka* (from 1862), *Satyanada Kahalam, Satyanadam,*[107] *Nazrani Deepika,* (from 1887, later *Deepika*),[108] *Kerala Mitram, Malayala Manorama* (from 1890)[109] and so on contributed greatly to political awakening and shaped public opinion and national consciousness. Christianity also moulded the minds of men, women, youth and children through their educational institutions.

Considering the numerical insignificance of the Christians in India in comparison with the Hindus who form the majority population, the Christian contribution to freedom struggle is indeed commendable and remarkable. In addition, we need to remember that the vast majority of the Christians of India belong to the lower classes and during the independence movement they were still struggling to emancipate themselves from the clutches of the upper castes of Hinduism.

Indian freedom movement was not the monopoly of the Hindus as Shourie would have us imagine. Kuldip Nayar maintains that the freedom struggle was secular in character. The Hindus, Muslims, Sikhs, Christians, Parsis and others all fought together shoulder to shoulder.[110]

Thus patriotism is indeed a Christian virtue. The Indian Christians *truly identified themselves* with the Indian national movement and demonstrated their deepest concern for the cause. In fact, they were among the prominent persons who pioneered and shaped the goals of Indian nationalism. Therefore, as George Thomas rightly observes, 'the Indian Christian community *was not behind any other community* in their desire for national freedom and in their readiness to work and make sacrifices for it'.[111]

Accusation: Missionary Scholarship Was a 'Holy War' Meant to Convert

Shourie holds that there was also a conspiracy between the Christian missionaries and foreign scholars. According to him, the missionary scholarship, or the scholarship inspired by the missionary impulse, has been even more lethal than the calumny against Indians, because its effects have lasted through the century.[112] He even calls it a 'Holy War' against Hinduism with the aim of ensuring that Christianity acquires dominion over the world.[113] He argues, for example, that the scholarship of the famous indologist Friedrich Max Müller (1823-1900), whose literary output was prodigious, had a commitment to the spread of Christianity in India. He further alleges that Max Müller eagerly awaited with great expectation for the ultimate and imminent triumph of Christianity in India.[114] Monier Williams is another scholar whom Shourie accuses of having had a sinister desire to convert India to Christianity.[115] There is no denying the fact that Max Müller greatly loved and respected the Indian cultural heritage. It is also a fact that Indians themselves knew little of their cultural heritage until the scientific research and the scholarship of men like Max Müller and Monier Williams revealed it to them.

Shourie is very *selective* in his reference to foreign scholars. He wrongly takes an individual scholar's opinion as the view of all scholars and of the Christian missionaries. Great personalities like Robert de Nobili (1577-1656) the 'father of Indian inculturation', Joseph Beschi (1680-1747) the Tamil scholar, Thomas Stephens (1549-1619) the English Jesuit who wrote a *Purana*,[116] the indefatigable Baptist missionary William Carey who himself translated the whole Bible into Bengali, Sanskrit, Oriya, Marathi and Hindi, Camille Bulcke who wrote a scholarly thesis on Ram for his Ph.D and who is also acknowledged as a great Hindi scholar, George Proksch (1904-1986), a scholar of Hindi, Sanskrit, and Hindustanti music, are but a few of the many eminent Christian missionaries who made great contribution to the development of Indian languages, the science of linguistics and Indian art.[117] Other important areas in which Christian contribution is significant are medicine and health, anthropology, philosophy, theology, mass media and social communication, inter-faith dialogue, art of printing, modern science, social service, development of human resource, preservation of indigenous cultures and development of languages both classical and modern. In fact, many modern regional languages were provided with grammars, vocabularies, alphabets and scripts by Christian missionaries.[118]

Again, there were also other great scholars of non-Indian origin – T.W. Rhys Davids, Paul Deussen, Richard Garbe, Theodore Stcherbatsky, Erich Frauwallner, A.B. Keith, H. Zimmer, V. de la Poussin, R. Antoine, J. Neuner, P. Fallon, R.V. De Smet, Bede Griffiths, Abbe J.A. Dubois, J. Dupuis, Sara Grant, to name a few – who scientifically studied the sacred texts, religions and philosophies of India with great respect and admiration. Unfortunately, the contribution of these missionaries is of little significance as far as Shourie is concerned. He *conveniently* makes no reference to them in his *Missionaries in India.* However – though it will be indignant to Shourie – we Indians need to be grateful to those noble-minded people who have helped us to discover ourselves, and to build up our self-confidence, rather than finding fault with them.

Accusation: Insurgency in Northeast India is Supported by Missionaries

Shourie maintains that certain missionary groups have been giving assistance to the secessionist activities in Northeast India. He says: "Intelligence agencies speak specifically of the role of missionaries in stoking unrest in the North-East."[119] He further argues that, while intelligence agencies have been warning government about the role of some missionary groups in fomenting secession in the Northeast, those dangers are never acknowledged in public by government and have not taken the necessary steps to put an end to the activities of such elements.[120] He also alleges that, it is the conversions that have led to social tensions and clashes between the various communities and tribes. They also prepare the ground for anti-national forces to secure allies and clients.[121]

According to Shourie, the support the Church gives to secessionist groups is the greatest in Nagaland, followed by Manipur. In Mizoram, he says, the role of the Church is overtly political. There are also intelligence reports to government of the secessionist groups receiving 'liberal financial contributions' from certain Church organisations. He accuses them of diverting funds meant for developmental programmes to certain insurgent groups.[122]

In speaking of the situation in Northeast India, Shourie frequently refers to the intelligence report as his source of information. But it is to be examined who forms these so-called intelligence agencies? In India much of the bureaucratic work is already in the hands of those who advocate Hindutva – from governors of states to Vice-Chancellors of the universities to clerks in the offices. In Northeast, there are also numerous business communities from 'outside' that strongly advocate the Hindutva ideology and give it full support, including funds. If some of these people form the so-called intelligence agencies, the reports against the Christian missionaries can hardly expect to be objective.

According to Shourie, much of what the missionaries are doing in Arunachal Pradesh is a violation of existing laws. Yet little is done to stem their violations. He also argues that it was because of the tensions which the aggressive missionary activities were causing in the areas that the Arunachal Pradesh Freedom of Religion Act was passed in 1978.[123] But it must be recalled here that, the so-called 'Freedom of Religion Act' in reality is a denial of a person's fundamental right to follow one's conscience in matters of religion. No civilised world will pass a law denying freedom of conscience to a human being. Besides, one should not obey an unjust and irrational law. In this connection, we must also add that, many tribal groups in Northeast India have been Hinduised by 'sanskritisation', 'absorption' and 'assimilation', i.e., through Hindu festivals, use of Hindu symbols, rituals and literature, promotion of Sanskrit language as well as through 'forced' conversions by some of the Hindu missionaries and rulers as in parts of Assam, Arunachal Pradesh, Manipur and Tripura.

Shourie alleges that in Northeast India, States are carved out on the basis of religion. He says: "The aim henceforth of an influential part of the Church was to carve out states, or area within states, in which the Christians would be in majority as Christians or, at the least, areas in which persons running the governments would be amenable to the influence of the Church. The effort has proceeded farthest in the North-East, and has become a cause of concern among the intelligence and defence service."[124] Anyone who is familiar with Indian politics, history and administrative system knows that for the creation of a new state many important criteria are followed other than religion, such as, administrative feasibility, geographical situation, population, ethnic and linguistic 'homogeneity', etc.

At this juncture, a question may be asked to Shourie – as he was a minister in the BJP-led NDA government – has he or the NDA governments in New Delhi ever seriously asked the question why is the Northeast in a condition of unrest? What has the government at the centre done for the educational, social, economic and human development of the people of the region? Vishal Mangalwadi who visited Nagaland some years ago was told by a Hindu from the Hindi belt who was an officer in the Indian army about the real condition of Nagaland. There is, he said, only one railway station and only one airport for the whole state. It has no rivers, no major industries, no mineral wealth and no commerce. In fact, the Government of India has done much to damage Nagaland's trade and tourism by enacting various travel restrictions.[125]

So, the root cause of the problem of 'political unrest', 'insurgency' and 'secessionism' in Northeast India lies mainly with the fact of long-standing neglect of the region by the various governments in New Delhi, and not with the Christian missionaries. Is the ULFA which is a powerful secessionist group of Assam a Christians movement? No. Its members are Hindus. There are over 19 major secessionist groups in Manipur valley and several of them are led by the Hindus. If we look at India as a whole we will discover that, as Mani Shankar Aiyar says, the Naxalites of Andhra Pradesh are Hindus, the Hurriyat gang in Kashmir are Muslims, and the Khalistanis are Sikhs.[126] Here the words of Archbishop Thomas Menamparampil of Guwahati seems appropriate: "Missionaries are often accused for the political unrest in the North-East. In fact, there are only a small number of Christians among the political activists there. An unfair share of blame is put on the Christians."[127]

Christianity has contributed much to the people of Northeast India:[128] the people there have not been allowed to be victims of the oppressive structures perpetuated by Hinduism, like, caste system, gender discrimination and untouchability, from many superstitious practices, the discriminatory laws of Manu, the hegemony of the Hindu upper castes, Zamindars and the Hindutva ideologues and organisations. They have received greater dignity as human beings, greater respect for human rights, greater gender equality, better educational and health care facilities, better prospects of poverty eradication, greater self respect, etc., than many of their counterparts in India, especially in the so-called 'cow-belt' of North India where Hinduism dominates. It is said, for example that, in many ways, women in Northeast are better off than their counterparts in the rest of India. Dowry deaths, female foeticide and infanticide hardly make headlines in newspapers.

It may be befitting to recall here an advice of Mangalwadi to Arun Shourie: "I wished you [Shourie] would stop worrying about what the missions [sic] have done to the North-Eastern tribes. You and I need rather to be concerned about what Hinduism is doing today, say, to the Tharu tribe in the UP."[129]

Shourie's Undisclosed Religious Allegiance

In the book *Missionaries in India* Shourie claims that he is a person with no definite religious allegiance. He says: "I am an ardent idolater: I bow to pictures and idols, I visit temples and Buddhist shrines and Sufi *dargahs* – especially Hindu temples."[130] He further affirms that, he practises daily meditation using the techniques set out in Buddhist texts, and believes that the essence of the Indian people is their inner quest and that, this quest is pursued first and the foremost by Hindus.[131] When in 1994, the organisers of the Catholic Bishops' Conference of India during their meeting in Pune invited Shourie to give a Hindu assessment of missionary work in India, he conveniently said: "I am, of course, nobody to speak on behalf of the Hindus. I am not even one who can report what the perception of the Hindus is of the work of the Christian Missionaries."[132] This ambiguous – or better stated undisclosed – religious identity of Shourie has been very advantageous to him for targeting certain religious groups. But the groups and the religious communities he attacks, the religious ideology he staunchly defends, and the government in which he has rendered his service as an important union cabinet minister, make it clear to any intelligent person, where Shourie's religious and ideological allegiances lie.

Use of Select, Outdated and Controversial Sources

Much of the source material that Shourie has used for writing the *Missionaries in India* has been highly selective and controversial in nature, besides being outdated. For example, he shows much dependence on *The Complete Works* of Swami Vivekananda, and *The Collected Works of Mahatma Gandhi*. But unfortunately, he is clearly *selective* and one-sided in his references to them. Sardar K.M. Panikkar's *Asia and Western Dominance* (1953) is another source to which he has recourse.[133] Another important source which Shourie frequently uses is the controversial *The Christian Missions Enquiry*

Committee's Report or *The Niyogi Committee Report* of the Madhya Pradesh Government which was released in 1956. It has been proved beyond doubt that, this report was prepared with the prejudice that, Christianity is a menace to India. The Niyogi Committee consisted of six members with Dr M. Bhawani Shankar Niyogi, a retired Chief Justice of the Nagpur High Court, and its Secretary, the only official representative of the government, all others being non-officials. The only Christian member of the Committee was a man from Kerala who had many grievances against the foreign missionaries and had often attached them publicly in the press. Thus the Committee gave the appearance of having a Christian representative among its members. Dr Niyogi himself was a man deeply prejudiced against the foreign missionaries.[134] Mani Shankar Aiyar calls him an intolerant Congress activist who made his life's mission to root out Christian missionary activity.[135] Therefore, we have serious reasons to question the objectivity of this report. In fact, when in 1955, the Niyogi report was presented in the parliament in Delhi, it was rejected outright as discriminatory towards the Christians. On that occasion, the then Prime Minister Jawaharlal Nehru said: "Christianity is one of the important religions of India, established here for nearly two thousand years. We must not do anything which gives rise to any feeling of oppression or suppression in the mind of our Christian friends and fellow-countrymen."[136] However, Shourie has found it very useful for his purpose of maligning the Christians and painting them in bad light.[137] Some of the other sources of Shourie are the 'Census of India', and the draft working documents used by the Catholic Bishops' Conference of India in their meeting of January 1994 – which again he has used in a one-sided and selective manner, in addition to quoting them out of context.

Shourie conveniently avoids making a study of the writings of those Indians who found in Christianity many things positive. For example, he neglects those to whom Christian social teaching was a source of inspiration, like Raja Ram Mohan Roy (1772-1833), Mahatma Phule (1827-1890), Gopal Krishna Gokhale (1863-1915). He does not consider those Hindus who were intensely committed to Christ though they may not have joined any formal Church organization, like, Keshab Chandra Sen (1838-1884), Pratap Chandra Mazoomdar (1840-1905) or those Hindus who claimed to remain Christians, such as Brahmabandhab Upadhyaya (1861-1907), Manilal C. Parekh (1885-1967), Narayan Vaman Tilak (1861-1919), Pandita Ramabai Saraswati (1858-1922) and the like.[138]

Shourie is a past master in quoting texts *out of context* and in selecting controversial Christian writers to support *his* views – for instance, he refers to Thomas Paine, Hans Küng and Edward Schillebeeckx.[139] It may be recalled that for Paine the Bible was more the work of a demon than the word of God; Küng is noted for his views against the doctrine of infallibility; Schillebeeckx was suspected of 'heresy' by the Catholic Church.

Shourie selects carefully *certain writings* from the British colonial period, such as, those of T.B. Macaulay, Charles Trevelyan and Richard Temple and quotes from them extensively.[140] Among the foreign scholars, he makes special mention of Krzenski, Max Müller and Monier Willams. Their views and writings are used by him in order to 'establish' his premise that there was a secret conspiracy between the colonialists, scholars and missionaries in order to Christianise India.

But Christian missionaries in India had more important and urgent things to do than 'playing politics'. It is evident from the quantity and the quality of their contribution to Indian culture. Mention has already been made to some of the outstanding Christian scholars and missionaries, and their contribution to Indian culture. In addition, it is an acknowledged fact that Christian missionaries and scholars made substantial contribution to Indian vernacular languages and dialects, by providing them alphabets, scripts, vocabularies and grammars.[141] The missionaries were also primarily responsible for the introduction of the art of printing, modern science, educational pattern, medicine and health, etc., in India.

Use of *Others* as Shourie's Mouthpiece

Shourie uses a clever method of using *others* to express *his* views. In fact, he effectively uses certain eminent personalities as *his* mouthpiece and quotes extensively from them. For example, he frequently uses the writings of Mahatma Gandhi and Swami Vivekananda, in order to impress upon the reader how badly Hinduism has been treated by the Christian missionaries. For instance, Shourie says: "The viciousness of the distortions and misrepresentations of the missionaries, the virulence of their abuse, the length of time over which they kept up the barrage – we cannot imagine these today. Swami Vivekananda had to face these at every turn, Gandhiji knew them well."[142] He says again: "Swami Vivekananda has given the most heart-rendering accounts of the calumnies that Christian missionaries spread about Hinduism, about India, about him personally."[143]

When Shourie wants to tell the Christians that Jesus Christ is not the Son of God, he uses the words of Mahatma Gandhi who said: "Jesus was the son of God only in the sense that we are all children of God, [...] The belief that Jesus is the only begotten son of God is to me contrary to Reason."[144] Elsewhere he uses the *Quran* to tell the same to Christians.[145] Again, when Shourie wishes to express the view that laws should be passed to prevent the so-called proselytisation he quotes Gandhiji again: "If I [Gandhiji] had power and could legislate, I should certainly stop all proselytising."[146] He further states: "Gandhiji said, it would be better for non-Indian missionaries to return to their countries and attend to problems there."[147] One wonders why Shourie does not state *his opinions* about Christianity on his own authority without employing *others as his mouthpiece* and quoting them selectively and often out of context.

Denial of Fundamental Rights to Minorities

Christianity neither accepts nor condones any conversion by force or fraud or allurement. Forced conversion is a contradiction in terms. It is totally against the basic principles of human rights and freedom of conscience. In fact, the Church explicitly forbids it. But Christians do try to witness to Christ and proclaim their belief in him. Similar things are also being done by almost all the religions of the world, including those of India. Freedom to profess, practice and propagate one's faith is guaranteed by the Indian Constitution as one of the fundamental rights. It says: "All persons are equally entitled to Freedom of Conscience and the right to freely profess, practise and propagate religion." (Article 25) Therefore, a Christian – for that matter the follower of any religion – if he or she proclaims his or her faith, it is not a violation of anyone's right, for he or she is only exercising one of his or her fundamental rights.

Shourie's *Missionaries in India* is written with the objective of denying the above stated fundamental right to the Christians. He also demands that, all cases of conversions be open to scrutiny by the state authorities.[148] He says: "The freedom of religion guaranteed by Articles 25 and 26 of the Constitution should be subject to the same sort of restriction as is a secular right like freedom of speech. [....] In a secular country, why should the right to practise and propagate religion not be subject to the same sorts of perimeters as applied to other secular rights?"[149]

Shourie goes on to accuse the Christians that the missionaries have successfully fought off every effort to enjoin on the State the duty to scrutinise conversions.[150] First of all, Shourie should know that the State has neither the duty nor the right to scrutinise the religious conversion of any person. Besides, if an ordinance or law is unjust or discriminatory towards a particular group, it is unacceptable and one is perfectly justified in disobeying it. In India, certain States want to scrutinise the practice and propagation of faith of *some selected minority religions only*, and not others who are engaged in similar activities. It is well known that practically all over India the Hindu missionaries and groups are seriously involved in propagating their faith. They may call it by different names such as, *shuddhi* ('purification'), *ghar vapasi* ('returning home'), *paravartan* ('turning back'), 're-conversion', sanskritisation, 'cultural integration', etc. They are also engaged in the same activity in North America, Europe and elsewhere. For example, the Rama Krishna Mission, International Society for Krishna Consciousness, Siddha Yoga Meditation, Integral Yoga, Movement of Satya Sai Baba, Sanatana Dharma Samgha, the Self-Realisation Fellowship of Yogananda, Ananda Margis, Transcendental Meditation of Maharishi Mahesh Yogi, the Centre of Aurobindo and Mère and so on, are agents for the propagation of Hinduism outside India especially in North America and Europe.[151] Besides, if all conversions are to be subject to scrutiny by the State, the so-called re-conversions in which many Hindutva organisations are engaged, should also be subject to the same scrutiny, for it is also conversion from one faith to another.

An observation made by Gurcharan Das, one of the leading thinkers of contemporary India, may be apt here. He asks: "The critics of the Christian missionaries in India complain that they not only engage in charity but also convert people to their faith. I ask, what is wrong with that? After all, freedom of thought and religion are guaranteed by our Constitution. If the marketing of ideas by Christians is more successful, it means merely that they are doing a better job than the Hindus and the Muslims. The persecution of the Christians by the Hindu fundamentalists only means that they suffer from an inferiority complex. They lack confidence in their own way, and its ability to hold people."[152]

Shourie's 'Feet of Clay' in Indian History

In the book *Missionaries in India,* Shourie deals with Christianity in India as if it is a vestige of British colonialism and nothing more. His historical treatment of it seldom goes beyond the period of British imperialism. Thus, he reduces the history of 2000 years of Christianity in India to 200 years of British rule. But in reality, Christianity in India is as old as Christianity itself. In fact, Benjamin Walker comments: "Christianity is of greater antiquity in India than in any other country in the world except Palestine – it is older in India than in Rome itself."[153]

Shourie's 'feet of clay' in Indian history is even more evident in what he says about the role of Christians in the Indian national movement and the relationship between missionaries and the British colonisers. According to him, the missionaries, even those of Indian origin, did not join the Independence Movement, and Christian missionary activity was inextricably tied up with British imperial control.[154] As we have already seen from our detailed discussion above, there was no such collaboration between missionaries and the British, and the true history of the Indian Independence movement presents us with a different story than that which Shourie provides. Many Christians actively participated in the freedom struggle.

Shourie's Superficial Knowledge of Christianity

Shourie examines the Bible, the New Testament in particular, in an extremely incompetent manner. Without being proficient in the science of hermeneutics and knowledge of Biblical languages, Shourie ventures to comment on the Christian Bible and its contents in an air of authoritativeness.[155] Shourie's *Harvesting our Souls* (2000) is the best example of his profession to be a 'Bible scholar'. According to Shourie, the command of Jesus to 'go into the whole world to preach the good news' is a later interpolation.[156] Unfortunately, he does not realise that, even if this verse is a later addition, it would not in any way change the basic belief of the Christians on the matter. Christians do not base all their activities of proclaiming their faith, on this one verse from the New Testament. There are other weighty reasons for proclaiming the message of Jesus Christ. Thus, in discussing the Bible, Shourie lacks scholarship and sensitivity. His cynicisms reveals his blatant fundamentalist leanings and anti-Christian mentality. Biblical books, some of which go back to more than 3000 years, and which continue to inspire millions of people all over the world, deserve greater respect than Shourie is willing to concede.

Shourie in his book discusses several Christian theological issues, such as, the inerrancy of the Bible, infallibility of the Pope, moral teachings of the Catholic Church, theology of Vatican Council II, salvation outside the Church, 'contextualisation' of the Church, inculturation, inter-religious dialogue, liberation theology, etc. His analysis lacks depth of scholarship. He often uses sources that are dubious. For example, when he discusses the doctrine of 'infallibility', first of all, he does not understand the concept correctly, for he says: "The history of the Popes and their actual conduct had left little ground for believing that, being the representatives of God on earth, they were infallible."[157] Secondly, it seems that he depends on Hans Küng – a theologian 'censured' by the Catholic Church precisely for his wrong views on the issue – as the *reliable authority* on the matter!

On the occasion of the CBCI meeting in Pune in 1994, the then Archbishop Alphonse Mathias of Bangalore told Bishop Valerian D'Souza of Pune, *teasing him and Shourie*: "'He [Shourie] knows more about Christianity than your students,' [...] 'He knows more about Christianity', [...] 'than many of our professors'."[158] From the manner in which Shourie discusses Christian theological matters and passes judgements on them, it seems that he took *too seriously* what was said as a 'joke'!

Missionaries in India is a Trust Betrayed

Shourie's book *Missionaries in India* (1994) is an epitome of a betrayed trust. In the introduction to his book, he states: "For some reason the organisers were so kind as to ask me to give the Hindu perception of the work of Christian missionaries in India. That lecture and the discussion which followed forms the scaffolding of this book."[159] Christians often have a quality to be open, welcoming, to think well of others, to be nice and courteous to people. Shourie concludes his *Missionaries in India* with these words: "They [Bishops, senior clergy and scholars gathered at Pune for the C.B.C.I meeting in 1994] heard me out in pin-drop silence, and with unbroken patience. [...] They were courteous and the very models of dignity and decorum throughout. *I left feeling I had been among friends.*"[160] Later, the same person who was treated as a friend by the Christian leaders wrote a book accusing, maligning and denigrating them, and it reveals his *level of culture*. The book also proves that, he neither had the magnanimity to return the courtesy shown to him nor the nobility to *respect truth* and to be *as objective as possible* in his evaluation of the Christians. Instead, he *betrayed their trust* by writing a book based on half-truths and distorted facts concerning them. The betrayal of trust was complete when Shourie published the seminar material of the Catholic Bishops Conference of India (1994) without formal authorisation from the organisers.[161]

Shourie's Anti-Christian Syndrome

It is said that, falsehood oft repeated, achieves the semblance of truth and some are sure to believe it. Shourie's *Missionaries in India* is a typical example of such an attempt at propagating falsehood with persistence and malice.[162] Thus, a bundle of partial truths, many distorted facts, several outdated sources and plenty of imagination form the source material for the above work. He also uses the writings of scholars, administrators and Christian missionaries of the *colonial India* in order to assess the Christianity of *today*, as if the same conditions and circumstances still prevail. Therefore, the arguments in the book carry little conviction. The work also epitomises his prejudices against Christianity, and in the process, reveals his 'anti-Christian syndrome'.

Shourie seldom has a good word for the services that the Christian missionaries have rendered to the nation, to himself personally and to his family. In this, he seems to make his own, the words of Swami Vivekananda who said: "The college founded by the missionaries are all right, so far as the education is concerned. But with religion it is different. The Hindu is acute; *he takes the bait but avoids the hook.*"[163] We may say that, Shourie has taken the bait in as much as he has benefited from the Christian institutions. He is not an exception. There are also many others who have benefited by the education provided by the Christian institutions. But what Shourie wants to tell the Christian missionaries is that Christian education is all right, their social and humanitarian services are welcome, but let them not utter the word 'Christianity' or the name of Jesus Christ. In other words, Shourie's philosophy is: let the Christians do *their duty to serve the nation* but let them *not ask for their rights*. But Shourie should know that, without Jesus Christ and Christianity, there is neither Christian education nor Christian service nor Christian humanitarian activity.

Many of Shourie's comments on Christianity and Christian missionaries are provocative, scornful, and provide a philosophy for religious fundamentalists to shatter the centuries old fabric of religious pluralism in India. He does not hesitate to say that, the Church is a vendor of goods,[164] that the Bible contains many contradictions and interpolations, that Jesus Christ is not the Son of God, that the objective of the Christian institutions and Christian humanitarian activities is to convert the non-Christians, that the Christians instigate and support the insurgency movements in Northeast India, that the focus of the Church is not depth of the spiritual search but numbers, that there was a conspiracy between Christianity and British colonialists, and between Christian missionaries and scholars to Christianise India, etc.

Therefore it takes little effort for a reader of *Missionaries in India* to understand that the picture of the Christians which Shourie paints is that, they are villains, criminals and anti-nationals and they deserve to be served notice to 'Quit India'. Shourie's book is a pre-meditated and well-calculated campaign of calumny against the Christian community. It may be noted that the Christian community though a minority, has a commendable record of patriotism and service and that it has not taken to violence or aggression in its 2000-year old existence in India.

Besides the *Missionaries in India* which we have analysed at some length, there is a formidable quantity of 'Shourie literature – most of them targeting religious minorities and secular ideologies with venom and aggression. He sows prejudices and harvests hatred. He breaks rather than builds. Basically Shourie is *a negative writer*. Yet his capacity as a 'pen-pusher' has won him readers who tend to credit him with scholarship. He has emerged as a theoretician and ideologue providing legitimacy to religious fundamentalism and Hindu cultural nationalism. His writings have contributed much to the crisis of secularism and religious tolerance in India, as was witnessed, for example, in the attacks against Christians in Gujarat in 1998, Orissa in 1999 (murder of the Graham Stains and his two sons),[165] against Muslims in Gujarat in 2002 (post-Godhra violence), the passing of anti-conversion laws in some of the States of India, etc. History bears ample testimony to the fact that acts of fascism is always preceded by carefully concocted ideological distortions. It is writings of people like Shourie which have rendered legitimacy to acts of violence, crime and murder carried out regularly by the foot soldiers of fundamentalist ideologies.

Conclusion

Shourie thrives by denigrating and maligning the minorities of India – be they Buddhist, Christian, Muslim, Communist, Dalit or Tribal. He stigmatises Christianity as a foreign religion propagated by missionaries. He approaches Christianity with the preconceived mindset that it is quintessentially destructive in nature. His *Missionaries in India* contains the stuff necessary to buttress all the more the Hindutva offensive against the Christian minority in India. The assumptions that underlie his presentation of distorted facts, irrational arguments, prejudices and calumny against Christianity are to be seen as part of a wider sinister design to cleanse India of the Christians. But Shourie should know that Indian Christians are Indian like every other Indian, and that their patriotism and loyalty to the nation can never be questioned by any right thinking person. But the real threat to India is that portion of the majority community in India which borrows from Italian fascism and Hitler's Nazism dangerous ideas and dubious techniques with the sinister intention to create out of the secular, pluralistic and democratic India a monolithic Hindu *rashtra* by wiping out the minorities.

Shourie's book *Missionaries in India* is deliberately political with decisive hegemonic objectives. It spurns the intellectual objective of searching for truth. It is communal in essence, and the intention of the author is to make Christians hate-objects of the Hindus and Hindutva organisations. Undoubtedly, Shourie is very familiar with the strategy of the fascists in propagating 'Big Lies' against their opponents. This being the case, the book of Shourie can be considered as a typical example of seditious literature, and sooner or later it would belong to the dustbin of history.

Notes

1. See A. Shourie, *Missionaries in India,* 3.
2. See K. Elst, *Decolonising,* 216-217.
3. See K. Elst, *Decolonising,* 216.
4. See http://.164.24.167:8080/members/website/Biodata.asp?no=72.
5. Shourie was elected to the Rajya Sabha in July 1998; from November 1991 to 31 August 2001 he was Minister of State in the ministry of Statistics and Programme Implementation and Minister of State in the Department of Administrative Reforms and Public Grievances of the Ministry of Personal, Public Grievances and Pensions; from 24 July 2000 to August 2001 Minister of State (Independent Charge) of the Department of Disinvestment; from 1 September 2001 onwards Minister of Disinvestment and Minister of Development of North Eastern Region (relinquished the charge of Minister of Development of North Eastern Region on 29 January 2003); from 9 November 2002 to 29 January 2003 Minister of Commerce and Industry; from 29 January 2003 to May 2004 Minister of Communications and Information Technology and from August 2004 onward member of the Committee on External Affairs. See http://164.24.167:8080/members/website/Biodata.asp?no=72.
6. See M.S. Ayar, *Confessions of a Secular Fundamentalist,* xii.
7. See K. Elst, *Decolonising,* 215-216.
8. A. Shourie, *Missionaries in India,* 9.
9. A. Shourie, *Missionaries in India,* 13. Elsewhere also Shourie says the same thing that conversion is the main activity and the principal business of Christianity in India. See ID., *Harvesting our Souls,* 2.
10. See A. Shourie, *Missionaries in India,* 13-14
11. See A. Shourie, *Missionaries in India,* 207-208.
12. A. Shourie, *Missionaries in India,* 15.
13. A. Shourie, *Missionaries in India,* 34.
14. See A. Shourie, *Missionaries in India,* 34.
15. In 1881 Christians in India were 0.71 per cent; in 1991 0.98 per cent; in 1941 1.91 per cent; in 1951 2.04 per cent; in 1991 2.04 per cent and in 2001 2.06 per cent. See A.P. Joshi, M.D. Srinivas and J.K. Bajaj, *An Illustrated Presentation on Religious Demography of India Updated up to 2001,* 9.
16. See M.S. Aiyar, *Confessions of a Secular Fundamentalist,* 94.
17. See M.S. Aiyar, *Confessions of a Secular Fundamentalist,* 189.
18. See A. Shourie, *Missionaries in India,* 168.

19. *Government of India, Ministry of I&B (1996), India 1995, 79,* as cited in *India at 50 Facts, Figures and Analysis 1947-1997*, 390.
20. A. Shourie, *Missionaries in India,* 6.
21. A. Shourie, *Missionaries in India,* 6.
22. A. Shourie, *Missionaries in India,* 3.
23. A. Shourie, *Missionaries in India,* 232-233.
24. M.S. Aiyar, *Confessions of a Secular Fundamentalist*, 190.
25. Aiyar names some of the top colleges of India run by the Christians, such as, St. Stephen's, Delhi, St. Xavier's, Kolkata, Loyola, Chennai, Sophia College for women, Mumbai, St. Columbas, Delhi, St. Xavier's, Ranchi, etc. See M.S. Aiyar, *Confessions of a Secular Fundamentalist*, 190.
26. A. Shourie, *Missionaries in India,* 6-7.
27. See A. Shourie, *Eminent Historians,* i.
28. A. Shourie, *Missionaries in India,* 3. (Emphasis added).
29. See A. Shourie, *Missionaries in India,* 24-28.
30. A. Shourie, *Missionaries in India,* 8.
31. See M.S. Aiyar, *Confessions of a Secular Fundamentalist*, 191.
32. Benedict XVI, *Deus Caritas est,* no. 31.
33. See "Whose Mother is She anyway?" 26.
34. See B.K. Punj, "The Mother Principle", 22.
35. See *Organiser,* 2 November 2003, 10.
36. P.S. Jha, "Who is an Indian?", 43.
37. *India Today,* 24 November 2003, 26.
38. See *India Today,* 18 August 2003, 106.
39. A. Shourie, *Missionaries in India,* 7.
40. G. Das, *The Elephant Paradigm,* 135.
41. See M.S. Aiyar, *Confessions of a Secular Fundamentalist*, 41.
42. A. Shourie, *Missionaries in India,* 20.
43. A. Shourie, *Missionaries in India,* 19.
44. See A. Shourie, *Missionaries in India,* 15.
45. A. Shourie, *Missionaries in India,* 235.
46. A. Shourie, *Missionaries in India,* 3.
47. A. Shourie, *Missionaries in India,* 235. (Emphasis added).
48. See A. Shourie, *Missionaries in India,* 51.
49. G. Das, *The Elephant Paradigm,* 135.
50. This is a widely publicised Hindutva allegation. For example, in the saffronised NCERT school textbook of Social Sciences for Class IX,

we read: "Trade led to political conquest and political power was used to propagate Christianity [...] The English East India Company in the name of religious neutrality was giving maximum support and encouragement to Christianity." B.S. Parakh (ed.), *Contemporary India*, 6; In a book published in 2005 on the religious demography of India we read: "The British, through their *patronage and propagation of Christianity*, introduced another source of religious heterogeneity." A.P. Joshi, M.D. Srinivas and NDJ. K. Bajaj, *An Illustrated Presentation on Religious Demography of India Updated up to 2001*, 9. (Emphasis added)

51. A. Shourie, *Missionaries in India*, 91.
52. See A. Shourie, *Missionaries in India*, 109.
53. See V. Mangalwadi, *Missionary Conspiracy*, 11-13.
54. See V. Mangalwadi, *Missionary Conspiracy*, 158.
55. See V. Mangalwadi, *Missionary Conspiracy*, 126.
56. See V. Mangalwadi, *Missionary Conspiracy*, 167.
57. See V. Mangalwadi, *Missionary Conspiracy*, 127.
58. See V. Mangalwadi, *Missionary Conspiracy*, 127, 161.
59. See S. Yechury, *What is this Hindu Rashtra?*, 7.
60. B.S. Moonje (P&J 5587), 1940, File 117/D-1, Hindu Mahasabha Copies of Resolution, etc, L/P&J/8/683, India Office, British Library, London, 1940. (Emphasis added).
61. See A. Shourie, *Missionaries in India*, 200.
62. A. Shourie, *Missionaries in India*, 200. (Emphasis added).
63. M.S. Golwalkar, *Bunch of Thoughts*, 141. What follows in this section is largely an answer given by the present author to Golwalkar elsewhere. See J. Kuruvachira, *Hindu Nationalists of Modern India*, 166-177.
64. See F. Wilfred, "Christians between Identity – Politics and Nationalism", 265 footnote 13.
65. See G. Thomas, "The Christians and the Freedom Movement", 63.
66. See G. Thomas, "The Christians and the Freedom Movement", 64-66. See also P.K.K. Menon, *The History of Freedom Movement*, vol. 2, 243 footnote 30.
67. See D.A. Jayakumar, *Christians and the National Movement*, 128.
68. See D.A. Jayakumar, *Christians and the National Movement*, 129-131. Kumarappa received degrees from Ohio Wesleyan University, Boston University and the Universities of Harvard and Columbia. He was professor of Philosophy for some time at Lucknow University. See ibid.

69. In July 1947 he joined the delegation nominated by Government of India to help India's economic interest in maritime transport at the meeting of shippers in London. Since he was also a prominent figure in Congress affairs, he was given a chance to be a member of the All India Congress Working Committee in place of Jay Prakash Narayan in 1947. But he rejected the offer in spite of Gandhi's persuasion. After the Independence of India Kumarappa was not interested in power politics. He chose Gandhi Niketan Ashram at Kallupatti (Madurai) to be his headquarters. But his health further deteriorated and was finally admitted to the Government General Hospital in Madras. People of national importance like Rajendra Prasad, Jawaharlal Nehru, Rajaji, Kamaraj and C. Subramanyan frequently visited him. He died on 30 January 1960.
70. See D.A. Jayakumar, *Christians and the National Movement*, 131.
71. See D.A. Jayakumar, *Christians and the National Movement*, 132.
72. See D.A. Jayakumar, *Christians and the National Movement*, 134. See also H.A Popley, *Builders of Modern India K.T. Paul Christian Leader* (1938).
73. See D.A. Jayakumar, *Christians and the National Movement*, 121.
74. See D.A. Jayakumar, *Christians and the National Movement*, 122.
75. See D.A. Jayakumar, *Christians and the National Movement*, 123.
76. See D.A. Jayakumar, *Christians and the National Movement*, 123.
77. See D.A. Jayakumar, *Christians and the National Movement*, 124.
78. See G. Thomas, "The Christians and the Freedom Movement", 64-67.
79. Philippose was born in 1903 in a well-known Jacobite Syrian Christian family of Kerala. He did his higher studies in England. His meeting with Mahatma Gandhi was a significant point in his life. He was one of those sent to Wardha on delegation to meet Gandhi, and spent about three months with him. See "Philippose Elanjikkal John (1903-1955)", 169.
80. Joachim Alva was born on 21 January 1907 at Udipi, South India. He was educated at St. Aloysius College Bangalore. He studied for his B.A. and L.L.B at the St. Xavier's College, Elphinstone College and Law College, Bombay. He served as Steering committee and the Executive Committee of the Bombay Congress Party. He was elected to the Lok Sabha from South Canara from 1952-1967. In 1969 he was a member of the Rajya Sabha. See "Alva Joachim (1907-)", 120-121.
81. "Alva Joachim (1907-)", 121.
82. "Alva Joachim (1907-)", 121.
83. See M.V. Kamath, *A Reporter at Large*, 15; 26-27, 106-107.

84. M.V. Kamath, *A Reporter at Large*, 27.
85. See P.K.K. Menon, *The History of Freedom Movement*,. vol. 2, 1-2.
86. See P.K.K. Menon, *The History of Freedom Movement*, vol. 2, 10.
87. See P.K.K. Menon, *The History of Freedom Movement*, vol. 2, 12 footnote 21.
88. George Joseph was born at Chengannur, Kerala, on 5 June 1887 in a prosperous middleclass family belonging to the Syrian Christian community of Kerala. He studied at Madras Christian College. Then he went to England in 1904 where he took an M.A. in Philosophy at the University of Edinburgh and later Law at Middle Temple in London in 1908. On his return he set up his law practice in Madurai. In 1931 he accepted Roman Catholicism. He was deeply rooted in his Christians principles and values. Among those who influenced his political philosophy mention may be made of Mrs. Annie Besant, Motilal Nehru, Mahatma Gandhi, C. Rajagopalachari, Dr. T.S.S. Rajan. See G.G. Jospeh, *George Joseph*, xxiii-xxiv, 2,8,214;"Joseph George (1887-1938)", 250-252.
89. See P.K.K. Menon, *The History of Freedom Movement*, vol. 2, 91-92 footnote 9a.
90. See G.G. Jospeh, *George Joseph*, 103. In a letter dated 6 February 1920 Motilal Nehru wrote to his son, Jawaharlal Nehru about making George Joseph the editor of the *Independent* 'I think you had better get Joseph for your Editor. You cannot have a better man'. See ibid.
91. See D.A. Jayakumar, *Christians and the national Movement*, 128-129.
92. See G.G. Jospeh, *George Joseph*, 3, 140. George Joseph's tenure as editor lasted about six months after which Gandhi returned to his editorial duties. See ibid., 140.
93. See P.K.K. Menon, *The History of Freedom Movement*, vol. 2, 91-92 footnote 9a.
94. See G.G. Jospeh, *George Joseph*, 3, 67.
95. See G.G. Jospeh, *George Joseph*, 3,158-159.
96. See P.K.K. Menon, *The History of Freedom Movement*, vol. 2, 91-92 footnote 9a.
97. See "Joseph George (1887-1938)", 252.
98. See P.K.K. Menon, *The History of Freedom Movement*, vol. 2, 221, footnote 11.
99. See P.K.K. Menon, *The History of Freedom Movement*, vol. 2, 223.
100. See P.K.K. Menon, *The History of Freedom Movement*, vol. 2, 224.
101. E.M. Gawne, Collector of Malabar requested Samuel Aaron to evict the *Satyagrahis* on the threat of prosecution. Samuel Aaron replied

that he was willing to face the prosecution though, he added, he could not guess what offence he had committed, for the Congress had not yet declared to be an unlawful organisation. He was charged under section 157 and sentenced to pay a fine of Rs 1000 or undergo rigorous imprisonment for six weeks in default. Since Samuel Aaron refused to pay the fine, he was taken to the Central jail at Cannanore. On 18 July the Payyannur police went to the weaving factory owned by Samuel Aaron at Pazhayangadi with a warrant for claiming his movable property to realise the fine of Rs 1000 imposed on him. They took car-loads of things found in the factory. See P.K.K. Menon, *The History of Freedom Movement*, vol. 2, 239 footnote 23.

102. See P.K.K. Menon, *The History of Freedom Movement*, vol. 2, 111 footnote 17.
103. See P.K.K. Menon, *The History of Freedom Movement*, vol. 2, 223, 256 footnote 4, 261, 302 footnote 25.
104. See P.K.K. Menon, *The History of Freedom Movement*, vol. 2, 263-266, 269, 273, 276 footnote 18, 277 footnote 20, 296.
105. See P.K.K. Menon, *The History of Freedom Movement*, vol. 2, 276 footnote 19.
106. See P.K.K. Menon, *The History of Freedom Movement*, vol. 2, 268.
107. Printing press had been introduced into Kerala by the Christian missionaries at the end of the sixteenth century. Probably *Rajya Samacharam* published by the Basel Mission at Tellicherry from June 1847 was the first journalistic publication in Malayalam and its virtual editor was the Christian missionary Herman Gundert. Next came *Paschimodayam*, a monthly, published by Basel Mission at Tellicherry from October 1847. It was followed by *Paschima Taraka* published from Cochin in 1862-1863 and later from Trivandrum. *Satyanada Kahalam* was published first from Koonamavu and later from Varapuzha and Ernakulam. This was the predecessor of *Satyanadam* which came to be published as a weekly, and a certain C. Varkey served as its editor for about 48 years. See P.K.K. Menon, *The History of Freedom Movement*, vol. 2, 580-581. However, a few scholars opine that *Gnananikshepam*, a newspaper published once a month from the C.M.S. Press Kottayam, was the first journal in Malayalam. Others hold that it was started only in 1848. See ibid., footnote 2.
108. See P.K.K. Menon, *The History of Freedom Movement*, vol. 2, 581.
109. In 1888 *Malayala Manorma* Company was started at Kottayam by Varghese Mappilla Kandathil (1858-1904). See P.K.K. Menon, *The History of Freedom Movement*, vol. 2, 581-582. He was first the editor of *Kerala Mitram*, a weekly newspaper, and later of *Malayala Manorama*

(1890 onwards). He was born in a rich Jacobite Christian family of Tiruvalla, Kerala. After his early education he joined the Government College, Trivandrum. He acquired a sound knowledge of Malayalam and Sanskrit. See "Varghese Mappila Kandathil (1858-1904)", 245.

110. See K. Nayar, "Burnt beyond Recognition", 49-50.
111. See G. Thomas, "The Christians and the Freedom Movement", 64-66.
112. A. Shourie, *Missionaries in India,* 159.
113. A. Shourie, *Missionaries in India,* 151.
114. A. Shourie, *Missionaries in India,* 133-151.
115. See A. Shourie, *Missionaries in India,* 152.
116. See N. Falcao, *Kristapurana: A Christian-Hindu Encounter* (2003).
117. See R.H. Lesser, *Some Eminent Missionaries of India,* 19-36.
118. For a detailed discussion on this topic see J. Kuruvachira, *Roots of Hindutva,* 115-118; See G. Plathottam, "Contribution of Christianity to Language and Literature", 334-362. See also S. Karotemprel, "Salesian Contribution", 130-132.
119. A. Shourie, *Missionaries in India,* 234.
120. See A. Shourie, *Missionaries in India,* 208.
121. See A. Shourie, *Missionaries in India,* 207.
122. See A. Shourie, *Missionaries in India,* 207-208.
123. See A. Shourie, *Missionaries in India,* 209.
124. A. Shourie, *Missionaries in India,* 205.
125. See V. Mangalwadi, *Missionary Conspiracy,* 312.
126. See M.S. Aiyar, "Arun Shourie and His Acolytes", 10.
127. Quoted in A. Shourie, *Missionaries in India,* 234.
128. For an account of the influence and impact of Christianity on the people of Northeast India see J. Puthenpurakal (ed.), *Impact of Christianity* (1996); G. Plathottam, "Contribution of Christianity to Language and Literature", 334-362; S. Karotemprel, "Salesian Contribution", 130-132; J. Kuruvachira, *Roots of Hindutva* 115-117; G. Maliekal, *History of the Catholic Church Among the Khasis* (2005); J. Thekkedath, *A History of the Salesians of Don Bosco in India,* 2 vols. (2005).
129. V. Mangalwadi, *Missionary Conspiracy,* 312.
130. A. Shourie, *Missionaries in India,* 2.
131. See A. Shourie, *Missionaries in India,* 2.
132. A. Shourie, *Missionaries in India,* 1.
133. See A. Shourie, *Missionaries in India,* 3-4.

134. See *The Niyogi Committee Report A Critical Appraisal*, 9, 13.
135. See M.S. Ayar, *Confessions of a Secular Fundamentalist*, 189.
136. J. Nehru, as cited in F.A. Plattner, *The Catholic Church in India*, 7.
137. For a critical study on the Niyogi report see A. Soares, G.X. Francis, W. Coelho, *et al.*, *The Niyogi Committee Report A Critical Appraisal*, Varanasi, n.d.
138. See H. Staffner, *The Significance of Jesus in Asia*, 5-168.
139. See A. Shourie, *Missionaries in India*, 211.
140. See A. Shourie, *Missionaries in India*, 60-105.
141. See G. Menacherry, "Cultural Contribution of Indian Church", 85-86; G. Plathottam, "Contribution of Christianity to Language and Literature", 334-362.
142. A. Shourie, *Missionaries in India*, 45-46.
143. A. Shourie, *Missionaries in India*, 3-4.
144. A. Shourie, *Missionaries in India*, 240.
145. See A. Shourie, *Indian Controversies*, 424-426.
146. *Collected Works of Mahatma Gandhi* 46, 110 as cited in A. Shourie, *Missionaries in India*, 37.
147. A. Shourie, *Missionaries in India*, 39.
148. A. Shourie, *Missionaries in India*, 40.
149. A. Shourie, *Missionaries in India*, 232.
150. See A. Shourie, *Missionaries in India*, 204.
151. See T.A. Tweed, S. Prothero (eds.), *Asian Religions in America*, 241-260; E. Fizzotti, F. Squarcini, (eds.), *L'Oriente che non tramonta*, 34-37;97-110; 131-242.
152. G. Das, *The Elephant Paradigm*, 135.
153. B. Walker, *Hindu World*, I, 238. For a full discussion on the topic of Christianity in India see also R. Thapar, *History of India*, I, 134-135; A.M. Mundadan, *History of Christianity in India*, ch.1; R.E. Frykenberg, "Christians in India: An Historical Overview of Their Complex Origins", 33-61; P. Carson, "Christianity, Colonialism, and Hinduism in Kerala: Integration, Adaptation, or Confrontation?", 127-154.
154. See A. Shourie, *Missionaries in India*, 200.
155. See A. Shourie, *Missionaries in India*, 141-142,211-213.
156. See A. Shourie, *Missionaries in India*, 212.
157. See A. Shourie, *Missionaries in India*, 212.
158. A. Shourie, *Missionaries in India*, 241-242.

159. A. Shourie, *Missionaries in India,* ix-x.
160. A. Shourie, *Missionaries in India,* 242. (Emphasis added)
161. See A. Shourie, *Missionaries in India,* 245-293.
162. For example Arun Shourie's *Harvesting Our Souls* (2000) has a chapter entitled 'An Echo Chamber' in which he presents *his version* of the atrocities committed against the Christians between 1998-1999, such as, the raping of nuns in Madhya Pradesh, the murder of Graham Stains and his two sons in Orissa by Hindu fanatics, and so on as mere fabrications of Christians and invention of the Christian media. See A. Shourie, *Harvesting Our Souls,* 7-24.
163. *Collected works* 8, 216 as cited in A. Shourie, *Missionaries in India,* 21. (Emphasis added)
164. Arun Shourie in another of his book says: "The Church is big business. Evangelisation is big business. And the business depends on the harvesting of souls". A. Shourie, *Harvesting Our Souls,* 25.
165. Shourie defended of Dara Singh and some of the Hindutva organisations that were accused of murdering the Stains in Orissa in 1999. See A. Shourie, *Harvesting our Souls,* 14-24.

V

Narendra Modi
The Icon of Contemporary Hindu Communalism

Narendra Damodardas Modi was born on 17 September 1950 at Vadnagar in Meshsana district of North Gujarat. He came to Ahmedabad in 1967 and approached the RSS office, and from there pursued his studies and obtained a Masters Degree in Political Science. He took part in the *Nav Nirman* ('construct anew', meaning 'a total revolution') movement started by Jayaprakash Narayan ('JP') in the early 1970s as a pressure group against corruption.[1] As an RSS *pracharak* Modi took active part in the movement which brought out the leadership qualities in him. In 1972 he became the leader of the Gujarat *Lok Sangharsh Samiti* (LSS, 'Committee for People's Struggle') initiated by 'JP' as part of the *Nav Nirman* movement. Modi also took part in the anti-emergency movement in 1975.[2]

In 1980 he joined the BJP which was a newly founded political party. When Shankarsinh Vaghela was the BJP president of Gujarat (1987-1992), he handpicked Modi with the aim to make BJP a political force in the state.[3] In 1988 Modi was elected the General Secretary of the BJP unit in Gujarat. But a year later he lost this post. From 1989 to 1995 he was in-charge of the election campaign, and in 1995 the BJP won the Assembly elections with a two-third majority in the State. In 1995 Modi was elected the National Secretary of the BJP in charge of various state units like, Haryana, Punjab, Himachal Pradesh, and Jammu and Kashmir. In 1999 he was the National General Secretary of the BJP, and from 2001 Chief Minister of

Gujarat. It was the first time that an RSS cadre being elected to such a post.[4] Modi was sworn in as Chief Minister of Gujarat on 7 October 2001 when the then Chief Minister Keshubhai Patel's popularity was going down dangerously. The BJP needed a charismatic leader to lead the party to victory in the Assembly elections which was then envisaged for 2003.

In 1990 Modi actively participated in the Somnath to Ayodhya *Ram Rath Yatra* led by L.K. Advani. It is said that Modi's prominence as an organiser began from this famous *Rath Yatra.* He also helped Murli Manohar Joshi in organising the *Ekta Yatra* in 1991-1992. In 1993, the U.S. government, under Young Political Exchange Programme, invited him to attend the meet. He also addressed the 'Global Vision 2000' in Washington D.C. where some 10,000 delegates from more than 60 countries participated. Modi belongs to the Other Backward Classes (OBC).[5] He is single[6] and a vegetarian.

Modi's Worldview as Shaped by the RSS

Modi is considered as a hardcore RSS cadre. He was a member of the *Akhil Bharatiya Vidhyarti Parishad,* a powerful student body affiliated to the RSS. In 1970 he officially joined the RSS. From 1972 he was already a fulltime RSS *pracharak.* But when he was a *pracharak* in the RSS he was different from others. It is said that he liked variety in the things he used, like sandals, watches and pens. But the conservative Maharashtrian RSS leaders did not approve of it.

Modi's political ethics is based on the principle of 'end justifies the means' which he seems to have inherited from the RSS. For example, according to M.S. Golwalkar, the long time leader and visionary of the organisation, killing of women is supposed to be against *kshatra dharma* (duty/morality of a worrier). It also ordains one to fight the enemy in the open. Nevertheless, Ram killed *rakshasi* (demoness) Taraka and shot Vali from behind a tree for Rama was aware of his ultimate duty of establishing the rule of righteousness by destroying the wicked. The slaying of an innocent woman is sinful but the same principle cannot be applied to a demoness. Golwalkar further argued that the technique of fighting also varies according to the nature of the enemy.[7] Elsewhere he said: "Our philosophy teaches us to fight with all our strength, [...] Sri Krishna commands Arjuna to fight, but without war-fever."[8] In the war of Mahabharata, Krishna told Arjuna that his duty was to achieve victory on the battlefield.[9] When the five Pandavas went to seek the blessing of their mother Kunti before the commencement of the Mahabharata war, she blessed them saying, "Go ye all to the battle. This is the occasion for which Kshatriya women give birth to sons. [....] Let every mother speak in the same heroic strain to her sons even now."[10] During the battle when Karna had got down to lift up the wheels of his chariot stuck in the mud, Sri Krishna commanded Arjuna to direct his arrows to him. Karna appeared to Arjuna in the name of *dharma* (morality/duty) saying that it was *adharma* (immoral) to strike at an unarmed and chariotless adversary.[11] One notices here an obvious *relativism* in Golwalkar's ethics, rationalisation of violence and a morality prompted by opportunism. As an RSS *pracharak* Modi's worldviews was shaped by principles such as these.

Modi as a Controversial Figure in Indian Politics

Modi is perhaps one of the most controversial figures in contemporary Indian politics. He is likened by his critics to notorious dictators like Adolf Hitler, Slobodan Milosevic and Augusto Pinochet. He catapulted to infamy in 2002 after 'presiding' over one of India's worst communal riots in recent years. The riots left more than 2000 people killed and over 1,000,000 homeless. The tragedy severely damaged India's credentials as a secular democracy and culturally pluralistic country and the event was described as genocide and ethnic cleansing by many Human rights organisations and activists.

Seldom Indian politicians have done so much to polarise pubic opinion in the name of religion as Modi. In the Assembly elections of December 2002 his biggest gains were in those areas of the State where inter-communal violence led to the deaths of thousands of people, mostly Muslims. All this leads one to argue that Modi may be considered as the perfect icon of Hindu communal politics, which no right thinking person would subscribe to. Below we examine some aspects of his political strategy in order to substantiate our argument. When in April 2006 Modi engaged in a 51 hour fast against stopping the work on the Narmada dam, *The Hindu* editorial argued that his fast was farcical because there is no contemporary politician in India who is further away from Gandhian philosophy than Modi.[12]

Godhra 2002: A Test Case of Modi's Hindutva

It may be argued that Modi's political ideology is best manifested in the manner in which he handled the tragic Godhra and post-Godhra events of 2002. The Godhra tragedy on 27 February 2002, which burned the S-6 coach of the Sabarmati Express train and killed as many as 58 *kar sevaks* (Hindu rightwing volunteers), put the spotlight on Modi in a manner none one would have anticipated. Godhra sparked the worst ever anti-Muslim violence in recent decades. On 27 February 2002, Modi as Chief Minister of Gujarat told in a press statement during his visit to Godhra: "It (burning of the Sabarmati Express train) was a pre-planned act. The culprits will have to pay for it. It was no communal violence. It was a violence, one-sided, collective act by only one community [meaning the Muslims]".[13] After Modi pronounced this verdict, the Godhra incident was used to carry out a retaliatory pogrom in which more than 2,000 persons lost their lives. In reality, what followed was not a clash between two communities but a Hindu rage against the Muslims. The consequence was the birth of Modi as the new force within the BJP.[14] Justifying the massacres, Modi also said, quoting Newton's third law, 'that every action has an equal and opposite reaction' – referring to the burning of the train and the backlash that followed. Many pro-Sangh Parivar 'investigators' zealously tried to prove Modi right and desperately attempted to corroborate his statements that there was a Muslim conspiracy in the burning of the train. For instance, the RSS chief K.S. Sudarshan argued that Godhra tragedy was a spontaneous reaction to the action of Muslim fundamentalists.[15] It is said that instead of trying to prevent the violence, Modi 'instructed' his administration to do nothing. The bloody events that followed established Modi as the new Hindutva hardline icon. He then manipulated the public sympathy and sense of insecurity generated in the post-Godhra phase to engineer a landslide state assembly election victory in December 2002.[16]

Modi Seeks Political Mileage: Gujarat Assembly Elections 2002

Asghar Ali Engineer who assessed the Gujarat pogrom of 2002 has discovered a clear political motive behind the event. The defeat of the BJP in the assembly elections in Uttar Pradesh and Punjab and Uttranchal and in the bye-elections for two assembly seats in Gujarat had created a great political crisis for the BJP leaders. The people of these states rejected the BJP because of its corruption and non-governance. Elections were also due in Gujarat in March 2003, and there were clear prospects of the party losing those elections. The only means at the disposal of the BJP was the polarisation of the Hindus and Muslims, and to do it, organise communal riots. All indications suggest that the carnage was well planned and executed with finesse for political mileage for the BJP under the leadership of Modi.[17]

Modi was seriously criticised by political parties, human rights activists and the intellectuals for his handling of the violence in the State of Gujarat. Even the Supreme Court of India in its verdict on the Best Bakery case[18] compared him to a modern day Nero. The court expressed its shock over the manner in which the State government came to the aid of the perpetrators of violence against the minority community during the riots. Although the Bench made a general observation, the reference was obvious. It said: "The modern-day 'Neros' were looking elsewhere when Best Bakery and innocent children and helpless women were burning, and were probably deliberating how the perpetrators of the crime can be saved or protected. Law and justice became flies in the hands of these 'wanton boys'. When fences start to swallow the crops, no scope will be left for survival of law and order or truth and justice."[19] But in Gujarat and among certain sections of the Hindus in the country Modi's popularity grew. Taking advantage of the communally polarised atmosphere in Gujarat after the Godhra and post-Godhra violence, Modi asked the authorities to dissolve the assembly in order to seek new elections in 2002 itself, six months ahead of the schedule.

While Gujarat was burning there were rumours that elections will soon be held, and if so, the BJP would win hands down. Modi dissolved the assembly though it had a comfortable majority and there was no crisis in the party. He wanted to hold elections before October 2002. The Gujarat State was, during those days, highly polarised, and the temptation to hold elections was too great for Modi to resist. However, the chief Election Commissioner J.N. Lyngdoh came in the way, and after assessing the Gujarat situation found an intense sense of insecurity among the Muslims. He, under section 174 of the Indian Constitution, recommended that elections could not be held in Gujarat immediately. Hundreds of Muslims were in refugee camps living in inhuman conditions and were not in a position to return to their localities.[20] Enraged at the refusal to hold early elections, Modi alleged that the Christian Lyngdoh had links with Sonia Gandhi and that both of them met sometimes in Church.[21]

During the Gujarat assembly elections of December 2002 Modi proved himself to be the greatest crowed-puller than even the then Prime Minister Atal Bihari Vajpayee or the then Deputy Prime Minister L.K. Advani.[22] In fact, Vajpayee avoided campaigning in Gujarat simply because the party felt that 'Moditva' would be sufficient to sweep the elections. Modi led the BJP to a sweeping victory in the assembly elections winning a record 128 seats in the 182 member assembly.

Modi had no qualms of conscience about arousing communal emotions during the assembly elections. The assembly was dissolved on 19 July 2002 to reap immediate rewards. But the elections were delayed thanks to the Election Commission.[23] Modi used Godhra as its main election plank and manipulated the fear and the feelings of insecurity following the Godhra tragedy. During the assembly election campaigns he frequently repeated: 'I can never forget Godhra' and at every election meeting he played on the public outrage caused by the burning of the Sabarmati Express train in order to stir insecurity and communal hatred.[24] To evoke communal emotions, Modi used election posters with pictures of the burning train. The Sangh Parivar distributed T-shirts with a picture of the burning train and slogan 'I will not let my village become another Godhra'.[25] Modi used to ask the people whether they should set up refugee camps and keep open baby producing centres? – a reference to the Muslims. He also told them that the Hindus must teach the Muslims a lesson who multiply their number without restrictions.[26]

Modi took out the *Gujarat Gaurav Yatra* ('pilgrimage for the glory of Gujarat') to mobilise the masses for the BJP with the assembly elections in view. It was expected to cover all the 182 assembly constituencies of the State and people were told about the achievements of Modi and of the BJP government.[27] During his election campaign he spoke of 'Gujarat pride'. At an election rally at Khambhat he said; "We Gujaratis were compared with killers, looters, rapists and killers of the Muslims [....] Madam (Sonia) is here. She should come here in Khmabhat. She too referred Gujarat as land of Godse instead of Gandhi. People of Gujarat will teach her a lesson."[28] Soon after the Best Bakery verdict, Modi planned a *Kesari*

Yatra of north and central Gujarat where the BJP could face some setbacks in the elections.[29]

The Sangh Parivar version of the truth behind Godhra was shown around on video cassettes in Gujarat and across the country to justify the post-Godhra violence. They were also used to garner electoral support in the Assembly polls of 2003 in other states of India. These cassettes not only depicted unsubstantial versions but also generated ill-will between the communities.[30] But after the elections, the BJP forgot all about Godhra. A senior BJP politician is reported to have said: "Why should we organise anything? There is no need for it now."[31]

After the elections in Gujarat, the RSS approved Modi's strategy and wrote in their weekly paper *Organiser* that Modi needs to be congratulated from the heart for his victory.[32] Seshadri Chari, editor of the same weekly, said: "Modi, a one-time pracharak of the RSS in Gujarat, knew the history, geography and chemistry of the state inch by inch. His magic worked and the party was galvanised."[33]

The BJP National Executive meeting in New Delhi from 23 to 24 December 2002 stated: "The election [in Gujarat] was considered a trial for cultural nationalism of the BJP [....] the people of Gujarat endorsed our commitment to cultural nationalism and voted us back for a third time in a row;"[34] "Let our critics remember that the BJP stands for the protection of each and every Indian and his right to religious freedom [....] We are confident that the Gujarat election will prove to be a turning point in India's history, and the ideology of cultural nationalism propagated by the BJP will find wide-scale acceptability all over the county."[35]

But critics outside the Sangh Parivar gave a different verdict on the election victory. G.M. Banatwala said: "Gujarat's electoral verdict, which conferred a landslide win to the BJP, is a victory of terror and fascism, consequent of the most vicious communal campaign ever since Independence [....] The electoral outcome is fraught with serious consequences. Secular democracy and the values cherished by the Indian constitution face grave challenge."[36]

Praful Bidwai observed that one of the main reasons for the dark victory of Modi was the electorate's polarisation along religious lines, which the BJP effected as well as the 'soft Hindutva' line of the Congress and the failure to confront the BJP on communalism and cultural nationalism.[37]

Similarity of Modi's Tactics with That of Adolf Hitler

Modi punishing Muslims for the Godhra tragedy evokes the memory of what Adolf Hitler did when the Reichstagsgebäude (German Parliament building; *Reichstag* = German Parliament from 1871-1945) was burned down by someone in 1933. On 27 February 1933 this building was set on fire, allegedly by a Communist from Holland. For this Hitler took serious action against all the Communists of Germany. It gave Hitler an *occasion* to retaliate against all the Communists who were his major political opponents. But even today it is not certain what was the real reason behind the fire. Concerning the fire Hermann Göring, a close collaborator of Hitler said: *"habe ich gewußt; Die Kommunistische Partei ist die Schuldige am Reichstagsbrand"*.[38] ('I have known that the Communist party is guilty of burning the Parliament building'). Again, when Göring was told that one person was responsible for the fire he retorted: *"Ein Mann? Das war nicht ein Mann. Das waren zehn, zwanzig Männer! Mensch, wollen Sie denn nicht begreifen?[....] Das ist das Signal zum kommunistischen Aufstand"*.[39] ('One man? That was not one man but ten, twenty men! Hey, do you not want to understand? That is the signal of the Communist revolt'). We may argue that, like Hitler who used the burning of the Reichstagsgebäude as an *occasion* to crackdown on the Communists of Germany, Modi used the burning of the Sabarmati Express train to initiate a pogrom against the Muslim community in Gujarat. In a report prepared by British diplomats it is stated that the post-Godhra incidents were planned. If the Sabarmati Express tragedy had not happened, another flashpoint would have been created to justify the premeditated violence as reaction.[40]

Various Reports on Godhra Tragedy

Modi announced that the burning of the train at Godhra railway station was the result of a pre-planned attack on the *kar sevaks* by the Muslims, before any worthwhile investigation was done. Initial reports by the railway police, the Special Investigation Team (SIT) and the Forensic Science Laboratory (FSL) on the Godhra tragedy also endorsed the conspiracy theory of Modi. However, both the interim and the final report of justice U.C. Banerjee Commission appointed by the UPA government in September 2004 showed that the fire was an accident.[41] The interim report of the Banerjee Committee was released in April 2005. On 16 May 2005, Justice S.C. Jain the Chairman of the Central Review Committee on the Prevention of Terror Act (POTA) gave a ruling that corroborated the interim findings of the Banerjee Committee, on the eve of the elections in Bihar in 2005. The BJP then dismissed the interim report as a gimmick resorted to by the Railway Minister and former Chief Minister of Bihar, Laloo Prasad Yadav, to woo minority votes in Bihar, and questioned the timing of its release.[42] Reports of the National Commissions, Women's Organisations, Independent Fact Finding Teams and Human Rights Groups also ruled out the conspiracy theory of Modi.

The Modi-led BJP government was in power in Gujarat at the time of the post-Godhra pogrom. The BJP which had been justifying the pogrom against the Muslims in Gujarat as a reaction to the Godhra 'conspiracy' probably felt that the findings, if sustained by facts, would turn public opinion against the party which is seen as responsible for the pogrom.

According to the version of the Modi government, the conspiracy was hatched on the night before the Godhra incident. The prosecution theory runs as follows: on learning about the return of *kar sevaks* from Ayodhya by train, a core group of conspirators purchased petrol in 20-litre carboys from a petrol pump at about 21.00 hours on 26 February 2002 and kept the tempo carrying the petrol behind a guest house. Later, these carboys were shifted to the home of one of the accused. Late in the night these conspirators met their co-accused and claimed that they had already met Maulavi Hussain Hazi Ibrahim Umerji, a local businessman and social worker, who ordered that coach S-6 of the Sabarmati Express train coming from Ayodhya be set on fire. The prosecution further claimed that the following morning when the train arrived at Godhra at 7.43 hours, the *kar sevaks* raised slogans while alighting from the train to have tea and breakfast and had altercations with tea hawkers. One of them tried to tease a Muslim girl who, along with her mother and sister ran to the booking office situated nearby. Taking advantage of it, one of the accused, Salim Panwala raised the alarm with a view to stop the train for more time, and gathered Muslim hawkers. As another accused ran towards the end of the platform and shouted, more people from his community gathered at the station as well as near the parcel office. Meanwhile the train started and Panwala falsely shouted that *kar sevaks* were beating the people of his community and were abducting a Muslim girl inside the train. With a *mala fide* intention – the prosecution said – he incited, mislead and pressured three hawkers, got the emergency chain pulled by them and got the train stopped on the platform. Muslim mobs of Signal Falia and surrounding areas then formed an unlawful assembly and started pelting the stationary train with stones. The train began moving again. Panwala and others again incited the hawkers to board the running train and pull the emergency chain. As the train stopped they ran and picked up the carboys filled with petrol from the home of another accused and went inside S-6 coach of the train and poured the petrol from the carboys into the coach and went out of the door. Some people made a hole near the lid on the upper side of the carboy from outside and poured petrol, lit rags and pushed them inside the coach by means of a stick and thereby set the coach on fire. Others chased passengers who escaped from the burning coach, and even intercepted and stopped the fire-fighters of the Godhra municipality.[43]

But the statements by local officials before the enquiry commission suggest that the Godhra incident occurred after a spontaneous fight between local Muslims and *kar sevaks* travelling on the Sabarmati Express on 27 February 2002. The assistant Station Master Rajendraprasad Mina testified that no crowd was waiting for the train to stop. The crowd gathered after the train stopped for the second time. He said that the mob did not arrive together. Groups of 10 to 15 persons gathered, including women and children. Raju Bhargava, the Police Superintendent of Panchmahal district said that passengers were injured on the upper part of the bodies. This raises questions about the Special Investigation Team (SIT) theory that petrol was poured through the aisle of the coach. If the petrol had been poured down the aisle, the fire would have spread bottom up, injuring people on the lower part of their bodies.[44] The reports of forensic experts who have stated that 60 litres of inflammable liquid simply could not have been flung from outside the compartment, given the topography of the area.[45]

Although the forensic laboratory report concludes that the fire started from inside with at least 60 litres of petrol, others feel that the report is based more on conjecture than on proof. Raju Bhargava states that he did not smell any inflammable fuel such as petrol, diesel or kerosene. According to Mukul Sinha, a human rights lawyer for the Jan Sangharsh Manch, there is no evidence of fluid fire. Nawab Singh Chowdhry, a Railway Police Force inspector, has also testified that he put out a part of the fire with water. But an expert in fire fighting, Chowdhry said that, oil fires are not extinguished with water. This proves that the coach did not burn because of a petrol fire. However, both the SIT's evidence and the FSL reports state that petrol was used. Several people, including Chief Minister Modi, State Home Minister Gordhan Zadafia and Vishva Hindu Parishad leader Jaideep Patel along with media crew and VHP volunteers were allowed inside the compartment before the forensic tests were done or the First Information Report (FIR) was filed. Hence people say that the investigation into the Godhra incident throws up more questions than answers. The SIT's story has some gaps that are not adequately explained. Many believe that with the Modi government in power the truth of what really happened at Godhra may never be known.[46]

Gujarat as BJP's Hindutva Laboratory

Gujarat was referred to as Hindutva's laboratory experiment, a pilot project on whose success was hinged plans to carry out cultural cleansing operations throughout India.[47] It was only after 19.00 hours – i.e. nearly after 12 hours after the Godhra train tragedy – on 27 February 2002 that the Gujarat Chief Minister Modi, began looking at the ISI conspiracy in the train tragedy. This was all that was needed to launch what was obviously a carefully orchestrated genocide and ethnic cleansing in at least 16 of the 24 districts of the State. Thereafter, the image of the burnt S-6 coach and the bodies within were used and re-used for mass mobilisation, especially to harvest votes in the Gujarat State elections.[48] According to a report published in the weekly *Outlook* on 3 June 2002, on the night of 27 February 2002 Modi summoned a late night meeting of high officials in his bungalow, and it was decided that there would be justice for Godhra the next day.[49]

Modi by his policy signalled the Sangh Parivar that they would not be called to account if they committed crimes against any minority community. Thus VHP and Bajrang Dal took law into their own hands. In a tape recorded interview to Rediff.com Prof. Keshav Ram Kashiram, the chairman of the Gujarat unit of the VHP stated that the shops in Ahmedabad were looted on the basis of a list prepared by the VHP in advance: 'in the morning we sat down and prepared the list', he revealed.[50]

Hardly any of the Hindu rioters who took part in the killing have been brought to justice, mainly because Modi's government consistently frustrated attempts to prosecute the guilty. The police handling of the riot cases in Gujarat point to a blatant attempt to shield the guilty while harassing the victims. According to a report in March 2003, of the 4,252 cases filed, the police have closed half the cases, citing lack of evidence. Witnesses who testified against powerful politicians have been put in jail while real criminals roam about free.[51] It was alleged that Modi transferred those police officials who did not only tried to control the mob but also booked cases against influential persons.[52] During the three weeks of violence in Gujarat Modi transferred 'punitively' as may as twenty-seven senior police officers, and he justified the action by arguing that they were routine promotions.[53] It was only after two and a half months after the communal riots broke out that Modi as Chief Minster of the State held a formal meeting with Gujarat Muslim leaders.[54]

When the post-Godhra pogrom was taking place police stood as spectators, allegedly at the request of the State government. A police officer was even seen giving petrol from a government vehicle for burning the victims.[55] Hate speech and hate writing not merely preceded the post-Godhra pogrom but actually made the carnage possible. The violence in Gujarat in 2002 was preceded for some months by the systematic distribution of poisonous material, some anonymous, that constantly spewed hatred and venom against the Muslim minority in the State. Even during the orgy of violence, thousands of these pamphlets could be found. Some pamphlets advocating systematic economic boycott of Muslims even carried the address of an office of the VHP. Others were even more graphic and vicious and advocated mutilation and rape.[56] Maheshweta Devi of Kolkata quotes from a typical leaflet that has been in circulation for months: "Policemen and jawans, wake up! You are Hindus. Be on the side of the Hindus."[57] It is said that the VHP and the Bajrang Dal marketed *trishuls* (tridents) in a big way in Gujarat 12 months prior to 27 February 2002.[58] On the 27 of every month meetings were organised at every street-corner to commemorate the burning of the train at Godhra. For many months people lived in abject dread, as mobs were aroused and incited afresh and sporadic violence recurred. Every festival, Hindu or Muslim, was no longer an occasion for rejoicing; it only filled people with dark foreboding of a perennial spectre of violence, says Harsh Mander.[59] The Concerned Citizens Tribunal in their report on 15 May 2002 argued that evidence was received accusing the VHP and the Bajrang Dal of recruiting and training young men in the use of arms and ammunition, collecting information about houses, shops and other business establishments of the minority community and effectively using them in the post-Godhra violence.[60]

Speeches made by Gujarat Chief Minister Modi and the VHP's working president were brought to the attention of the court. Modi had publicly declared that he wanted to teach the Muslims a lesson. We may compare Modi's stand with regard to the police assistance to the victims in the words of Hemann Göring of the Nazi regime. Göring said: "We must put an end to the absurdity of every rogue shouting for the police. The police are not there to protect rogues, vagabonds, usurers and traitors. If people say that here and there someone has been taken away and maltreated, I can only reply: You can't make omelettes without breaking eggs. Don't shout for justice so much."[61]

It was reported that when Modi realised that his five and a half months in office as Chief Minister was not working to win the masses in favour of the BJP, he decided on a religious polarisation between the Hindus and Muslims as the only way to political success. Anything would have served as a trigger for it, and the Godhra tragedy provided the opportunity. But there was talk of making an issue of a cow slaughter video the party had got, but that plan was cancelled.[62]

The fact finding teams and civil enquiries probing the anti-Muslim violence in Gujarat found compelling evidence of the most extreme form of sexual violence against women during the first few days of the Gujarat carnage.[63] In 2002 after a visit to Gujarat Kuldeep Nayar wrote:

> I just listened to their harrowing tales, of murder, rape, people burnt alive, looting. After sometime I felt that I could not take it anymore. Sorrow beyond a point dulls your sensitivity. Chief Minister Narendra Modi was away to Rajkot. But I gave a bit of my mind to the chief secretary and the home secretary. Why didn't any official in Gujarat resign? Was there nothing called

> conscience, not even in the land of Mahatma Gandhi? Why had none of them gone round the refugee camps? Must a BJP-run government be saved from dismissal because the Centre is led by the BJP?.[64]

What took place in Gujarat in 2002 is well documented in studies, analyses, reports by fact-finding teams, human rights groups, statutory bodies like the National Human Rights Commission, the media and others.

Harsh Mander, one who has served in the Indian Administration Service (IAS) for over two decades, reports that in Ahmedabad most people he met – social workers, journalists, and survivors of the violence – agree that what Gujarat witnessed was not a riot but a sort of terrorist attack followed by a systematic, planned massacre, a pogrom. Everyone spoke of the pillage and plunder being organised like a military operation against an external armed enemy: an initial truck would arrive broadcasting inflammatory slogans, soon followed by more trucks with disgorged young men, mostly in khaki shorts and saffron sashes. They were armed with sophisticated explosive materials, country weapons, daggers and *trishuls* (tridents). The leaders were seen communicating on mobile telephones from the riot venues, receiving instructions from and reporting back to a co-ordinating centre. Some were seen with documents and computer sheets listing Muslim families and their establishments. They had detailed and precise knowledge about buildings and business held by members of the minority community. Mosques and *dargahs* (monuments of Sufi saints) were razed, and were replaced by statues of Hanuman and saffron flags.[65]

International working president of the VHP, Ashok Singhal, was explicit in linking Gujarat pogrom with Hindutva ideology: He said at a large public meeting at Shivala Bhaiyan temple in Amritsar on 4 September 2002: "People say that I praise Gujarat. Yes I do. Gujarat has been a successful experiment. Godhra happened on February 27 [2002] and the next day, 50 lakh Hindus were on the streets. We were successful in our experiment of raising Hindu consciousness, which will be repeated all over the country now."[66] The VHP even went to the extent of proposing an *asthi yatra* (carrying the Godhra victims' ashes) to 750 different places all over the country.[67] The then BJP president Venkaiah Naidu also spoke about replicating the Gujarat experiment in States going to the polls in 2003 but later backtracked and clarified that he only referred to repeating the party's experience of ensuring a cohesive campaign.[68]

In executing the Hindutva project the Hindutva organisations have been supported by the Sangh Parivar Diaspora. Harsh Mander after his visit to the USA wrote in June 2003: "The visit confirmed to me how closely the turbulent recent history of the dramatic rise of right-wing religious fundamentalism and the politics of hatred in India, is related to and nourished by the Indian Diaspora in the US an influential segment of this Diaspora is ideologically committed to the politics of Hindutva. They receive enormous financial support exposed by the Stop Funding Hate Campaign."[69] Asghar Ali Engineer observes that the middle castes in Gujarat are extremely conservative and unhesitatingly align themselves with the BJP. Most of the Gujarati NRIs in the UK and the USA also belong to these castes and help the Sangh Parivar generously with donations that have really helped make Gujarat a laboratory of Hindutva.[70]

Harsh Mander has summed up the ultimate results of the Hindutva lab experiment in Gujarat as follows: stunning brutality of the mass violence, the impunity of the state authorities, the depths of the social divide, the success of the economic boycott and above all the electoral endorsement of the massacre.[71] The European Union diplomats dismissed the Government of India's position that the Gujarat violence constituted an 'internal affair' of the country and affirmed their right to comment on the issue saying that the Gujarat events are a threat to the international order.[72]

The National Human Rights Commission (NHRC) requested the Supreme Court to take all the key riot-cases out of the state of Gujarat. In a separate application it also sought transfer of four other serious cases for trial outside the state. In 2003 the Gujarat government was told by the Supreme Court that it may monitor the Best Bakery trial and other riot-related cases. The state was also given orders to provide security to witnesses.[73]

In December 2005 a mass grave of the victims of a communal pogrom in Lunawada, Gujarat, was unearthed by CBI officers and policemen, and skulls found in the grave are believed to be those of the people killed in the 2002 riots. The Gujarat High Court passed an interim order directing the CBI to conduct DNA tests in a laboratory in Hyderabad. The victims did not trust the Gujarat police or the Gandhinagar laboratory to carry out the tests.[74]

When Modi offered to step down as Chief Minister of Gujarat after the pogrom, the BJP National Executive meeting at Panjim, Goa, in April 2002, unanimously rejected it and asked him instead to seek dissolution of the assembly and go to the people and ask for their verdict. But such a response to Modi was criticised as a negative development in Indian democracy.[75] The pre-requisite for obtaining the people's mandate in a democracy is the holding of free and fair elections, which was not possible then in Gujarat.

Gujarat Pogrom as a State Sponsored Genocide

It has been argued that the burning alive of 58 passengers in coach S-6 of the Sabarmati Express at Godhra on 27 February 2002 was used to justify genocide violence against Gujarat's Muslims.[76] In what were clearly three of the worst carnages – 87 persons were burnt alive in the Limadiya Chowkey, Kidiad incident, while over 70 persons were killed and burned in two separate carnages in Pandharwada village, Panchmahal district – the Gujarat government effectively ensured acquittals of all the accused, through the appointment of public prosecutors with questionable political backgrounds and wilfully negligent investigations.[77]

In the post-Godhra pogrom over 10,000 homes were shattered and businesses were destroyed and agricultural lands were seized. Despite the fact that the Prime Minister had announced Rs150 crore in central aid for survivors of the pogrom, the Gujarat government remained adamant in not even disbursing the available resources. No less than 1,16,000 persons were internal refugees, thrown out of home and hearth, living in relief camps. During this period the Gujarat government refused to give them food, water and medicine despite their constitutional obligation to bear the cost of their internal displacement. Here again it took legal interventions in the Gujarat Court before the government was forced to act.[78] Many relief camps were also forcefully disbanded by the Modi government. Reports say that no less than 200-300 Muslim women were subjected to brutal sexual violence and no less than 270 mosques and *dargahs* were desecrated and then destroyed. The calculated state-sponsored attempt to ravage the dignity of a community was evident.[79]

After the Godhra incidents people lived in fear and humiliation. They dared not to step out of their homes in dread of taunts and humiliation.[80] People who have lived together in peace and friendship for generations were turned coldly like strangers. They heard drunken threats of men from their villages at night. People of certain villages did not allow Muslims to their villages. A film on the Godhra incident entitled *Godhra Tak – The Terror Trail?* was produced by Shubradeep Chakrovarty. But he had to face the wrath of the Sangh Parivar, especially the VHP.[81]

The *Mille Gazette* reported that the leaked report conducted by the British High Commission in New Delhi said that the Gujarat pogrom of 2002 in which more than 2000 Muslims died, hundreds of women were mass raped and properties worth millions of pounds were plundered and destroyed, had all the hallmarks of genocide.[82] The attackers caused serious bodily and mental harm to them and inflicted 'conditions of life' to bring about their destruction. No less significant were measures imposed to prevent births within the group and 'use rape as a means to change the identity of a group, and impart to the child an identity that is different from the one acquired at birth'.[83] The unearthing of the mass grave at a government wasteland at Lunawada, Gujarat, on 27 December 2005 is seen as one more evidence of the complicity of the Gujarat police in the 2002 pogrom, and those buried there are alleged to be killed by Hindu fanatics.[84]

A book entitled *Threatened Existence: A Feminist Analysis of the Genocide in Gujarat* was published 22 months after the Gujarat pogrom. Praful Bidwai who analysed the study observes that it is a serious reminder of the violence and climate of fear and intimidation that prevailed in Gujarat as well as the exceptional nature of the orgy of killing, rape, plunder and arson that took place following the Godhra train tragedy. The authors of *Threatened Existence* visited Gujarat nine months after the worst phase of anti-Muslim violence. The team consisted of feminist jurists and scholar activists from the United States, Algeria/France, United Kingdom, Germany, Sri Lanka and India. Its members are known for their writings on women, conflict and violence.[85] *Threatened Existence* rigorously establishes that the post-Godhra pogrom was organised and directed by the BJP-controlled state led by Modi and that it constitutes a crime against humanity under international law.[86]

Bidwai notes that *Threatened Existence* shows how rape, especially gang rape, and defiling and mutilation of the female body were central planks of the sexualised violence in Gujarat. Thousands of Muslim women suffered horrible forms of bestiality when they were raped to the shouts of *Har Har Mahadev* and 'Go to Pakistan, why are you in Hindustan'?. The cutting of women's breasts, the splitting open of their bellies and burning of their foetuses were virtually ubiquitous in Gujarat.[87] It is said that 'mass has no conscience and no responsibility'88 and it is verified in this case.

According to Bidwai, *Threatened Existence* argues that the Gujarat violence conforms to the notion of crimes against humanity because it was 'part of a widespread or systematic attack against a civilian population, carried out by the perpetrators with knowledge that his or her acts were part of the larger attack. The violence was carried out by Hindu communalists with the full awareness that their acts are part of a broader game plan. There is no doubt that both state and Hindutva leaders, Hindutva organisations and those who joined the mobs or who participated in the persecution of the Muslim community for the most part, knew that their activities were part of a bigger plan. Bidwai maintains that the notoriousness of the violations, their concerted nature, the number of participants and the scale of the attack make ignorance virtually impossible.[89]

Reports in *Threatened Existence* methodically show that the violence fits the legal criteria of Article 2 of the Genocide Convention. It says that Genocide means any of the following acts committed with intent to destroy, in whole or in part, a national, ethnical, racial or religious group; causing serious bodily or mental harm to members of the groups; deliberately inflicting on the group conditions of life calculated to bring about its physical destruction in whole or in part; imposing measures intended to prevent births within the group; forcibly transferring children of the group to another camp.[90]

According to Cedric Prakash, an internationally acknowledged human rights activist.[91] what took place in Gujarat was not merely communal violence or riots. It was a *genocide,* a carnage, an ethnic cleansing designed to wipe out or ostracise a whole community. It was well planned and well executed. It was not a 'spontaneous' reaction as it was made out to be. The preparations must have taken several months. A year earlier, a widely circulated Gujarati daily listed several hotels run by the Chilya community which had non-Islamic names. Most of them were razed to the ground during the carnage. A meticulous census was conducted on the Muslims and Christians of Gujarat in 1999. That data was sufficient to help the rampaging mobs to know exactly whom to attack and where.[92] In some areas Tribals and Dalits were very effectively used in the arson and looting of Muslim homes and establishments.[93]

According to Cedric Prakash, today the general opinion about the Gujarat pogrom is that it was a state-sponsored genocide. The Citizens' Tribunal has clearly indicated, besides the Chief Minister Modi and several politicians, several high-ranking bureaucrats and police officials were part of it. The Sangh Parivar was given a free hand to do what they wanted. The police were apparently given clear instructions not to take any action. There is also evidence to show that some were encouraged to join in the violence which they did, with ruthless finesse. Some BJP state ministers and leaders of the Sangh Parivar were seen leading the mobs.[94]

Discrimination Against the Minority Religions

The BJP Government in Gujarat under Modi discriminates against Muslims and Christians. V.P. Singh, the former Prime Minister of India, referring to the adherents of Hindu right-wing ideology and organisations, once said: "Their Hindutva is only hatred of the minorities. If you are a Hindu, then you have to hate the minorities, that seems to be their credo."[95] This is aptly applicable to Modi, evident as it is from his attitude towards minority religions in his state, especially the Muslims and Christians.

In 2002 Gujarat's Muslims were targeted and killed on the basis of religious affiliation. The post-Godhra violence followed from the Hindutva project of cleaning India of the non-Hindus. *Threatened Existence* convincingly relates this genocidal violence based on the Hindutva ideology – which proclaims that the Hindus alone are the legal citizens of India and that the non-Hindus may stay in this country but wholly subordinated to the Hindu nation, claiming nothing, deserving no privileges, far less any preferential treatment, not even citizen's rights[96] – to the building of a Hindu *rashtra* in India. In the RSS ideology one finds a prescribed treatment for the non-Hindus, particularly Muslims. It has a parallel in Nazism which wanted to purge Germany of the Jews.[97] Golwalkar praised Hitler for keeping up the 'purity of the German race and its culture by 'purging the country of the Semitic races'. Similar sentiments were expressed by the Sangh Parivar in its 18 March 2002 resolution in Bangalore: "Let Muslims understand that their real safety lies in the goodwill of the majority."[98]

Discrimination Against the Muslims

The BJP's dislike for the Muslims is proverbial and long standing. Already in 1999 the BJP government in Gujarat conducted a meticulous census on the Muslims (and Christians) of the state.[99] When Modi became the Chief Minister of Gujarat he intensified his 'persecution' of the Muslims and made efforts to polarise the state on the basis of religion, namely, Hindu and Muslim. In 2003 he conducted a survey of Muslim *madrasas,* the ostensible purpose was to see that the *madrasas* provide modern education.[100]

In 2004 he announced the formation of a commission on population control headed by him soon after the religion-wise census data was released.[101] Conducting surveys of homes and address of people on communal basis is a dangerous idea as it is a typical prelude to focus violence against minority communities. The Jews were targeted thus in Nazi Germany, and the non-Muslim communities of Afghanistan in the Taliban years and more recently in Bangladesh and Gujarat itself went through a similar experience in 2002.[102]

The Karmayogi School Activity Calendar 2004-2005, issued on behalf of the Gujarat Secondary and Higher Secondary Education Board, Gandhinagaram comfortably did away with the minority Muslim and Christian festivals, out of the listed 50 days of celebrations.[103]

When the top BJP leaders such as Vajpayee and Advani have been trying to win over Muslim voters, Modi made no such attempts. When Arif Mohammad Khan joined the BJP and visited Gujarat, Modi did not even grant him an appointment. He does not want to welcome Muslims into the party.[104]

Modi as Chief Minister publicly manifested his dislike for the Muslims in his pronouncements. For example, 9 September 2002 during the *Gujarat Gaurav Yatra* he said, insulting the Muslims: *"What should we do? Run relief camps for them? Do we want to open baby-producing centres?* Ham paanch, hamare pachhees *[We five and our 25]. Gujarat has not been able to control its growing population and poor people have not been able to get money.... We have to teach a lesson to those who are increasing population at an alarming rate."*[105]

The Sangh Parivar has constantly tried to project the Muslim community as one that is illiterate and underdeveloped. But the census proves the contrary. The Census of 2001 shows that the Muslim literacy rate (73.47%) in Gujarat is higher than the Hindu literacy rate (68.31%), and the state average was 69.14 per cent. The annual growth of the Muslims was 2.7 per cent, slightly higher than the Hindus' at 2.2 per cent. However, the demographer Leela Visaria points out that Kutch and two districts in Rajkot were not counted in 2001 because of the earthquake and many have not been included in the new Census data. If they were, it would have pushed up the Hindu growth rate.[106]

Modi's inherent Islamophobia seems to be inherited from the RSS, and he is one of those who keep this trend alive in the Sangh Parivar. On 8 December 1947, Golwalkar, the supreme chief of the RSS, stated unequivocally his dislike for the Muslims in one of his public addresses: "The Sangh will not rest content until it had finished Pakistan. If anyone stood in our way we will have to finish them too."[107] "No power on earth could keep them [Muslims] in Hindustan. They should have to quit this country."[108] He argued that, all the pro-Pakistani elements did not go to Pakistan at the time of the independence of India in 1947. Many of them remained back in India even after the partition of the country.[109]

Bidwai reminds us that for more than a thousand years the Muslims have been inseparable from India's material life: languages, arts, crafts, economic practices, literature, music, administrative system, forms of social intercourse and politics. The Muslim's integration in Independent India and their commitment to it is one of the greatest stories of cultural and political assimilation anywhere. It is also truly remarkable that not a single Indian Muslim has recently joined a violent Islamic movement anywhere in the world.[110] About the contribution of Islam to Indian culture, Benjamin Walker observes: "So considerable has been the influence of Islam, that there is not an aspect of Hindu life, including its religion and domestic routine that has not been touched by it."[111] Science, art, architecture, music, astronomy, ayurveda, fashion, vernacular languages and literature came under the Muslim influence. In fact, its influence is found even in the intimate details of the domestic life of the Hindus.[112]

Modi's aversion for Muslims is internationally known. In 2003 he was invited to England by the Overseas Friends of the BJP (OFBJP). The visit was kept as a top secret. But as soon as the visit was confirmed the Indian Muslim organisations in the U.K started writing to the British government to take action against the visit.[113]

Muslim and non-Muslim organisations in the UK quoted from the Islamophobic speeches of Modi and stressed that he could be expected to do nothing but to preach hatred among peaceful communities also in the U.K. They also questioned the reasons for giving visa for an anti-Muslim like Modi.[114] Some of the placards carried by the protesters read: 'Arrest Modi for Genocide and Crimes Against Humanity now.' 'Narendra Modi the Butcher of Gujarat.' 'Mr.Modi you are Murderer not Friend of Gujarat.' 'Arrest and jail Modi, etc.'[115]

Economic Boycott of the Muslims

According to Cedric Prakash, the Gujarat carnage was meant to break the backbone of the Muslim economy and it has succeeded to a great extent.[116] Harsh Mander writing one year after the Gujarat pogrom observes that the re-opened business establishments of the Muslims were boycotted by non-Muslim clients. Rival shops are run by new caste Hindus and tribal entrepreneurs, and they thrive. In some non-vegetarian wayside hotels run by the Muslims hardly a day passes without a gang of hoodlums eating a hearty meal and then threatening to pull down his shop again if he has the 'audacity' to ask them to pay the bill. The economic boycott works in many other ways. None will either buy or sell animals to any Muslim trader. Hindu autorickshaw owners no longer rent their rickshaws to Muslim drivers. Many Muslim factory workers have been summarily dismissed and replaced by others. Daily-wage workers who gather each morning to look for work are picked up for employment only on days when every non-Muslim worker is employed. Tenants are evicted from agricultural land. Farmers are unable to cultivate because their bore-wells are stuffed with stones, their pump houses destroyed. None can rent a house except from another Muslim. In some villages people are not allowed to speak when they go to shop. They are allowed to point to what they wish to purchase, place their money on the shop shelf and meekly await the time when the shop owners choose to pick up their money and give them what they wish to buy, at a price they are no longer permitted to negotiate.[117] The economic boycott of the Muslims in Gujarat reminds one of what Hitler did to the Jews in Germany.

It has also been reported that some weeks prior to the Godhra tragedy thousands of copies of a circular letter, allegedly from the

VHP were distributed in Ahmedabad and other places in Gujarat, calling for an economic boycott of the Muslims and their establishments. Translation of a leaflet reads as follows:

> Vishva Hindu Parishad
> Satyam Shivam Sundaram!
> Jai Shri Ram!
>
> Wake up! Arise! Think! Save the country! Save religion!
>
> Economic boycott is the only solution! The anti-national elements use the money earned from the Hindus to destroy us! They buy arms! They molest our sisters and daughters! The way to break the backbone of these elements is:
>
> An economic non-cooperation movement!
>
> Let us resolve:
>
> 1. From now on I will not buy anything from a Muslim shopkeeper!
> 2. I will not sell anything from my any shop to such elements!
> 3. Neither shall I use the hotels of these anti-nationals nor their garages!
> 4. I shall give my vehicle only to Hindu garages! From a needle to gold, I shall not buy anything made by Muslims, neither shall we sell things made by us to them.
> 5. I shall boycott wholeheartedly films in which Muslim heroes and heroines act! Throw out films produced by these anti-nationals!
> 6. We shall never work in offices of the Muslims! We will not hire them!
> 7. We will not let them buy offices in our business premises nor sell nor rent out houses to them in our housing societies and colonies.
> 8. I shall certainly vote, but only for him who will protect the Hindu nation.
> 9. I shall ensure that our sisters and daughters do not fall into the 'lovetrap' of Muslim boys at schools, colleges and workplaces.

10. I shall not receive any education or training from a Muslim teacher.

Such a strict economic boycott will throttle these elements! It will break their backbone. Then it will be difficult for them to live in any corner of this country. Friends, begin this economic boycott from today! Then no Muslim will raise his head before us! Did you read this leaflet? Then make ten photocopies of it and distribute it to our brothers. The curse of Hanumanji be on him who does not implement this and distribute it to others! The curse of Ramchandraji will also be on him! Jai Shri Ram!

A true Hindu patriot.[118]

Discrimination Against the Christians

Already in 1999 a survey of the Christians was done by the BJP government in north and central Gujarat, which was later withdrawn due to protest.[119] In 2003 the police once again embarked on a clandestine survey of Christian institutions in several parts of Gujarat.[120] The Modi government asked the police to find out how many people they had converted to Christianity. This was just before the government announced its decision to table the so-called 'Freedom of Religion Bill' (Anti-Conversion Bill) in the Gujarat Assembly which would have made it mandatory for those changing their religion to seek the permission of the district collector.[121]

The Hindu reported that, the survey was ordered by the Modi government in Gujarat to collect information about Christian families and organisations, and it had all the trappings of a covert operation.[122] Policemen, sometimes in plain clothes, enter institutions at midnight by jumping over the gates and ask questions about the institution's source of funds: 'From which country are you getting the foreign contribution; what do you do with this foreign contribution; if you are not getting any foreign funds and getting money only from Gujarat, which part of the state is helping you, etc.[123] In Patan district police authorities questioned a priest of the Catholic *ashram* in a Saturday midnight raid. The priest was asked about the antecedents of some students living in the *ashram*, the kind of food and facilities the inmates get at the institution and whether any of them had been converted to Christianity. The police team in mufti also went to the 'Daughters of the Cross', a Christian institution run for the uplift of illiterate rural women, and made similar queries there too. The Christian community feared that the Gujarat government will target it in the same manner it victimised the Muslims after the Godhra train tragedy.[124]

In May 2003 the highest court in India issued notices to the Gujarat State Home Secretary, Director General of Police and others asking them to be present on 24 June 2003 in connection with hearing of a petition filed by All India Christians Council (AICC) alleging clandestine survey of the Christian community in the villages of the Patan district.[125]

In April 2004 Modi declared 'Good Friday' – which is a very sacred day for all the Christians, and traditionally a national holiday in India – as a working day.[126] On 1 April 2006 the Modi government sent out nuns who have selflessly served the leprosy patients for 57 years from the Leprosy hospital in Ahmedabad on behalf of the Catholic diocese of Ahmedabad.[127]

Modi's Gujarat as a Communally Polarised State

Modi's Gujarat continues to be a communally polarised state along religious affiliations, thanks to the systematic work done by Sangh Parivar organisations. Forced separation of couples belonging to different religious communities is a fact and this mindset is most prevalent in Gujarat.[128] People refuse to sell to the Muslims' houses in 'Hindu' areas. Unwanted anywhere outside their own community, Muslims tend to cluster together. There are some large Muslim pockets in each big city of Gujarat, which some Gujarat press call 'mini Pakistans'. The term connotes that everyone living there is an 'enemy'.[129] The segregation means less communication and this makes it easier for Sangh Parivar organisations to propagate prejudice and stoke the fear of 'the other'. Even in elite areas Muslims are not allowed to buy property. When for instance Muslims bought flats in Paldi, an upmarket area of Ahmedabad, Bajrang Dal activists ransacked the building and threw a bomb that blasted the lift. Later they forced the Muslim owners to sell their flats at a pittance. In Ahmedabad's walled city, the Bajrang Dal attacked traders who sold property to Muslims.[130]

In Modi's Gujarat even schools are ghettoised. After the communal carnage of 2002 several schools asked Muslim students to leave. In Naroda Patiya, where some of the worst killings occurred, children refused to go back to school after teachers made them sit separately. Many Muslim parents withdrew their children from good schools and admitted them to substandard ones in Muslim neighbourhood just because they felt that their children were safe in schools closer to home.[131] After hounding on Muslim residents of villages, local Bajrang Dal units have put up banners proclaiming 'Muslim free'.[132] Elderly Muslim residents who tried to return to their homes in Pavagadh, a village adjoining a temple in Panchmahal were beaten up and chased out.[133] Hindu festivals are used to give trouble-makers an opportunity: they often shout slogans against or antagonise the Muslims with the intention of creating trouble and then blame them for attacking the Hindus.[134] Dionne Bunsha says about Modi's Gujarat that the killing may be over, but the injustices continue.[135] Zahir Janmohammed, a 25 year-old graduate and third-generation expatriate from India in the USA says: "I have been searching for Gandhi for several years. But after spending months in Gandhi's homeland, Gujarat, I fear he may be dead."[136] I.K. Shukla remarks: "In Gujarat, if Hinduism was ruthlessly decapitated, humanity was savagely desecrated too. Hindutva has re-defined patriotism and pride as Rape, Loot, Arson, Kleptomania, Genocide of the Innocents – the Muslims. Christians, Dalits, and Adivasis."[137]

Ashis Nandy reminds us that hate becomes respectable especially when it is directed against the hateful, and Savarkar, the 'father of Hindutva', is one of those who understood it long ago.[138] In Gujarat, under the direction of Modi as Chief Minister, hate did become respectable, especially when it was directed against the Muslims and Christians!

In 2003 *India Today* reported: "The Godhra carnage changed Gujarat – politically as well as socially. If Narendra Modi is ruling over Gujarat today, it is perhaps a direct fallout of the Godhra case."[139]

Teesta Setalwad says: "Today's Gujarat is no longer the Gujarat we had known and lived in. Never before has Gujarat been so demeaned as by this regime. There is distance and hatred every-where."[140]

Gurcharan Das observes: "His [Modi's] hands are covered in blood and he should be sacked. But once he is gone, what happens next? Whom will we blame for the next communal riot? Communalism is more than a governance issue."[141]

Modi as the Mascot of Virulent Hindutva

Bidwai argues that Gujarat is unique for the sheer spread and power of the VHP with branches in 55 per cent of the 18,000 villages. Along with religious cults and *gurus*, the VHP bas drummed up an aggressive form of Hindu identity assertion. Its penetration of schools and textbooks is extensive. Given the weakness of Gujarat's Left wing political parties and of its liberal intelligentsia there has been little resistance to Sangh Parivar's growth, and a decade of BJP's rule in Gujarat has consolidated Hindutva's hold. No other state matches Gujarat in its ideological hold over civil society and state institutions, including the police.[142]

After the spectacular victory of the Assembly elections in Gujarat in December 2002 BJP said that the 'road map for the future is clear'. The BJP national Executive meeting in Panjim, Goa, on 23-24 December 2002 declared the Gujarat election verdict as a mandate for and an endorsement of its core ideological positions. Bidwai notes that Modi was seen not just as Chief Minister of Gujarat rather as the mascot of a new, virulent Hindutva. BJP also attributed, among other things, the victory of Modi in Gujarat as punishment to secularists for their Hindu bashing.[143] It is also argued that the RSS's slogan "one village, one *shakha*" was aimed at saffronising the entire Gujarat state by 2005.[144]

It has been remarked by critics that Modi won the election on the corpses of the thousands who died in the Gujarat carnage.[145] When Modi visited London he invoked a militant God. In his speech he said that people have been worshipping Krishna so far as the playful God, the one who played the flute and sang with the *gopis*. But times have changed. The time has come to worship Krishna who wielded the Sudarshan Chakra.[146]

Modi's *Panchamrit* scheme announced soon after taking over as the Chief Minister never mentioned communal harmony as a goal to be achieved in a blatantly communally torn and culturally polarised State. Instead he spoke of education, irrigation, power, public security and people's power.[147]

Modi's Use of Language Without Refinement

Use of slanderous campaign and hate-language is part of Modi's culture. His employment of crude language is deliberate, intended to malign his opponents. He made several objectionable speeches against the Muslims during his Assembly election campaign of 2002. The vulgar and indecent campaign was neither accidental nor the result of individual hallucination. It was the outcome of deliberate planning. For example Modi said:

> "What should we do? Run relief camps for them [Muslims] do we want to open baby-producing centres?."[148]

> "In order to progress, every child born in Gujarat needs education, manners and employment ... that is the economy we need... and for this we will have to teach a lesson to those who are increasing the population [a reference to the Muslims] at an alarming rate."[149]

> "I got the Narmada water in the month of Shravan, if they [Congress] had it their way ... they would have got it in Ramzan."[150]

According to K.N. Panikkar, no electoral campaign had touched such low level of decency and public morality as that of the BJP as in the general elections of 2004.[151] The abysmal levels to which the BJP can plunge was revealed by none other than Modi in the distinguished and attentive presence of L.K. Advani during his *Bharat Uday Yatra's* Gujarat leg. Modi stooped low with his language without refinement with his comments on Sonia Gandhi and Rahul Gandhi. He said that earlier the Congress election had a cow and a calf and people used to say that a cow and calf are fighting election (reference to Indira Gandhi and son Sanjay Gandhi). But now a farmer told him that a hybrid calf (Rahul) is going to fight election. On 31 March 2004 in Patan, Modi called Sonia Gandhi a 'Jersy cow' and Rahul a 'hybrid calf'. He said that he had 'conducted a random survey in Kheeda'. He asked 20 shopkeepers if they would employ Sonia Gandhi as a clerk. None said they would. Similarly, he asked people if they would like to give Rahul a chauffeur's job. Nobody said yes. It is such unworthy leaders who wish to be Prime Minister of India – Modi said.[152]

On another occasion Modi stated: "For Sonia, if in power, *Vande Mataram* might sound different."[153]

"Let a standard four student and Sonia sing 'Vande Mataram' together without a sheet of paper for reference. A kid from Khambhat will win this contest. All our freedom fighters [...] have died for Vande Mataram. But she does not know the national song."[154]

In November 2003 Modi alleged that Sonia, while in Mizoram and Chhattisgarh, struck a deal with Christian missionaries to influence voters and results. He said; "The nation wants to know from Sonia Gandhi the objective of her meeting with foreign missioners."[155]

When Modi was cornered by the Chief Election Commissioner Lyngdoh, he spread the canard to demoralise the person saying that both Sonia and the Election Commissioner Lyngdoh met in church. But the fact is that neither Lyngdoh nor Sonia is a Churchgoer. On another occasion he said: "The motto of the Congress had degenerated from Vande Mataram to Vande Mata-Rome after Sonia Gandhi became its president."[156]

The BJP, to which Modi belongs, seems to have a basic dislike for Sonia Gandhi and her family. In fact, his party accused Sonia to be a spy of Italy. *BJP Today*, published the following, maligning her: "She [Sonia] was in touch with Italian spies. An innocent and devout housewife, unconcerned about politics and state, was deep in her contact with the Italian spy agencies."[157] It also alleged that Sonia was an adept in bringing about spy connections, a highly skilled and scary business, as early as the early 1980s. Yet she pretended, even now does, to be an innocent housewife.[158]

The slanderous campaign against Sonia Gandhi and her family was a deliberate, planned attempt to exploit xenophobic prejudices and reaffirm a dangerous notion of nationalism, to which ethnicity, not citizenship, is central.[159] Bidwai argues that Sonia Gandhi chose to become an Indian citizen. She has as much right to hold public office as any other Indian. The BJP's denial of that right and its hysterical anti-'foreigner' campaign puts it in the same league as ethnic chauvinist parties such as the Nazis in Hitler's Germany, the Likud in Sharon's Israel, the British National Party in the U.K or Jean-Marie Le Pen's National Front in France.[160]

N. Jamal Ansari argues that both Sonia Gandhi and Hindutva have connections with Italy. Ms. Gandhi is by birth Italian but has adopted Indian values whereas the Hindutva ideologues are born Indians but ape fascist ideology (It may be recalled that the first Hindutva leader to establish contacts with Italy's fascists forces was B.S. Moonje, who later became the mentor of K.B. Hedgewar, the founder of the RSS). In his opinion Ms Gandhi is more Indian than the Hindutva ideologues.[161]

When people questioned her patriotism Sonia said: "Those who question my patriotism should first point out when, from the time I became Indiraji's daughter-in-law until now, have I ever failed to conform to Indian traditions; what fundamental values of a secular Indian family have I failed to adopt?."[162]

The emergence of Sonia Gandhi-led Congress as the single largest party after the General Elections of 2004 made it clear that an overwhelming mass of people in India rejected the campaign against her on the basis of her foreign origin. That also indicated that they do not see her as unfit to hold constitutional office in India.[163] K.N. Panikkar says: "The common man in India values civilised behaviour and disapproves indecency, particularly if it is against women."[164] He adds: "The way the 'foreign origin' issue was handled by the BJP leadership not only betrayed the anxiety for survival, but a lack of elementary courtesy and decency."[165]

Bidwai rightly says that the Indian people simply did not fall into the xenophobic trap set by the BJP. For them, a person who was born abroad, but have voluntarily chosen to be an Indian and to live here, is as authentic a national as any other. What matters is citizenship, not ethnicity. Accepting the naturalisation of people of foreign origin is part of the agenda of inclusion. And it was this agenda that the electorate of 2004 has strongly endorsed.[166]

Prem Shankar Jha has also provided a fitting reply to Modi and those like him who questioned Sonia's foreign origin. He says that he cannot see how Sonia is a foreigner. There are millions of people from India who now live in and work in the USA and Canada. Barring the very rare exception they can hardly claim to be contributing to India's GNP or to its pool of knowledge and enterprise. A disproportionate number earn quarter million dollars plus salaries designing the weapons and software systems that are being used to terrorise the world. Not one of these, to his knowledge, has come back to India and offered his expertise to the Indian government, let alone spied for it as Israelis and Chinese scientists have done for their countries of origin. Are they Indians? By the same token was Mother Teresa a foreigner? It is true, she was born in the Balkans and came to India via Belgium. But none since Mahatma Gandhi has poured forth his or her love, caring and compassion on India's poor and needy as she did. It is not the accident of birth that determines nationality, but the positive, unstinting commitment of one's adult life. One has absolutely no control over the former, but a large measure of control over the latter. By that measure the NRIs/PIOs in North America do not qualify as Indians. Mother Teresa d[illegible]. So does

Sonia Gandhi. Mrs. Gandhi is not the same league as Mother Teresa, but no one can deny the depths of her attachment and her commitment to India. She gave up her country decades ago to live in a strange land because of her love for her husband; her children are Indians by birth and race and they have not become NRIs. She is indissolubly linked to this country by love and pain.[167]

Modi as an Icon of Hindu Communalism

Today Modi is an icon of Hindu communalism. According to Chunni Bhai Vaid, a prominent Gandhian leader, it is the rumours and machinations of the VHP and the RSS that have totally communalised Gujarat.[168]

It was reported that in August 2003, Modi planned to make the Independence Day celebrations of India into a Hindu-style celebration. Accordingly, 15 August would be greeted by chimes of temple bells and '*prabhat pheris*' by Hindu organisations like the Gayatri Parivar, the Brahmakumaris and the Swaminarayana sect, and the government would follow their lead with Ganesh Vandana, Shiva Vandana and Shiva Tandav.[169] Prominent Muslim leaders, human rights activists and the Congress reacted sharply to such a move arguing that Independence Day is meant for all Indians and that it cannot be converted into a Hindu 'festival' because such an attempt would subvert the long cherished secular principles of the country.[170]

Modi's services were used by BJP in its election campaigns to play the communal card in several states. In 2003 the BJP high command fielded Modi as the star campaigner in the four states that went to polls – Himachal Pradesh, Madhya Pradesh, Delhi and Rajasthan. Commenting on this Bidwai observed that the fielding of fiery Hindutva icons like the saffron-clad Uma Bharati and Narendra Modi as campaign leaders conveyed an unambiguous message because Modi is not just another BJP leader or Gujarat Chief Minister. In the public mind, he is the organiser of the Gujarat pogrom.[171] In the same year a host of Hindutva leaders had even planned to take Modi to Kerala in a bid to communalise the State and to divide its people.[172] During the general elections of 2004 Modi campaigned in Uttar Pradesh in select seats where Hindutva has a greater emotive appeal.[173] In 2006 he campaigned for the BJP in Assam which went to polls.[174]

In the general elections of 2004 BJP was defeated, and many considered the Gujarat pogrom as one of the reasons for the party's debacle. In fact, BJP's distinguished leader Vajpayee himself said at Manali where he had gone for a holiday that Gujarat riots was one of the causes of BJP's defeat in the elections and that Narendra Modi's removal from government was one of the options that would be discussed at the Mumbai meeting of the National Executive of the BJP. This send shockwaves in the Sangh Parivar and many refused to accept it as a correct analysis of the party's defeat.[175] But the pressure from the RSS, exerted directly by K.S. Sudarshan, forced the BJP to repudiate Vajpayee publicly. BJP president Venkaiah Naidu spoke to Vajpayee who was in Manali three times over telephone on 14 June 2004 and secured his consent for a statement 'clarifying' his views. Naidu denied that the Mumbai National Executive would have Modi on its agenda.[176]

The RSS leader Sudarshan's intervention in the case of Modi made the valid point that he should not be made a sacrificial goat. The RSS and the VHP felt that the dismissal of the Gujarat Chief Minister would signify that the party was moving away from Hindutva. In fact, at the Mumbai meet Vankaiah Naidu and L.K. Advani highlighted the need to 'rededicate' themselves to their ideology, without 'being apologetic about Hindutva'.[177] When senior BJP leader Madan Lal Khurana demanded the removal of Modi as the Chief Minister of Gujarat disciplinary action was served against him.[178]

Modi as a Hardcore Hindu Nationalist

At the root of the Gujarat pogrom there was an 'experiment' to build a Hindu *rashtra* in India as envisaged by the Sangh Parivar. After the election victory of Modi in Gujarat in December 2002, the VHP leader Pravin Togadia stridently declared that India will become a Hindu *rashtra* in two year's time.[179] Some say that today Gujarat is a Hindu *rashtra* in one State. After the victory in the Gujarat Assembly elections of December 2002 the slogan of the saffron group was 'Godhra to Gandhinagar and Gandhinagar to Delhi'.[180] There are even some people who envisage Modi as a future BJP candidate for Home Minister or Prime Minister of India.

BJP to which Modi belongs is a Hindu nationalist political party and the political arm of the RSS which is adamant on building a

Hindu *rashtra* in India. The BJP's Election Manifesto of 1996 stated: "Hindutva or cultural nationalism, shall be the rainbow which will bridge our present to our glorious past and pave the way for an equally glorious future [....] Hindutva is a unifying principle, which alone can preserve the unity and integrity of our nation. It is a collective endeavour to protect and re-energise the soul of India, to take us into the next millennium as a strong and prosperous nation."[181]

Deepal Trevedie calls Modi 'Narendra the Nazi', and an RSS *pracharak* camouflaging as a Chief Minister.[182] Because of his Hindutva hardline stand even today Modi enjoys the full support of the RSS and the VHP in all his undertakings. Gujarat has become synonymous with 'anti-Muslim' and if Modi goes this issue will lose political relevance.[183] The RSS has always stood by Modi and has defended him as an uncompromising icon of Hindutva ideology. In the RSS mouthpiece *Organiser* we read: "Narendra Modi, Chief Minister of Gujarat has been nailed to the cross. Indirectly he was called a modern-day Nero who fiddled while the Best Bakery and its inmates burnt."[184] Defending his ideological hero Modi and sympathising with him, the RSS ideologue and 'eminent' journalist M.V. Kamath wrote in *Organiser*, "No man in recent times indeed since Independence has been more reviled, demonised and hated than Gujarat's Chief Minister Narendra Modi. Since 28 February 2002 the English language newspapers, especially have gone at him hammer and tongs, and with very respect, with a wilfulness that has had no parallel in journalistic history. Every possible weapon including half-truths and downright lies were used both by the electronic and print media to condemn Modi and his government as fascist, bloodthirsty and vicious".[185]

Some Comments on Modi's Character and Personality

After the Godhra pogrom of 2002 Modi was rated as the most controversial politician India has seen in recent years. Secularists saw him as the hatchet man of the RSS who 'conducted' the carnage of Gujarat. The reputed Indian weekly in English *The Week* of 28 April 2002 published 50 reasons why Modi should be dismissed from his office as the Chief Minister of Gujarat. Some of the reasons are the following:

Vishnu Bhagat, a retired admiral said: "Modi, who has committed worse crimes than a Nazi, should be tried by an international criminal court for premeditated mass murder of women and children."[186]

U.R. Ananthamurty, a writer, confessed: "Modi has made me ashamed of my Hindu identity. I am a Hindu. I believe it is a great religion. But, it is very difficult to be a Hindu if there is a man like Modi around. He should go in order to save Hinduism."[187]

Rajmohan Gandhi, historian and grandson of Mahatma Gandhi, lamented: "The Gujarat carnage besmirched India's name. I personally have not been so shaken in years. The Hindu militants destroyed every Hindu and human value."[188]

J.N. Dixit, India's former foreign secretary, argued: "The Modi government should go because of these reasons. Firstly, he didn't take any pre-emptive action to prevent the Godhra incident. Secondly, after the incident, he did nothing to control communal violence. Further, he did not allow the police to act effectively and those who acted were transferred."[189]

Swami Agnivesh, social activist, stated: "Modi should be tried as a criminal in an international court for the systematic pogrom he carried out in Gujarat."[190]

Sophia Khan, Ahmedabad-based lawyer-activist, noted: "Modi was behaving more like an RSS *pracharak* than a chief minister. His statements from day one justified all sorts of violence."[191]

Ananada Shankar, dancer and choreographer, affirmed: "A person who professes violence in the name of religion does not belong to this country."[192]

Anjolie Ela Menon, activist, stated: "It is a clear case of genocide. The groundswell of opinion against Modi throughout India is the only source of hope in an otherwise hopeless situation."[193]

Gautam Navlakha, human rights activist, opined: "Modi should be prosecuted for failing to stop the violence after February 27 [2002]. It is clear that the post-Godhra violence was planned, and so the failure is all the more serious."[194]

We have also other eminent personalities who have pronounced verdicts on Modi. For example, writer and social activist Arundhati Roy has called Modi 'the overseer of mass murder in Gujarat.[195]

Chief Justice V.N. Khare said: "I have no faith left in the Gujarat government. You have to protect people and punish the guilty. What else is raj dharma?."[196]

Seema Mustaffa wrote: "The Gujarat government under the ugly Indian, Narendra Modi, left no stone unturned to ensure that the victims of his violence were isolated, and that the goons who killed and maimed innocent citizens of this country were left free to take the law into their own hands again."[197]

Some say that Modi suffers from a superiority complex and is a die-hard believer in himself.[198] According to some, with paranoid security concerns, as Chief Minister, his office premises resemble a modern fortress complete with high-tech security including closed-circuit TV. Sources say that Modi wants to keep a close watch on visitors and even the security staff.[199]

Haren Pandya who as the former Home Minister of Gujarat was Modi's fierce opponent. Many see his murder as politically motivated. Haren Pandya's father Vithalbhai Pandya said: "I am of the firm opinion that this was an intentional political murder [....] The murderers may have killed because of money. But the real political culprit must be arrested. No real inquiry can be made until the person in power [Modi] steps down."[200]

It is amazing how in Gujarat there was an unrest of BJP MLAs within the party itself. Modi was accused of arrogance and inaccessibility even to his party workers. In 2003 nearly 80 per cent of the BJP's MLAs in Gujarat wanted Modi's removal, the main reason being his autocratic style of functioning. Yet the party deferred any action against him in view of the Lok Sabha elections of 2004.[201] A Modi supporter remarked: "What they [opponents of Modi] should not, however, forget, is that Narendara Modi is a fighter and a hardcore nationalist. Getting rid of him is easier said than done."[202]

Modi's critics say that he promotes only himself. Many consider him as an arrogant, egoistic and rancorous person.[203] He is also described as a self-righteous leader lacking in humility and courtesy. Capitalising on his self-trumpeted simplicity and abstinence he projects himself as the unrivalled leader of Gujarat BJP.[204] Some allege that he is a narcissist. Every state-level BJP party propaganda material invariably carries his picture. All state transport buses have his picture on the rear. In all announcements of the government and the party Modi comes first, then the event. He has a skilfully crafted image for public consumption and spends a lot of time managing it.[205]

Anita Pratap observes that Modi's intolerance to criticism has repeatedly manifested itself in despotic lashings. Instead of engaging his opponents in debate and discussion, he resorts to strong-arm tactics to muzzle, browbeat and malign. Dissenters are jailed, roughed up or physically thrown out from conference rooms by flunkies. No other Chief Minister in recent times has crossed swords with every major democratic institution in the country, the Election Commission, the media, the National Human Rights Commission, NGOs, the Women's Commission and the Apex Court. The message implied in this is that that Modi is bulldozing a course antithetical to everything that is Indian, democratic and acceptable.[206]

V.D. Savarkar, 'the father of Hindutva' advocated that Indian's should shed the soft values like, humility, self-surrender and forgiveness and cultivate sturdy habits of hatred, retaliation and vindictiveness'.[207] Modi seems to have assimilated these 'values' more than any Hindutva ideologue in contemporary times.

Eminent journalist Bhaskar Ghose argues that Modi together with Pravin Togadia of the VHP have tried to create an identity for the Hindus defined by hatred and intolerance, and should that gain acceptance among a large number of people, they will be taking India into a holocaust from which we will never emerge whole again.[208]

The judgement on the Best Bakery case delivered on 12 April 2004 by Justice Doraiswamy Raju and justice Arijit Pasayat stated – which was a reference to the state of affairs in Modi's Gujarat – "When the ghastly killings take place in the land of Mahatma Gandhi, it raised a very pertinent question as to whether some people have become so bankrupt in their ideology that they have deviated from everything which was so dear to him. When a large number of people, including innocent and helpless children and women, are killed in a diabolic manner it brings disgrace to the entire society."[209]

In March 2005 the United States denied Modi a diplomatic visa and revoked his tourist/business visa under a law that bars such a privilege to anyone who caries out severe violations of religious freedom.[210] It was a mirror as to how the international community envisages Modi.

Judging from what has been said above we may maintain that Modi is a master political strategist whose worldview is guided by the ethics of end justifies the means. He rationalises violence and rejects truth and justice, especially when it concerns the Muslim and Christian minorities whom he cannot tolerate. Suffice it to say that Modi has become a symbol of shame and disgrace to India and to Indian values of non-violence, tolerance, cultural pluralism, democracy and search after truth.

Gujarat pogrom 2002 had much to do with Hindu religion. In fact, those responsible for it are alleged to be religious people and religiously oriented organisations. Modi is an ardent supporter of Hinduism, and he polarised Gujarat State on religious lines – Hindu and Muslim – and won the state assembly elections in 2002. During and also in 2007 the election campaigns he strongly endorsed militant Hindu nationalism. In 2003 in Gujarat, the independence day celebration of India was celebrated in Hindu style. He passed the so-called 'Freedom of Religion Bill' ('Anti Conversion Bill') in the state soon after the elections which in every sense favours Hinduism.

Heinich Himmler (1900-1945), the one who was responsible for the genocide and the architect of mass murder of Jews under the Nazi regime was a 'religious' person and a believer in God. In fact, belief in God was demanded of the members of the *Schutz-Staffel* (SS) which he directed. A prospective member had to answer 50 questions. The first was: '*Also glaubst du an Gott*' ('Well, do you believe in God?'), and the expected answer was: '*Ja, Ich glaube an einen Herrgott*'. ('Yes, I believe in one Lord, God'). Another question was: '*Was haltest du von einem Menschen, der an keinen Gott glaubst?*' ('What do you think of a man who does not believe in God?'). The expected answer was: '*Ich halte ihn fur uberheblich, grosswahnsinnig und dumm; er ist für uns nicht geeignet*' ('I consider him to be arrogant, awfully crazy and stupid; he is not suited for us).[211] Paradoxically, the same Himmler who was responsible for the extermination of millions of Jews and others of the so-called non-pure race was a convinced vegetarian and one who was passionately in love with animals.[212]

Conclusion

In contemporary Indian politics Narendra Modi is considered as a Hindu communalist and a Hindutva hardliner. According to K.N. Panikkar, Modi is a blue print of the future, if the Indian State comes fully under the control of the Sangh Parivar.[213] So many credible voices are arrayed against Modi, yet he survives – nay he thrives – and anyone who criticises him is often condemned as anti-Hindu, anti-national, anti-BJP and pseudo-secularists.[214] As Chief Minister of Gujarat, Modi now finds himself in the same situation as during the riots in February-March 2002 – a hero for the adherents of Hindu cultural nationalism but a villain for everyone else.[215]

The Gujarat pogrom of 2002 has lead many people to lose faith in the ideal of a secular and culturally pluralistic India. When recalling the pogrom some people doubt whether Mahatma Gandhi would have been safe in Modi's Gujarat, and consider the Mahatma as an accident that happened to that State.[216] The present Prime Minister of India, Man Mohan Singh, created history by apologising to the nation for the anti-Sikh carnage of 1984. But it has been asked whether Modi would apologise for the genocide in Gujarat in 2002?[217] Every right thinking person in India knows that if any government should resign on the basis of truth and justice and Constitutional principles, it is Modi's. But so far such a thing has not happened and very little is being done by the concerned authorities of India to dismiss Modi and his government to ensure justice, human rights and democracy in Gujarat.

The Congress-led UPA government came into power in New Delhi after the general elections of 2004 with the promise of restoring secularism, democracy, communal harmony, justice and punishing those responsible for communal riots and violation of human rights. But so far hardly anything has been done by the central government in this direction. Consequently, Modi marches on unhampered, and probably many in the present UPA government look upon him with secret admiration, for there are not a few in the Congress and other political parties who endorse Hindu cultural nationalism and advocate 'soft Hindutvə'. But handling Modi and his government could turn out to be the acid test of the secular credentials of the Congress-led UPA government. India today needs leaders of the calibre of Jawaharlal Nehru, who, according to Mani Shankar Aiyar, was a 'secular fundamentalist', and vanquished the soft Hindutva school from the Congress and saved India from succumbing to Hindu communalism.[218]

In 2005, sustained campaign against Modi in the USA by secular Indian organisations and effective lobbying, led the US government to keep Modi out of the country. It is said that about 60-70 e-mails were sent out daily and 125 academics signed a letter to the State department,[219] and their efforts bore fruit, Modi was denied US visa, and he remained at home. This only shows that if there is a political will, and concerted effort, the government of India can ensure justice to all the victims of the communal riots in Gujarat and punish the guilty, even if they appear to be above the law. Does the Congress-led UPA government have such a will? Or has it fully succumbed to 'soft Hindutva'?

Notes

1. Jayaprakah Narayan (1902-1979) launched the *Nav Nirman* movement – generally understood as movement for a 'total revolution' in the political scenario of India – basically against the corrupt regime of Chimanbhai Patel. The movement was soon captured by the RSS. Since Narayan was consumed with anti-Congress sentiments he did not mind taking the help of the RSS to ensure the downfall of Indira Gandhi, the then Prime Minister of India. This provided the RSS and the members of the Sangh Parivar with an opportunity to capture the movement. Besides, by associating with an anti-corruption movement they could also acquire respectability. It is said that Narayan took a liking to Modi, a dynamic young leader, during the days of the *Nav Nirman* movement. See A.A. Engineer, "The Gujarat Carnage", 15.
2. See D. Bunsha, "An Ambitious Pracharak", 8.
3. See *Asian Age,* 12 September 2002.
4. See T. Otto, "Narendra Modi: ein Portrait", http://www.suedasien.net/bios/modi_narendra.htm
5. See B. Puri, "BJP's Problems and Prospects", 123.
6. Reportedly Modi married a lady working as a teacher in a poor Muslim area about 100 kilometres from Ahmedabad. But his official biography makes no mention of it. Critics say that the omission is in keeping with the value that orthodox RSS members place on a life of bachelorhood, allowing in their view true dedication to work as an RSS leader. See http://news.bbc.co.uk/l/hi/world/south_asia/1958555.html
7. See M.S. Golwalkar, *Bunch of Thoughts*, 286.
8. M.S. Golwalkar, *Bunch of Thoughts*, 342.
9. See M.S. Golwalkar, *Bunch of Thoughts,* 286.
10. M.S. Golwalkar, *Bunch of Thoughts*, 291.

11. See M.S. Golwalkar, *Bunch of Thoughts*, 286-287.
12. See "People's Needs over Party Politics", 10.
13. See D. Bunsha, "The Mystery of the Godhra Fire", 37.
14. See " Gujarat Riots Glaring Fault Lines", 102.
15. See *The Indian Express*, 30 January 2003.
16. See D. Bunsha, "The Mystery of the Godhra Fire", 37.
17. See A.A. Engineer, "The Gujarat Carnage", 18.
18. For details on the Best Bakery case see U. Mahurkar and S. Mitra, "Wanted Justice", 27-36. (27-36)'; "The Disaster that Followed Tragedy", 28-29.; "Best Bakery Case; PYCL Demands Fresh Trial", 16-22.
19. V. Ventatesan, "A Judicial Stricture", 35.
20. See A.A. Engineer, "The BJP and Gujarat Elections", 42.
21. See *Vir Arjun*, 23 August 2002.
22. See V. Venkatesan, " The Road from Gujarat", 127.
23. See A.G. Noorani, "The Man Behind the Image", 5.
24. See "A Quiet Anniversary", 40.
25. See "A Quiet Anniversary", 40.
26. See T. Otto, "Narendra Modi: ein Portrait", http://www.suedasien.net/bios/modi_narendra.html
27. It has been observed that the motorised chariot designed for the *Gujarat Gaurav Yatra* of Narendra Modi in 2002 was a 'marvel of design and innovation' with hydraulic lifts, domed podium with a lotus in front on which Modi could rest his hand while addressing the public, digital photographs detailing Gujarat's achievements stuck on the two sides of the van, lights and a public address system and a toilet. The van was also air-conditioned. See "Yatra on a Mazda Rath", 32.
28. D. Bunsha, "Advantage Modi, Thanks to Congress", 24.
29. See D. Bunsha, "Advantage Modi, Thanks to Congress", 24.
30. See "Godhra: Who's afraid of Facing Facts?", 12.
31. D. Bunsha, "A Quiet Anniversary", 40.
32. See M.G. Vaidya, "Elections in Gujarat and After", 10.
33. S. Chari, "Religious Retort", 56.
34. V. Venkatesan, " The Road from Gujarat", 126.
35. V. Venkatesan, "The Road from Gujarat", 126-127.
36. G.M. Banatwala, "Challenge of Faith", 54.
37. See P. Bidwai, "A Long haul for Secularists", 108.

38. H. Höhne, "Biedermänner Banausen Brandstifter", 50.
39. H. Höhne; "Biedermänner Banausen Brandstifter", 50.
40. See "Riots were Planned", 1.
41. See N. Oza, "Fire and Storm", 60.
42. See V. Venkatesan, "Busting a Conspiracy Theory", 38.
43. See V. Venkatesan, "Busting a Conspiracy Theory", 38-39. Interestingly, it may be added here that, Pravin Togadia of the VHP claimed that a mob of 2000 Muslims burned down the coach S-6 of the Sabarmati Express. See P. Togadia, "Final Warning", 35.
44. See D. Bunsha, "The Mystery of the Godhra Fire", 38.
45. See T. Setalvad, "Godhra Revisited", 7.
46. See D. Bunsha, "The Mystery of the Godhra Fire", 38. It is reported that many *kar sevaks* travelling in the Sabarmati Express train behaved in an aggressive and 'uncivilised' manner as is evident from the reports. Several passengers reported that they were harassed by the *kar sevaks* travelling in Sabarmati Express throughout the journey. Many *kar sevaks* travelled without tickets and took over the reserved compartments, packing the train to thrice their capacity. They threw out ticket checkers who attempted to enter the compartment. At every station they shouted anti-Muslim slogans. At Godhra station they refused to let a passenger buy tea from a Muslim vendor and pushed him out of the coach, while abusing him. At the Godhra station some *kar sevaks* tried to pull into the compartment a girl. They let her go after the mother screamed for help.
47. See M. Majumdar and V. Menon, "This Man is the Real Culprit", 404.
48. See T. Setalvad, "Godhra Revisited", 8.
49. See M. Joseph and S. Anand, "A Plot from the Devils Liar", 423-424.
50. See E. Faleiro, "Faleiro's Letter to Advani", 438.
51. See D. Bunsha, "Blocking Justice", 39.
52. See *The Gujarat Pogrom*, 12.
53. See "The Will is Lacking", 223.
54. See *The Gujarat Pogrom*, 19.
55. See A.A. Engineer, "The Gujarat Carnage", 21.
56. See "The Long Road to Justice", 11.
57. S. Sanyal, "Modi Ilk's Bigoted Pogrom", *The Statesman*, 9 April 2002.
58. See K.G. Kannbiran, "Ungodly Act", 17.
59. See H. Mander, "Inventing Borders in Gujarat", 93.
60. See "Concerned Citizens Tribunal", 422.

61. Quoted by Johannes Hohlfeld (ed.), *Deutsche Reichsgeschicte in Dokumenten*, vol. 4, as cited in J.C. Fest, *The Face of the Third Reich*, 121, 487 note 24.
62. See M. Joseph and S. Anand, "A Plot from the Devils Liar", 425.
63. See "Rape as Community Punishment", 17-18.
64. K. Nayar, "The Road Taken from Sialkot to Ahmedabad", *The Indian Express*, 3 April 2002.
65. See H. Mander, "Cry, the Beloved Country", 41-42.
66. V. Venkatesan, "A Test Case in Supreme Court", 41.
67. See *The Gujarat Pogrom*, 11.
68. See V. Venkatesan, "Winning without Hindutva?", 11.
69. H. Mander, "In Search of Gandhi and Godse", 103.
70. See A.A. Engineer, "BJP's Riot-Free India", 82.
71. See H. Mander, "In Search of Gandhi and Godse", 102.
72. See *The Gujarat Pogrom*, 16.
73. See A. Malekar, "It's a Legal Battle, 32-33.
74. See D. Bunsha, "Digging up the Truth", 36.
75. See *The Gujarat Pogrom*, 14.
76. See T. Setalvad, "Godhra Revisited", 6.
77. See "The Long Road to Justice", 10.
78. See "The Long Road to Justice", 11.
79. See "The Long Road to Justice", 11.
80. See H. Mander, "Inventing Borders in Gujarat", 91
81. See "Godhra: Who's afraid of Facing Facts?", 12. See also "Rape as Community Punishment", 17-18. All of them contain terrible stories of rape during the Post-Godhra days.
82. See http://www.millegazette.com/dailyupdate/2003/20030823.htm
83. See P. Bidwai, "For Justice in Gujarat", 122.
84. See N. Oza, "Grave Reminder", 10.
85. See P. Bidwai, "For Justice in Gujarat", 121
86. See P. Bidwai, "For Justice in Gujarat", 122.
87. See P. Bidwai, "For Justice in Gujarat", 122.
88. See J. Poonthuruthil, *Growth and Responsibility*, Shillong, 2006, 201, 284.
89. See P. Bidwai, "For Justice in Gujarat", 122.
90. See P. Bidwai, "For Justice in Gujarat", 122. See also R. Bonney (ed.), *Harvest of Hatred*, 186-187.
91. See "France Honours Fr. Cedric Prakash", 17.

92. See C. Prakash, "Gujarat: The Embers Still Burn", 18-19.
93. See C. Prakash, "Gujarat: The Embers Still Burn", 19.
94. See C. Prakash, "Gujarat: The Embers Still Burn", 19.
95. V. P. Singh, "Hindus are Next", 32.
96. See M.S. Golwalkar, *We*, 47-48.
97. See P. Bidwai, "For Justice in Gujarat", 122.
98. P. Bidwai, "For Justice in Gujarat", 122.
99. See C. Prakash, "Gujarat: The Embers Still Burn", 18-19. In 2003, when the BJP-led NDA was in power in New Delhi, in Kerala a census of Churches and Mosques and all the institutions connected with them, was made. In the State both are minority communities. See M.C. Menon, "Central Census on Kerala Churches and Mosques", 9-10.
100. See *The Statesman*, 13 March 2003.
101. See D. Bunsha, "Narendra Modi's 'Concerns'", 19
102. See *The Hindustan Times*, 12 March 2003.
103. *The New Leader*, 16-31 August 2004, 32.
104. See D. Bunsha, "Silenced into Submission", 31.
105. D. Bunsha, "Narendra Modi's 'Concerna'", 19.
106. See D. Bunsha, "Narendra Modi's 'Concerns'", 19.
107. R. Guha, "They too Wrote our History", 52.
108. R. Guha, "They too Wrote our History", 52.
109. See M.S. Golwalkar, *Bunch of Thoughts*, 177.
110. See P. Bidwai, "A Long Haul for Secularists", 109.
111. B. Walker, *Hindu World*, vol. II, 100.
112. See B. Walker, *Hindu World*, vol. II, 100-102.
113. See http://www.millegazette.com/dailyupdate/2003/20030823.htm
114. See http://www.millegazette.com/dailyupdate/2003/20030823.htm
115. See http://www.millegazette.com/dailyupdate/2003/20030823.htm
116. See C. Prakash, "Gujarat: The Embers Still Burn", 19.
117. See H. Mander, "Inventing Borders in Gujarat", 92.
118. A. Mitra, "Shall Nobody Save Us?", 400-401.
119. See *The Hindustan Times*, 13 June 2003.
120. For example, in the districts of Rajkot, Patan, Vadodara, Anand and Banaskantha. See *The Hindustan Times*, 13 June 2003
121. See D. Bunsha, "Narendra Modi's 'Concerns'", 19.
122. See *The Hindu*, 14 March 2003.
123. See *The Statesman*, 17 June 2003.

124. See "Modi Government still Surverying Christians", 8-9.
125. See *The Hindustan Times*, 30 May 2003.
126. See "Friday Eve Fever", 10.
127. See C. Prakash, "Nuns Get Marching Orders", 24-26.
128. When childhood lovers Reema and Anthony of Ahmedabad eloped to Mumbai the conservative family of Reema engaged Bajrang Dal and VHP to separate the couples. See D. Bunsha, "Organised Intolerance", 17.
129. See D. Bunsha, "Organised Intolerance", 17.
130. See D. Bunsha, "Organised Intolerance", 17.
131. See D. Bunsha, "Organised Intolerance", 17-18.
132. See D. Bunsha, "Organised Intolerance", 18.
133. See D. Bunsha, "Organised Intolerance", 18.
134. See D. Bunsha, "Organised Intolerance", 18.
135. See D. Bunsha, "Organised Intolerance", 18.
136. H. Mander, "In Search of Gandhi and Godse", 102.
137. I.K. Shukla, "Gujarat was Gifted to Godse", 6.
138. See A. Nandy, "Allure of the Demonic", 38.
139. U. Mahurkar, " On the Fast Track", 34.
140. T. Setalvad, "Godhra Revisited", 8.
141. G. Das, *The Elephant Paradigm*, 81.
142. See P. Bidwai, "A Long haul for Secularists", 108.
143. See P. Bidwai, "A Long haul for Secularists", 107.
144. See *The Gujarat Pogrom*, 1.
145. See "Hindutva'a Triumph", 114.
146. See S. Suri, "Now We Wait for the Light", 30.
147. See P. Kumar, "Modi Announces Panchamrit Scheme", 8.
148. See V. Venkatesan, "A Test Case in Supreme Court", 41.
149. V. Venkatesan, "A Test Case in Supreme Court", 41.
150. V. Venkatesan, "A Test Case in Supreme Court", 41.
151. See K.N. Panikkar, "Down, but not Out", 122.
152. See P. Bidwai, "'Vision' and Vitriol", 128. During the general election campaign of 2004 the BJP leader Pramod Mahajan said that only a person who is 100 per cent Indian should be the Prime Minister of India. See "Atal Sandesh Yatra in Orissa", 7.
153. A. Roy, "'Exit' Politics", 2.

154. Chief Minister Narendra Modi at an election rally in Khambhat, Anand, Gujarat as cited in D. Bunsha, "Advantage Modi, Thanks to Congress", 23.
155. *The Indian Express*, 20 November 2003.
156. See *India Today*, 26 December 2005, 246.
157. S. Gurumurthy, "Unmasking Sonia Gandhi", 20.
158. See S. Gurumurthy, "Unmasking Sonia Gandhi", 21.
159. See P. Bidwai, "'Vision' and Vitriol", 128.
160. See P. Bidwai, "'Vision' and Vitriol", 128.
161. See N.J. Ansari, "Foreign Bodies", *Pioneer*, 19 September 2002.
162. Sonia Gandhi in Jaipur on 16 October 2003, as cited in B. KANG, "Origins, Destinations", 28.
163. See V. Ramakrishnan, "The Return of the Congress", 4.
164. K.N. Panikkar, "Down, but not Out", 122.
165. K.N. Panikkar, "Down, but not Out", 122.
166. See P. Bidwai, "Liberation at Last!", 126.
167. See P.S. Jha, "Who is an Indian?", 43.
168. See P. Palety, "Sixty per cent Say VHP, State Connived in Riots", 381.
169. See *India Today*, 4 August 2003, 14.
170. See *India Today*, 4 August 2003, 14.
171. See P. Bidwai, "More then Just a Wake-up Call", 123.
172. See *Indian Currents*, 23 February 2003, 39.
173. See V. Ramakrishnan, "The Battle for U.P.", 9.
174. See "Give us a Chance, Say BJP", 8.
175. See S. Khosla, "No Mudslinging, Please", 2.
176. See V. Venkatesan, "Alone at the Top", 14.
177. See D. Bunsha, "A Second Wind for Modi", 17.
178. See "BJP Suspends Khurana, Hints at Expulsion", 1.
179. See P. Bidwai, "A Long haul for Secularists", 107.
180. See D. Desai, "Will Modi's Magic Show Get Going?", 10.
181. As cited in *The Gujarat Pogrom*, 1.
182. See D. Trevedie, "Divide and Rule: Modi Offers Recipe of Hate", 67.
183. See htttp://www.rediff.com/news/2004/jun/21spec2.html
184. Narad, "Modi being Unfairly Vilified", 17.
185. M.V. Kamath, "Of Modi-Meters and Other Fairly Tales", 17.
186. "Fifty Reasons". 35.
187. "Fifty Reasons". 35.

188. "Fifty Reasons". 36.
189. "Fifty Reasons". 36.
190. "Fifty Reasons". 37.
191. "Fifty Reasons". 38.
192. "Fifty Reasons". 38-39.
193. "Fifty Reasons". 39.
194. "Fifty Reasons". 40.
195. See A. Roy, "'If Bush is So Acceptable", 72.
196. S.N. Bhaumik and S. Mukerjee, "The Big Fish Escapes", 40.
197. S. Mustafa, *Deccan Chronicle*, 17 April 2004, as cited in Narad, "Modi being unfairly Vilified", 17.
198. See htttp://www.rediff.com/news/2004/jun/21spec2.html
199. See "Big Bro watchin'[sic]", 12.
200. D. Bunsha, "Probe or Persecution?", 40.
201. See V. Venkatesan, "Alone at the Top", 14.
202. S. Sharma, "Congress even Condones Terror", 2.
203. See A. Malekar, "Quest for Justice", 30.
204. See A. Kulkarni, *The Advent of Advani*, 240.
205. See htttp://www.rediff.com/news/2004/jun/21spec2.html
206. See A. Pratap, "A Spoonful of Dissent", 50.
207. See A. Nandy, "Allure of the Demonic", 38.
208. See B. Ghose, "Questions of Identity", 91.
209. "Crime and Complicity", 97.
210. See htttp://www.expressindia.com/fulllstory.php?newsid=43432 The Sangh Parivar reacted sharply to the US government for denying Modi – their poster boy – the diplomatic visa. See Raghavendra, "Who Worked against Modi Visas?", 1-2; S. Jain, "US Duplicity in Denying Visa to Modi", 5.
211. See V. Trimondi and V. Trimondi, *Hitler, Buddha, Kriahna*, 24.
212. See V. Trimondi and V. Trimondi, *Hitler, Buddha, Krishna*, 33.
213. See K.N. Panikkar, "The Agony of Gujarat", 93.
214. See A. Prtap, "A Spoonful of Dissent", 50.
215. See U. Mahurkar and S. Mitra, "Wanted Justice", 35.
216. See R. Sharma, "Would Mahatma have been Safe", 236.
217. See R. Sharma, "Would Mahatma have been Safe", 236.
218. See M.S. Aiyar, *Confessions of a Secular Fundamentalist*, 3.
219. See S. Sirohi, "All-American Grand Slam", 9.

Conclusion

Political Leaders Who Failed India

We have briefly analysed the worldviews and identities of five leading Hindu rightwing political leaders of India belonging to the Bharatiya Janata Party – Atal Bihari Vajpayee, Lal Krishna Advani, Murli Manohar Joshi, Arun Shourie and Narendra Modi. Individually taken, these leaders are capable, intelligent, experienced and well informed persons with admirable administrative abilities. But unfortunately, they have been deeply rooted in an ideology that is narrow-minded, communal, undemocratic, anti-secular and negative, namely, Hindutva or Hindu cultural nationalism. During their tenure of office as national political leaders, union cabinet ministers, heads of governments and key administrators, they misled millions of Hindus both in India and abroad, rationalised violence, encouraged communal clashes and promoted religion-based politics and denied justice to thousands belonging to the minority communities. They neglected their duty to promote religious tolerance and communal harmony and failed to concede to the people what the Indian Constitutions guarantee as their fundamental right. Thus they wilfully rejected truth and refused to listen to the voice of conscience. The only thing that mattered for them was their pet idea of creating a Hindu *rashtra* in India.

Barun De, an eminent historian, assesses the 1990s as a time of a major national change in Indian culture and social outlook and an increase of political religion. A new effort to incorporate religious emotion into political sympathy waves infiltrated major party programmes. Ideas were taken from Khomeini in Iran or Zionists in Israel or fundamentalist Republicanism in the USA. Hindu fanaticism seeped into the propertied classes and aspirants for participation in the consumer culture. With the installation of the first BJP government in New Delhi in 1996 for the first time since Independence, Muslims faced the prospect of being governed by a party that avowedly represented the majority community, which was not just pro-Hindu but a party that wanted to usher in a new Hindu millennium at the expense of the minority communities of India. Thus the educational curricula, concept of Indian culture and scientific achievements were given a non-Muslim and non-Christian tinge. But it was a too costly step that took India not forward but backward.[1]

In the early years of the BJP it was very much people oriented and open to many noble ideals, at least theoretically, and it even considered itself as an alternative to the Congress Party. Christopher Jaffrelot reminds us that in the original constitution of the BJP the word 'Hindu' did not make a single appearance.[2] It emphasised such values and principles as integral humanism, Gandhian socialism, decentralised economy, positive secularism, nationalism and national integration, democracy, value based politics and unity and diversity of India.[3] All these resulted in a certain alienation of the party from the RSS. The ideological dilution manifested by the BJP and its set back in the elections in the early years left the RSS in doubt whether the organisation is capable of promoting the Hindu nationalist cause. But in the subsequent years a radical change took place in the party and it became the extended arm of the RSS in politics.

Vajpayee, Advani, Joshi, Shourie and Modi have been in the field of active politics for several decades, and for some, politics has been a lifetime commitment. Probably right from their early years their mindset has been shaped by the worldviews of such organisations as Arya Samaj, RSS, ABVP, VHP, Jan Sangh, etc, which advocate a narrow political philosophy centred around the creation of a Hindu *rashtra* in India founded on the concepts of one nation (Hindu), one culture (Hindu), one language (Sanskrit) and one religion (Hinduism).[4] Consequently, for them, all those who do not conform to it are enemies and traitors of the Hindu *rashtra*.

The Greek Philosopher, Plato, in his *Gorgias* 525-526[5] describes the qualities of a good ruler. According to Plato, he is essentially a

Philosopher King whose responsibility consists in promoting what is true and good. But if one is indoctrinated in some vicious ideology for a long time and accepts subjective truth as absolute, and refuses to listen to the voice of conscience, it is impossible to discover what is objectively true and good. The result is ethical and epistemological relativism.

A true Hindu can never be a religious fanatic or fundamentalist. In this sense those who advocate Hindu cultural nationalism are to be considered as pseudo-Hindus. Today Hindutva ideologues are trying to impose a new identity on the Hindus, which will affect their cultural, social and political worldviews. They have no qualms of conscience to mix Hindu religion with politics for the sake of power. In fact, all the five leaders we have discussed above have liberally mixed Hindu religion and politics, manipulated the illiterate masses, and played on their emotions and gained political mileage. They have shown themselves to be ideological dictators who advocate, either openly or tacitly, communalism, violence, hatred and even genocide in order to consolidate their power and to maintain the same.

We may ask what is the aim of politics? Is it meant to destroy a nation and its people? Or is it meant to maintain order in society, dispense justice, assure peaceful co-existence of peoples and guarantee human rights?

Sataymeva jayate ('truth alone triumphs') is the motto of India. The ancient sages of India sang: 'Lead me from untruth to truth, from darkness to light'. The great teacher Jesus Christ said: 'You shall know the truth and the truth shall set you free'. Mahatma Gandhi, the father of the nation, believed that 'truth is God and God is truth'. A close examination of the political philosophy of the five leaders examined in this study and their political strategies reveal that they are persons who refused to accept truth and chose darkness rather than light.

In a political system that functions on lies it is difficult to recognise truth or listen to the voice of conscience. It hardens human hearts, and people live by false certainties founded on subjective truth and imagined good. Adolf Hitler and his collaborators had absolute certainty that they were doing the right thing by exterminating the six million Jews and many others who did not belong to the 'pure race'. But their subjective certainty did not save them from being judged by the world and criminal and unjust. A similar situation exists in India where the Hindutva ideologues function as political leaders, administrators and dispensers of justice.

Vajpayee, Advani, Joshi, Shourie and Modi and several others like them, are falsely convinced that India is a Hindu nation from time immemorial, that the minorities in India are second class citizens, that the future of the Muslims should depend on the goodwill of the majority Hindu community, that Christians are the greatest internal threat to India, that they should make the Church in India indigenous by subjecting it to the state as in China, that end will always justify the means so that even murder, militancy, arson, riot, rape and genocide are permitted provided they serve to attain the ultimate goal of creating the Hindu *rashtra*. These were the teachings with which the personalities we have analysed in this study have been indoctrinated from their early youth by virulent Hindu cultural nationalist organisations and hardcore Hindutva ideologues. In essence their political philosophy was basically that of the RSS. Perhaps, more than anyone, it is Nehru who assessed the real character of the RSS. As early as 1947 he called it an organisation which has the nature of a private army that is proceeding on strictest Nazi lines.[6]

What is known as Machiavellianism in the West – i.e., the use of force and any form of repression by a ruler for the purpose of safeguarding his rule and the continuance in power is seen as an end in itself[7] – has a parallel in India in 'Chanakyanism'. Chanakya (Kautilya, 4th century B.C.) wrote a treatise on statecraft entitled *Arthasastra* which contained a code of conduct for rulers that justified force, cunning and ruthlessness and endorsed real politic and dismissed considerations of morality in public life, which ranged from spying to assassination.[8] In other words, they openly taught that end justifies the means. The political leaders who follow the ethics of Machiavelli and Chanakya are many in India as has been demonstrated in this study.

In the recent decades clash of religions has become a common occurrence in India. There is hardly a day without some form of violence taking place in the name of religion. But it is important to note that they are not organised by religions themselves but by politicians or politically oriented organisations. Religion *per se* does not give rise to communalism but a religious community does, when it mixes religion with politics. Religion, since it has a powerful emotional appeal, is used to mobilise the believing masses by political parties. For example, the single most factor for the rise of BJP in politics is its linking of Hindu religion with politics. The common people in India do not always think critically enough to understand the ulterior motives behind the so-called clash between religions. It is the same with the so-called religion-related issues. Did the people really understand the political motives behind the Advani's *Ram Rath Yatra* or Joshi changing of school textbooks or Modi blaming the Muslims community for Godhra train tragedy? Did the people really see through the real intention of Vajpayee's statements after the Gujarat pogrom of 2002 that 'wherever there are Muslims, they do not want to live with others" or Arun Shourie's accusation that conversion is the central activity of Christianity or the BJP's stand on cow slaughter or religious conversion or in projecting almost every problem in India as caused by Pakistan's ISI? Apparently, these are religious questions. But at the bottom they are political issues generated, promoted and sustained by politicians and political parties for gaining political mileage. No wonder once George III of England said that 'Politics are a trade for a rascal, not a gentleman'.[9]

Religion has given meaning to humanity since the dawn of civilisation. They are potential sources of tremendous power. But the same power can be utilised for good or evil. How religion can be utilised for evil has been repeatedly demonstrated in India by many political leaders. They have frequently manipulated the masses calling on the name of religion through their rhetoric, use of mass media and powers of persuasion. In the last two decades or so Hindutva politicians like Vajpayee, Advani, Joshi, Shourie and Modi and many others like them, have used Hindu religion for creating in India an atmosphere of hatred, revenge, vindictiveness, cultural narrow-mindedness and xenophobia against the minority communities. In their hands Hindu religion has turned aggressive and destructive. Opportunism, double talk and political calculations outweighed ethical considerations. Under their leadership India witnessed the dark side of religion – communalism, intolerance, murderous wars and narrow-minded nationalism. Here it is opportune to refer to Kuldip Nayar who says that Advani's *Ram Rath Yatra* marked the beginning of the assault on India's secular polity. It sowed seeds of hatred.[10] Abu Abraham notes: "I wish religion were the opium of the people, as Marx described it. But it is far worse, more deadly than opium. Religion, unlike opium does not put people to sleep. It excites them to persecute one another to make a virtue of lawlessness, to claim for themselves an exclusive possession of the truth."[11]

The founding fathers of independent India took pains to separate religion and State in the Constitutions, and advocated secularism and democracy as cherished goals. According to Jawaharlal Nehru, the first Prime Minister of India, communalism has striking resemblance to the various forms of fascism. In fact, he called it the Indian version of fascism. Hence for him, there was no question of a compromise with it, and he denied it a place in secular India.[12] He vanquished the 'soft Hindutva' within the Congress party by his hard secularist stand.

As an ideology Hindutva is clearly fascist, communal, violent, dictatorial and a bourgeois device to control the masses. It is a conspiracy of a certain section of the Hindu upper caste elite. What they propagate is the utopian vision of creating a Hindu *rashtra* in India where religion and politics are inexorably linked. But such an ideal is anti-modern and backward looking and is obsessed with Hindu culture and everything Hindu.

Sang Parivar's exclusionary and militant brand of Hindu nationalism cannot be acceptable to India. Their religion ought not to intrude into the public life. They should not politicise Hindu religion. Nehru affirmed that it is incorrect and undesirable to use 'Hindu' or 'Hinduism' for Indian culture, even with reference to the distant past, although the various aspects of thought as embodied in ancient writings were the dominant expression of that culture.[13]

Yet, unfortunately, creation of a Hindu *rashtra* in India is the ultimate goal of the Sangh Parivar. Contrary to this Kuldip Nayar argues that had the Hindu *rashtra* been India's aim, it would have established it after winning independence. With the 80 per cent Hindu population in the country, there was nothing to stop it from doing so. Instead, the most democratic and secular constitution was adopted. That represented the ethos of our national movement and what India stood for.[14] In 1951 Nehru wrote: "It may sound very nice to some people to hear it said that we will create a Hindu *rashtra*, etc. I cannot understand what it means [....] Hindu *rashtra* can only mean one thing and that is you leave the modern way and get into a narrow, old-fashioned way of thinking, and fragment India into pieces."[15]

The acid test of any democracy is the way in which the minority groups are treated in a country. If this rule is applied, leaders like Vajpayee, Advani, Joshi, Shourie, Modi and others like them fail the test. The RSS leader and ideologue Golwalkar had given two options to non-Hindus residing in India which are known to every informed Indian: either to glorify Hinduism or stay on in the country as second class citizens. Today, the Hindu rightwing nationalism of the Sangh Parivar poses an inherent danger to Indian democracy, secularism and cultural pluralism. In fact, writer and social activist Arundhati Roy rightly affirmed that the general elections of April-May 2004 was fundamentally about two issues: the economy and right-wing nationalism.[16] The rightwing nationalists led by Vajpayee lost the elections of 2004.

Education of the masses in political consciousness is an urgent need in India. Asghar Ali Engineer has correctly analysed the situation of Indian education. He says that, the educational system in India could never rid itself of the trappings of communalism. Even today textbooks are a fundamental source of communal divide.[17] There is an undercurrent of co-operation and mutual support among the various organisations in the name of religion, especially at the time of elections and discussions on national issues.

Sangh Parivar and its leaders do not care to discuss important issues before the nation like, economic reforms, social change, elimination of poverty, malnutrition, abolition of caste system, eradication of illiteracy, gender discrimination, untouchability, promotion of health care, national integration, science and technology, modernisation of India, and the like. Instead the issues dear to them are parochial and narrow, like, cow protection, beef eating, re-conversion, anti-conversion laws, Astrology, Christian missionaries, Pakistan, ISI, Ram temple at Ayodhya, Hindu *rashtra*, *rath yatra*, discussion on religious demography, re-writing Indian history, saffronisation of education, etc. But are these the real issues affecting the nation? They have definitely missed the point and are out of the track.

Hindu cultural nationalism has a poor intellectual background. There is poverty of thinking and critical reflection in its ranks. Even their best think tanks cannot envisage India beyond the narrow confines of the Hindu *rashtra*. None of the leaders examined in this study are noted for their originality of thinking or trail blazing initiatives in any field. They simply took the much trodden path delineated by their ideological mentors like Savarkar, Hedgewar, Golwalkar, S.P. Mukherjee, and others, without serious critical reflection. Their ideology survives not because of the power of thinking of their leaders or the strength of its cause but by tapping into the religious feelings of the Hindus and hatred towards the minorities of the Indian society. Way back in 1954 Nehru said: "The Hindu communal organisations are definitely aggressive and they can play on the religious or other feelings of the majority community."[18] Noted columnist Anita Pratap observes that a Hindu nationalists dismiss rather than discuss, abuse rather than argue, deride rather than debate. Every weapon, from the internet to word-of-mouth is used to malign, poison and attack those who don't conform.[19]

There is an acute intellectual poverty among the Hindu nationalists and that is evident also from the fact of them engaging themselves in the literal reading of Hindu scriptures and religious myths, uncritical adherence to superstitious beliefs, sentimentalism and 'follow the leader mentality'. Koenraad Elst, who is himself a pro-Hindutva writer, commented on the state of Hindutva saying: "There is not much of a think-tank culture in India, much less in the organised Hindu movement."[20] Such a lack of intellectual engagement and critical thinking itself is a factor that has contributed to the growth of Hindutva. In fact, Hindutva thrives where ignorance, illiteracy and superstition dominate. Aurobindo Ghose said as early in 1920: "I believe that the main cause of India's weakness is not subjection, nor poverty, nor a lack of spirituality or Dharma, but a diminution of thought power, the spread of ignorance in the motherland of knowledge. Everywhere I see an inability or unwillingness to think."[21]

The ideological and intellectual expose of Hindutva must continue and secularists must work united to cleanse Indian politics and institutions of communalism and Hindu cultural nationalism. Hindutva elements need to be purged out of the numerous Central and State structures and institutions which they have infiltrated. They must be replaced by people of high integrity and proven secular credentials. There should be no place in India for any organisation which preaches violence and promotes communal hatred in any form. The Sangh Parivar must be told to put reason into what they preach, and morality into what they do. It should be asked to disband its many private armies that are capable of demonstrating only their muscle power.

Today Hindutva is a problem related to Hindu religion. The answer to problems due to religion must come from religion itself. Gurucharan Das says that communal harmony in India will not come from converting people away from religion as the secularists had hoped. It will come when moderate religious leaders come forth in public life and begin to lead ordinary, decent people in the direction of a secular polity, and snuff out the evil voices of fundamentalism.[22]

Unfortunately, the minorities in India today are divided without enlightened and courageous leadership. They cannot easily come together to defend themselves, demand justice or fight for their rights. Very little pressure is made on the international community regarding the plight of the minorities in India. The Hindutva ideologues and their organisations have taken advantage of this deplorable situation.

The UPA government came to power after the general elections of 2004 with the promise of rectifying the wrongs done by the BJP-led NDA government, especially in matters regarding communalism and politicisation of religion. But so far it has done pretty little to address these issues. In the Congress-lead UPA government there are numerous 'soft-Hindutva' ideologues and Hindu elites who subtly endorse Hindu cultural nationalism. These people would not easily let the government function in a democratic and secular way. We may note here that it was the Congress governments that passed the anti-conversion law in Madhya Pradesh and Orissa in 1967 and 1968 respectively. This tells us plainly that many in the Congress cannot be trusted with secularism and democracy.

There are many examples of the non-functioning nature of democracy in India. Narendra Modi, the Chief Minister of Gujarat made Gujarat into a Hindutva lab in 2002. But paradoxically he was rated as the best Chief Minister of India by some of the opinion polls in 2005 – a typical case of Indian hankering for sycophancy; Vajpayee as Prime Minister did nothing to take action against Modi for the post-Godhra communal riots; Advani and Joshi who were seriously implicated in the destruction of the Babri mosque in 1992 have been acquitted under questionable circumstances, and they ride on triumphantly on chariots and address mammoth rallies thereby sending a message to everyone that if one has political connections and power any crime can be committed and can get away with it. Everyone knows that Babri mosque is a case of justice delayed beyond limits to the advantage of the Hindutva groups and ideologues and people in power. The same is true with cases relating to the Gujarat pogrom 2002. Both are glaring examples of justice purposely delayed. One is then led to ask a question: is there justice in India? Will the victims of political crimes ever get their grievances addressed? Nani Palkhivala seems to have analysed the Indian situation well when he said that a sense of justice and fairness is not inherent in the Indian psyche.[23] T.N. Seshan, the former Chief Election Commissioner of India reminds us that a society or a community based on as much injustice as we are in India is unlikely to succeed. Injustice is not in the court of law. Injustice in the sense that there is no court to which you can convey a sense of grief.[24] The cases of justice denied or delayed are also proofs that our democracy does not work the way it should. Seshan was right when he said that until and unless we rectify this decayed, damaged, dilapidated empire called Indian democracy all that we may do will be like painting a picture on water.[25] Probably, for many years to come it is futile to expect anything in the form of justice from the democratically elected Government of India, be it Congress or BJP or any other party for that matter. The kind of political leaders we have today may not save India or the Indians. We may need to look elsewhere for a solution.

It may be recalled here that in the heyday of Hitler's power in Europe, the Catholic Church was not a mere spectator to the Nazi atrocities. She intervened in every possible way she could, in the circumstances of the rule of a dictator. Pope Pius XI wrote an encyclical entitled *Mit brennender Sorge* ('With burning Concern') in 1937 in German, smuggled it into Germany, got it printed secretly and distributed to all the Churches for reading. In a state of dictatorship it was indeed a very dangerous act and it involved great risk for the Church. But the action of the pope was appreciated by people of good sense all over especially in France, USA, Italy, Poland, Hungary, Brazil. They said 'finally there is an opposition (*Widerstand*)'.[26] In fighting the Nazi dictatorship the Church also lost thousands of priests, religious and lay persons. This is something which the Church and her hierarchy in India could take note of and emulate.

Aggressive promotion of Hindu nationalism by political leaders like Vajpayee, Advani, Joshi, Shourie and Modi, has already inflicted much damage to India as a nation. These Hindu rightwing political leaders consciously encouraged and supported Hindu nationalism while they were in power. But today, nearly sixty years after the Independence of India, it is preposterous to speak of a Hindu *rashtra*. As Nehru said, we have always to remember India as a composite country, composite in many ways, in religion, in customs, in languages and in ways of life. Any attempt by the majority group to impose itself on others can only lead to inner conflicts, which are as bad as outer conflicts.[27] Everyone knows that BJP appeared on the political scenario of India as an alternative to the Congress Party. But it has proved to be more oppressive and sectarian than the Congress. The BJP has failed India and her people. In as much as BJP champions the cause of Hindu cultural nationalism it has no future. It is destined to irrelevance and posterity will remember the party and all its leaders as protagonists of a dark phase in the political history of India.

What Gurcharan Das observes is something which every patriotic Indian should take to heart. He says that Jawaharlal Nehru had bequeathed a cosmopolitan attitude that all human beings are equal and that all differences of colour, caste and religion are superficial and has little impact on the human capacity for living a good life. Now Hindu nationalism seems to challenge these ideals. Nationalism might have had a place in the first half of the twentieth century when we were fighting for Independence; it might even have made sense when we were building a nation in the fifties. But now, many decades later, when we should have been more confident and secure in our nationhood, its value seems to be doubtful. And when that nationalism is linked with religion it seems to have a sinister quality.[28]

A nation cannot rise on average persons and narrow-minded visionaries like Vajpayee, Advani, Joshi, Shourie and Modi. They were puppets in the hands of their ideological organisations that dictated to them policies for the government, code of conduct in public life and treatment of their real or imagined enemies. We need men and women of steel with clear sightedness, broad vision, unalloyed secular credentials, sense of truth, justice and courage. Evidently such persons are not likely to be found in any of the numerous organisations and institutions that uphold Hindu cultural nationalism. What we see around are blind men and women with puny minds fighting to paint India in saffron colour.

Principles of democracy and secularism have never been so weak in India as in these days. The frequency with which communal riots have been taking place in India shows that there is something fundamentally wrong with our political and administrative system as well as our understanding and practice of secularism. The growth of communalism, religious fundamentalism and cultural nationalism seems to be due to at least three major factors. We shall examine them briefly.

First, in India, religion – rather the so-called religion – has a deadly hold over people, even on the well-educated middle and upper classes. Today religious hatred seems to be the secret of success of any mass movement organised by political parties. People will spontaneously respond positively in the name of religion and they are ready for a *dharma yudha* or *jihad* or crusade. Religions seems to have lost their creative impulse to promote peace, justice, harmony and culture. Indians need to free themselves from a so-called religiosity that makes them slaves of religious and political leaders through a process of rational thinking, critical reflection and personal decision on religious and political matters. We may say that in the present context of India, the greatest enemy of India is, unfortunately, religion itself. It has been the common denominator practically in all the major incidents of violence in the country especially in the past 200 years or so.

Secondly, the Indian administrative system is so weak that it cannot intervene effectively and promptly to prevent communal riots and religious fundamentalism. In the administration itself there are people who subtly support one religious group or the other or are cowards afraid of taking strong actions when required. We may say, for example, that, if Shah Bano case[29] related to the Muslim Personal Law had been handled more intelligently, if the gates of the Babri mosque at Ayodhya had not been opened for the Hindus to worship,[30] if the Indian government had not permitted the screening of the TV serials *Ramayana* and *Mahabharata,*[31] if L.K. Advani had been prevented from taking out the *Rath Yatra* in 1990,[32] if the *kar sevaks* had been blocked from reaching Ayodhya intent on destroying the Babri mosque in 1992,[33] if the communal organisations and political parties had been banned from public life, if zero toleration had been shown to anyone disrupting communal harmony, if the Congress had stopped playing the 'soft Hindutva' card and refrained from appeasing certain minority groups, and if India had political leaders of the calibre and convictions of Nehru, probably the political history of India would have been different from what it is now.

It would be rewarding to recall here what Khushwant Singh, one of the eminent journalists and champions of secularism in contemporary India, has to say about Nehru and his attitude towards religion, secularism and democracy. Singh affirms that Nehru was above prejudices of any kind: racial, religious or caste. He refused to compromise his secular beliefs by indulging in religious rituals to gain acceptance. He was convinced that religion had played a very negative role in Indian society. But his successors exploited religious sentiments to gain political mileage. He was a visionary with precise notions of India of the future. Being a leader in the true sense of the term he forced Indians to accept, at times unwillingly, his ideas of modernising the country. He was the father of Indian constitutional democracy, of universal adult franchise, the five-year plans, giving equal rights to women. This was largely due to the fact that he was better educated than any of his successors with the exception of Manmohan Singh and spent nine years in jail reading and writing and thinking about his country's tomorrows. He worked hard from early morning to well past midnight He coined the slogan *aaraam haraam hai* ('to laze about is a sin'). His name will go down in history among the greatest rulers of India.[34] He put into practice what Pope Benedict XVI has propounded, that the State may not impose religion, yet it must guarantee religious freedom and harmony between the followers of different religions.[35]

Dipankar Gupta and Romila Thapar remind us how Nehru handled the RSS and the Hindu Mahasabha in 1947. The partition of India had just happened and the Hindu sectarians went on a rampage in many places, even in the city of Delhi. Nehru did not reason or plead with them. He put them behind bars whenever they broke the law. When Mahatma Gandhi was assassinated, Nehru again acted swiftly and unambiguously. He banned the RSS and other allied organisations and exposed their shallow rhetoric.[36] Unfortunately, today, there is *none* in this country having the stature and convictions of Nehru. There is no real political will to act. The entire system is fragile, weak and timid, and if the criminals and murderers have political links, the system is totally paralysed.

India's fate seems to be to endure the criminally negligent administration and permit political dwarfs and communalists to rule over her for many more years to come.

Thirdly, there is a serious erosion of secularism. There are many who boast of being secularists but without understanding its true significance. There are political leaders with passionate sympathy for Hindutva masquerading as secularists in almost every political party be it the Left parties or the Congress or others. So far, there has been no real popular resistance whether spontaneous or organised by these parties in defence of secularism. Everyone knows that the Communists are capable of filling the streets with thousands of their ranks and followers at the blow of a whistle for a cause that is *dear to them.* Muslims seems to have the greatest capacity for mass mobilisation in the name of religion, as it was clearly demonstrated when they reacted against the cartoons that appeared somewhere far away in a Danish newspaper denigrating Prophet Muhammad.[37] The tidal waves of the reaction reached also the Indian shores and did much damage to the Indian psyche. Will the Muslims leaders in India use the power to mobilise their followers to promote secularism and democracy? Christians in India invest much in education and they have some of the best educational institutions in the country. Will they take the trouble to impart to the young generation the true meaning and the importance of secularism and cultural pluralism with the same keenness with which they work to produce good academic results?

There is a pressing need in India today for a correct understanding of secularism and new methods to promote it in order to prevent the country from disintegrating. In secular India the State does not subscribe to any religion but all religions are respected and are given equal opportunity and equitable benefits. Nehru has already clarified what secularism means for India. It means that India is a country which honours all faiths equally and give them equal opportunities, that is, as a State it does not allow itself to be attached to one faith or religion. He said: "We call our state a secular one [....] It does not obviously mean a state where religion as such is discouraged. It means freedom of religion and conscience, including freedom for those who may have no religion. It means free play for all religions, subject only to their not interfering with each other or with the basic conceptions of our state."[38] He considered narrow religious nationalism as a relic of the past age and is no longer relevant today. It represents a backward and out of date society.[39]

It would serve well to recall here the advice of Gurcharan Das to the Hindu nationalists of India who still insist on building a Hindu *rashtra* at the expense of the minorities and at the sacrifice of secular and democratic values. He says: "My advice to Hindu nationalists is to get on with building a great country and forget the minorities [....] What a wasted life, hating others when you could spend it living with plenitude and producing happiness for others."[40] We earnestly wish that the Hindutva ideologues and political leaders, from Vajpayee to Modi, and all Indians for that matter, reflect over this wise piece of advice.

Notes

1. See B. De, "The BJP Wanted", 204.
2. See C. Jaffrelot, *The Hindu Nationalist Movement*, 316.
3. See C. Jaffrelot, *The Hindu Nationalist Movement*, 316-317 and footnote no.8.
4. S.M. Pandya, the head of the department of Sanskrit, at St. Xavier's College, Ahmedabad, says that the need of the moment is not one religion, but mutual respect and tolerance of the devotees of the different religions. For Hindus to expect Islam, Christianity or Zoroastrianism to be driven out of India is an idle dream. See S.M. Pandya, "A New Way of Living", 82.
5. Plato, *Gorgias* 525-526.
6. See J. Nehru, *Letters to Chief Ministers*, vol. 1, 33-34 (letter of 7 December 1947) as cited in C. Jaffrelot, *The Hindu Nationalist Movement*, 87, footnote 38.
7. See T.J.S. George, *The Enquire Dictionary*, 301.
8. See T.J.S. George, *The Enquire Dictionary*, 28. 302. See also S.R. Goyal, *The Kautilya Arthasastra*, 166-174.
9. See S. Gopal and U. Iyengar (eds.), *The Essential Writings of Jawaharlal Nehru*, vol. 1, 636.
10. See K. Nayar, "Burnt Beyond Recognition", 49.
11. A. Abraham, *The Tribune*, 10 March 2002.
12. S. Gopal and U. Iyengar (eds.), *The Essential Writings of Jawaharlal Nehru*, vol. 2, 121.

13. See J. Nehru, *The Discovery of India*, 71.
14. See K. Nayar, "Burnt beyond Recognition", 50.
15. S. Gopal and U. Iyengar (eds.), *The Essential Writings of Jawaharlal Nehru*, vol. 1, 186.
16. See A. Roy, "'If Bush is so Acceptable", 64.
17. See A.A. Engineer, "The Gujarat Carnage", 6.
18. S. Gopal and U. Iyengar (eds.), *The Essential Writings of Jawaharlal Nehru*, vol. 1, 190.
19. A. Pratap, "A Spoonful of Dissent", 50.
20. K. Elst, *Decolonising*, 226.
21. Spoken in April 1920, quoted in Abhas Chatterjee, *Concept of Hindu Nation*, p. 67 as cited in K. Elst, *Decolonising*, 229.
22. G. Das, *The Elephant Paradigm*, 81.
23. See N. Palkhivala, *We the Nation*, 105.
24. See T.N. Seshan. *A Heart Full of Burden*, 43.
25. See T.N. Seshan. *A Heart Full of Burden*, 95.
26. See "Mit brennender Sorge", *Das Reich*, 496; "Viele Wollten damals", *Das Reich*, 526.
27. S. Gopal and U. Iyengar (eds.), *The Essential Writings of Jawaharlal Nehru*, vol. 1, 188.
28. G. Das, *The Elephant Paradigm*, xii. (Emphasis added)
29. The Shah Bano case triggered two of the hottest political legal battles in India, namely on women's rights and the desirability of a common civil code. As orthodox Muslims raised the slogan of 'Islam on danger' the Congress government of Rajiv Gandhi introduced the Muslim Women's (Protection of Rights on Divorce) Bill, which the government passed on 5 May 1986. The most controversial provision of the Act limited Muslim women's right to alimony to three months after the divorce. Thereafter, it would be the responsibility of the family or Wakf Board to support her. The case was also a test for the secular ethos of the country. It was asked whether a secular State could become an arbiter of religion? See K. Bhattacherjee, "Fair Judgement", 42; C. Jaffrelot, *The Hindu Nationalist Movement in India*, 334-346. See also "Shah Bano Case Code of Conflict", 63; A.T. Embree, "The Function of the Rashtriya Swayamsevak Sangh", 618.
30. For details see C. Jaffrelot, *The Hindu Nationalist Movement*, 370-374.
31. Between 1987 and 1990 on Sunday mornings the serialised versions of the great Indian epics the *Ramayana* and *Mahabharata* were shown on national television. They transformed the psyche of millions of Hindus and paved way for a 'renaissance' of Hindutva. It also

fuelled the Sangh Parivar campaign for the demolition of the Babri mosque at Ayodhya. See C. Shattuck, *Hinduism*, 11-12; *India Today*, 15 September 1988, 140; C. Jaffrelot, *The Hindu Nationalist Movement*, 389-390; "Screen Gods", 43. Three of the stars in *Ramayana* serial went on to become Lok Sabha members on behalf of the BJP: Arvind Trivedi (Ravana), Deepika Chikaliya (Sita) and Dara Singh (Hanuman). See S. Murthy, "Serial Valmiki", 162. "Telecasting the Ram story also subtly changed Ram's icnography from the pose of a detached god (shanta) to that of an active warrior". P. van der Veer, "Hindu Nationalism", 665.

32. It is said that Advani's *rath yatra* changed the course of India's political history. The Ram wave overnight transferred the BJP into the largest political party. See *The Indian Express*, 1 February 2004. About this *yatra* of Advani we read: "Communal tensions hit fever pitch during his kitschy chariot's journey across large parts of India on its way to Ayodhya. Hindu-Muslim riots erupted everywhere. In order to stem the violence. V.P. Singh [the then Prime Minister] goaded Lalu Prasad Yadav to arrest Advani as soon as he entered Bihar". D. Padgaonkar, "In 1990, Politics Metamorphosed", 172. See also "Rath Yatra Rallying Ram", 76.

33. About the destruction of the Babri mosque on 6 December 1992 Sunil Khilnani, the author of *The Idea of India* writes: "[6 December] 1992 did increase the insecurity of all Indians who do not subscribe to the syndicated Hinduism of the Sangh Parivar and its political representatives – and it created the conditions that made possible Gujarat 2002 [....] it has challenged our political identity, our convictions about who we are [...] that December day diminished us, in our own eyes and in the eyes of others". S. Khilnani, "The Rubble at Ayodhya", 182.

34. See K. Singh, "Like a Storm in a Gandhi Cap", 70.

35. See Benedict XVI, *Deus Caritas est*, no. 28.

36. See D. Gupta and R. Thapar, "Who are the Guilty?", 110.

37. Twelve cartoons on Prophet Muhammad appeared in the Danish newspaper *Jyllands Posten* on 30 September 2005. But the reaction against them came months later in early 2006. See "In the Name of Free Speech", 78. J. Kattoor, "Fire and Fury over a Cartoon", 27.

38. S. Gopal and U. Iyengar (eds.), *The Essential Writings of Jawaharlal Nehru*, vol. 1, 192.

39. S. Gopal and U. Iyengar (eds.), *The Essential Writings of Jawaharlal Nehru*, vol. 1, 194.

40. G. Das, *The Elephant Paradigm*, 134-135.

Glossary

Acharya	Teacher
Advaita	Non dualism, monism.
Advaita Vedanta	A school of Hindu theology of non-dualism.
Agnihotra	Vedic sacrifice.
Ahimsa	Non-violence.
Akhand Bharat	Undivided India.
Ananda Marga	A controversial spiritual-political movement started in 1955 by Prabhat Ranjan Sarkar (b. 1921) who assumed the name of Amandamurti.
Antyodaya	Rise of the lowest or the last.
Anushilan Samiti	Disciplinary Organisation.
Arjuna	One of the five Pandava brothers who was known for his martial skill, and who is Krishna's interlocutor in the *Bhagavadgita*.
Arya	Noble.
Aryans	A family of people belonging to the Indo-European linguistic group.
Arya Samaj	Noble Society or Society of Aryas. A crusading reform movement founded in 1875 by Swami Dayananda Saraswati.
Ashram	Hindu stages of life; hermitage.
Avatar	Descent of God.
Ayurveda	Divine knowledge of life, ancient Indian science of health
Bajrang Dal	The Force of Strong-Bodied Hanuman or the Army of Hanuman; the VHP youth wing.
Bharata Dharma Mahamandala	All India Religious Association.

Bharat Mata	Mother India.
Bharat Ratna	Jewel of India.
Bhakti	Loving devotion to God.
Brahman	A concept which designates the Ultimate Reality in the Hindu thought.
Brahmin	One who belongs to the priestly class of the Hindu society.
Caste	A hereditary stratification of society defining status, occupation and inter-group ranking in Hindu tradition, namely: *Brahmins* (priests), *Kshatriys* (warriors), *Vaisyas* (merchants, cultivators) and *Sudras* (labourers). Those who are outside these four classes form a fifth caste called the untouchables.
Dalit	Those placed outside the classical Hindu caste hierarchy – the untouchables.
Devadasis	God's maidservants, a caste of women dedicated to temples.
Dharam Sansad	Parliament of Hindu religion.
Dharma	Traditional Indian term for religion, code of conduct, duty, cosmic order and virtuous action.
Dharna	sit-in
Diaspora	Dispersion. The membership of a religion scattered outside its main homeland: for example, the Jews outside Israel.
Dravidian	A linguistic group believed to have been the original inhabitants of India, and whose early civilisation reaching its apogee in the Indus Valley or Harappan culture in third millennium B.C.
Durga Vahini	Brigade of the Tiger-Goddess.
Durgahs (*Dargahs*)	Religious and religio-cultural shrines; monuments of Sufi saints.
Ekal Vidyalayas	Single teacher schools.
Ekatmata yatra	Chariot procession for national unity.
Fascism	A hyper-nationalist, totalitarian ideology. An ideology that advocates extreme right-wing views under one party or leader. For example, the ideology of Mussolini and Adolf Hitler's Nazism.
Gayatri mantra	Invocation to the Sun as part of daily ablution by the Hindus.
Ghar vapasi	Home coming, re-conversion to Hinduism.
Gita	Short form for *Bhagavadgita* ('The Song of the Lord'), which is one of the most famous Hindu scriptures.
Gitarahasya	The Secret of the *Gita*. A celebrated commentary on the *Gita* by B.G. Tilak.
Guru	'The weighty one', spiritual teacher.

Gurukul	*Gurukul* system was the name given to the ancient Indian method of education. *Guru* is a spiritual preceptor. In ancient India the *guru* received pupils in his own *ashram* (hermitage). The pupil (*chela* or *shishya*) gave him implicit obedience, worked for him in the household and paid him great reverence.
Hanuman	The monkey-god who assisted Ram in his struggle against Ravana.
Hindu rashtra	Hindu nation.
Hindu Sangathan	A movement launched in the 1920s with the aim of uniting the Hindus by transcending divisions of caste and sect.
Hindutva	A term coined by V.D. Savarkar to indicate 'Hindu-ness'. As an ideology it stands for Hindu fundamentalism and Hindu cultural nationalism.
Janmabhoomi	Birth place.
Jati	subcaste.
Jihad	'Effort', the struggle for Islam, interpreted either as righteous war against 'infidels' or as a spiritual striving.
Karma Yoga	Way of action.
Kar seva	Rendering physical service as a sign of devotion to God.
Karsevak	A volunteer who took part in the movement to build a temple at Ayodhya.
Kranti Dal	Party of the Revolution.
Krishna	The incarnation of Vishnu.
Kshatriya	The warrior caste of Hindu society.
Lathi	Stick, rod.
Lok Sabha	People's Assembly, the Lower house of Indian Parliament.
Machiavellianism	The art of government based on the principles enunciated by Niccolo Machiavelli which justifies the use of force and any form of repression in order to safeguard his rule.
Madrassa	Islamic religious school.
Mahabharata	An abbreviated form of *Mahabharata-yudha* ('The Great Battle of the Bharatas'). One of the great Indian epics.
Mandir	Temple.
Manu	The author of the Manusmriti or system of Hindu Law.
Manusmriti	'The Law of Manu'.
Masjid	Mosque.
Mein Kampf	'My Struggle'. Adolf Hitler's biography and ideological tract, which contains the essence of Nazism.

Nazism	The exaggerated nationalist ideology of Adolf Hitler's Germany. A racist German-first ideology.
Nirman	Construction
Om	An important auspicious and sacred syllable in Hindu, Buddhist and Jain traditions.
Parivar	Family.
Pitrubbu	Fatherland.
Pracharak	trained full-time worker or volunteer of the RSS
Pseudo-secularism	A term used by Hindu nationalist to denote the alleged practice of favouritism toward the non-Hindus under the cover of 'secularism.
Rajya Sabha	The upper house of Indian parliament.
Rama	Incarnation of Vishnu, hero of the *Ramayana*.
Ramayana	One of the great Indian epics.
Ramlila	Annual *dassera* festivity signifying victory of Ram over Ravana.
Ram Rajya	Ram's kingdom.
Rashtra	Nation.
Rath yatra	Chariot procession.
Rigveda / Rig Veda	The main collection of the Vedic hymns in ancient India.
Sadhu	Hindu monk or ascetic.
Sadhvi	Female ascetic.
Saffronisation	Imposition of Hindu cultural nationalist ideology on aspects of Indian life.
Sammelan	Conference, convention.
Samiti	Committee.
Samskara	Ritual. A rite by which a person is sanctified and raised to a special state
Sanatana Dharma	Eternal religion, Eternal Law. Orthodox Hinduism which does not accept the various socio-religious reforms of A.D. 1900.
Sangh	Community, association.
Sanghatan	Organisation.
Sangh Parivar	Affiliates of the RSS family.
Sanskar Kendras	Centres for inculcating Hindu religious and cultural values
Sanskritisation	Originally it meant a process by which a lower-caste Hindu changes his customs, rituals, ideology and way of life in the direction of a higher caste. Today the term stands for any effort at Hinduisation of a non-Hindu group through changing their way of life and culture.
Sanyasi	A person who has renounced the world.

Sarsanghchalak	Supreme chief of the RSS.
Sati	The ignominious practice of burning of widows on their husbands funeral pyre.
Satyagraha	'Holding on to truth'. In the Gandhian sense it means relying on the truth and justice of a cause rather than force to achieve one's goal. Non violent protest.
Sena	Army.
Sevika	Woman volunteer.
Shakha	Local branch of the RSS.
Shibir	Camp.
Shilayana	Ceremony of laying foundation.
Shiv Sena	Army of Shivaji. A militant parochial organisation set up in Mumbai in the 1960s by Bal Thackeray.
Shuddhi	Purification; re-conversion ceremony.
Swadeshi	'One's own country'. An ideology which favours indigenous means of production of goods or knowledge over those imported from abroad.
Swaraj	Self-rule.
Swastika	A Sanskrit symbol signifying prosperity, auspiciousness and well-being. Nazis in Germany used it as their party's emblem because of its Sanskrit-Aryan connection.
Swayamsevak	literally, a volunteer; RSS activist.
Tirthankaras	'Ford-makers' who enable the faithful to cross the stream of existence to the other shore, namely, liberation.
Upanishads	A major philosophical section of the Vedic revelation.
Vanavasi	Forest-dweller. Tribal
Vande Mataram	A hymn which celebrates India as Divine Mother.
Veda	Knowledge. The corpus of revealed texts that belonged to the Aryans.
Vedanta	End of the Veda or the Upanishads.
Yajna	Sacrifice.
Yatra	Pilgrimage, journey, march.
Yoga	System of physical and mental discipline, one of the six orthodox schools of Hindu philosophy.
Yudha	Warfare.
Xenophobia	A pathological dislike for 'outsiders'.
Zamindar	literally 'possessor of land'. A landlord.

Bibliography

Abey, K., "The Doctrine of Deception", *Indian Currents*, 26 October 2003, 50.

Abraham, A., *The Tribune*, 10 March 2002.

Achievements of NDA Government. A Pocketbook, Delhi: Ministry of Information and Broadcasting, Government of India, 2004.

"Advani Calls upon Manmohan Singh to Restore Savarkar Plaque", *BJP Today*, 1-6 October 2004, 21.

Advani, L.K., "Let us Re-dedicate Ourselves to Service to Motherland", *BJP Today*, 1-15 November 2004, 12-17.

——, "National Security in Jeopardy", *BJP Today*, 1-15 October 2005, 12-17.

——, *People Betrayed*, Delhi 1979.

——, *A Prisoner's Scrap-Book*, (1978) New Delhi 2002.

"Advani Regrets Babri Masjid Demolition", *The Hindu*, 2 June 2005, 12.

Against Communalisation of Education New Delhi 2001.

Agnivesh, Swami, "Agnivesh Vs PM?", *Indian Currents*, 4 April 2001, 4[illegible].

Ahmed, F.B., "Poet Prime Minister T[illegible]", *Organiser*, 5 January 2003, 9.

Aiyar, M.S., "Arun Shourie and His Acolytes", *Sunday*, 25 April–1 May, 1999, 8-10.

——, "BJP and the Hindu State", *The Indian Express*, 26 November 2002.

——, *Confessions of a Secular Fundamentalist*, New Delhi 2004.

——, *The Telegraph*, 9 March 2004, 9.

"Aksharadaan Abhiyan in North-East Villages", *Organiser*, 18 July 2004, 12.

"All Parties must Back It", *Outlook*, 18 August 2003, 23.

"Alva Joachim (1907-)", in N.K. Singh (ed.), *Encyclopaedia of the Indian Biography*, vol. 1, New Delhi, 2000, 120-121.

Ambroise, Y., "Hindutva's Real Agenda and Strategies", in *Hindutva: An Indian Christian Response*, J. Mattam and P. Arockiadoss (eds.), Bangalore 2002, 11-102.

Andersen, W. K. and Damle, S. D., *The Brotherhood in Saffron*, New Delhi 1987.

Ansari, N.J., "Foreign Bodies", *Pioneer*, 19 September 2002.

Arackal, F., "Double Talk", *Indian Currents*, 7 March 2004, 42-44.

The Asian Age, 12 September 2002.

The Asian Age, 20 February 2003.

"Atal Bihari Vajpayee in His own Words: 'The Sangh is My Soul'", in *Gujarat 2002 Untold and Re-told Stories of the Hindutva Lab*, J. Dayal (ed.), Delhi 2002, 1024-1027.

"Atalji one of the Ablest Prime Ministers of India – R. Ventakataman, former President of the Republic of India", *BJP Today*, 1-15 January 2004, 8.

"Atalji Rules out Modi Factor for NDA's Defeat", *BJP Today*, 16-30 June 2004, 12-13.

"Atal Sandesh Yatra in Orissa", *Organiser*, 8 February 2004, 7.

"Atalji Seeks Two-Thirds Majority in Lok Sabha", *BJP Today*, 16-29 February 2004, 5.

"Attack on Bishop a New Strategy", *Indian Currents*, 12 February 2006, 27-28.

Aurobindo, *India's Rebirth*, Mysore, 3rd edition, 2000.

"Back to the Basics: We are what we are because of the Party", *BJP Today*, 1-15 July 2004, 4-10.

Bamzai, K., "Elementary Failure", *India Today*, 8 September 2003, 54-56.

Banatwala, G.M., "Challenge of Faith", *India Today*, 30 December 2002, 54.

"Ban, Excise, Punish, Gag", *Outlook*, 12 December 2005.

Batra, D.N., "Reject Unpatriotic Textbooks", *Organiser*, 11 June 2006, 20.

Bavadam, L., "The Son Rises", *Frontline*, 28 February 2003, 49-50.

Baxter, C., *The Jana Sangh. A Biography of an Indian Political Party*, Philadelphia 1969.

Benedict XVI, Encyclical Letter *Deus Caritas est* of the Supreme Pontiff Pope Benedict XV, Rome 25 December 2005.

"Best Bakery Case; PYCL Demands Fresh Trial", *Harvest of Hatred. The Concerned Citizens' Tribunal Report on Gujarat, 2002*, R. Bonney (ed.), Delhi 2004, 16-22

Bhambhri, C.P., "Parivar Versus Dynasty", *The Pioneer*, 17 January 2004.

——, "Sangh Parivar in Government", *The Hindu*, 14 April 2003, 10.

Bhaumik, S. N., "Hawk Flock", *Outlook*, 26 June 2000, 26-28.

Bhaumik, S. N. and Mukerjee, S., "The Big Fish Escapes", *Outlook*, 29 September 2003, 36-40.

Bhattacherjee, K., "Fair Judgement", *The Week*, 29 January 2006, 42.

Bhattacharya, S., "NCERT: Rewriting Indian History, Xeroxing World History", in *Plagiarised and Communalised*, New Delhi 2003, 14-16.

——, *Vande Mataram. The Biography of a Song*, New Delhi 2003.

Bhishikar, C.P., *Shri Guruji Pioneer of a New Era*, Bangalore 1999.

Bhushan, R., "Joshi's Class of 2000", *Outlook*, 27 November 2003, 20-22.

Bidwai, P., "Between Despair and Hope", *Frontline*, 10 October 2003, 125-126.

——,"But who Lit the Fire?", *Frontline*, 11 February 2005, 92-94.

——, "The BJP's Second Mascot", *Frontline*, 26 March 2004, 119-120.

——, "The BJP's 'Plan B'?", *Frontline*, 5 December 2003, 110-111.

——, "Convulsions in the Parivar", *Frontline*, 6 May 2005, 115-117.

——, "Jinnah's Ghost Haunts the Parivar", *Frontline*, 1 July 2005, 114-116.

——, "For Justice in Gujarat", *Frontline*, 13 February 2004, 121-122.

——,"Liberation at Last!", *Frontline*, 4 June 2004, 126.

——, "A Long Haul for Secularists", *Frontline*, 17 January 2003, 107-109.

——, "More than Just a Wake-up Call", *Frontline*, 2 January 2004, 123-124.

——, "Politics and Culture as Blind Sport", *Frontline*, 17 March 2000, 108.

——, "Sanskrit and *Sanskriti* as Weapons", in *Against Communalisation of Education*, New Delhi 2001, 33-38.

——, "A Tilting of the Scales", *Frontline*, 21 May 2004, 106-107.

——, "'Vision' and Vitriol", *Frontline* 23 April 2004, 127-128.

"Big Bro watchin'[sic]", *Outlook*, 4 August 2003, 12.

"Bishop Deplores Harassment of Christians", *Indian Currents*, 16 April 2006, 46.

"BJP Destined to be Stronger for a Stronger India", *BJP Today*, 16-30 April 2005, 12-21.

"The BJP has Evolved", *Frontline*, 23 April 2004, 32.

"BJP-ruled States Urged to Address RSS Concerns", *The Hindu*, 26 January 2006, 5.

"BJP Seeks Superpower Status for India", *BJP Today*, 16-30 April 2004, 24.

"BJP Sights Chance to Get Kerala Toehold", *The Telegraph*, 17 May 2003, 7.

"BJP Suspends Khurana, Hints at Expulsion", *The Hindu*, 21 August 2005, 1.

"BJP's Minority Development Convention, February 25", *BJP Today*, 16-31 March 2004, 23.

"BJP Succeeded in Unleashing Potential of India", *BJP Today*, 16-29 February 2004, 6-10.

BJP Today, 1-15 May 2004 (cover page)

"BJP Upbeat about Its Future", *BJP Today*, 16-30 April 2005, 4.

Bonney, R. (ed.), *Harvest of Hatred: The Concerned Citizens' Tribunal Report on Gujarat, 2002*, Delhi 2004.

——, "Introduction" to J.P. Hartung, G. Hawkes and A. Bhattacharjee, *Ayodhya 1992-2003: The Assertion of Cultural and Religious Hegemony*, Delhi 2004.

Brahmachari, R., "India: The Mother of Western Civilisation", *Organiser*, 10 October 2006, 11.

——, "Yoga Craze of the West", *Organiser*, 11 September 2005, 14.

Bramsted, E.K., "Fanatisch und Bedingungslos. Goebbels und die NA-Propaganda", *Das Reich*, Band 1, (1936/37), 472-477.

"Breeding Bigotry", in *Against Communalisation of Education* New Delhi 2001, 126-130.

Boro, H., "Free Education from Western Bonds", *Organiser*, 19 January 2003, 20.

Bryant, E., *The Quest for the Origins of Vedic Culture The Indo-Aryan Migration Debate*, New Delhi 2001.

B.S. Moonje (P&J 5587), 1940, File 117/D-1, Hindu Mahasabha Copies of Resolution, etc, L/P&J/8/683, India Office, British Library, London, 1940.

Bunsha, D., "Advantage Modi, Thanks to Congress", *Frontline,* 7 May 2004, 23-24.

——, "An Ambitious Pracharak", *Frontline,* 3 January 2003, 8.

——, "Blocking Justice", *Frontline,* 28 March 2003, 39-41.

——, "Digging up the Truth", *Frontline,* 27 January 2006, 36-37.

——, "The Mystery of the Godhra Fire", *Frontline,* 28 March 2003, 37-38.

——, "Narendra Modi's 'Concerns'", *Frontline,* 8 October 2004, 19.

——, "Organised Intolerance", *Frontline,* 26 March 2004, 17-18.

——, "Probe or Persecution?", *Frontline,* 23 May 2003, 39-40.

——, "A Quiet Anniversary", *Frontline,* 28 March 2003, 40.

——, "A Second Wind for Modi", *Frontline,* 16 July 2004, 16-17.

——, "Silenced into Submission", *Frontline,* 21 May 2004, 30-31.

"The Burning of Bombay", *Sunday,* 24-30 January 1993, 29-37.

Carson, P., "Christianity, Colonialism, and Hinduism in Kerala: Integration, Adaptation, or Confrontation?", in R.E. Frykenberg (ed.), *Christians and Missionaries in India. Cross-Cultural Communication since 1500,* London 2003, 127-154.

"CBCI Decries Burning of Cardinal's Effigy", *Indian Currents,* 1 January 2006, 13.

Chandrasekhar, S., "Shun Western Approach", *Organiser,* 17 September 2003. 20.

Casolari, M., "Hindutva's Foreign Tie-ups in the 1930s", in J. Dayal (ed.), *Gujarat 2002,* New Delhi 2002, 1028-1057.

"Charges Framed against Advani, Seven Others", *The Hindu,* 29 July 2005, 1.

Chari, S., "Indian Americans should Utilise their Heritage to Show World a New Path", *Organiser,* 24 August 2003, 10-11.

——, "Religious Retort", *India Today,* 30 December 2002, 56.

Chawla, P., "And Beyond", *India Today,* 30 December 2002, 30-31.

Cherian, J., "Advani's Crusade", *Frontline,* 4 July 2003, 25.

Chowdhury, S.R., "'The Killing of Gandhi'", *The Hindu,* 15 February 2003, 9.

Chitkara, M.G., *Rashtriya Swayamsevak Sangh National Upsurge,* New Delhi 2004.

Clarke, N.G., *Hitler's Priestess. Savitri Devi, the Hindu-Aryan Myth, and Neo-Nazism,* London 2000.

"Coalition Politics – a Challenge", *Organiser,* 12 September 2004, 20.

"Communalisation of Education and Culture: A SAHMAT Statement", in *Against Communalisation of Education,* New Delhi 2001, 9-22.

Communalisation of Education. The Assault on History, New Delhi 2002.

Communalism Combat, June-July 2003, 19-20.

"Concerned Citizens Tribunal", in A. A Engineer (ed.), *The Gujarat Carnage,* New Delhi 2003, 420-423.

"Connecting Northeast with Rest of the Country", *Organiser,* 22 January 2006, 17.

The Constitution of India, Delhi, 5th edition 2002.

Crasta, J., "Hindutva Ado about Nothing", *Indian Currents*, 26 February 2006, 18-22.

"Crime and Complicity", *Frontline*, 4 June 2004, 97-99.

Daily, 12 July 2000.

Das, G., *The Elephant Paradigm India Wrestles with Change*, New Delhi 2002.

——, *India Unbound*, New Delhi 2000.

Das, N., "Ministry Re-scuffle", *Indian Currents*, 9 February 2003, 15-19.

Dass, S.K. (ed.), *Atal Bihari Vajpayee Prime Minister of India*, Delhi 2004.

Dayal, J., "Will CBI ever Catch Advani?", *Indian Currents*, 9 February 2003, 10-13.

De, B., "The BJP Wanted to usher in a New Hindu Millennium", *Indian Today*, 26 December 2005, 204.

"Demonising Christianity, Islam: How Textbooks Teach Prejudices", in *Against Communalisation of Education* New Delhi 2001, 124-125.

Desai, D., "Will Modi's Magic Show Get Going?", *Outlook*, 24 November 2003, 10.

Deshpande, R., "Advani's Ordeal", *India Today*, 4 August 2003, 26-31.

De Souza, D., "Goa New Hindutva Lab", *Indian Currents*, 25 March 2006, 224-229.

Devi, S., *A Warning to the Hindus* [1939], New Delhi 1993.

"The Disaster that Followed Tragedy", *India Today*, 21 July 2003, 28-29.

Domarus, M., *Hitler Reden und Proklamationen 1932 bis 1945*, vol.1, Leonberg 1987.

"Dr. Joshi Integral Modern Education and Science with Indian Traditions", *Organiser*, 19 January 2003, 18.

Elst, K., *Decolonising the Hindu Mind*, New Delhi 2001.

Embree, A.T., "The Function of the Rashtriya Swayamsevak Sangh: They Define the Hindu nation", in M. E. Marty and R.S. Appleby (eds.), *Accounting for Fundamentalisms. The Dynamic Character of Movements*, Chicago 1994, 617-652.

Engineer, A.A., "The BJP and Gujarat Elections", *Indian Currents*, 1 December 2002, 42-44.

——, "BJP's Riot-Free India", in A.A. Engineer, (ed), *The Gujarat Carnage*, New Delhi, 2003, 80-84.

——, "The Gujarat Carnage", in A. A Engineer (ed.), *The Gujarat Carnage*, New Delhi, 2003, 1-24.

——, "Secularism's Victory", *Indian Currents*, 6 June 2004, 6-10.

Eraly, A., "Cry Babies", *Outlook*, 22 August 2005, 92.

"Expectations from a Visionary PM", *BJP Today*, 16-31 January 2004, 19-20.

"Exploring Scientific Basis of the Content of the Vedas", *Organiser* 4 July 2004, 12.

Falcao, N., *Kristapurana: A Christian-Hindu Encounter*, Anand: 2003.

Faleiro, E., "Faleiro's Letter to Advani", in A. A Engineer (ed.), *The Gujarat Carnage,* New Delhi 2003, 436-438.

"Fatal Factor", *Indian Currents,* 23 May 2004, 9.

Fest, J.C., *The Face of the Third Reich,* Munich 1963.

"Fifty Reasons Why Modi should Go", *The Week,* 28 April 2002, 34-40.

Fizzotti, E. and Squarcini, F., (eds.), *L'Oriente che non tramonta. Movimenti Religiosi di origine orientale in Italia,* Roma 1999.

"France Honours Fr. Cedric Prakash", *Indian Currents,* 28 May 2006, 17.

Frank, W. A., "Wer Jude ist Bestimme Ich", *Das Reich,* Band 1 (1936/37), 312-318.

"Friday Eve Fever", *Outlook,* 19 April 2004, 10.

Frykenberg, R.E., "Christians in India: An Historical Overview of Their Complex Origins", in R.E. Frykenberg (ed.), *Christians and Missionaries in India. Cross-Cultural Communication since 1500,* London 2003, 33-61.

"Future of India in Learning Sanskrit", *Organiser,* 30 October 2005, 17.

Gandhi, R., *Revenge and Reconciliation,* New Delhi 1999.

Ganguli, A., "The Fuehrer Rides Again", *The Hindustan Times,* 20 May 2002.

George, S.K., "Christian Women Paraded Naked in MP", *Indian Currents,* 11 June 2006, 11.

George, T.J.S., *The Enquire Dictionary,* New Delhi 1998.

Gatade, S., "Enter 'Hero Hitler!", *Communalism Combat,* June-July 2003, 21-22.

Ghose, B., "Questions of Identity", *Frontline,* 2 January 2004, 90-91.

Ghose, A., "Stability and Development, Atalji's Two Gifts to India", *BJP Today,* 15-31 December 2003, 7.

Ghose, B., "Senora [sic] Sonia vs India's Atalji", *BJP Today,* 1-15 May 2004, 27.

"Gib mir Vier Jahre Zeit Nationalsozialistischc Bilanz 1937", *Das Reich,* Band 1, (1936/37), 532-535.

"Der Giftpilz Wie Kinder Hassen Lernen", *Das Reich,* Band 1 (1936/37), 208-209.

"Give us a Chance, Say BJP", *The Hindu,* 27 March 2006, 8.

"Godhra: Who's afraid of Facing Facts?", *Communalism Combat,* October 2003, 12.

Goebbels, J., *Goebbels Reden 1932-1939,* Band 1, München 1971.

Goel, S.R., *Hindu Temples What Happened to Them,* 2 vols. New Delhi, 1993, 1998.

"Going over the Top", *The Week,* 31 August 2003, 10.

Golwalkar, M.S., *Bunch of Thoughts,* Bangalore, 3rd edition 1996.

——, *We or Our Nationhood Defined,* Nagpur 1939.

Gopalakrishnan, A., "A New Head for the Akademi", *Frontline,* 14 March 2004, 87-88.

"Gopal Godse" 'Nathuram did not Leave the RSS'", *Communalism Combat,* August 2004, 27-28.

Gopal, S. and Iyengar, U., (eds.), *The Essential Writings of Jawaharlal Nehru,* vols. 1 and. 2, New Delhi 2003.

Govnda, R., "Class Struggle", *India Today,* 17 April 2006, 2006, 51.

Goyal, S.R., *The Kautiliya Arthasastra,* Jodhpur 2000.

Guha, R., "They too Wrote our History", *Outlook,* 22 August 2005, 44-52.

The Gujarat Pogrom, New Delhi 2002.

"Gujarat Riots Glaring Fault Lines", *India Today,* 18 August 2003, 102.

Gupta, D. and Thapar, R., "Who are the Guilty?", *The Hindu,* 2 April 2002, in A. A. Engineer (ed.), *The Gujarat Carnage,* New Delhi 2003, 108-111.

Gurumurthy, S., "Unmasking Sonia Gandhi", *BJP Today,* 16-31 October 2004, 21.

Habib. I., "The Rewriting of History by the Sangh Parivar", in *Against Communalisation of Education* New Delhi 2001, 39-46.

Hartung, J.P., Hawkes, G. and Bhattacharjee, A., *Ayodhya 1992-2003: The Assertion of Cultural and Religious Hegemony,* Delhi 2004.

Hebbar, N., "Caste as Priests", *The Week,* 14 July 2002, 20-21.

The Hindu, 21 March 2002.

The Hindu, 14 March 2003.

The Hindu, 20 November 2002.

"Hindu Hopes Rise in Kerala SNDP-RSS Come Closer", *Organiser,* 1 June 2003, 7.

Hindu Mahasabha Ideals, The Central Parliamentary Board, Akhil Bharat Hindu Mahasabha, Calcutta, December 1950.

"Hindus in Russia", *Organiser,* 25 December 2005, 9.

The Hindustan Times, 22 April 2002.

The Hindustan Times, 30 May 2003.

The Hindustan Times, 13 June 2003.

The Hindustan Times: 29 July 2000.

The Hindustan Times, 12 March 2003.

"Hindutva is Consciousness of the Country", *Organiser,* 27 April 2003, 7.

"Hindutva's Triumph", *Frontline* 17 January 2003, 114.

"His Love for Another Parivar", *Outlook,* 15 September 2003, 8.

Hitler, A., *Mein Kampf, Zwei Bände in einem Band Ungekürzte Ausgabe,* München 1942.

Höhne, H., "Biedermänner Banausen Brandstifter", *Das Reich,* Band 1 (1936/37), 47-52.

"'Hitler, Godse Idolised, not the Mahatma'". *The Asian Age,* 19 October 2004, 2.

"Hitler a Hero in NCERT Books: Members", *The Sentinel* 29 April 2003, 5.

"HRD Ministry Its Master's Voice", in *Against Communalisation of Education* New Delhi, 2001, 131-134.

"'I am still Active in Politics'", *Indian Currents,* 15 February 2004, 32-35.

"Ideologue Dossier", *India Today,* 16 January 2006, 40-41.

"'I Became the Prime Minister because of Advaniji' – Atalji at Lucknow", *BJP Today,* 16-30 April 2004, 25.

"I have Come here to Felicitate Advaniji" – Atalji at Amritsar", *BJP Today,* 16-30 April 2004, 9-10.

The Indian Currents, 23 February 2003, 39.

The Indian Express, 26 November 2002.

The Indian Express, 22 January 2003.

The Indian Express, 30 January 2003.

The Indian Express, 20 November 2003.

The Indian Express, 30 December 2003.

The Indian Express, 1 February 2004.

India at 50 Facts, Figures and Analysis 1947-1997, Chennai 1997.

"India Slips on Human Development Index", *The Hindu*, 9 July 2003, 1.

India Today, 15 September 1988, 140-141.

India Today, 4 August 2003, 14.

India Today, 18 August 2003.76.

India Today, 18 August 2003, 106.

India Today, 20 October 2003, 44.

India Today, 24 November 2003, 26.

India Today, 26 December 2005, 246.

India Today, 26 December 2005, 307.

"Intellectuals' Forum for Pro-Hindu Government in India", *Organiser*, 27 March 2005, 14.

"In the Name of Free Speech", *Frontline*, 7 April 2006, 78-83.

Jaffrelot, C., *The Hindu Nationalist Movement and Indian Politics*, New York 1996.

Jain, S., "US Duplicity in Denying Visa to Modi", *Organiser*, 3 April 2005, 5.

Jayakumar, D.A., *Christians and the National Movement: The Memoranda of 1919 and the National Movement with Special Reference to Protestant Christians in Tamil Nadu: 1919-1939*, Calcutta 1999.

Jha, P.S., "Who is an Indian?", *Outlook*, 3 November 2003, 43.

Jha, V.M., "A New Brand of History", *Frontline*, 28 February 2003, 87-89.

Joglekar, J.D., "Veer Savarkar: Profile of a Prophet", in V. Grover (ed.), *V.D. Savarkar*, New Delhi 1993, 305-341.

"Joseph George (1887-1938)", in N.K. Singh (ed.), *Encyclopaedia of the Indian Biography*, vol. 1, New Delhi 2000, 250-252.

Joseph, G.G., *George Joseph. The Life and Times of a Kerala Christian Nationalist*, New Delhi 2003.

Joseph, M. and Anand, S., "A Plot from the Devils Liar", *Outlook*, 3 June 2002, in A. A. Engineer (ed.), *The Gujarat Carnage*, New Delhi 2003, 423-426.

Joshi, A.P., Srinivas, M.D and Bajaj, J.K., *An Illustrated Presentation on Religious Demography of India Updated up to 2001*, Chennai 2005.

Joshi, M.M., "My Days with Deendayalji", *BJP Today*, 1-15 October 2005, 30-31.

Joshi, R., "Look Delhi, Aim Rome", *Outlook*, 10 July 2000, 22-26.

"Kalam Unveils Savarkar Portrait", *The Hindu*, 27 February 2003, 1.

Kamath, M.V., "Five Years of Vajpayee Rule", *Organiser*, 13 April 2003, 6.

——, "Of Modi-Meters and Other Fairly Tales", *Organiser*, 28 October 2003, 17.

——, *A Reporter at Large*, Mumbai, 2002.

Kang, B., "Origins, Destinations", *Outlook*, 3 November 2003, 28-29.

Kannbiran, K.C., "Ungodly Act", *Communalism Combat*, May 2003, 17.

Kant, K.S., "Wake up from Slumber and Face New Challenges", *Organiser*, 31 August 2003, 13.

Kanungo, P., *RSS Tryst with Politics From Hedgewar to Sudarshan*, Delhi 2002.

Kapoor, R.S., *Failing the Promise. Irrelevance of the Vajpayee Government*, New Delhi 2003.

Karotemprel, S., "Salesian Contribution to Culture in North-East India", in *Don Bosco in India*, Madras 1989, 130-132.

Katakam, A., "Muscle Power and Parochial Projects", *Frontline* 23 April 2004, 12-13.

——, "Polarised State", *Frontline*, 26 March 2004, 124-125.

Kattoor, J., "Big Joke or Joker?", *Indian Currents*, 11 July 2004, 39-41.

"Fire and Fury over a Cartoon", *Indian Currents*, 26 February 2006, 27-30.

Kaur, N., "To Undo the Damage", *Frontline*, 18 June 2004, 21-22.

Keim, W., *Erziehung unter der Nazi-Diktatur*, Band 1, Darmstadt 1995.

Keshav, A.R., "Why not Make Sanskrit the Official Language?", *Organiser*, 29 August 2004, 15.

Khare, N.B., *Presidential Address, Akhil Bharat Hindu Mahasabha*, 28th Session, Calcutta, 1949.

——, *Presidential Address, Akhil Bharat Hindu Mahasabha*, Special Session, Jaipur, 28 April 1951.

Khilnani, S., "The Rubble at Ayodhya Represents Conflicting Views of Indian History", *India Today*, 26 December 2005, 182.

Khosla, S., "No Mudslinging, Please", *Organiser*, 27 June 2004, 2 and 9.

"The 'King, the 'Prince' and Shri Vajpayee", *BJP Today*, 1-15 April 2004, 21-23.

Koonz, C., *Mütter im Vaterland. Fraeun in Dritten Reich*, Freiburg 1991.

Kulkarni, A., *The Advent of Advani. An Authentic Critical Biography*, Bombay 1995.

Kulkarni, S., "Victim of the Juju Syndrome", 1-8 September 2004, *BJP Today*, 14-15.

Kumar, A., "Modi Promises", *Organiser*, 5 January 2003, 5.

Kumar, K., "Hindu Revivalism and Education in North-Central India", in *Fundamentalisms and Society*, Martin E. Marty and R. Scott Appleby (eds.), Chicago 1993, 536-557.

——, "Modi Promises", *Organiser*, 5 January 2003, 5.

Kumar, P., "Agni Fights for Hindu Interests Globally", *Organiser*, 9 May 2004, 7.

——, "A Brand India School Network", *Organiser*, 13 June 2004, 4.

——, "Modi Announces Panchamrit Scheme", *Organiser*, 19 January 2003, 8, 19.

——, "Stop Criticising RSS or Try to Create an Organisation like RSS", *Organiser*, 2 January 2005, 10.

Kumar, P. and Kumar, D., "I Prefer to Die rather than Eat Beef", *Organiser*, 2 March 2003, 9.

Kumar, R., "Diaspora India", *Organiser*, 22 August 2004, 14.

Kuruvachira, J., *Hindu Nationalists of Modern India. A Critical Study of the Intellectual Genealogy of Hindutva*, Jaipur 2006.

——, "The New UGC Philosophy Curriculum: A 'Saffron' Conspiracy?". *Indian Currents*, 7 July 2002, 40-44.

——, *Roots of Hindutva. A Critical Study of Hindu Fundamentalism and Nationalism*, New Delhi 2005.

"Lack of Proper Political Conduct of MLAs and MPs Major Failure-Causing Factor in Elections", *BJP Today* 1-15 July 2004, 11-13.

Lakhani, J.D., "Promoting Education the Hindu Way", *Organiser*, 8 May 2005, 11.

Langour, F., "Anschleichen Tarnen Melden". *Das Reich*, Band 1 (1936/37), 400-409.

"Lathis against Trishuls", Interview with Laloo Prasad Yadav, *Frontline*, 23 May 2003, 6.

The Laws of Manu, G. Biihler (trs.), Delhi 2001.

Lesser, R.H., *Some Eminent Missionaries of India*, Varanasi 2001.

Lewis, B.R., *Hitler Youth. The Hitlerjugend in War and Peace 1933-1945*, Osceola 2000.

"The Long Road to Justice", *Communalism Combat*, October 2003, 9-12.

"A Longstanding but Flawed Democracy", *The Statesman*, 27 February 2004.

"'The Lotus will Bloom', Atalji Predicted in 1980", *BJP Today*, 1-15 April 2005, 4-6.

Madhok, B., *Portrait of a Martyr Biography of Dr. Shyama Prasad Mookerji*, Bombay 1969.

Mahurkar, U., "On the Fast Track", *India Today*, 21 July 2003, 34.

Mahurkar, U. and Mitra, S., "Wanted Justice", *India Today*, 21 July 2003, 27-36.

Majumdar, M. and Menon, V., "This Man is the Real Culprit. He Got Our People Killed", in A. A Engineer (ed.), *The Gujarat Carnage*, New Delhi 2003, 403-410.

"Making Sanskrit a Language of the Masses", *Organiser*, 12 December 2004, 13.

Malekar, A., "It's a Legal Battle", *The Week*, 24 August 2003, 32-33.

——, "Quest for Justice", *The Week*, 19 October, 2003, 30.

Maliekal, G., *History of the Catholic Church Among the Khasis*, Shillong 2005.

Mander, H., "Cry, the Beloved Country", in A. A. Engineer (ed.), *The Gujarat Carnage*, New Delhi 2003, 40-44.

——, "Inventing Borders in Gujarat", *Frontline*, 28 March 2003, 91-93.

——, "In Search of Gandhi and Godse", *Frontline*, 20 June 2003, 102-104.

Mangalwadi, V., *Missionary Conspiracy Letters to a Postmodern Hindu*, Mussoorie, 2nd edition 1996.

"The Many Children of the Sangh Parivar" in J. Dayal (ed.) in *Gujarat 2002*, New Delhi 2002, 1058.

"Massive Literacy Drive by Sewa Bharati in Delhi", *Organiser*, 12 February 2006, 17.

McDonough, F., *Hitler and the Rise of the Nazi Party*, London 2003.

Menacherry, G., "Cultural Contribution of Indian Church", in *Indian Christian Directory for the New Millennium*, Kottayam 2000, 85-87.

"Men, Muscle and Money", *Paronarama*, 29 September 2003, 2.

Menon, M.C., "Another Blow to VHP", *Indian Currents*, 29 May 2005, 19-22.

——, "Central Census on Kerala Churches and Mosques", *Indian Currents*, 13 July 2003, 9-10.

——, "RSS in US Terror List", *Indian Currents*, 28 December 2004, 23-24.

Menon, P., "Books of Bias and Errors", Book Review, *Frontline*, 12 September 2003, 75.

——, "Concerns of History", *Frontline* 30 January 2004, 40, 42.

——, "A Debate on Historians", *Frontline*, 30 January 2004, 41.

Menon, P.K.K., *The History of Freedom Movement in Kerala*, vol. 2 (1885-1938), Trivandrum 2001.

Mishra, B.R., "Won Won't Let You Go", *BJP Today*, 16-31 May 2004, 17-18.

"Mit brennender Sorge", *Das Reich*, Band 1 (1936-37), 496.

Mitra, A., "Shall Nobody Save Us?", in A. A. Engineer (ed.), *The Gujarat Carnage*, New Delhi 2003, 400-403.

Mitra, C., "Why", *BJP Today*, 1-15 June 2004, 21-22.

"Modi Government still Surveying Christians", *Indian Currents*, 8 June 2003, 8-9.

"A Move to Revive Sanskrit", *Organiser*, 29 February 2004, 15.

Mukerji, D., "Popularity Test Ride", *The Week*, 16 April 2006, 32-33.

Mukherji, S., "The NCERT Conspiracy", *Indian Currents*, 27 July 2003, 29.

Mukherjee, S.P., *Leaves from a Diary*, New Delhi 1993.

Mundadan, A.M., *History of Christianity in India. From the Beginning up to the Middle of the Sixteenth Century*, Bangalore 1984.

Muralidharan, S., "Bankrupt Campaign", *Frontline*, 7 May 2004, 4-5.

——, "The History Project", *Frontline*, 15 March 2003, 28-29.

Murthy, S., "Serial Valmiki", *The Week*, 25 December 2005, 162.

Mustafa, S., "Far from Home", *Indian Currents*, 27 July 2003, 8-9.

Naipaul, V.S., *India: A Wounded Civilisation*, New Delhi 1977.

Nair, P., "RSS' Godse Shrine", *Indian Currents*, 19 September 2004, 47.

Nanda, M., "Postmodernism, Hindu Nationalism and 'Vedic Science'", Part I, *Frontline*, 2 January 2004, 78-82

Nandy, A., "Allure of the Demonic", *Outlook*, 22 August 2005, 38-39.

——, *Bonfire of Creeds*, New Delhi 2004.

Narad, "Modi being unfairly Vilified", *Organiser*, 16 May 2004, 17.

"Nationalism is another Word for Hindutva", *The Hindu*, 4 August 2004, 11.

Nayar, K., "Burnt beyond Recognition", in A. A. Engineer (ed.), *The Gujarat Carnage*, New Delhi 2003, 48-50.

——, Road Taken from Sialkot to Ahmedabad", *The Indian Express*, 3 April 2002.

"NDA Protest Against Tainted Ministers", *BJP Today*, 16-30 June 2004, 9-11.

Nehru, J., *The Discovery of India* [1946], New Delhi 2004.

The New Leader, 16-31 August 2004, 32.

News Time, 9 July 2003.

The Niyogi Committee Report A Critical Appraisal, Varanasi 2000.
"No Alternative to BJP: Only Alternative, a 'Terrible Alternative'", *BJP Today*, 1-15 February 2004, 12-14.
"No Dilution of Hindutva", *Frontline*, 27 January 2006, 26-27.
Noorani, A.G., "The BJP-RSS Equation", *Frontline* 20 May 2005, 47-52.
——," Hindutva, not Hinduism", *Frontline*, 26 March 2004, 122.
——, 'How Advani Went Scot-Free", *Frontline*, 30 January 2004, 47-51.
——, "Lessons from History", *Frontline*, 18 June 2004, 125.
——, "The Man Behind the Image", *Frontline*, 16 July 2004, 4-13.
——, "A Man of the Parivar", *Frontline* 15 November 1966, 98-100.
——, "Modi and His Visa", *Frontline*, 2 April 2005, 47-50.
——, "The Real Vajpayee", *Hindustan Times*, 30 April 2002.
——, "Savarkar and Gandhi", *Frontline*, 28 March 2003, 34-36.
"One Lakh Ekal Vidyalyas by 2011", *Organiser*, 16 May 2005, 9.
Organiser, 18 April 2004, 20.
Organiser, 14 March 2004, 2.
Organiser, 2 November 2003, 10-11.
Organiser, 29 February 2004, 1-2.
Organiser, 5 January 2003, 15.
Otto, T., "Narendra Modi: ein Portrait", http://www.suedasien.net/bios/modi_narendra.htm
Outlook, 21 July 2003, 21.
"Overseas Friends of BJP", *BJP Today*, 16-31 January 2004, 24.
Oza, N., "Fire and Storm", *The Week*, 19 March 2006, 60-62.
——, "Grave Reminder", *The Week*, 8 January 2006, 10-13.
——, "The Hindu Way", *The Week*, 22 January 2006, 27.
Padgaonkar, D. "In 1990, Politics metamorphosed into a farce and a tragedy at a Dizzying Speed", *India Today*, 26 December 2005, 172.
Palety, P., "Sixty per cent Say VHP, State Connived in Riots", *Outlook*, 15 April 2002, in A. A. Engineer (ed.), *The Gujarat Carnage*, New Delhi 2003, 380-382.
Palkhivala, N., *We the Nation*, New Delhi 1994.
Pandya, S.M., "A New Way of Living One's Religious Faith in the Context of Religious Pluralism in India: Hindu Perspective", in *Sarva-Dharma-Sammelana 1998 (National Inter-faith Assembly)*, A. Suresh (ed.), New Delhi 1999, 75-85.
Panikkar, K.N., *Before the Night Falls. Foreboding of Fascism in India*, Bangalore, 2002.
——, "The Agony of Gujarat", in A. A. Engineer (ed.), *The Gujarat Carnage*, New Delhi 2003, 93-96.
——, "Down, but not Out", *Frontline*, 18 June 2004, 121-124.
——, "In the Name of Nationalism", *Frontline*, 26 March 2004, 4-8.
——, "Outsider as Enemy", in *Against Communalisation of Education*, New Delhi 2001, 47-57.

——, "The Sangh Strikes", *Frontline,* 1 July 2005, 19-22.

——, "Whither Indian Education", 23 in *Against Communalisation of Education,* New Delhi 2001, 23-32.

Parakh, B.S. (ed.), *Contemporary India Textbook in Social Sciences,* New Delhi, NCERT, 2002.

Parihar, R. and Deshpande, R., "Forward March", *India Today,* 25 August 2003, 24-25.

"People's Needs over Party Politics", *The Hindu,* 17 April 2006, 10. (Editorial)

"Philippose Elanjikkal John (1903-1955)" in N.K. Singh (ed.), *Encyclopaedia of the Indian Biography,* vol. 6, New Delhi 2000, 169.

"Pictorial Exhibition on Savarkar in UK", *Organiser,* 22 June 2003, 20.

Pintchman, T., "The Ambiguous Female: Conceptions of Female Gender in the Brahmanical Tradition and the Role of Women in India", in N. Smart and S. Thakur (eds.), *Ethical and Political Dilemmas of Modern India,* New York 1993, 144-159.

The Pioneer, 3 November 2003.

Plagiarised and Communalised. More on the NCERT Textbooks, New Delhi 2003.

Plathottam, G., "Contribution of Christianity to Language and Literature", in J. Puthenpurakal (ed.), *Impact of Christianity on Northeast India,* Shillong 1996, 334-362.

Plato in Twelve Volumes, III, Lysis, Symposium, Georgias, Eng. tra. W.R.M. Lamb, Massachusetts, 1925.

Plattner, F.A., *The Catholic Church in India,*

Poonthuruthil, J., *Growth and Responsibility,* Shillong, 2006.

"Pope Interferes in India's Internal Affairs", *BJP Today,* 1-15 June 2006, 10.

Popley, H.A., *Builders of Modern India K.T. Paul Christian Leader* (1938).

Prakash, C., "Anti-Conversion Law. Gujarat Govt. in Limbo", *Indian Currents,* 26 March 2006, 31-32.

——, "Gujarat: The Embers Still Burn", *Indian Currents,* 22 February 2004, 18-21.

——, "Nuns Get Marching Orders", *Indian Currents,* 16 April 2006, 24-26.

"A Project to Explore British Hindu Identity", *Organiser,* 12 March 2006, 3.

Prtap, A., "A Spoonful of Dissent", *Outlook,* 1 September 2003, 50.

"Proper Use of Resources not Made – Atalji", *BJP Today,* 16-30 April 2004, 11-12.

Punj, B.K. "The Mother Principle", *Outlook,* 4 December 2003, 22. (22).

——, "Understanding Hindutva", *Pioneer,* 11 July 2002.

Puri, B., "BJP's Problems and Prospects", *Frontline,* 8 October 2004, 123-125.

Pushparajan, A., "A Secular Critique of Hindutva", in J. Mattam and P. Arockiadoss (eds.), *Hindutva. An Indian Christian Response,* Bangalore 2002, 223-258.

Puthenpurakal, J., (ed.), *Impact of Christianity on Northeast India,* Shillong 1996.

Putra, B., "BJP's Problems and Prospects", *Frontline,* 8 October 2004, 123-125.

——, "Hubris at Hubli", *Indian Currents,* 29 August 2004, 18-20.

——, "Punish the Collaborators", *Indian Currents,* 17 October 2004, 17-20.

"A Quiet Anniversary", *Frontline*, 28 March 2003, 40.

Rai, L.L. *The Arya Samaj*, New Delhi 1991.

Raja, A., "NDA Agenda: Promise of a Developed India", *Organiser*, 18 April 2004, 1 and 20.

Rajalakshmi, T.K., "For a Holistic Curriculum", *Frontline*, 1 July 2005, 85-87.

——, "Removing an Irritant", *Frontline*, 2 January 2004, 125-126.

"Rajasthan Passes Anti-Conversion Bill", *The Hindu*, 8 April 2006, 5.

Rajgopal, A., "Non-Resident Nationalism", *Frontline*, 26 March 2004, 127-129.

Raghavendra, "Who Worked against Modi Visas?", *Organiser*, 3 April 2005, 1-2.

Rmachandran, R., "Astrology on a Pedestal", 48, *Frontline*, 18 July 2004, 48-49.

Ramakrishnan, V., "The Battle for U.P.", *Frontline*, 21 May 2004, 4-6.

——-, "Battles Within", *Frontline*, 1 July 2005, 4-7.

——, "Hindutva Institutions in Education The spreading network of RSS", *Frontline*, November 07-20, 1998. (from http://www.sacw.net/HateEducation/Ramak101198.html.)

——, "The Return of the Congress", *Frontline*, 4 June 2004, 4-6.

——, "A Rough Ride Ahead", *Frontline*, 27 January 2006, 24-26.

——, "Yatra Challenge", *Frontline*, 24 March 2006, 26-28.

Rao, C.R., *RSS and Jana Sangh A Menace to the Unity, Integrity, Secular Democratic Set-up and Progress of our Motherland*, New Delhi 1969.

Rath, D.K., "A Centre for Dialogue on Civilisations", *Organiser*, 7 March 2004, 17.

Rath, D.K., "Mission Mandate", *Organiser*, 14 March 2004, 1 and 19.

"Rajnathji Lodges Protest with the Pope", *BJP Today*, 1-15 June 2006, 11.

"Rath Yatra Rallying Ram", *India Today*, 18 August 2003, 76.

"Rape as Community Punishment", *Indian Currents*, 29 June 2003, 17-18.

"Recognize Your Glorious Heritage", *Organiser*, 13 February 2005, 9.

"Revolutionising Literacy in Remote Rural India", *Organiser*, 23 May 2004, 6.

"Riots were Planned", *Hindustan Times*, 15 April 2002.

Röhrich, W., *Die Macht der Religionen. Glaubenskonflikte in der Weltpolitik*, München 2004.

Roy, A., "Democracy: Who's She when She's at Home?", in S. Agnivesh and V. Thampu (eds.) *Harvest of Hate Gujarat under Siege*, New Delhi 2002, 113-132.

——, "'Exit' Politics", *Organiser*, 9 May 2004, 2-3.

——, "'If Bush is So Acceptable to Manmohan and the Congress, Why Lose Sleep over Modi'", *Outlook*, 22 August 2005, 64-74.

"RSS 'Pracharaks' made BJP Regional Secretaries", *The Hindu*, 7 August 2004, 11.

RSS Resolves. Full Text of Resolutions from 1950 to 1983, Bangalore 1983.

Ruthven, M., *Fundamentalism. The Search for Meaning*, Oxford 2004,

Sadgopal, A., "Gender and Education", *Frontline*, 5 December 2003, 100.

The Saffron Agenda in Education. An Exposé, New Delhi 2001.

Saffronised Substandard A Critique of the New NCERT Textbooks, New Delhi 2002.

"Saffronising Goa: RSS Invades the Classroom", in J. Dayal (ed.), *Gujarat 2002*, New Delhi 2002, 1109-1134.

"*Sakhi Sammelan*: A Unique Experience for Women", *Organiser*, 24 Aril 2005, 17.

"Sangh Parivar Targets K.N. Panikkar", *The Hindu*, 4 July 2003, 13.

"Sanskar Bharati to Celebrate *Sanskritik Navchetana Varsha*", *Organiser*, 20 November 2005, 17.

"Sanskrit Going Global", *Organiser*, 10 October 2004, 12.

"Sanskrit Training Camp in Karnavati", *Organiser*, 12 September 2004, 13.

Sanyal, S., "Modi Ilk's Bigoted Pogrom", *The Statesman*, 9 April 2002.

Saraswati, D., *Satyartha Prakash*, G.P. Upadhyaya (tr.), *The Light of Truth*, Allahabad 1956.

Sarkar, S., *Beyond Nationalist Frames. Relocating Postmodernism, Hindutva, History*, New Delhi 2002.

Savarkar, G.D., "Foreword" to *A Warning to the Hindus* (1939) by S. Devi, New Delhi 1993, 9-11.

Savarkar, V.D, *Hindu Sanghatan. Its Ideology Immediate Programme*, Bombay 1940.

——, *Hindutva. Who is a Hindu?*, (1923) New Delhi 2003.

——, *Historic Statements*, Bombay 1967.

——, "Problems Before Hindudom After Bloodless(!) Vivisection", in V. Grover (ed.) *V.D. Savarkar (Political Thinkers of Modern India-14)*, New Delhi 1993, 174-178.

——, "Then Who is Who, Pray?", in V. Grover (ed.), *V.D. Savarkar (Political Thinkers of Modern India-14)*, New Delhi 1993, 165-169.

Scaria, M., "Christians at the Receiving end in Rajasthan", *Indian Currents*, 2 April 2006, 8-10.

"Screen Gods", *The Week*, 29 January 2006, 43.

Seshan, T.N., *A Heart Full of Burden*, New Delhi 1995.

"Seminar on Miraculous Effects of *agnihom*", *Organiser*, 12 September 2004, 12.

Sengupta, P., "Russians Seek Solace in *Bharatiya Gurukula*", *Organiser*, 11 May 2003, 8.

Seshadri, H.V., *Hindus Abroad – Dilemma: Dollar or Dharma?*, New Delhi 1990.

—— (ed.), *RSS A Vision in Action*, Bangalore, 2nd edition 1998.

Setalvad, T., "Godhra Revisited", *Communalism Combat*, October 2003, 6-8.

"Shah Bano Case Code of Conflict", *India Today*, 18 August 2003, 63.

Shanmuganathan, V., "Indians in USA Command more Respect than Before", *Organiser*, 28 October 2003, 4.

Sharma, J.K., "Brazil Resonant with Jai Shri Ram", *Organiser*, 21 September 2003, 15.

Sharma, K., "Blot on History", *The Week*, 9 December 2001, 43.

Sharma, R., "Would Mahatma have been Safe in His Own State?", *India Today*, 26 December 2005, 236.

Sharma, S., "Congress even Condones Terror in Their 'Damn Modi' Campaign", *Organiser*, 27 June 2004, 1-2.

Shetty, A.V., "Vedic Astrology in Indian Universities, in *Against Communalistion of Education*, New Delhi 2001, 66-71.

"The Shiv Sena Indicted", *Frontline*, 28 August 1998, 20-23.

Shourie, A., *Eminent Historians*, New Delhi 1998.

——, *Harvesting our Souls. Missionaries their Design their Claims*, New Delhi 2000.

——, *Indian Controversies*, New Delhi 1993.

——, *Missionaries in India*, New Delhi 1994.

Shukla, I.K., "Gujarat was Gifted to Godse", *Indian Currents*, 1 December 2002, 6-7.

——, "Informer of '42'", *Indian Currents*, 9 May 2004, 29-30.

Shukla, S., *India Abroad Diasporic Cultures of Postwar America and England*, New Delhi 2003.

Shattuck, C., *Hinduism*, New Jersey, 1999.

Singh, K., *The End of India*, New Delhi 2003.

——, "Like a Strom in a Gandhi Cap", *Outlook*, 12 December 2005, 70-71.

——, "The Next Heir to the Throne", *Panorama*, 21 July 2002, 2.

——, "One-eyed Justice", *Hindustan Times*, 11 March 2006, 10.

Singh, T., *Lollipop Street Why India will Survive Its Politicians*, New Delhi 1999.

——, "Missing the Point", *India Today*, 3 September 2001, 16.

Singh, V.P., "Hindus are Next", *India Today*, 30 December 2002, 32.

Sirohi, S., "All-American Grand Slam, *Outlook*, 4 April 2005, 9-12.

Six, C., *Hindu Nationalismus und Globalisierung. Die Zwei Gesichter Indiens: Symbole der Identität und des Anderen*, Frankfurt A. M 2001.

Smith, D., *Hinduism and Modernity*, Oxford 2003.

Soares, A., Francis, G.X. and Coelho, W., *et al.*, *The Niyogi Committee Report A Critical Appraisal*, Varanasi, n.d.

Srinivas, C., "Textbooks Sectarian Story or History?", *Indian Currents*, 12 January 2003, 19-21.

"Standing Ovation", *BJP Today*, 1-15 June 2004, 23.

Staffner, H., *The Significance of Jesus Christ in Asia*, Anand 1985.

"A State-funded Hindu School in Britain", *Organiser*, 10 July 2005, 7.

The Statesman, 17 June 2003.

The Statesman, 13 March 2003.

"The Statesman Speaks", *BJP Today*, 16-31 January 2004, 3.

"Still in the Race", *Frontline*, 27 January 2006, 29.

Subrahmanyam, V., "Lal Krishna Advani's War with the *Parivar*", *The Hindu*, 20 July 2005, 10.

Suri, S., "Now We Wait for the Light", *Outlook*, 1 September 2003, 30-32.

——, "Vote's the Good News", *Outlook*, 3 November 2003, 38-39.

Surya, V., "Bitter Lessons", *Frontline*, 30 December 2005, 84-86.

——, "Strong on Slogans", *Frontline*, 30 December 2005, 86-87.

Swain, P.C., *Bharatiya Janata Party*, New Delhi 2001.

Swain, S., "Involve Entire Society in Sangh Work", *Organiser*, 16 March 2003, 20.

Swami, P., "A Campaign of Sabotage", *Frontline*, 13 February 2004, 33-34.

"Talks only Solution: Advani", *The Hindu*, 2 August 2003, 1.

Talreja, K.M., *Triumphant March to 'Param Vaibhav' (Supreme Glory)*, New Delhi 2004.

Taneja, N., "A Saffron Assault Abroad", *Frontline*, 27 January 2006, 77-78.

The Telegraph, 4 February 2003.

Thakur, A., "Ramayana in the Global Context", *Organiser*, 12 June 2005, 20.

Thampu, V., "No, Prime Minister", in A. A Engineer (ed.), *The Gujarat Carnage*, New Delhi 2003, 124-128.

Thapar, R., *History of India*, vol. 1, London 1966.

Thekkedath, J., *A History of the Salesians of Don Bosco in India*, 2 vols. Bangalore 2005.

"This is the First Election without any Tension and Cut-throat Competition", *BJP Today*, 1-15 May 2004, 4-7.

Thomas, G., "The Christians and the Freedom Movement" in *Indian Christian Directory for the New Millennium*, Kottayam 2000, 63-67.

Tilak, B.G., *Selected Documents of Lokamanya Bal Gangadhar Tilak (1880-1920)*, 4 vols., R. Kumar (ed.), Delhi 1992.

The Times of India, 25 April 2004.

Today's 'Iron Man' Life and Times of Lal Krishna Advani, New Delhi 2002.

Togadia, P., "Final Warning ", *India Today*, 30 December 2002, 35.

Trevedie, D., "Divide and Rule: Modi Offers Recipe of Hate", in A. A. Engineer (ed.), *The Gujarat Carnage*, New Delhi 2003, 62-67.

Trimondi, V. and V. Trimondi, *Hitler, Buddha, Krishna. Eine unheilige Allianz vom Dritten Reich bis Heute*, Wien 2002.

Tripathi, P.S., "Aftershocks of a Verdict", *Frontline*, 10 October 2003, 18-19.

——, "The Blitz in Lucknow", *Frontline*, 21 May 2004, 6.

——, "A Law unto Itself", *Frontline*, 23 April 2004, 41-42.

——, "Strategic Voting", *Frontline*, 21 May 2004, 12-14.

Tripathi, P.S., "A Trial Run", *Frontline*, 12 September 2003, 25-26.

Tweed, T.A. and Prothero, S., *Asian Religions in America. A Documentary History*, New York, 1999.

"Unifying Varsities through Uniform Syllabus", *Organiser*, 29 May 2005, 16.

"Unmasked Truth", in A. A. Engineer (ed.), *The Gujarat Carnage*, New Delhi 2003, 228-229.

"'Untold Story of Hindujaan'", *Indian Currents*, 15 January 2006, 17-19.

Vaidya, M.G., "Elections in Gujarat and After", *Organiser*, 12 January 2003, 10.

Vajpayee, A.B., *Decisive Days*, N.M. Ghatate (ed.), Delhi 1999.

——, *Four Decades in Parliament*, vol. 1, N.M. Ghatate (ed.), Delhi 1996.

"Vajpayee Visits RSS Headquarters", *The Hindu*, 28 July 2004, 3.

"Varghese Mappila Kandathil (1858-1904)", in N.K. Singh (ed.) *Encyclopaedia of the Indian Biography*, vol.8, New Delhi 2000, 245.

Vasudev, S. and Mishra, N., "Its' Not in Your Stars", *India Today*, 20 October 2003. 86-88.

Vedantam, S., "Tamil Nadu is not an Atheistic State", *Organiser*, 23 March 2003, 11.

"Venkaiah Naidu Proposes Compulsory Military Training for Youth", *BJP Today* 16-30 June 2003, 13.

Venkatesan, V., Advani's Yatra and Other's Fears", *Frontline*, 26 March 2004, 28-29.

——, "Alone at the Top", *Frontline*, 16 July 2004, 14-16.

——, "BJP As Big Brother", *Frontline*, 20 June 2003, 30-32.

——, "Busting a Conspiracy Theory", *Frontline*, 1 July 2005, 38-39.

——, "Image and Reality", *Frontline*, 1 July 2005, 14 and 16.

——, "A Judicial Stricture", *Frontline*, 7 May 2004, 34-35.

——, "The Road from Gujarat", *Frontline*, 17 January 2003, 126-129.

——, "A Secular Veneer", *Frontline*, 31 January 2003, 37-39.

——, "Tainted Credibility", *Frontline* 2 July 2004, 126-128.

——, "A Test Case in Supreme Court", *Frontline*, 28 March 2003, 41-42.

——, "Winning without Hindutva?", *Frontline*, 2 January 2004, 11-12.

Veer, Peter Van Der, "Hindu Nationalism and the Discourse of Modernity: The Vishva Hindu Parishad", in M. E. Marty and R.S. Appleby (eds.), *Accounting for Fundamentalisms. The Dynamic Character of Movements*, Chicago 1994, 653-668.

"VHP to Triple Its Service Projects in Vanvasi Areas", *Organiser*, 20 June 2004, 12.

"Viele wollten damals wenigstens im Gottesdienst Ihre Ruhe Haben", *Das Reich*, Band 1 (1936/37), 526-528.

Vindicated by Time. The Niyogi Committee Report on Christian Missionary Activities, New Delhi, 3rd edition 1998.

Vir Arjun, 23 August 2002.

Vishwanahan, S., "The Spread in the South", *Frontline*, 26 March 2004, 9-11.

Vyas, N., "BJP in a State of Siege", *The Hindu*, 7 June 2006, 11.

——, "No Change in the Advani Persona", *The Hindu*, 16 July 2005, 11

Walker, B., *Hindu World. An Encyclopedic Survey of Hinduism*, vols. I & 2 (1968), New Delhi 1995.

"We are there to Support them; help them Preserve their Heritage", *Organiser*, 4 July 2004, 13.

The Week, 15 November 1998.

"We shall Return – Advaniji", *BJP Today*, 16-30 June 2004, 14-16.

"We will not be allowed to Sit in the Opposition for Five years", *BJP Today*, 16-30 June 2004, 17.

"What's the Party Line?", *The Week*, 16 November 2003, 48.

"When Advani was Unmasked", *Indian Currents*, 9 February 2003, 14.

"Whose Mother is She anyway?", *Outlook*, 3 November 2003, 26.

"The Will is Lacking", in A. A. Engineer (ed.), *The Gujarat Carnage,* New Delhi, 2003, 222-223.

"Winning without Hindutva?", *Frontline,* 2 January 2004, 11-12.

Wilfred, F., "Christians between Identity – Politics and Nationalism", in J. Mattam and P. Arockiadoss (eds), *Hindutva An Indian Christian Response,* Bangalore 2002, 259-281.

Yadev, S., "Face Off", *India Today,* 6 October 2003, 26-27.

"Yatra on a Mazda Rath", *Outlook,* 5 July 2002, 32.

"Yatra's Aim to Highlight Threat to Nation's Security, says Advani", *The Hindu,* 10 April 2006, 12.

Yechury, S., *What is this Hindu Rashtra? On Golwalkar's Fascistic Ideology and the Saffron Brigade's Practice,* Madras 1993.

"'3030 1000' – BJP's Phone in Service," *BJP Today,* 1-15 May 2004, 25.

Internet Sources

http://newsanalysis-intl.tripod.com/astrology.html

http://news.bbc.co.uk/l/hi/world/south_ asia/1958555.html

http://pib.myiris.com/profile/article.php3?fl=b9416

http://timesofindia.indiatimes.com/articleshow/27950.cms

http://www.awaazsaw.org/ibf/appendix6.html

http://www.bjp.org/leader/mmjoshi.html

http://www.countercurrents.org/comm-chatterji080106.html

http://www.cpiml.org/liberation/year_2003/July/commentary2_advani.html

htttp://www.expressindia.com/fulllstory.php?newsid=43432

http://www.foil.org/newsflash/appendixg.html

http://www.hindustantimes.com/news/5922_808914,0015002200000057.html

http://www.hinduismtoday.com/archives/2005/1-3/62-65_traditions. html

http://www.hssworld.org/seva/sevadisha/sevadisha1/vanavasi_kalyan_ashra m.html

http://www.hvk.org/articles/1198/0005.html

htttp://www.rediff.com/news/2004/jun/21spec2.html

http://www.milligazette.com/Archives/01062001/07.html

http://www.millegazette.com/dailyupdate/2003/20030823.html

http://www.sacw.net/HateEducation/Ramak101198.html.

http://www.sriramakrishna.org/education.html

http://www.vhp.org/englishsite/d.Dimensions_of_VHP/aSewa/NSNS/ intheserviceofpoor.html

http://www.vidyabharati.org/kendras.asp

http://www.vskgujarat.com/like_minded_organization/ vanvasi_kalyan_ashram.html

http://164.24.167:8080/members/website/Biodata.asp?no=72

Index

E

F

H

S